The Eagle and the Elephant

The Eagle and the Elephant

Strategic Aspects of US-India Economic Engagement

Raymond E. Vickery Jr.

Woodrow Wilson Center Press
Washington, D.C.

The Johns Hopkins University Press
Baltimore

EDITORIAL OFFICES

Woodrow Wilson Center Press
One Woodrow Wilson Plaza
1300 Pennsylvania Avenue, N.W.
Washington, D.C. 20004-3027
Telephone: 202-691-4029
www.wilsoncenter.org

ORDER FROM

The Johns Hopkins University Press
Hampden Station
P.O. Box 50370
Baltimore, Maryland 21211
Telephone: 1-800-537-5487
www.press.jhu.edu/books/

Library of Congress Cataloging-in-Publication Data

Vickery, Raymond Ezekiel, 1942–
   The eagle and the elephant : strategic aspects of U.S.-India economic
engagement / Raymond E. Vickery.
      p. cm.
   ISBN 978-1-4214-0073-0 (hardback) — ISBN 978-1-4214-0145-4 (paperback)
   1. United States—Foreign economic relations—India.   2. India—Foreign
economic relations—United States.   3. United States—Foreign relations—India.
4. India—Foreign relations—United States.   I. Title.
   HF1456.5.I4V53 2011
   337.73054—dc22
                                                        2011007551

Contents

Acknowledgments   ix

1 Economic Engagement: The Engine of Strategic Cooperation   1
2 Economic Engagement and Civil Nuclear Cooperation   32
3 Services Outsourcing and Economic Development   87
4 Economic Engagement and Preserving the Peace: The Reaction to Terrorism   115
5 Economic Engagement, Electric Power, and the Environment   129
6 Energy and Defense Security: The Iran Pipeline Example   172
7 Economic Engagement and Multilateralism: Meeting the Financial Meltdown   189
8 Economic Engagement and Food Security: Green Revolutions   210
9 Economic Engagement and Health Security: The Fight against HIV/AIDS   243
10 Conclusion: Where Do We Go from Here?   270

Notes   285
Index   317

Acknowledgments

This book was conceived as the central project for my tenure as a Public Policy Scholar at the Woodrow Wilson International Center for Scholars in 2008 and 2009. I am indebted to the Woodrow Wilson Center, its president, Lee Hamilton, and his deputy, Michael Van Dusen, for the opportunity of association with them. Although as of this writing Lee is stepping down as director of the Center, his positive imprint on the Center and the character of our nation is permanent.

I was introduced to the Center by my dear friend Ellis Mottur. His comments upon reading the manuscript for this work were insightful and extremely helpful. Although Ellis passed away before the publication of this book, I will always be grateful for the insights and support he gave me in making this Woodrow Wilson Center project a reality.

Robert Hathaway was my chief mentor at the Woodrow Wilson Center. With his keen intellect and good judgment, Bob has given generously of his time in reading and rereading the manuscript of this book and providing guidance at each step in the process. Kent Hughes was instrumental in my taking up this project, and I am grateful to him. Other scholars at the Center were particularly helpful, including Dennis Kux, Samuel Wells, William Milam, and Kathryn Lavelle. I am grateful to Joe Brinley, director of the Woodrow Wilson Center Press, for his guidance and persistence, as well as Yamile Kahn, managing editor of the Press. I have enjoyed support for this project from Michael Kugelman and Susan Levenstein, and Bryce Wakefield of the Asia Program office and able research assistants Daniel Greenberg, Rory Lin, and Ritodhi Chakraborty. Lucy Jilka, Kimberly Conner, and especially Lindsay Collins of the Scholar Administration Office were extremely helpful.

At Albright Stonebridge, Sandy Berger and Tony Harrington have been instrumental in providing support for bringing this project to fruition. Sandy gave his time directly in interviews, guidance, and the remembrance of details about the shaping of the Clinton administration's economic engagement strategy. Richard Celeste was kind enough to share his perspectives on the US-India relationship from his vantage point as ambassador during the second term of the Clinton administration. Mona Sutphen was an early source of inspiration. John Schlosser was an important source of wisdom about strategic matters involving the region.

My service in the Clinton administration is a basis for most of the case studies in this book. For this opportunity to serve, I am deeply grateful to President Bill Clinton as well as the late secretary of commerce, Ron Brown. Had he not died so tragically, Ron would have made further important contributions to the US dialogue about the advantages for the United States of international economic engagement. I am also indebted to Ron's successors under whom I served, Mickey Kantor and Bill Daley, as well as undersecretaries for international trade Jeffrey Garten and Stuart Eizenstadt. I was privileged to receive the assignment of interfacing with India and working with Michael Copps, David Rothkopf, Lauri Fitz-Pegado, Susan Esserman, the late Charles Meisner, and David Marchick in carrying out the "Big Emerging Markets" strategy. Ken Juster and Brian McCormack were generous in sharing their perspectives from the George W. Bush years. From the legislative branch, Jonah Blank was generous with his experience not only about the US-India relationship but also the process whereby one can actually produce a book.

Frank Wisner has been a constant source of information, support, and encouragement in my attempts to better the US-India relationship. Ashley Wills was generous in his sharing with me his vast knowledge of South Asia and the conduct of US foreign policy in that part of the world, as was Matthew Daley.

At the US-India Business Council (USIBC), Michael Clark and Ron Somers understood the deep relationship between the economic interests of their USIBC members and the overall growth in the US-India relationship. I am grateful to them for sharing their insights and recollections. I am particularly grateful to Ron for including me as a part of the USIBC team advocating the US-India civil nuclear initiative. In this capacity, I was the beneficiary of associations with Bruce Fein and Graham Wisner. Sanjay Bhatnagar was kind enough to review chapter 5 from the perspective of his long experience with energy and environmental matters in India. I am grateful to the president and chief executive officer of the US Chamber of Commerce, Tom Donohue, and his senior vice president for international affairs, Dan Christman, for their support. Tom Campbell was especially helpful with his insights on the food security issues dealt with in chapter 8.

During the past fifteen years, I have been privileged to work closely with the Indian American community and I am grateful to them. Swadesh Chatterjee has played a key role in the political development of the community and has been most helpful in delineating the role of Indian Americans in US-India economic engagement as it affects strategic matters. I would also like to thank Ramesh Kapur, Prakash Ambegaonkar, and Aziz Haniffa for their personal support.

At the law firm Hogan Lovells, David Hensler guided my thinking about this book, and Marcia Wiss and Robert Pender readily shared with me their wealth of knowledge on India.

From the Indian side, I am grateful to Meera Shankar, the present ambassador of India to the United States, and her mentor in Washington, the late S. S. Ray. Shankar, Ray, and each of the Indian ambassadors subsequent to him—Naresh Chandra, Lalit Mansingh, and Ronen Sen—have been incredibly generous over the years in sharing their knowledge and experience. Amit Mitra gave freely of his views and critiques from his perspective as secretary-general of the Federation of Indian Chambers of Commerce and Industry. Amit's deputy, Vijay Topa, was always willing to provide helpful guidance from his marvelous store of good judgment and understanding. I was fortunate to have the help of the Confederation of Indian Industry's chief mentor, Tarun Das, and deputy director-general, Kiran Pasricha.

I would like to thank Walter Andersen for his careful readings of the manuscript and his many helpful comments and suggestions. And I am grateful to Teresita Schaffer, Howard Schaffer, Karl "Rick" Inderfurth, Stephen Cohen, and Tim Roemer.

The first person to read the manuscript for this book was my beloved wife, Ann. Being familiar with her expertise—honed as a copy editor for the *Public Papers of President Harry S. Truman,* as a member of President Richard Nixon's speechwriting staff, and as a partner at Hogan Lovells—it was with some trepidation that I awaited her comments. Without her view that this book would be worth publishing, her editorial assistance, and her love and support throughout the process of production, this book would have been impossible. My mother, Clarene Vickery, as of this writing is ninety-two years of age, is still sharp as a tack, and has encouraged me at every step in writing this book. My brothers Donald, Kenneth, and Steve have all written books of their own and have provided advice and guidance, for which I am grateful. I am blessed with two adult sons, Morgan and Philip, whose constant interest and inquiries concerning this project have been an incentive to keep going. There are many others to whom I owe much in connection with this book. However, I had best stop now or the acknowledgments may become longer than the work itself.

The Eagle and the Elephant

Chapter 1

Economic Engagement:
The Engine of Strategic Cooperation

I told the Prime Minister that we heartily support his ambitious program of economic reform that brings India's economy into the global marketplace. This important reform plan will be the engine of growth in our relationships.

—President William J. Clinton, news conference with
Prime Minister P. V. Narasimha Rao, May 19, 1994

During the night of November 26–27, 2008, terrorists moved methodically through the Taj Mahal and Oberoi hotels in Mumbai. Spreading mayhem, they looked especially for Americans and Britons to murder. The terrorists attacking Mumbai picked these luxury hotels as prime targets for a compelling strategic reason. The Taj and the Oberoi are icons of Indian economic prosperity and commercial relations between Indian and foreign companies. These hotels are known as places where Indian businesspeople gather with their counterparts from the United States and the United Kingdom. A third target, the Leopold Café, where a dozen were killed, was chosen for similar reasons.

The linkage between US-India economic engagement and these targets of the Mumbai terrorists was palpable. The Mumbai terrorists sought icons in order to denigrate India's economic engagement with the United States and other such countries. In seeking to promote an international conflagration, these economic targets were on a par with the murders of peaceful Indian travelers at a train station, the infirm at a hospital, and Jews at an international hospitality center. These were all targets chosen to shock and offend. The terrorists apparently hoped to set off a war between India and Pakistan, a conflict that would work against the strategic interests of both the United

1

States and India. However, against the background of a maturing economic and strategic relationship between the United States and India, no such war occurred. Instead, US-India cooperation against terrorism, including that emanating from Pakistan, became closer than ever.

On July 18, 2005, President George W. Bush and Prime Minister Manmohan Singh entered a news conference in the White House's East Room to endorse the Joint Statement they had just issued. The statement covered many areas of existing and potential cooperation between the United States and India. However, the pronouncement that caught the world's eye and captured the attention of strategic thinkers in both the United States and India concerned the possibility of civil nuclear cooperation. By 2005, the level of trade and investment between the United States and India had risen exponentially since India had made significant moves to open its economy in 1991. This economic engagement had built a community of shared interests that contributed greatly to the feasibility of making this Joint Statement on civil nuclear cooperation. These shared economic interests were fundamental to the subsequent passage of legislation enabling the implementation of civil nuclear cooperation and the ending of India's nuclear isolation. Had the Mumbai terrorists struck a week later, they would have encountered a business delegation from the United States seeking to implement the US-Indian civil nuclear agreement. Many members of that delegation represented companies and business interests long involved in both US trade and investment with India and the push for civil nuclear cooperation.

On October 1, 2008, less than two months before the Mumbai attack, the US Congress gave final legislative approval to the US-India civil nuclear initiative. In that same year, the United States and India signed agreements worth billions of dollars to provide military transport and naval patrol aircraft. The rising tide of US-India trade and investment made possible the civil nuclear agreement. In turn, the agreement was instrumental in creating an atmosphere of trust conducive to defense acquisitions and closer ties across the board. US export controls generally flow down from nuclear transfer restrictions. Revising these restrictions for civil nuclear technology had an impact on regulations that have long restricted transfers of other high-technology products. Other instances of US-India economic engagement have had less fortunate consequences.

In 1993, for instance, a subsidiary of Enron signed an agreement to build near the coastal village of Dabhol in Maharashtra State one of the world's largest gas-fired electrical power plants. This was to be the first of eight so-called fast-track projects. The fast-track program was an initiative the Indian minister of power designed to promote foreign direct investment in India and to relieve the country's chronic shortage of electric power. As eventually renegotiated, the Dabhol contract called for the building of a 2,000-megawatt plant and payment to Enron of some $35 billion over the life of the contract. The Enron investment in Dabhol was to be the largest single foreign direct investment in India. Unfortunately, in 2001, Enron and the Dabhol power project collapsed amid allegations of fraud, corruption, and price gouging.

The collapse of the Dabhol project caused hundreds of millions of dollars in losses to lenders and investors all around the world and soured the appetite for foreign investment in India's conventional power sector. Seeing this collapse of a flagship investment between the United States and India and experiencing problems of their own, major US power developers pulled out of India. Others refused to invest. Economic engagement between the United States and India on power development ground to a halt. The fast-track program failed. The disastrous Dabhol/fast-track experience has been a significant factor in the failure of the United States and India to cooperate significantly on conventional power development. This lack of successful engagement has adversely affected cooperation on the related issues of environmental protection and climate change.

These episodes concerning terrorism, civil nuclear engagement, and power development indicate that the linkage between economic engagement and strategic issues is sometimes direct and forceful. More often, however, the linkage is indirect and remote, although no less forceful in the long run. These episodes also show that the impact of economic engagement can be both positive and negative. When economic engagement supports initiatives like civil nuclear cooperation, the effects on strategic cooperation are manifest and positive. However, the sad history of the Enron power project at Dabhol and the whole fast-track program provides a cautionary example of the negative effects on strategic cooperation that can come from economic engagement.

Definitions of "Strategic Issues" and "Economic Engagement"

Economic engagement has profound effects on the ability of nations to cooperate on strategic issues. For the purposes of this book, the term "strategic" is used in its broadest sense to denote major issues of transnational significance. These issues require the use of political strategy for their solution or amelioration. From this perspective, defense and military security matters are certainly strategic issues. However, the transnational issues of energy, the environment, economic development, food, and health also require strategic approaches if they are to be addressed successfully. Therefore, these issues are also strategic aspects of international relations.

The "economic engagement" under consideration here happens in both the public and private sectors. Trade and investment are the most prominent categories of economic engagement, and the ones usually cited for their political effects. Trade and investment in turn can be divided into component parts. Because trade in goods is more easily and more accurately measured than that in services, trade in goods is the type of trade usually referenced for its political effect. But this convention is outdated. Services now tend to hold a dominant position in most developed economies. As a developing economy, India prides itself on having a world-class information technology services industry. Information-technology-enabled services are arguably now preeminent in their political impact on the abilities of India and the United States to cooperate strategically.

Similarly, international investment can be broken down into foreign direct investment (FDI) and foreign portfolio, institutional or indirect investment (FII). FDI involves some management of the enterprise in which an equity interest is acquired. FDI is usually thought of as being a more stable and longer-term investment providing greater opportunities for technology and management skill transfer. FDI is viewed by many government officials as having a greater political impact on the ability of the United States and India to cooperate strategically on issues of broad transnational importance. FDI in plant and equipment, infrastructure, and other projects continue to be viewed favorably by both Indian and US officials. In particular, Indian officials see the United States' FDI in a positive light and profess to encourage more of it.

FII seems less welcome in India. FII is viewed as being less stable and more likely to cause domestic dislocation. Heavy US investor withdrawals from the Indian stock market in 2008 and 2009 were subject to political criticism. However, in 2010 the Indian economy was on a sharper growth path than that of the United States and was likely to remain so for the foreseeable future. Indian commentators took pride in the return of international institutional investors to the Indian market. Although Indian officials resisted calls to restrict FII, the influential Indian elite involved in these markets seemed to give the United States little credit for this inflow of FII.

Public and private lending also play a role in US-India economic engagement. Bilaterally, public lending is chiefly through the subsidized mechanism of the US Export-Import Bank. In effect, the Ex-Im Bank's program allows Indian purchasers of US exports to borrow at below-market rates. The international lending agencies such as the World Bank and the Asian Development Bank are usually not thought of as bilateral instrumentalities. Yet the reality is that because of US influence in the lending operations of both institutions, the funds they provide are significant in the US-India relationship. However, lending from private sources is vastly larger than public lending. Even so, the potential importance of private lending for economic engagement has been held down in the case of India by restrictive Indian laws and regulations. These strictures have been credited by many Indians with helping India avoid some of the worst aspects of both the Asian financial crisis of the 1990s and the recent international financial crisis that began in the United States.

Aid flows can also have a significant effect on the ability and willingness of the United States and India to address strategic issues. Historically, US government aid to India has been a fundamental type of US-India economic engagement and has had a direct impact on US-India strategic cooperation. US aid has been both monetary and in kind. Monetary aid has gone to projects ranging from health to energy to child labor. The most outstanding example of in-kind aid has been the so-called Public Law 480 sale of US agricultural commodities for Indian currency that could only be spent within India. With the diminution of US government aid to India during the past two decades, private assistance has become more important. The Bill & Melinda Gates and William J. Clinton foundations, along with numerous India-centric charities such as the American India Foundation, constitute a subcategory of US-India economic engagement particularly important to US-India strategic cooperation in health and education.

On a macroeconomic level, the various government actions affecting currency valuations may also be seen as a type of economic engagement that affects strategic cooperation. Certainly, the struggles at the Group of Twenty and elsewhere to deal with imbalances and stimulus measures are a type of engagement central to international relations. In the case of the United States and India, the strength and mutuality of the underlying trade, investment, lending, and aid relationships seem to have driven the two countries in the direction of cooperation in their efforts to meet the most recent worldwide financial and economic crisis.

In summary, "economic engagement" includes trade, investment, lending, aid, and the monetary and regulatory interactions that affect these categories of engagement.

Methodology

This book explores the strategic aspects of economic engagement within the context of the US-India relationship through a series of case studies. This exploration will show that economic engagement directly affects the political ability of the United States to cooperate with India in addressing strategic issues. The instances of US-India economic engagement are set forth in this book as case studies showing that economic engagement is fundamental to the ability of the United States and India to cooperate politically. In turn, the political ability of the United States and India to cooperate is vital to the solution of issues fundamental to the peace and prosperity of the United States, India, and the world.

The case studies in this book are vehicles for exploring US-India cooperation on major strategic issues. Although the case study method is a common methodology in schools of law and business, the approach here to constructing these cases is often personal. The episodes under consideration draw on my involvement with the United States–India experience dating back over the past forty-five years. My contact with India began in 1964. As a participant in the Fulbright program, I went to South Asia to do research on the role of the press in the politics of the region. In India, Sri Lanka, and Pakistan, I was impressed with the political role of newspaper publishers not just as purveyors of news and opinion but also as major players in the economies of their countries. Plainly, the economic roles of the publishers affected what happened politically on issues of concern to the United States.[1] Later, as a lawyer and elected official, I saw firsthand the relationship between the growing economic engagement of Indian Americans in US-India trade and the impact of that engagement on US politics. During the past fifteen years, I have been intensely involved in US-India economic engagement as a government official and then as a consultant advising United States–based entities involved in US-India trade and investment.

I have drawn on this personal experience while attempting to place this work in the broader framework of descriptive, normative, and prescriptive inquiry. This framework is indicated by considering, within the context of the US-India relationship, the following questions:

- What is the impact of economic engagement on strategic relations?
- What should be the impact of economic engagement on strategic relations?
- What, if anything, should the US government do to make the impact of economic engagement work more fully to the benefit of the US national interest?

The responses to these questions are explored more deeply in the concluding chapter of this book. However, it can be stated at the outset that the cases presented here show that US-India economic engagement is fundamental to the two countries' strategic relationship.

Recognition of the Relationship between Economic Engagement and Strategic Issues

Many have recognized a relationship between economic engagement and strategic issues. The relationship has been described in both positive and negative terms. The liberal philosopher John Stuart Mill spoke of international trade as being the "principal guarantee of the peace of the world."[2] Mill perhaps borrowed from Thomas Hobbes, who listed "the desire of such things that are necessary to commodious living" among "the passions that incline men to peace."[3] In a negative vein, David Hume found that "nothing is more usual among states which have made some advances in commerce, than to look on the progress of their neighbors with a suspicious eye, to consider all trading states as their rivals and to suppose that it is impossible for any of them to flourish but at their expense." Vladimir Lenin took this jealousy to its extreme conclusion when he characterized World War I as an "imperialist war" and blamed this "highest stage of capitalism" for "years and even decades of armed struggle between the 'great' powers for the artificial preservation of capitalism by means of colonies, monopolies, privileges, and national oppression of every kind."[4]

In the modern literature, the political economist Harold Lasswell identifies economics as one of the four primary instruments through which governments pursue foreign policy. Lasswell distinguishes this use of goods and money from information, diplomacy, and force as the other primary instruments of foreign policy.[5] However, information and diplomacy are most often ways in which messages about force and economics are communicated and manipulated, rather than primary instruments.[6] Seen in this perspective, force and economics are the two preeminent instruments of foreign policy.

Economics as a primary instrument for the pursuit of foreign policy can be characterized as an instrument of "statecraft." According to Benn Steil and Robert Litan, David Baldwin provides the "single classic text" on "economic statecraft."[7] Although there are other valuable texts, most of these tend to concentrate on the efficacy of sanctions[8] or narrower concepts such as "commercial diplomacy."[9] Baldwin's work is a leading text on the full range of economic engagement as an instrument of foreign policy.[10] The fact that in the last twenty-five years there has appeared no other such work is demonstrative of the paucity of attention given economic engagement as an instrument of foreign policy.[11] Steil and Litan's work on financial statecraft is itself a rather unique exposition of a segment of economic engagement as an instrument of foreign policy.

Among the US presidents and Indian prime ministers who have served during the focus period of this book—1991 to 2010—there has been widespread recognition of the importance of economic engagement to foreign policy. In welcoming Prime Minister Manmohan Singh to Washington in November 2009 as the first official state visit of his presidency, President Barack Obama said of the United States and India, "It's the story of two economic marvels fueled by an ethic of hard work and innovation. And today, our nations are two global leaders driven not to dominate other nations but to build a future of security and prosperity for all nations."[12] A year later, as a member of the private-sector presidential executive mission, I watched as Obama implemented this vision. He moved from a meeting with business in Mumbai to a joint statement and address to Parliament in New Delhi stressing economic engagement and then moving to strategic cooperation. In dealing with the Afghanistan crisis, he has pledged to "work with our partners" (including India) "to pursue a more effective civilian strategy" that features agricultural assistance as a means to make "an immediate impact in the lives of the Afghan people."[13]

On his 2009 trip to Washington, Prime Minister Singh described economic relationships as "the bedrock upon which social, cultural, and political relationships are built." He continued, "A strategic relationship that is not underpinned by a strong economic relationship is unlikely to prosper."[14] With regard to Afghanistan, he also stressed the economic dimension of Indian policy. Citing the lesson of history that "peace, security, and prosperity are indivisible," he pledged India to "continue to assist Afghanistan in building its institutions and its human resources."[15]

President George W. Bush has been criticized for an overreliance on military means in launching a "war on terror" as a response to the attacks of

September 11, 2001. This criticism has been particularly harsh with regard to the invasion of Iraq. However, President Bush fully grasped the relationship between economic engagement and strategic cooperation in US-India relations. At the press conference announcing the historic Joint Statement of July 18, 2005, Bush said, "We're also committed to increasing the prosperity of the people of India and America alike. Today marks the completion of the next steps in strategic partnership. Completing this partnership will help us further cooperation in the areas of civil nuclear, space, and high-technology commerce."[16]

During his second visit to Washington as prime minister in 2000, Atal Bihari Vajpayee noted, "Economic and business cooperation is the critical pillar of our relations."[17] Vajpayee's remark echoed the thoughts of the prime minister who first fostered abolition of the "License Raj," P. V. Narasimha Rao. In addressing the US Congress in 1994, Rao used "democracy and development" as the metaphorical "fingers" for sustaining positive US-India relations.[18]

Thus, the question is not whether economic engagement plays a role in strategic cooperation but the nature of that role.[19] Economic engagement has been characterized as the "foundation" or "ballast" for the US-India bilateral relationship. The "foundation" concept is that of a less-noticed economic structural component that keeps the political superstructure standing. "Ballast" invokes the image of a ship more easily kept on course in the midst of changing political winds because of the "weight" of economic engagement. Both these metaphors fail to capture the dynamic, active role played by economic engagement. Perhaps the metaphor that best captures the role of economic engagement in promoting US-India strategic cooperation is that used by President Clinton in the opening quotation above—"engine of growth."

Economic Engagement and Foreign Policy in the Clinton Administration

President Clinton saw economic engagement as the "engine" for foreign policy.[20] Samuel R. ("Sandy") Berger, first deputy national security adviser and then the national security adviser to Clinton, says that the role of economic engagement in Clinton's foreign policy was prompted in part by what Clinton knew best about foreign policy. Coming from a background as governor of Arkansas, an exporting state, Clinton was familiar with the role of trade development as a primary international function of government. He came to office as the first post–Cold War president of the United States. As Berger has said, "Clinton inherited a world quite different from that of his presidential predecessors. Clinton's presidential world was not defined by two rival security blocs. Clinton saw a world defined in large part by global economics—a world in which economics could drive political and security issues. Commerce was a legitimate part of diplomacy, and he was willing to use his authority to advance the interests of the United States through economic engagement." According to Berger, "Clinton probably sold more planes for Boeing than Boeing sold for itself during Clinton's years in the White House." From his experiences as the former governor who had sought to sell Arkansas' products abroad and solicit foreign direct investment, it was natural for Clinton to view economic engagement as a tool of diplomacy.[21]

Whatever the roots of President Clinton's international outlook, his actions in setting up a National Economic Council (NEC) and using it as a primary part of the national security apparatus were innovative and significant. My former colleague at the Department of Commerce, David Rothkopf, comments in his landmark study of the National Security Council (NSC) that the Clinton era was marked by a shift of focus to "prosperity and growth as engines of personal advancement, social harmony, justice and peacekeeping."[22] In this respect, the agreement of Tony Lake and Sandy Berger at the NSC with Robert Rubin and Bowman Cutter at the NEC to have a common international economic staff for the NSC and the NEC was fundamental.[23] Certainly, from my perspective at the Commerce Department, the fact that the department was dealing at the White House with the same set of international economic staff members handling both security and commercial matters made a significant impact. This commonality of staff confirmed that the administration was committed to the same vision of economic engagement we were seeking to implement at Commerce. Further, Vice President Al Gore, with his interests in the Internet and international competitiveness issues, was intimately involved in international economic matters through his national security adviser, Leon Fuerth, and domestic policyadviser, David Beier. This involvement further strengthened the view at Commerce of the link between economic engagement and international strategic cooperation.

The Clinton emphasis on economic engagement as the engine of strategic cooperation was made plain to all of us when the Commerce Department, in league with the NEC, brought about a reversal of the policy conditioning renewal of China's most-favored-nation trade status on a revision of its human rights policies. China had reacted negatively on a range of strategic cooperation matters, most notably in a less-than-successful trip by Secretary of State Warren Christopher to Beijing in March 1994. Secretary of Commerce Ron Brown and the Commerce Department argued that the strategic relationship with China was more likely to be furthered through economic engagement than ultimatums. We at the department were able to provide data and analysis that showed the harm to ordinary Americans from nonrenewal of most-favored-nation status for China. The May 1994 policy change fit well with India's economic emergence and new openness to the world.[24] The shift set the stage for business development initiatives not only with China but also India and other major developing nations.

In retrospect, the initiatives of President Clinton in setting up the NEC and upgrading the role of economic engagement can be seen as both a revival of policies employed by his predecessors during the Cold War and a precursor for those used in the George W. Bush and Obama administrations. President Richard Nixon had established a Council on International Economic Policy in January 1971. This council was established to "achieve consistency between domestic and foreign economic policy." Its avowed purpose was to "provide a clear top-level focus for the full range of international economic policy issues; deal with international economic policies—including trade, investment, balance of payments, finance—as a coherent whole; and consider the international economic aspects of essentially foreign policy issues, such as foreign aid and defense, under the general policy guidance of the National Security Council."[25]

Joseph Nye, dean of the John F. Kennedy School of Government at Harvard University and a former assistant secretary of defense, coined the term "soft power" to signify power based on the power of attraction or attractiveness. Nye places sanctions, payments, and bribes in the category of "hard power" and concentrates on institutions, values, culture, and policies as "soft power."[26] However, as the Obama administration began, the terminology had changed. "Soft power" changed into "smart power," with a strong, positive economic content concentrating on global development, economic integration, and technology and innovation.[27]

In the first years of the Obama administration, this concept of "smart power" appeared to gain momentum. For example, at the Department of State, there was a concentration on "five pillars" of US-India relations. Four of these five pillars involved economic engagement. At the Treasury, there was involvement with India at the Group of Twenty and with the US-India CEO Forum. The deputy secretary of the Treasury, Neal Wolin, said in discussing Treasury's relations with the Department of Defense, "It's always been true, since the beginning of nations, that economic relations between nations, mercantile relations between nations, have been right in the core of their broader relations. And that economic policy globally has always been deeply intertwined with the politico-military piece of foreign policy."[28] At the Department of Defense, Secretary Robert M. Gates proposed three multi-billion-dollar funds that, in addition to training security forces, would concentrate on prevention and stabilization through largely economic means.[29] The Obama administration's "National Security Strategy," sent to Congress in May 2010, placed a renewed emphasis on the economic component of foreign policy.[30]

Thus, for all its innovation, Clinton's establishment of the NEC and use of economic engagement can also be seen as both a return to and a precursor of methods for using the economic tools of statecraft.

The Interactive Relationship between Economic Engagement and Political Action on Strategic Issues

As taken from the case studies in the chapters that follow, the thesis of this work is that economic engagement most often drives political strategic cooperation, not vice versa. Certainly, economic engagement and political action on strategic issues are interactive and interdependent. As discussed below, the interaction between the political and economic may be characterized as "feedback loops." It is also true that once organized violence commences, the immediate role of economic engagement changes in character. However, this does not indicate that economic engagement is subordinate to force as an engine of foreign policy. Economic engagement does not cease to be the engine of international strategic cooperation when there is a September 11, 2001, terrorist attack or a "war on terrorism." The economic role is certainly changed but is ultimately no less vital. Put another way, "the end of history," using Francis Fukuyama's phrase, is not required for economic engagement to become the engine of foreign policy.[31] "History" is of course as much the record and interpretation of economic occurrences as it is those of force and violence. Economic engagement should not be considered a category of foreign policy separate from security considerations. Rather, as we shall see, the two are so closely intertwined as to be inseparable at the strategic level. The duality in strategic thinking and bureaucratic organization that tends to place economics and security in separate realms is inadequate to furthering the national interest in the most effective manner. Placing economic engagement into a subordinate role can be equally harmful.

Objections to Linking Economic Engagement with Strategic Issues

Nevertheless, there are those who argue that economic engagement, particularly commercial engagement, should be separated insofar as possible from strategic relations, especially questions of military security and human rights. During my tenure at the Department of Commerce, there was considerable surprise among the leadership when the eminent national security pundit Jim Hoagland wrote a column criticizing the emphasis on trade development and commercial diplomacy as a detriment to progress on human rights.[32] *The Economist,* with a cover that portrayed a hand with money and implied governmental bribery, likewise criticized the concept of national promotion of international economic engagement as a tool of foreign policy. The criticism seemed to be that particularly matters involving national defense and security should be separated insofar as possible from economic considerations in order to keep the national interest from being sold out for material gain. The argument is that strategic matters involve existential and moral issues that are best kept separate from those of economic engagement, lest economics take precedence over defense security or moral values. It is argued that relating economic and security interests can only bring about confusion in the furtherance of a nation's strategic interests.[33] The cases reviewed in this book will show, however, that economic engagement can be instrumental in providing levers that are positive alternatives or supplements to other tools of statecraft.

Others object to the use of economic engagement as an instrument of diplomacy because such use interferes with the operation of the international market for goods and services. When I arrived at the Department of Commerce, one of my first objectives was to establish an "Advocacy Center." This center was to be a part of implementing the Clinton administration's National Export Policy, which outlined the objectives for the interagency Trade Promotion Coordinating Committee, chaired by the secretary of commerce. This kind of interagency advocacy on behalf of US companies for major projects and contracts was to be a positive way to "level the playing field" against foreign competitors and build jobs in the United States.

In preparing to set up the Advocacy Center, I was challenged by members of the Commerce Department's professional staff who had just completed twelve years of service under the Ronald Reagan and George H. W. Bush administrations. They objected to the use of economic engagement through advocacy on particular deals as an "interference with the market." These internal critics argued that although it may be legitimate to try to promote the preconditions and environment for economic engagement, specific advocacy and promotion can only have a distorting effect.[34] According to some, if there is to be a government role in economic engagement, it should only be in those areas where the market does not operate. From this perspective, governmental aid, particularly military aid or aid that has a direct security linkage, is a legitimate instrument of statecraft, but other types of economic engagement should be left to the market. Trade is best left to the market, and aid should have only the limited utility of meeting needs that by definition cannot be met by the market.

From an expansive perspective of the sanctity of the market, governmental aid to other countries, or organizations within those countries, may be an appropriate use of economic engagement to promote national strategic interests, but government assistance to the private sector to further strategic objectives is inappropriate—whether in the form of guarantees from the US Export-Import Bank, insurance from the Overseas Private Investment Corporation, grants from the Trade Development Agency, contract advocacy, or otherwise. However, this view fails to attribute sufficient importance to the primary economic role played by the private sector in the United States. In terms of economic engagement and development, government acting on its own cannot hope to match the aggregate economic resources and impact of the private sector.

In each of the case studies set forth in this book, the government acting with only public resources could not expect to achieve the bilateral cooperation necessary to effectively address the strategic issues under consideration. Strong "public-private" partnerships are the only effective way for the United States to make full use of economic engagement as a powerful tool of its foreign policy. This public-private partnership means more than consultation for advice from business executives. The promotion of a confluence of interests between the private sector and government is a prerequisite for making effective use of economic engagement as an instrument to promote strategic cooperation.

Positive and Negative Uses of Economic Engagement

Economic engagement can be used as a tool of US foreign policy both positively and negatively. Unfortunately, the negative use of economics in the form of supposedly punitive sanctions has received the most attention as a tool of US foreign policy. Negative sanctions too often have been a mainstay of the United States' foreign policy discourse. This has been particularly true in the US Congress, where negative sanctions have often been the preferred way to show action on foreign policy problems. At times, Congress seems to view such sanctions as the easiest way to approach foreign policy issues. Negative sanctions require no appropriations or taxes. Legislation of a sanctions regime can be accomplished without the expenditure of apparent blood or apparent treasure.

As will be discussed, India particularly has felt the pressure of the actual or threatened withdrawal of economic engagement as a sanction for unwanted conduct. The most obvious case of such US sanctions against India has been the measures imposed in response to the 1998 Indian nuclear tests. In that instance, the so-called Glenn Amendment activated a variety of sanctions in an attempt to affect Indian behavior on a matter of extreme strategic importance to the United States and India. The Glenn Amendment sanctions failed spectacularly and were eventually withdrawn. The United States' threat of economic sanctions to modify Indian conduct toward Iran will also be analyzed. Historically, the cases show that a positive use of economic engagement is far more effective than a negative approach.

Economic Engagement and the US Government's Conduct of Foreign Policy

Given the importance and desirability of economic engagement, the United States has far to go in integrating economic engagement into its foreign policy apparatus. As pointed out above, there is not now nor has there been during the focus period of this study any lack of recognition of economics as an important factor in securing strategic cooperation. Public policy difficulties in this field revolve around the incomplete elaboration of the economic component of US foreign policy strategy and utilization of the entire range of governmental and private resources in the pursuit of strategic goals.

There are many US government councils, offices, departments, and bureaus that can provide public resources for using economic engagement to accomplish strategic cooperation. The National Security Council and its Office of International Economics has been commented on above, as has the National Economic Council and its staff. Also within the Executive Office of the President, the Office of the US Trade Representative has a fundamental role to play with regard to economic engagement. Beyond the White

House, the State Department's Bureau of Economic, Energy, and Agricultural Affairs, Treasury's Office of International Affairs, and the Defense Department's Defense Security Cooperation Administration all have resources that are traditionally viewed as supportive of using economic engagement to support US international strategic goals.

However, the available resources within the federal government to be used in pursuing economic engagement as an instrument to promote strategic cooperation go far beyond these organizations. Other executive branch departments have resources that are often more effective in promoting economic engagement than those federal agencies usually thought of as relevant to the international strategic interests of the United States—including the Department of Commerce, with its International Trade Administration and Bureau of Industry and Security; the Department of Agriculture, with its Foreign Agricultural Service; the Department of Energy, with its Bureau of Policy and International Affairs; the Department of Transportation, with its International Aviation Office and International Transportation and Trade Office and the Federal Aviation Administration; and the Department of Health and Human Services, with its Food and Drug Administration. In addition to these departments, the Environmental Protection Agency, the Export-Import Bank, the Overseas Private Investment Corporation, and the Trade and Development Agency all have relevant resources.

With many federal agencies having resources highly relevant to the use of economic engagement as a tool of foreign policy, the chief challenges are (1) how to draw effectively on these resources and (2) how to integrate these resources into an economic component of strategic policy. Bureaucratic "turf wars" are legendary in Washington. When I was at the Department of Commerce attempting to put together interagency programs on advocacy and trade promotion, interdepartmental bureaucratic warfare was endemic. Observations since then have confirmed that this rivalry is a major consumer of governmental attention and energy. This rivalry takes two forms. First, there is a reluctance to concede or share functions. Second, where there is a shared function, it is routine to actively undermine another agency's execution of its efforts.

The State Department bureaucracy is particularly infamous for its unwillingness to allow others to share in foreign affairs or to concede any aspect of foreign affairs to non–State Department actors. One of the undersecretaries of commerce for international trade with whom I worked was Stuart Eizenstat, who had served as President Jimmy Carter's domestic policy adviser. Under Carter, the Foreign Commercial Service (FCS) had been moved from State to Commerce. Eizenstat pointed out to me that two decades after the transfer, State was still smarting from the loss of FCS. State still seems intent on maintaining a priority for its economic officers at the embassy level over FCS officers.[35] Likewise, when I was involved in establishing the Advocacy Center in Commerce as a function of the interagency Trade Promotion Coordinating Committee, State was intent on establishing its primacy on project advocacy.

With each of these relevant agencies, there are difficulties in melding a comprehensive, integrated economic engagement component into the policies on international strategic issues facing the United States. For example, at the State Department, economic matters are clearly viewed as of secondary importance. Even though Secretary Hillary Clinton has tried to elevate a variety of economic, educational, health, and human rights concerns as elements of foreign policy, the path to power within the department remains through the political affairs wing. Political affairs positions are filled, while economic offices remain empty. Matters involving guns and bombs far outweigh those having to do with trade and investment. At the embassies, those coming to talk about matters with a military relationship take precedence over those with an economic brief. The Treasury Department too often focuses on macroeconomic matters as if they were divorced from strategic considerations. The Commerce Department is often viewed as a dumping ground for political operatives instead of an integral part of strategic policy-making and policy implementation. At Commerce, there is a decades-long turf feud within the International Trade Administration; its three bureaus—United States and Foreign Commercial Service, Market Access and Compliance, and Manufacturing and Services—constantly jockey for advantage. The Office of the US Trade Representative is too often seen as a tool solely to further domestic interests and is insufficiently integrated into foreign policy strategic planning.[36] And even though food security is a key initiative of the Department of State, there seems to be little appetite at State for working in partnership with the Department of Agriculture and drawing on its resources to implement the initiative.

The Private-Sector Resource

On the private-sector side, there are resources that the government can use to build the public-private partnerships necessary to use economic engagement as an instrument for promoting strategic cooperation. Some of these resources will be utilized by contracting with for-profit corporations and with nonprofit nongovernmental entities. The primary example of this sort of relationship occurs when the Department of Defense or the US Agency for International Development contracts with the private sector for goods and services to be used in economic engagement with foreign entities. However, the great strength of the private sector in supporting the United States' foreign policy goals in partnership with the government comes not from commercial contracts but from voluntary participation. For example, there is a network of unpaid private-sector committees advising the US trade representative on trade policy matters. Most of these committees are administered jointly with the Department of Commerce, and some are administered with the participation of the Department of Agriculture, the Department of Labor, and the Environmental Protection Agency.[37] The president and department heads often consult with industry representatives. At Commerce during the Clinton administration, "CEO Breakfasts" involving business executives with diverse perspectives were particularly helpful in promoting economic engagement abroad.

There has been criticism that US private-sector participation in facilitating international economic engagement is a conflict of interest. The argument is that such participation is only undertaken for self-gain at the expense of the public. Of course, there is self-interest involved. One of the objects of such participation is to harness private interest to produce a public benefit. However, it is a mistake not to recognize that there is a willingness in the private sector to undertake difficulties and risks that is not driven simply by the profit motive. The US business community has shown itself willing to go beyond the profit motive and to act in the national interest in promoting international strategic cooperation through economic engagement. The role of public-private partnership in the crucial Presidential Business Development Mission to India in 1995 is discussed below. However, a non-Indian example illustrates the point more saliently. The example is that of the business executives who partnered with Secretary Ron Brown on his ill-fated mission to Bosnia and Croatia and, perhaps more especially, those who later returned with Secretary of Commerce Mickey Kantor.

We at Commerce's Trade Development Bureau recruited most of the US business executives to travel with Secretary Brown to Bosnia and Croatia and the mission resumed by Secretary Mickey Kantor. The immediate commercial value of projects in this war-torn area was not great by international standards. However, the promotion of economic engagement could help bring peace and stability to the states of the former Yugoslavia.

All involved knew that there was a physical risk in both the Brown and

Kantor missions. In fact, an earlier date for the Brown mission had been scrubbed. As one Commerce official put it to me, "I don't want to lose a secretary of commerce on my watch." The Brown trip was rescheduled for April 1996. The mission took place not long after the army of the former Yugoslavia had withdrawn from Bosnia and Croatia. In the waning days of open warfare, a Serbian-Montenegrin force had crossed the maritime mountains along the Croatian coast to destroy the antique city of Dubrovnik. Dubrovnik is one of the most perfectly preserved Medieval/Renaissance cities in the world, with a history extending back to ancient times. Set on a small peninsula jutting into the crystal-clear, blue-green waters of the Dalmatian Coast, the walled city is a United Nations World Heritage Site and was a major center for national tourism in the old Yugoslavia.

The army marching north from Montenegro had burned and otherwise destroyed many of the villages between their place of crossing the mountains and Dubrovnik. At the time Dubrovnik had, just south of the city, a modern airport capable of handling international jet traffic. When the army reached the airport, the soldiers looted radar and other air traffic control apparatus. They then marched on to Dubrovnik. From a ridge overlooking the medieval walled port city, the Serb-Montenegrin force commenced to shell one of the jewels of Western culture. It was only thanks to a heroic Croatian defense and the influence of US diplomatic efforts that the city was saved and the Serbs withdrew.

As we at the Department of Commerce recruited a business delegation to go with Brown, the Government of Croatia pushed to have Dubrovnik included as the first stop on the mission. The Croatians' plea was that the possibilities for economic revival through tourism to Dubrovnik were significant. The revival and expansion of this tourist trade would be a major factor in promoting stability along the Dalmatian Coast and in neighboring Bosnia. There were US companies represented on the mission with expertise in real estate development and air travel. However, not knowing exactly the security situation in the Dubrovnik area, there was a reluctance at the Department of Commerce to include Dubrovnik on the itinerary. The Croatians insisted that the airport was safe for Brown, a dozen or so of our colleagues at Commerce, and the business delegation of twelve US executives. There was one electronic beacon still operative and, besides, the airport would be used during the daylight for only a short visit. The visit would symbolize that the public and private sectors of the United States and Croatia could partner together to restore peace and prosperity in that part of the world through the rehabilitation of a major tourist attraction. Secretary Brown agreed that the Presidential Business Development Mission to Bosnia and Croatia would go to Dubrovnik.

April 3, 1996, the Wednesday before Easter, proved to have most unusual weather for a spring day along the Dalmatian Coast. Severe thunderstorms rolled in from off the Adriatic. These storms were not continuous but isolated in cells of exceptional darkness and heavy rain. Coming in from the Croatian capital of Zagreb, the plane transporting the Croatian prime minister, members of his Cabinet, and the Croatian ambassador to the United States landed at Dubrovnik safely and without incident. The Brown plane with the US business delegation was to land shortly after the Croatian plane. As the Brown plane approached the airport, it flew into a storm cell that eliminated visibility. Unwisely, the US Air Force crew of the Brown plane attempted to make a landing with the assistance of the single nondirectional beacon. Instead of being lined up on the Dubrovnik runway, the plane was off course by 8 degrees. By the time the pilot realized his mistake and was attempting to pull up, it was too late. The Brown plane plunged into Saint John's Mountain just short of its crest. The twenty-seven government and private-sector passengers were killed, along with the six US Air Force crew members and two Croatians.

President Clinton was particularly concerned that the work that Brown and his delegation had commenced in support of building stability in the former Yugoslavia be continued. Although Clinton was personally "devastated" by the loss of Brown as his friend and "best political advisor in the Cabinet," he recognized that Brown had been using Commerce "to further not only our economic objectives but our larger interests in the Balkans."[38] Vice President Gore felt that, both for substantive and symbolic reasons, this continuity should be shown as soon as possible and volunteered to lead a return mission. Instead, it was decided that Mickey Kantor would be installed as the new secretary of commerce as soon as possible. Kantor would lead the return mission as soon as it could be assured that the effort would be both safe and substantive.

I was asked to begin preparations for the mission immediately. Most of the Commerce officials who had been instrumental in planning and implementing the Brown mission had been killed along with Brown. So I went to Bosnia and Croatia to pick up the pieces of the mission and meet with Bosnian and Croatian officials. The difficulty of the situation was brought home to me in Sarajevo. There I stayed in a hotel the front of which had been blown off by Serbian cannon fire. The elevator was still operative, but it opened onto a hallway with no outside wall. Fortunately, my room was at the rear of the building, which, being away from the impact area of Serbian fire, was still intact. There were shots fired during the night. However, my meetings with officials, particularly those of the NATO-led Implementation Force (IFOR) in Bosnia, convinced me that the return mission could be both safe and substantive. The mission of IFOR was to separate the warring factions and establish the security necessary for peace. The IFOR officials were particularly anxious that private-sector economic activity be restarted to support their efforts at building the peace.

Upon my return to Washington with a favorable report and an outline for Secretary Kantor's return mission, we began recruiting in earnest for a private-sector delegation. Instrumental in this effort and the organization of the return mission was Assistant Secretary Lauri Fitz-Pegado, director general of the US and Foreign Commercial Service and a close friend of Ron Brown. Kantor's return mission was to carry forward the vision of public-private partnership in support of the United States' strategic goals in the Balkans.

Of the twelve companies that had lost executives on the Brown mission, all but one were willing to send another one of their top executives to the Balkans with Kantor. Another five companies not represented on the Brown mission agreed to send executives as well. Among these representatives, two had been scheduled to be on the plane with Brown, but they had withdrawn at the last minute for scheduling reasons. Except for these last-minute withdrawals, they, of course, would have been killed along with Brown, and yet they were willing to participate. The Kantor mission took place in July with sixteen private-sector participants. This time the landing at Dubrovnik was safe and without incident. However, for the second stop in Sarajevo, bad weather set in again. As we dipped below the mountain ridges to land at Sarajevo, we lost all visibility, and instead of landing, the plane pulled up and went to Zagreb. The entire private-sector delegation later continued with us to Bosnia and the completion of the mission.

With the full participation of the business delegation, the Kantor mission lived up to its substantive as well as symbolic goals in support of a public-private partnership to promote the United States' strategic goals in the Balkans. Kantor's speech to the IFOR command in Tuzla was particularly impressive. Before the assembled troops, he drew together the strands of economic engagement and strategic cooperation. One particularly meaningful result of the mission was US-Croatian private-sector cooperation in replacing the radar and air traffic control apparatus at the Dubrovnik airport. Today Dubrovnik is an international tourist destination of major proportions. The airport is the economic mainstay of a region that remains peaceful.

Recently, the United States' foreign policy and national defense apparatus seems to have found a new appreciation for the role of economic engagement in promoting the nation's strategic interests. The use of military force in Iraq to effect "regime change" has brought neither peace nor stability. In Afghanistan, force brought the removal of the Taliban government. However, in both instances, the inability of the United States, its allies, and the governments it has helped install to create viable economies has been a clear detriment to the achievement of US goals. With regard to the conflicts in both Iraq and Afghanistan/Pakistan, the Obama administration's approach contains a more robust recognition of the key role that economic development must play. With regard to India, Obama and Singh agreed during Singh's 2009 visit to hold a "Strategic Dialogue," the first of which was held in June 2010 and overtly included economic matters. Secretary of State Clinton has revived and strengthened the US-India CEO Forum that brings together chief executives from the United States and India to discuss and advise on issues between the two countries.

However, it is not clear whether the Obama administration intends to utilize the strong public-private partnership approach necessary for the effective use of economic engagement as a primary tool of foreign policy. President Obama has frequently been criticized for the use of harsh rhetoric with regard to business. As discussed below, the Obama administration has attempted to proceed with tax changes aimed at doing business abroad. In any event, there still does not exist the integration across departments and agencies necessary to making economic engagement a fully effective component of foreign policy. The number and seriousness of present international crises make this weakness prominent in the Obama administration.

Economic Engagement and the Government of India's Conduct of Foreign Policy

The relationship between economic engagement and strategic cooperation from the Government of India's perspective is largely beyond the scope of this book. As stated, the methodology for relating and analyzing case studies is highly dependent on personal experience. Because that experience has been in the context of my service for the US government and private sector, it would be presumptuous at this point to attempt an analysis of the way the Indian government uses economic engagement in its conduct of foreign policy. However, from the perspective of having observed the Indian government from outside, a few comments may be in order.

The Indian economic reforms begun in 1991 provided the opening for both India and the United States to use economic engagement as an instrument for achieving greater cooperation on strategic issues. During the focus period of this book, Indian governments have generally recognized the importance of economic engagement for strategic cooperation. These governments have reciprocated the United States' appreciation for the importance of economic engagement and have recognized its role in shaping the strategic relationship. This has generally been true regardless of the party in power in New Delhi. For example, in working with the Bharatiya Janata Party–led government of Prime Minister Atal Bihari Vajpayee on the visit of President Clinton in 2000, the Government of India was as receptive to US-India economic engagement as the Congress Party–led government of Narasimha Rao was for Secretary Brown's Presidential Business Development Mission in 1995.

However, special recognition must be given to the influence of Manmohan Singh on the policy of the Government of India toward economic engagement as a tool for promoting cooperation on strategic issues. Although the actions of the business community and the sentiment of the Indian electorate have played the roles discussed below, the influence and leadership of Manmohan Singh and his economic lieutenant Montek Singh Ahluwalia have been instrumental. Some observers have designated India's use of economic diplomacy to promote engagement with both the United States and China as the "Manmohan Singh Doctrine."[39]

That Singh and Ahluwalia should exercise influence to promote economic engagement as a tool of Indian diplomacy is not surprising. Both Singh and Ahluwalia are world-class economists. Singh earned his master's and doctoral degrees at Oxford University and had a distinguished career as an economist at Indian universities before becoming involved in government.[40] The influence of Singh during the focus period of this book (1991–2010) has been in his roles as finance minister (1991–96), as leader of the opposition in the Rajya Sabha (1996–2009), and as prime minister (2009–present). Montek Singh Ahluwalia, eleven years junior to Singh, similarly received his master's and doctoral degrees at Oxford University. He was Singh's secretary at the Ministry of Finance and is the deputy chairman of the influential Government of India Planning Commission, of which the prime minister is titular chairman. Ahluwalia is often the prime minister's chief economic spokesperson in such forums as the US-India Strategic Dialogue noted above.

During the visit of President Obama to India in November 2010, the Singh government continued the post-1991 tradition of emphasizing the importance of US-India economic engagement to relations between the two governments.

In spite of leadership at the top of the Government of India and widespread support within the democratic system of India, very considerable Indian discontinuities hinder the optimum use of economic engagement as a means for reaching India's strategic goals. Chief among these is the failure to complete the structural reforms initiated in 1991. Large portions of the Indian economy remain under government ownership or direct control. Instead of enhancing the ability of India to use economic engagement, these controls often make it more difficult to interact with the private-sector, market-oriented US economic system.

Perhaps of even more concern in its effect on US-India economic engagement is the operation of the Indian bureaucracy. Although there are many fine, honest Indian civil servants in tune with the demands of a modern, largely market-driven economy (particularly at top levels), the Indian bureaucracy has a reputation as a drag on free market economic engagement. Indians from the Prime Minister on down recognize this problem. Perhaps this difficulty is the historical hangover of an Indian bureaucracy originally structured to run a colonial administration or a top-down, command-and-control economy. Even where reforms have been successful in allowing or moving economic activity into the private sector, there still remain bureaucrats in number and attitude suited for the pre-1991 system. Many such officials are simply redundant. Their lack of functionality is a chief factor in India's inability to make the progress it would like in wringing corruption from government. Having no positive role to play, some officials turn to negative exercise of authority. From the nonfunctional negative exercise of authority, it is but a short step to the solicitation and acceptance of compensation for the selective removal of such a barrier.

· As discussed below, particularly in the case study on food security (see chapter 8), the Indian economic system is also riddled with the remnants of the autarkical policy that prevailed during the first forty-four years of Indian independence. The concept of India functioning without foreign goods or services still has a powerful attraction for many Indians. As a result, tariff and nontariff barriers remain at levels higher than those for the United States and other developed countries. Restrictions on investment by US and other foreign investors abound in activities ranging from financial services to defense contracting.

India's British colonial experience was one of the foreign power coming as a trader and staying as ruler. This experience is fading as a salient election issue. However, the history of British colonization, and that of previous invaders, is indelibly etched in the psyches of many in India's foreign policy elite and contributes to the attractiveness of autarky. Complete Indian autonomy in dealing with issues having foreign implications is a litmus test applied by some to international engagement of any kind. During the Cold War, this approach, along with other considerations, was a driver in India championing nonalignment and an Indian third way on most international issues. Even with the advent of economic liberalization, the growth of economic engagement is still inhibited on the Indian side by the specter of economic imperialism.

Economic-Political Interaction

A factor in the initial reluctance of the Obama administration to emphasize private sector international economic engagement as a primary tool of foreign policy may be the political disfavor into which foreign trade and investment have fallen. This is particularly true among the core constituencies of the Democratic Party. In the context of democracies like India and the United States, the strategic impact of economic engagement is affected by electoral and legislative politics.

For example, when presidential candidate Senator John Kerry labeled American enterprises shipping jobs abroad "Benedict Arnold" companies in the 2004 presidential campaign, that statement resounded among the electorates in both the United States and India. Likewise, when President Obama renewed his campaign pledge to end "tax breaks for corporations that ship our jobs overseas," this language became an issue in the Indian parliamentary elections. US voters are concerned about losing jobs to Indian outsourcing operations, and offshore outsourcing becomes a campaign issue. Indian voters are concerned about Indian service providers being locked out of access to the United States. The availability of visas thus became a campaign issue in the Indian elections of 2009. In his first State of the Union Address, President Obama renewed his call for ending tax deferral on profits not repatriated to the United States at the same time as he expressed a commitment to the successful completion of the Doha Round of negotiations for the World Trade Organization. He also mentioned trade with Colombia, South Korea, and Panama, but without calling for approval of the pending trade agreements with those countries. Doubtlessly, Democratic Party politics prevented his going further on trade issues at that time. In conjunction

Figure 1.1. Economic Engagement Feedback Loops

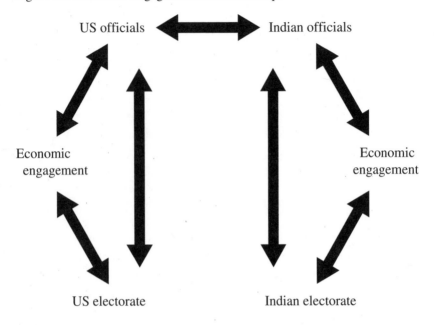

with a push for more US exports, he announced his intention to move forward with the South Korean free trade agreement. This announcement was received with a lack of enthusiasm among Democratic members of Congress and outright hostility from many of his supporters among organized labor.

Thus, US-India economic engagement has an impact on the behavior of both US and Indian electorates. These electorates then affect the behavior of the elected officials who deal with strategic issues. Economic engagement may also affect government officials directly in their strategic decisionmaking. Both elected and appointed officials may change their perspectives or actions on strategic issues based on their own perceptions of the economic impact on the national interest. Interactions between Indian and US officials on economic issues may affect their abilities to cooperate on a wide range of strategic issues. The interactive nature of democratic political considerations is illustrated in figure 1.1 as "feedback loops" that run (1) between economic engagement and the electorates, (2) between electorates and officials, (3) between economic engagement and officials, and (4) between US and Indian officials.

The impact of economic engagement on these feedback loops influences the behavior of the two nations both toward each other and toward third parties. In democracies, the interests created by economic engagement affect the electorate, and the electorate influences officials through the power of the ballot box. In turn, US elected officials may pass laws or cause regulations to go into effect that constrict or promote economic engagement.

For example, economic engagement in the form of outsourcing may cause a segment of the US electorate to oppose outsourcing. This opposition may be expressed through electing officials who are willing to pass laws or cause regulations to go into effect that constrict outsourcing. However, at each level, influence runs both ways. Not only does economic engagement affect the electorate, but the attitudes of the electorate also affect economic engagement. Executives involved in outsourcing may build a constituency in favor of US-India trade and investment. However, experience shows that an electoral constituency may also constrict economic engagement directly by opposing a particular type of engagement, for example, outsourcing. This can happen directly when a significant constituency's adverse attitude inhibits the willingness of corporate executives to be involved in an activity that may engender negative publicity and hostility. Also there may be a "flow-down" effect as officials take their case for or against economic engagement to the electorate. This leadership on economic issues may affect how the electorate uses its influence to affect economic engagement.

Economic engagement can also affect the actions of government officials directly. For example, nascent or prospective trade and investment can cause officials to change export and import regulations. Conversely, direct interaction between US and Indian officials can affect economic engagement. Using the civil nuclear example, interaction between US and Indian officials can result in the modification of US export controls. These controls will affect, in turn, not only trade in nuclear goods and technology but also the transfer of an entire range of high-technology goods and services between the United States and India. Civilian nuclear trade and investment will also affect such US-India joint actions as the interdiction of unauthorized nuclear transfers by a third nation.

The Historical Context

The importance of historical context must be appreciated in examining the case studies presented in this book. The focus period of this book is 1991 through 2010. This is the period that runs from the institution of broad economic reforms in India through the greatest economic decline faced by the United States since the Great Depression. However, the impact, positively and negatively, of economic engagement on US-India strategic cooperation is nothing new. Even through the distorting lens of the British Empire, the sister colonies of North America and India had some economic engagement of political significance. The Boston Tea Party, a precipitating event for the American Declaration of Independence and the ensuing Revolutionary War, was probably conducted with tea from India. Shortly after the United States declared its independence from Britain, it established consulates in Bombay and Calcutta, which have facilitated trade and investment between the United States and India for more than two hundred years. The early establishment of these consulates is indicative of economic engagement that began shortly after US independence and continued throughout the period when India was a colony.

From Indian independence in 1947 until the comprehensive Indian economic reforms of 1991, US-India economic engagement actually deteriorated in comparison with the nineteenth century and the first part of the twentieth century. This deterioration was largely based on Prime Minister Jawaharlal Nehru's vision of a Fabian socialist and import-substitution economic system for India. As US-India trade and investment dried up, about all that was left of economic engagement was the US-India aid portfolio. Even that aid portfolio at times seemed to be counterproductive to US-India cooperation on strategic issues. As discussed below, with regard to the "green revolution," the US administration of President Lyndon Johnson had increased food aid to India under the Public Law 480 program in the 1960s. Johnson had used this aid to try to force Indian domestic policy changes and movement away from the USSR on foreign policy issues. This heavy-handed attempt initially produced some movement in the direction Johnson wanted India to go. However, these tactics also produced a reservoir of bad feeling in Indian ruling circles. Nehru's daughter, Indira Gandhi, shared these feelings, and after becoming prime minister she attempted to take India further into socialism. As a result, such iconic US firms and leading foreign investors in India as Coca-Cola and IBM left the country in the 1970s.

In the 1950s, the United States transferred certain civilian nuclear technology to India under the US "Atoms for Peace" program. Even this limited economic engagement went bad when the Indians allegedly used some of the technology from this engagement and from a Canadian reactor to build their own nuclear weapons program. In 1974, India conducted a "peaceful" nuclear weapons test. This 1974 test ushered in a regime of US trade restrictions and sanctions that inhibited US-India trade and investment in virtually all types of high-technology goods and services. Although it is difficult to separate cause and effect, the deterioration of US-India economic engagement occurred in parallel with political deterioration. Cooperation between the two countries on strategic matters virtually ceased.

In 1991, the Indian economy reached its lowest point since the country achieved independence. India had barely enough foreign exchange for a week's worth of imports. After some two years of political turmoil following the assassination of Rajiv Gandhi in 1989, Narasimha Rao became prime minister, only to find the country nearly bankrupt. The new prime minister departed from precedent and brought in as his finance minister an academic economist who one day would be prime minister, Manmohan Singh. Under Singh's tutelage, the Rao government enacted economic reform measures that did away with many of the laws and rules that had established the Indian economy as one of the most tightly regulated economies in the world. The Indian economy took a significant turn toward free markets and the opening of the country to international trade and investment. The Rao government took steps to abolish the "License Raj," whereby detailed governmental approval controlling all facets of operations was required to conduct virtually any type of organized private economic activity. Tariffs were lowered and thousands of items were taken off the so-called restricted list. Being on this list meant that imports of the item were restricted to trade by the government. For the most part, the government refused to import items on the list. Thus, these items were for all practical purposes banned from importation.

The result of liberalization was immediate economic improvement. US-India economic engagement began to grow. The US-India political relationship began to become less adversarial and more positive. The nuclear tests by India in 1998 resulted in some slowdown in the economic engagement between India and the United States. However, as will be discussed below, neither US sanctions nor the slowdown lasted long. In general terms, the political relationship between India and the United States grew in tandem with the increase in economic engagement during the period from 1992 through 2008.

In 2010, India and the United States reached an economic crossroads. The international financial crisis that originated in the United States had seriously compromised the economies of the two countries. Markets eroded. Although India rallied in 2010 to forecast significant growth, the United States continued to wrestle with unemployment at levels not seen for decades.

The shifting of economic realities caused the beginning of serious macroeconomic engagement between the United States and India. As will be seen, the Group of Eight, which excluded India, was basically abandoned as the premier forum for macroeconomic interaction in favor of the Group of Twenty, in which India plays a significant role.

Thus, 1991 and 2010 are years of changed circumstances demarcating the beginning and end of a period of relative stability in the regulatory and international economic framework for observing a growing US-India economic engagement. This period serves as the environment for examining case studies that illustrate and illuminate the effects of US-Indian economic engagement on major strategic issues. The immediate post-2010 period will be a time of turbulence and challenge. Challenge always presents opportunity. The process of turning this period of challenge into change that takes advantage of the opportunity for US-India strategic cooperation will be driven ultimately and in major part by how the United States and India engage economically. There is always the possibility that episodes of force and violence will obscure the importance of economic engagement as the primary driver of the ability of the United States and India to cooperate strategically. Another India-Pakistan war, the fall of Pakistan to the Taliban, or the outbreak of war between the United States and/or its allies with Iran, North Korea, or another credible military power are examples of such possible events. However, even if one or more of such unlikely events should occur, economic engagement ultimately will be a driver of the strategic relationship. Episodes of force and violence will only change the timing, form, and perception of economic engagement as a strategic factor—not its fundamental role. Under any circumstances, the United States and India will need to integrate economic engagement into their respective policies for strategic cooperation.

The Bottom Line

Economic engagement is the engine of strategic cooperation. US-India case studies focused on the transition period 1991–2010 show that economic engagement has been the engine for moving the United States and India from estrangement to cooperation on strategic issues. Economic engagement and political actions are interactive. Economic engagement affects the political actions of US and Indian electorates and officials. Conversely, the political actions of electorates and officials affect US-India economic engagement.

During the focus period of this book, the United States and India have shared (1) an appreciation for the importance of economic engagement in defining their relationship; and (2) the impact of the economic engagement on strategic issues. However, there are difficulties and discontinuities—for example: (1) the inadequacy of the US bureaucracy for handling economic engagement issues; (2) the weakness of the US government in making use of public-private cooperation; (3) the inability of India to complete the economic and bureaucratic reforms that will move it beyond its command-and-control economic past; and (4) continuing Indian concerns about foreign influence in its economy and its strategic autonomy.

The quintessential case for studying the relationship between economic engagement and strategic cooperation is the US-India civil nuclear initiative. This case shows emphatically the relationships between economic engagement and such strategic issues as national and international security, energy, the environment, and economic development. Accordingly, let us turn to an examination of the US-India civil nuclear initiative.

Chapter 2

Economic Engagement and
Civil Nuclear Cooperation

It has freed India-US relations from the baggage of the past. You can't over-estimate its importance both in terms of symbolism and substance. The deal has opened the door to new opportunities ranging from cooperation in fighting climate change and nuclear nonproliferation to trade and investment.

—Ambassador Ronen Sen, describing the 2008 US-India civil nuclear agreement in an address to the US-India Business Council, March 4, 2009

On the morning of September 11, 2001, I went to the offices of Senator Richard Lugar (R-Ind.), then chairman of the Senate Foreign Relations Committee, in the Dirksen Senate Office Building. I was there to discuss the lifting of the few Glenn Amendment sanctions remaining against India for having tested nuclear devices some three years before. On the way into the Lugar offices, I noticed several assistants watching television. I jokingly asked what could be so important as to distract them from their work. I was told that an airplane had hit one of the towers of the World Trade Center in New York. An accident, I assumed. Probably a private plane had strayed off course. But I thought it strange. The weather in Washington was that of a beautiful day in late summer—not a cloud in the sky. The day seemed perfect for flying. I did not give the matter further thought as our staff host came out and led us into a conference room for the meeting.

One of the first questions asked by the Lugar staff member assigned to the India sanctions matter was why the nuclear issue was so important to US-India relations. I was about to respond when another staff assistant opened the door to the conference room. "A second plane has hit the World Trade Center," he said. "Another has crashed into the Pentagon. We have reason to believe that another plane is headed toward the Capitol. I suggest you not walk away from this building, but run." The meeting was over. We fled the building.[1]

The Historical Context

Why is the nuclear issue so important to US-India relations? The response to the question I never got to answer at that September 11, 2001, meeting has deep historical roots. These historical roots of the US-India nuclear controversy show how fundamental economic engagement is to strategic issues.

President Dwight D. Eisenhower had a keen interest in supporting the fledgling democracy of the newly independent India. In 1959, he had become the first American president to visit the new Republic of India, even though his "Cold War warrior" secretary of state, John Foster Dulles, and the secretary's brother, Allen, director of the Central Intelligence Agency, were deeply skeptical of the "nonaligned" foreign policy of India's first prime minister, Jawaharlal Nehru. Nehru's tilt toward the Soviet Union as a hedge against "neo-imperialism" seemed, at best, nonsense to the Dulles brothers and, at worst, a serious detriment to the US policy of containing the spread of communism from the Soviet Union and China. Nevertheless, with the support of a nascent US civil nuclear industry, Eisenhower had proposed the "Atoms for Peace" initiative to benefit countries like India.

The Atoms for Peace proposal came in a landmark 1953 speech at the United Nations. The proposal was aimed specifically at developing countries desperately in need of energy to fight their way out of poverty. India was one of the first nations to show interest in the proposal. Under the program, Indian scientists and engineers were given access to declassified US nuclear documents and US training at the Argonne Laboratory School of Nuclear Science and Engineering and other such US facilities.[2] However, given the skepticism toward India of the Dulles brothers and others in the Eisenhower administration, progress was slow at first on direct US-India civil nuclear engagement.[3] The United States did agree to provide, outside the Atoms for Peace program, "heavy water"[4] as a moderating element for a research reactor called the "Canadian-Indian Reactor, US" (CIRUS). This reactor was provided by Canada under an international South Asian aid initiative called the Colombo Plan.[5] The United States' role of supplying heavy water was to become a US political issue after the events of 1974.

Although Eisenhower had concluded in 1957 that India's nonaligned policy was not against US interests, the US government's view of India became more favorable under John F. Kennedy, who had been a strong advocate of India while serving in the US Senate. As president, he implemented this outlook, and Lyndon Johnson continued the approach. The Kennedy and Johnson administrations looked on India more as a fellow democracy than as a country refusing to be a partner in the fight to contain the Soviet Union and prevent the spread of Communism.[6] By 1964, the attitude of Indians toward the United States generally seemed positive and upbeat.[7] There were several components to this attitude. The effect of US food and agriculture assistance is discussed below. The 1962 offer of assistance against the Chinese during the short India-Chinese border war of that year was also a factor. However, even among students there was some understanding that India and the United States had begun to cooperate on civil nuclear matters in an important way. The signings of the first civil nuclear agreement between the United States and India in 1963 and the contract for American construction of two light-water reactors near the village of Tarapur in Maharashtra State were no small matters. Under a contract with India, American companies were to supply enriched uranium fuel to the Tarapur plant for a period of thirty years. Support for the initial 1963 US-India civil nuclear agreement was driven by economic engagement, just as was the agreement to be reached in 2008. General Electric was to build the Tarapur plant. The eminent historian of Indian nuclear policy George Perkovich has commented in regard to Tarapur that "the [US] desire to promote nuclear power overcame all doubts."[8]

Coming after the United States had assisted India at the time of the Chinese border incursion in 1962, the civil nuclear agreement of 1963 marked the most cordial relations between India and the United States since Indian independence. Aid flows, particularly under the Public Law 480 program (see chapter 8), added to the feeling that US-India relations were on a new and upward trajectory. However, this break in the estrangement of the world's two largest democracies did not last. Although there were a number of reasons for the end of the period of closeness and resumption of estrangement between the United States and India, one of the chief reasons was disagreement on nuclear matters.

India and the Non-Proliferation Treaty

In 1968, India resisted US pressure and refused to sign the Non-Proliferation Treaty (NPT). From the Indian perspective, this refusal to sign was completely justifiable. Section 3 of Article IX of the NPT defined a "nuclear-weapon State" as "one which has manufactured and exploded a nuclear weapon or other nuclear explosive device prior to 1 January, 1967."[9] Because India had not yet manufactured and exploded such a device on the specified date, agreeing to the treaty would have meant acceptance of the status of a "non-nuclear-weapon State Party to the Treaty" while its rival China would be recognized as a legitimate nuclear power. As a non-nuclear-weapon state, India would have agreed under Article II "not to manufacture or otherwise acquire nuclear weapons or other nuclear explosive devices." Many Indians believed that great nations had nuclear weapons as one of the characteristics of greatness. Although there were divisions of opinion as to whether India should develop nuclear weapons, most Indian leaders felt it was simply wrong to ask India to disown the possibility of developing nuclear weapons and relinquish its ambitions to become a great power. India refused to accept what it regarded as a second-class status. Under leadership and pressure primarily exerted by the United States, most nations of the world went ahead on the NPT without India.

The NPT experience was a significant setback for US-India relations. To many Indians, the experience placed the United States in a neo-imperialist posture by attempting to restrain India from becoming a great power. In a demonstration of its prowess, India conducted a nuclear test in 1974. The reaction of the United States was one of shocked amazement. Many American foreign policy leaders believed that India had broken its commitments to peacefully use the technology, equipment, and fuel sold to India under the Atoms for Peace program and the similar transaction pursuant to the CIRUS project. India denied any breach of its obligations. To deflect such criticism, India denominated its test as "peaceful" and designed only for civilian purposes. However, because the "peaceful" explosion was indistinguishable in all practical aspects from a weapons test, this labeling failed to satisfy US critics. When the United States retaliated by stopping shipments of nuclear fuel for the Tarapur plant, the Government of India viewed the action not only as a breach of contract but also as a breach of faith. Many Indians felt the stoppage of fuel showed that the United States was unreliable at best and treacherous at worst. This theme of unreliability based upon the failure to fulfill the fuel supply agreement for Tarapur became a continuing complaint of India in regard to doing business with the United States.

Even worse in the eyes of India was the concerted attempt by the United States to build a comprehensive international regime to prevent the flow of nuclear material to countries that refused to sign the NPT. The United States amended its atomic energy statutes to make it a violation of US law to transfer nuclear technology, equipment, or material to a country, like India, that was not a party to the NPT. The Atomic Energy Act as amended,[10] and the Nuclear Nonproliferation Act of 1978,[11] made it virtually impossible as a matter of US law for the United States to cooperate with India on nuclear matters. Internationally, the United States formed a Nuclear Suppliers Group with guidelines to prevent any transfer of nuclear materials or technology to nonsigners of the NPT. India rightly saw these actions as pointed specifically toward keeping it from obtaining the technology, equipment, and fuel that it needed for its civil nuclear program. In the eyes of many Indians, by implication, the United States was denying India the right to claim for itself not only equality with the United States but also equality with China and the three other states declared to be nuclear powers under the NPT—the United Kingdom, France, and the Soviet Union.[12]

The Glenn Amendment Sanctions

Differences over India's nuclear policy remained a constant in US-India relations for the next two decades. These differences came to be symbolized in the Indian mind by actions of Congress threatening sanctions if India should proceed with an overt nuclear program. Senator John Glenn (D-Ohio) had been instrumental in crafting the legislative responses leading to the Nuclear Nonproliferation Act of 1978, including 1977 legislation that dealt with the cutoff of international security assistance in the event of nuclear testing.[13] Concerned about reports of the continuation of India's and particularly Pakistan's nuclear ambitions, Glenn proposed further legislation designed to stop the testing of nuclear devices by states other than the declared nuclear powers. Formally titled the Nuclear Proliferation Prevention Act of 1994,[14] but better known as the "Glenn Amendment," this legislation provided for further sanctions to be imposed on states designated under the NPT as "non-nuclear-weapon states" that, nevertheless, detonated nuclear devices.

Under the Glenn Amendment, the detonation of a nuclear device by a "non-nuclear weapons state," as defined by the NPT, would trigger a long list of sanctions. Many of these involved the cutting off of US military and civilian aid. Cooperation in the form of financing assistance from the US Export-Import Bank, the Overseas Private Investment Corporation, and the US Trade and Development Agency would also be prohibited. Sanctions were not limited to actions of the US government. The Glenn Amendment also sought to reach loans from the World Bank and other international financial institutions and to stop loans or credit from US banks to any government responsible for exploding a nuclear device.[15]

The View from the Commerce Department

In the same year the Glenn Amendment became law (1994), I was commencing my duties as assistant secretary of commerce for trade development.[16] From this midlevel position, I saw firsthand the interrelationship between US-India economic engagement and the nuclear issue. In my first interview with Secretary Ron Brown in February 1993, he had made plain his plans for an expansive role for the department in international matters. A major field for implementation of this vision was to be US-India relations.

The relationship between President Bill Clinton and Secretary Brown was strong both personally and politically. Brown had been chairman of the Democratic National Committee during Clinton's campaign for the presidency. Brown handled both the nominating convention and the Democratic Party's role in the campaign with competence and vigor. As an African American, Brown was a key interlocutor with this important Democratic constituency. Clinton credited Brown with being a chief architect of the Clinton victory in 1992 and looked forward to a similar performance in his 1996 campaign for reelection.[17] Brown had expected a prominent Cabinet post for his service and political value. He had not expected to be offered the post of secretary of commerce. Rather, he thought of himself as a contender for secretary of state or another high post centering on foreign policy. Clinton's willingness to use economic engagement as a tool of foreign policy was a factor in Brown's willingness to accept the Commerce position.

The "Big Emerging Markets" Initiative

Upon my arrival at the Commerce Department, Clinton's (and Brown's) choice as the new undersecretary for international trade, Jeffrey Garten, impressed upon the International Trade Administration's assistant secretaries the importance of the department's "Big Emerging Markets" initiative. Garten had formulated and Brown had adopted as his international policy centerpiece this initiative targeting the ten largest markets outside the Organisation for Economic Co-operation and Development and Russia for special trade and investment development efforts. As export destinations for US goods, services, and investments, these developing markets were to be engines for creating economic growth in the US while strengthening bilateral political ties.[18]

Secretary Brown's Mission to India

As a part of the Big Emerging Markets initiative, Secretary Brown was to lead a "Presidential Business Development Mission" to India in January 1995. The designation "Presidential" was insisted upon by Brown. Brown said that his flying into India on a plane with the American flag painted on its tail and with the designation "Presidential" for his delegation was crucial to the success of the mission. However, the designation "Presidential" was more than symbolism and indicated the reality of the Clinton-Brown relationship. Brown discussed such missions as the one to India with Clinton before he left and debriefed him upon his return.[19] The announcement of India as a Big Emerging Market preparatory to Brown's trip to India made news in India. Now, the concept that India can be considered prominent based on its economic prowess is commonplace. But in 1994 and 1995, the concept was considered remarkable.

When responsibilities for the various Big Emerging Markets were assigned among the assistant secretaries in the Commerce Department's International Trade Administration, I was the only one interested in India. Other officials at the department admonished that I would be wasting my time trying to promote US-India economic engagement. Nonetheless, I persisted, and Garten designated me as a principal point of contact for India in the Big Emerging Markets initiative. He asked me to help in the preparation for Secretary Brown's trip and the follow-up to the trip. In this capacity, I began to work with US companies investing in or trading with India on a continual basis. Brown was to be accompanied on his mission to India by a delegation of business chief executive officers (CEOs). Contrary to some critics, these executives were recruited strictly on a nonpartisan basis. Active persuasion was necessary in many instances. The value of taking CEOs' time to go to India with a secretary of commerce was not obvious to many of the busy executives. The argument that participation would serve both the national and company interests was not always appreciated.

Chief among the business officials who saw the value of public-private cooperation in the endeavor was Scott Bayman, CEO of GE India and a resident in New Delhi, who made a special trip to Washington to brief Brown and work on trip preparation. According to Bayman, "Since the Clinton Administration wanted to improve relations with India, economic relations was an obvious place to start. The Indians needed to be shown that they could benefit from improving the relationship. India was desperate for liquidity and needed technology. If two-way trade could be improved, we all stood to benefit."[20] In conversations with executives going on the mission and their staffs, I began to understand the impediment to the realization of the US-India economic potential created by the nuclear issue. For example, GE had built the Tarapur nuclear power plant. Although GE was not responsible for the termination of the Tarapur nuclear fuel contract, GE was still affected by the bad feeling created from the termination.

The Advocacy Center was instrumental in organizing advocacy for projects that would be placed in the spotlight on the Brown mission. Projects were sought that would be indicative of the potential of US-India economic engagement. As noted in chapter 1, I had set up the Advocacy Center as one of my first jobs at the department. The Advocacy Center was essentially a group of twenty professionals selected from the Trade Development Bureau and assigned to specific US industrial sectors. The center was to serve as a mechanism for coordinating the efforts of the Clinton administration in support of securing for US companies significant overseas projects that would create employment in the United States. By tearing out walls, a special open architecture office was created in which the professionals worked with the most advanced computer and telecommunications equipment the department was able to obtain. In the first instance, the Advocacy Center drew upon the resources of the industry desks in trade development. Deputy assistant secretaries were key in providing this support from within their own offices and assisting in liaison with other departments. For example, Michael Copps, former chief of staff to the then–chairman of the Senate Commerce Committee, Ernest "Fritz" Hollings, was in charge of the energy and infrastructure desks.[21] Ellis Mottur, former director of the Congressional Office of Technology Assessment, was in charge of technology and aerospace.[22] These offices were the initial conduits for projects that went to the Advocacy Center, where I worked with other US departments and foreign agencies to vet them for advocacy efforts.

In preparing for the India mission, the Advocacy Center worked especially on power and other infrastructure projects originating through Copps's office and telecommunications and aerospace deals that came through Mottur's operations. As we worked these projects through the bureaucracies, the effects of the antagonistic relationship between the United States and India on civilian nuclear power became clear. The resentment based on the nuclear experience was palpable from both US and Indian officials. From the

US side, career officials at the Department of Commerce's Export Administration (now the Bureau of Industrial Security), the State Department, and the Department of Energy made plain that a discussion with Indians that might lead to the subject of nuclear power for India was out of bounds. There seemed to be an institutional perception left over from the 1974 test that India had betrayed the United States. I was repeatedly given to understand that the Indians were duplicitous and not to be trusted based on the nuclear experience.

On the Indian side, the lack of trust created by the US-India history over nuclear matters was much the same. The Indian officials were less direct than their US counterparts, but the message of mistrust was similar. At the Indian Embassy in Washington, Ambassador S. S. Ray and his minister for commerce (later ambassador to the United States) Meera Shankar welcomed the Brown mission enthusiastically and worked tirelessly for its success. However, others at the embassy obliquely questioned whether US companies could be trusted to fulfill their obligations.

In late 1994, I went with Garten to India in preparation for the Brown mission. There, Government of India officials at the Ministry of External Affairs raised the nuclear issue by comparing India's treatment with that of China. The Indian officials seemed to be reciprocating comments I had heard about India with implications that US trustworthiness was uncertain. Some Indian officials questioned whether US interest in Indian welfare was sincere and wondered aloud about the real object of our discussions. With the Indians, we had tried to stress that our trade mission was designed to create "win-win" situations that benefited both India and the United States. Unfortunately, against the background of our nuclear impasse, these representations were taken at less than face value.

However, there were officials on both sides who were already considering ways to bridge the nuclear divide. One of these was Ambassador Frank G. Wisner. According to Wisner, the US-India dispute over nuclear matters was one of the "three great divides" separating the United States and India when he took over as US ambassador in 1994.[23] I recall my surprise in a meeting with Wisner and Indian officials on the trip preparatory to the Brown mission that he did not rule out a suggestion from an Indian official to discuss civil nuclear cooperation. In fact, Wisner did talk with Indian officials about civil nuclear matters. However, the discussions at that time were only in the context of an inducement to India's joining the Comprehensive Test Ban Treaty. Wisner was correct in his assessment that India would be unwilling to join the treaty in return for US-India civil nuclear cooperation.[24]

Also in conjunction with the Brown trip, Garten asked me to organize a "US-India Commercial Alliance." This was to be an organization composed of US and Indian business executives supported by relevant trade associations in both countries. Secretary Brown and his counterpart, Minister of Commerce and Industry Palaniappan Chidambaram,[25] were to be personally involved in the alliance. The concept was to have an organization to continue addressing commercial issues raised during the mission. In working on the Brown trip and the follow-up US-India Commercial Alliance, I came in contact with the leaders of the two largest Indian trade associations, the Federation of Indian Chambers of Commerce and Industry (FICCI) and the Confederation of Indian Industries (CII). The secretary-general of FICCI, Amit Mitra, made plain that the nuclear issue represented a difficulty for creating closer economic relations between the United States and India. Tarun Das, secretary-general and then chief mentor of CII, expressed similar thoughts. Thus, even in 1995 Americans and Indians interested in the prospects for greater US-India trade and investment engendered by the Indian financial reforms of 1991 felt the impact of hostility over nuclear issues. As they sought the additional measures necessary to realize the full potential of these prospects, US-India estrangement over nuclear matters was a constant irritant.

In spite of behind-the-scenes tensions over nuclear matters, the January 1995 Presidential Business Development Mission to India was a considerable success. Billions of dollars worth of US-India deals were signed or announced. Brown went on nationwide television with an interactive, audience participation show that was very well received. A US-India Commercial Alliance agreement was signed. Homage was paid to Mohandas Gandhi and the link with Martin Luther King Jr. through the doctrine of nonviolence. The mission was one of the first to highlight internationally the growing economic prowess of India. After the mission, the Clinton administration and the government of Prime Minister Narasimha Rao were both ready to move forward on strategic matters. However, the next major steps in strategic cooperation would be delayed and, because of the delay, would not involve Rao.

A Time of Political Uncertainty

In 1996, both Rao and Clinton faced elections and a period of uncertainty that hindered the cause of US-India economic engagement. The Rao government's constitutional term of five years was up, and India went to the polls. In view of the significant economic progress that had been made under Rao and his government, many observers felt that a Congress Party government return to power was assured. The Bharatiya Janata Party (BJP) was the leading opposition as it campaigned on a platform of Hindu nationalism ("Hindutva") and national security. The electorate seemed unimpressed with both the leading contenders. The results of the election were unclear, with no party even close to obtaining a parliamentary majority. The BJP put together a loose coalition that formed a government led by Atal Bihari Vajpayee. This first Vajpayee government lasted only thirteen days, and it was followed by a "United Front" left-of-center government that was also manifestly unstable.[26] Two United Front governments failed within the next two years.

For Clinton's part, he not only had to contest the election of 1996 but also was soon embroiled in a scandal that led to his trial and acquittal on impeachment charges. By 1998, he was prepared to move forward with a trip to India.[27] However, the impeachment imbroglio was not over, and the political instability of the Indian Parliament made early elections likely. A Clinton mission to India was delayed. India went to the polls again in the spring of 1998. The BJP emerged as the single largest party in the Lok Sabha (House of the People, the directly elected lower house of Parliament). As the leader of a thirteen-party coalition, the BJP again formed a government under the leadership of Vajpayee.[28]

The "Induction" of the Nuclear Option and Sanctions

The BJP had campaigned on a manifesto, or platform, that included an intention "to induct the nuclear option." US government observers, including the Central Intelligence Agency, thought that this verbal formulation might indicate an intention to negotiate or at least delay further nuclear activity. Several Clinton administration officials felt they had been given Indian assurances to this effect. Thus, it was much to the surprise of the United States that India conducted a series of five nuclear tests on May 11 and 13, 1998, just days after the new BJP-led government took office.[29] The Indian government confirmed by action and words that "to induct the nuclear option" meant both to test nuclear weapons and to integrate them into the Indian military arsenal.

The effect of these tests on US-India trade and investment was swift. Clinton and his national security adviser, Samuel R. ("Sandy") Berger, felt let down by the Indians,[30] and that the administration had no choice but to follow the Glenn Amendment in imposing sanctions. Their judgment was that there was no legal justification for not acting. Further, Glenn was still in the Senate, where he exercised considerable influence on nonproliferation issues. Although Clinton had grave doubts about the rigidity of the Glenn sanctions regime and wanted to move forward with building US-India relations, he imposed the sanctions.[31]

On May 13, 1998, Clinton issued a presidential determination carrying out the Glenn Amendment. The determination simply ordered the relevant agencies and instrumentalities of the US government to impose the sanctions described in Section 102(b)(1) of the Arms Export Control Act.[32] The president also made a determination under the Export-Import Bank Act that no credits or guarantees would be extended to India. The sanctions imposed fell into four categories. First, there were the terminations of defense sales, licenses, and financing. These terminations were not particularly significant in economic terms because there was then very little defense trade between India and the United States. Second, there was the termination of foreign assistance, which included denial of governmental credit, credit guarantees, and other financial assistance. The denial of credit guarantees and financial assistance could be significant, because these availabilities amounted to some $14 billion. However, that amount was for availability, and actual transfers would be considerably less. Third, there was a prohibition against any US bank making loans or providing credits to the Government of India. Fourth, opposition by the United States to the extension of loans to India by any multilateral financial institution was required. This latter restriction was particularly galling to India because it appeared to be an attempt to extend US control to supposedly independent international lending institutions. Fourth and finally, there was a prohibition on exports to India of specific licensed goods and technology. Because only $151 million in such licenses had been granted in 1997 and pending licensing requests were only $12 million for 1998, this prohibition also was not particularly significant in economic terms.[33]

Thus, the Glenn Amendment sanctions as specified by the Clinton order had a limited direct impact on US-India economic relations. The Glenn Amendment was posited on a view of India as needing US assistance. This view of India as an aid-dependent country had largely become obsolete since India had begun to liberalize and grow rapidly. However, the damage from sanctions went beyond the direct effect of the items spelled out in the amendment and presidential order. There was a broad chilling effect felt by almost all US companies trading or investing with India or using the credits affected by the Glenn Amendment.

Looking to Congress for Sanctions Relief

Because the Glenn Amendment passed by Congress was the genesis of the linkage between economic engagement and nuclear policy, the affected US companies looked to Congress for relief. The trade association to which many of these companies belonged, the US-India Business Council (USIBC), would serve as a forum for coordinating this effort.

The USIBC is administratively a division of the US Chamber of Commerce. However, it is independent in matters of policy and functions with its own board of directors. The board determines policy and advises on the running of the USIBC. The USIBC was formed in 1975 at the request of Henry Kissinger as an outcome of his visit to India as secretary of state in the Gerald Ford administration.

By 1998, the USIBC was only active on a rather modest scale and had little policy influence. In fact, some of the leading traders and investors with India were disillusioned with its effectiveness. Under the leadership of General Electric and its vice president for public policy, Michael Gadbaw, some of these traders and investors had formed an "India Interest Group" for the purpose of playing a more active role in US government policy toward India. However, in 1998, just before the Indian nuclear tests, the USIBC hired Michael Clark, a young assistant professor of government at the College of William and Mary, as its executive director. Clark's main interest was policy. He was determined to meld the trade promotion functions of the USIBC with public policy interests in the US-India relationship. The invocation of sanctions provided the opportunity to build action for policy change through the growing economic engagement between the United States and India.

Many members of the US Congress were unhappy with the imposition of sanctions. Chief among these was Senator Sam Brownback (R-Kan.), who chaired the Subcommittee on Near Eastern and South Asian Affairs of the Senate Foreign Relations Committee. As a senator from Kansas, Brownback, of course, was concerned with agricultural exports. Under his leadership, Congress intervened almost immediately to provide relief to US wheat growers. That amendment to the Arms Export Control Act exempted forms of US Department of Agriculture–backed financial support from sanctions.

This legislation was signed into law by President Clinton on July 14, 1998.[34] However, the leading export of Kansas is not cereal grains. Aircraft and industrial machinery are both of more export importance to Kansas than wheat.[35] Accordingly, a range of USIBC members wider than those involved in agribusiness approached Brownback and other members of the Senate and House of Representatives with company assessments of the adverse impact of sanctions on their businesses. The result, the India-Pakistan Relief Act of 1998, which came to be known as Brownback I, authorized but did not require the president to waive sanctions for a period of one year as they related to civil foreign assistance, government nonmilitary transactions, opposition to India assistance from the World Bank and other international financial institutions, and US commercial bank transactions. Brownback I was eventually incorporated into the Omnibus Consolidated and Emergency Supplemental Appropriations Act of 1999 and was signed into law on October 21, 1998.[36]

President Clinton made use of the Brownback I authority almost immediately. He announced on November 7, 1998, that most sanctions involving civilian foreign assistance would be lifted. Prominent exceptions were the maintaining of US opposition to Indian projects of the multilateral lending agencies such as the World Bank and the Asian Development Bank and assistance from the Export-Import Bank, the Overseas Private Investment Corporation, and the Trade and Development Agency. The administration continued to talk about sanctions as if they were a significant incentive to India to agree to rein in its nuclear program. However, the passage of waiver authority and the immediate utilization of Brownback I by the president revealed sanctions as weak incentives for India to modify its nuclear behavior.

Brownback I had only allowed a one-year waiver. In 1999, permanent waiver authority was inserted in the Department of Defense Appropriations Act for fiscal year 2000. This legislation, referred to popularly as Brownback II, provided permanent authority for waiving the economic sanctions imposed against India and Pakistan in response to the nuclear tests.[37] President Clinton used this authority on October 27, 1999, just two days after signing it into law. In a memorandum for the secretary of state, Clinton waved the sanctions for (1) the activities of the Export-Import Bank, the Overseas Private Investment Corporation, and the Trade and Development Agency; (2) assistance under the International Military Education and Training program; (3) the making of any loan or the providing of any credit to the government in India by any US bank; (4) assistance to certain environmental funds; and (5) credits and other financial assistance provided by the

Department of Agriculture to support the purchase of food or agricultural commodities.[38]

The Clinton memorandum of October 27, 1999, left in place sanctions having to do with military items, transfers to certain specified Indian entities, and some high-technology or "dual-use" items (i.e., items that could have both civilian and military uses). Though symbolically important to India, these remaining sanctions did not have much practical effect on existing economic engagement. Militarily, the United States and India had almost no supply relationship. The Indian entities specified were involved with the Indian nuclear or space programs that had long been off limits for US export programs. India did not expect the United States to be supporting these programs. The high-technology or dual-use items were restricted by export controls generally, and a waiver under Brownback II was of little significance.

In essence, Brownback II brought the US legal constraints on US-India economic engagement back to where they had been before the imposition of the Glenn Amendment sanctions. However, the fact that these sanctions technically remained in effect, reflecting constraints in underlying US law and regulations, worked to highlight these constraints for the Indian foreign policy elite. We shall see below that even since all the remaining Glenn Amendment sanctions were lifted in 2001, these underlying constraints on economic engagement have continued to be an issue for US-India strategic cooperation. However, for the time being, Brownback II had basically removed the Glenn Amendment sanctions as an impediment to most US-India economic engagement.

US business had played a major role in bringing about Brownback II. According to Clark, the key breakthrough had been the ability to insert the amendment into the Department of Defense Appropriations Act. This appropriations bill was sure to pass and would not require a separate vote on what was likely to be a divisive issue. For this purpose, marshaling the contacts of US aerospace companies, chiefly Boeing, with the House Appropriations Subcommittee on Defense was key. Clark knew of the interests of Representative Charlie Wilson (D-Tex.) in gaining the full support of Pakistan for the fight against the Soviet occupiers of Afghanistan. Wilson became convinced that lifting sanctions against India was a prerequisite to doing the same for Pakistan. He spoke to the chairman of the Subcommittee, Representative Jerry Lewis (D-Calif.), who agreed to insert the measure. However, this could not have been accomplished unless the chairman of the

House Foreign Affairs Committee, Representative Ben Gilman (D-Md.), could be persuaded to waive his committee's jurisdiction over the measure. For this purpose, Clark called on Swadesh Chatterjee (see below) and the India American activists with whom he worked politically to intercede with Gilman. Gilman had significant Indian Americans supporters, and he agreed to the waiver.[39]

The Talbott-Singh Talks

During the period of the dance between the Clinton administration and Congress over the Glenn Amendment sanctions, the administration undertook an initiative to engage India directly on the issue of nuclear policy. The US deputy secretary of state, Strobe Talbott, conducted a series of discussions with the Indian minister for external affairs, Jaswant Singh. These discussions were premised, from the US perspective, on the need to achieve five nuclear "benchmarks": (1) the signing of the Comprehensive Test Ban Treaty (CTBT), (2) cooperation in negotiating a Fissile Material Cutoff Treaty, (3) agreeing to a "strategic restraint regime" that would limit the types and placement of nuclear weapon delivery vehicles, (4) putting in place a "world-class" export control system for nuclear-related technology, and (5) resuming negotiations with Pakistan over Kashmir.[40]

From the outset, the legitimacy of the "benchmarks" premise was not shared by the Government of India. The Indians did not have any problem with putting into place an effective export control regime. However, all the rest of the benchmarks were basically nonstarters with the Indians. Although Singh evidently portrayed at one point a willingness to enter into the CTBT under some vague circumstances, this position went beyond that of his government and served as little more than an inducement for Talbott to keep talking. Thus, while Talbott was attempting to engage India on the benchmarks, the business community and Indian Americans were working together with Congress to dismantle the Glenn Amendment sanctions.

The president was complicit in this dismantling. The president signed into law and, in fact, welcomed waiver authority. In the whole time I spent working on Capitol Hill on this issue, I did not encounter any administration official opposing the waiver legislation. The president exercised the waiver authority almost entirely as soon as it was given to him. The sanctions simply were contrary to the fundamentals of the underlying economic engagement that was driving relations between the United States and India. This engagement translated into political reality. Conducting negotiations on "benchmarks" without regard to this political reality driven by economic engagement was fruitless.

The Clinton administration apparently hoped that India could be induced to meet at least the CTBT benchmark by promising to conduct a presidential trip to India in the fall of 1998, if Vajpayee would announce India's adherence to the CTBT to the United Nations in September 1998. This hope produced nothing. In part, this may have been due to the Indian's understanding of the strong opposition growing in the US Senate to confirmation of the CTBT. As chairman of the Senate Foreign Relations Committee, Senator Jesse Helms (R-N.C.) led the fight against CTBT confirmation. In this effort, he was aided and abetted by Indian American activists who were just beginning their involvement in the US political process.

On October 13, 1999, the US Senate effectively wrote the end to this unsuccessful strategy of attempting to get the Government of India to agree to benchmarks. The US Senate rejected the CTBT. As to the only prominent benchmark for which Singh had offered hope, there was now no equitable underpinning for Indian agreement. The concept that India would agree to a treaty rejected by the Senate was not grounded in reality. With no equity, no economic basis, and virtually no US domestic political support, the benchmark engagement strategy was at an end. It was time to try a new approach with more possibility of success in building US-India strategic cooperation.

A New Approach to India

Fortunately, this new approach was already in the making. The president and Berger had been deeply impressed by India's conduct and restraint during the crisis created when Pakistan crossed the Kashmir Line of Control at Kargil in 1999. After President Clinton successfully negotiated a Pakistani pullback that kept India and Pakistan from possibly resorting to nuclear war, Berger followed Clinton's predilections to find a more productive way of dealing with the US-India nuclear relationship. Under Berger's guidance, the United States began to set a new course in the US-India relationship. The United States would not remain mired in a policy headed by sanctions over the nuclear issue.

Talks were begun with the Indian government concerning the scheduling of a visit to India by President Clinton and the themes for this visit. As indicated above, there had been consideration in the White House of a presidential trip to India since early in Clinton's first term. The 1998 nuclear tests and resulting sanctions had caused the postponement of this trip. With the Talbott talks going nowhere, the president and Berger were intent on rescheduling the trip. On October 15, 1999, just two days after ratification of the CTBT failed in the Senate, the first presidential mission to India since a stopover by President Jimmy Carter in 1978 was set for March 2000.

This new approach to US-India strategic cooperation combined an emphasis on the two nations' common ties of democracy with a focus on US-India economic and social engagement in a globalizing world. Supporting these themes were the same two forces that had decimated the Glenn Amendment sanctions. The first of these was US-India economic engagement, which had been key to forming opposition to the sanctions from the business community involved in trade and investment with India. The second component was the political activism of the Indian American community.

The Indian American activism component was related to economic engagement. Many Indian Americans of prominence were deeply involved in building US-India economic engagement. This was particularly true of Indian Americans in the information technology industry. Indian Americans were playing a vital and highly lucrative leadership role in the US information technology boom of the 1990s. Foreign-born Americans were founders in approximately a quarter of all technology startups in the United States from 1995 to 2005. By far the largest group of these foreign-born Americans were Indian Americans. Thus, 15.5 percent of all Silicon Valley startups during the period 1995 to 2005 had been by Indian American immigrants.[41] Many of the leaders of the Indian American community had been instrumental in the increasing US-India trade in software and information-technology-enabled services. A common pattern had been for an Indian American entrepreneur with a technical background to outsource some parts of his or her business to India. These outsourcing contracts usually went to Indian companies with which the Indian American entrepreneur had some relationship. Added to the political importance of Indian American information technology entrepreneurs were Indian Americans who ran a huge segment of the US hotel and hospitality industry, along with Indian American doctors and medical professionals in every state of the union.[42]

President Clinton Goes to India

President Clinton started his mission in India on March 21, 2000. In US statements issued to commence the visit, there were references to nuclear policy and nonproliferation that showed the continuing chasm between the United States and India on these issues. However, both sides agreed to place the public emphasis elsewhere. The major event dramatizing the themes of the trip was President Clinton's address to the Indian Parliament on March 22. Clinton opened his speech with a tribute to India and three "very basic lessons India teaches" "us": "confidence in democracy," "tolerance for diversity," and a "willingness to embrace social change" brought about by globalization.

The remainder of Clinton's address was built around four "challenges." The first three of these challenges were based on economic engagement. Clinton described these challenges as (1) "to get our own economic relationship right," (2) "to sustain global economic growth in a way that enriches the lives of rich and poor alike," and (3) "to see that the prosperity and growth of the information age require us to abandon some of the outdated truths of the Industrial Age." The fourth challenge concerned defense matters. This challenge was denominated "to protect the gains of democracy and development from the forces which threaten to undermine them."[43]

The president's speech was transforming. At the close of the speech and after the prime minister's reply, Parliament went into pandemonium. Legislators climbed over desks in their eagerness to shake hands with the president. This speech was a perfect example of using economic engagement as a theme for supporting cooperation on strategic issues. From the reaction of Parliament, it was evident that this was certainly a more fruitful approach to India than a negative use of economics through sanctions.

The themes of Clinton's speech to Parliament set the agenda for the rest of his visit. The US secretary of commerce, Bill Daley, had accompanied Clinton. A series of US-India private-sector roundtables was organized by the USIBC in conjunction with the Federation of Indian Chambers of Commerce and Industry and the Confederation of Indian Industries.[44] Nine roundtable meetings organized by industry sector resulted in a series of recommendations on economic topics. These recommendations were presented to Daley and the Indian minister of commerce and industry for discussion with the president and prime minister. Among these recommendations were several concerning cooperation on energy and power. Though the participants were given to understand that specific recommendations on nuclear power were not to be aired publicly, there was considerable discussion behind the scenes of this topic. The Government of India, impressed by the success of US business in the Brownback II battle of the previous year, had approached Clark before the trip about raising civil nuclear cooperation as an element of the Clinton mission. Clark's reaction at the time was that this was too early to do this. The Indians continued to raise the issue privately.[45]

After addressing Parliament, President Clinton proceeded to Hyderabad, where an event at the so-called High-Tech City building complex stressed economic engagement themes pertaining to information technology. The official part of the trip concluded with a presidential address at the Bombay Stock Exchange. The organizers of the presidential mission had called on CII to organize the Hyderabad event and FICCI to organize the Mumbai event. A USIBC delegation participated in both events. These events symbolized the growing importance of economic engagement to the overall US-India relationship. The mission resulted in the signing of agreements on cooperation in energy and the environment and an India-US science and technology forum. An elaborate US-India architecture of high-level consultations and joint working groups was put in place. These included regular bilateral "summits," as well as an annual foreign policy dialogue at the level of the secretary of state and minister of external affairs. Continuation and upgrade of a joint working group on counterterrorism and a dialogue on security and nonproliferation were agreed to. Major emphasis was placed on enhancing economic and business relations. A high-level group was to develop a common economic agenda. Tasks were set forth for a US-India Financial and Economic Forum, a US-India Commercial Dialogue, and a US-India Working Group on Trade.[46] Though the names and emphases changed in the George W. Bush and Barack Obama administrations, the architecture for continuing bilateral engagement between US and Indian governmental agencies is still largely the architecture established during the visit of President Clinton to India.

The George W. Bush Administration Seizes the Strategic Opportunity

The Clinton mission closed the chapter in US-India relations centered on attempts to coerce India through negative economic means to alter its policy positions on its nuclear status. A new administration under George W. Bush would seize the bipartisan implications of the Clinton initiative to thoroughly change the relationship of the United States and India on civil nuclear matters. But before this change could become a reality, history intervened in the form of the events of September 11, 2001. The United States felt it needed the immediate and full cooperation of India in the war on terrorism, and on September 21, 2001, the few remaining Glenn Amendment sanctions against

India were lifted. However, because the remaining sanctions against Pakistan were lifted at the same time, not all Indian opinion makers approved of this development. Some Indian critics decried the Bush administration's actions as less than represented because export controls continued on a range of goods and services that had dual civilian and military applications. These Indian critics confused sanctions with the nuclear weapons and dual-use technology export controls to argue that Bush was actually continuing to sanction India. These export controls had been in effect before the Glenn Amendment sanctions and continued in place. These controls generally flowed down from the controls and regulations of the Atomic Energy Act, and they were separate from sanctions as a matter of US law. These export controls were still of great concern to the Government of India. FICCI particularly would continue to support the Indian government in its protests against a US "technology denial regime." Modification of these controls would become a centerpiece of President Obama's 2010 mission to India.

Thus, over the years, the US-India dispute over India's right to nuclear weapons and nuclear technology became a defining point in US-India relations. The lack of cooperation on civil nuclear power became symbolic of the estrangement of India and the United States. This symbolism took on an importance out of proportion to the role that civil nuclear power might play in ameliorating the electrical power deficiencies of India. India has never envisaged that its energy needs will be met mostly through nuclear power, which has been considered too expensive to be the primary source for meeting the country's demand for electrical power. India has always envisaged that its cheaper coal- and petroleum-fueled electrical power plants would be the main sources of electric power. However, as environmental concerns about air quality and the costs of petroleum have risen, India has looked to nuclear power to play a greater role in meeting its demands for electricity. After September 11, 2001, the George W. Bush administration began to take a new look at tackling the civil nuclear issue as a means to define and symbolize a vastly changed strategic relationship between the United States and India.

A chief proponent of the complete removal of nuclear sanctions and widespread nuclear cooperation was Bush's new ambassador to India, Robert D. Blackwill. Blackwill, a former career Foreign Service officer and faculty member at Harvard's John F. Kennedy School of Government, had been one of the primary foreign policy advisers to candidate George W. Bush during his run for the presidency. These advisers became known as the "Vulcans." Vulcan, the Roman god of fire and metalworking, was an appropriate namesake for the group. A huge statue of the god dominates the skyline of Birmingham, Alabama, hometown of the Vulcans' leader, Condoleezza Rice, who was to become George W. Bush's national security adviser and then secretary of state. Further, the group was very much enamored of military might, including nuclear weapons—the ultimate in firepower.[47] The Vulcans' opposition to the CTBT and antipathy toward China made India a logical partner, in their view, for the United States on military security matters. Blackwill, first as ambassador, then as deputy national security adviser, would push the Bush administration toward resolution of the nuclear issue and a closer security relationship with India.

Prime Minister Vajpayee Returns to the United States after 9/11

In November 2001, Prime Minister Vajpayee again visited the United States. This time the major emphasis was on terrorism and an ideal time for Rice, Blackwill, and the other Vulcans to press for greater US-India cooperation on security matters. In support of their mutual condemnations and expressions of solidarity on terrorism, the leaders reiterated their commitment to the wide-ranging bilateral dialogue architecture established during the Clinton visit of March 2000. The leaders noted that India's interest in purchasing arms from the United States would be discussed by the Defense Policy Group. They agreed to expand the Bilateral Economic Dialogue. However, US nuclear law and the restrictions on high-technology and dual-use products that flowed from the anti-India nuclear regime were a major impediment to reaching the goal of closer cooperation on strategic issues. Accordingly, they also agreed to "begin a dialogue between the two governments with a view toward evaluating the processes by which . . . [the United States and India] transfer dual-use and military items, with a view towards greater transparency and efficiency."[48] This dialogue would continue the utilization of economic engagement as the chief tool to bring the US-India relationship to a fuller strategic partnership.

Through the dialogue, India sought to press the United States on a "trinity" of strategic issues.[49] These three issues were trade in items with defense implications, civilian space, and civilian nuclear cooperation. The Bush administration was prepared to move forward on the defense and dual-use trade issue immediately. The implication was that if sufficient progress were made on the defense / dual-use issue, then the civilian space and nuclear issues could be addressed.

The Formation of the Public-Private High-Technology Cooperation Group

Kenneth Juster, US undersecretary of commerce for industrial security, was chosen to head the effort to reach accommodation on the defense / dual-use trade issue. Juster had served as senior adviser to the deputy secretary of state, Lawrence Eagleburger, and as acting legal counselor to the Department of State during the administration of President George H. W. Bush. This experience had brought him into contact with Steve Hadley, who was to become first deputy national security adviser and then national security adviser to George W. Bush. In November 2002, Juster decided to make the founding of a High-Technology Cooperation Group (HTCG) the centerpiece of his first trip to India and a public-private mechanism to move forward the agenda on trade in defense and dual-use items. The HTCG was to give the Government of India and Indian business a positive stake in increased high-technology trade with the United States.[50] The two governments announced the formation of the HTCG while Juster was in New Delhi.

Juster's Government of India counterpart was the foreign secretary, Kanwal Sibal, a career diplomat ideally situated to bring export controls into the mainstream of Indian foreign policy considerations. A significant breakthrough came in February 2003. Juster and Sibal issued a "Statement of Principles" to govern their work and provide a road map for the activities of the group. The Statement of Principles emphasized the role of the private sector. The USIBC was responsible for the private sector on the US side. On the Indian side, the two governments obtained the participation of the three leading national trade associations, FICCI, CII, and the National Association of Software and Services Companies.[51] The statement stressed trade facilitation and trade in dual-use items. However, references to nonproliferation and export controls indicated that the work of the group would have implications beyond the defense and dual-use conundrum.[52]

The HTCG's first meeting took place in Washington in July 2003. Perhaps the most important part of the meeting occurred on July 1, when more than 140 representatives of US and Indian industries met in a public-private forum on US-India trade and investment. In addition to Juster, Deputy Secretary of Commerce Sam Bodman (who was later to become secretary of energy) and Undersecretary for Technology Phil Bond participated from the US government. The HTCG continued to meet alternatively in the United States and in India throughout the Bush administration.

The pattern for the HTCG's meetings was a private-sector forum, in which both company and government officials participated, followed by government-to-government meetings. Meetings usually dealt with four industrial sectors—information technology, nanotechnology, biotechnology, and defense technology. In all cases, a discussion of Indian access to US dual-use items and measures to enhance the confidence of Indian buyers of US goods and technologies was on the agenda. From my experience in participating in these meetings and leading sessions upon occasion, this agenda item often related back to the cancellation of the Tarapur nuclear fuel contract some thirty years earlier, as well as the US history of imposing sanctions for nuclear testing.

The Next Steps in the Strategic Partnership

By January 2004, enough progress had been made for Prime Minister Vajpayee and President Bush to announce a follow-on initiative termed "Next Steps in Strategic Partnership." The announcement took place January 12 by means of nearly identical statements issued simultaneously in New Delhi and Washington. The statements made it plain that among the "trinity" of issues, civilian nuclear activities were a primary focus. Civilian space programs and high-technology trade were mentioned, along with "our dialogue on missile defense." However, India intended to press the nuclear cooperation point, and the Bush administration was prepared to reciprocate. The experience gained through the meetings of the HTCG were now merging into a process that would set the stage for civil nuclear cooperation.

The announcement of the Next Steps in Strategic Partnership also had implications for Prime Minister Vajpayee and his National Democratic Alliance (NDA) coalition partners in setting the stage for their planned re-election. Within the NDA's strategy, the Next Steps in Strategic Partnership would provide an example of Indian progress in dealing with the world's remaining superpower as an equal. In April 2004, Vajpayee called for elections. The year 2004 seemed an auspicious time for the NDA coalition government to go to the polls. The growth of India's gross domestic product was at an all-time high, and its prestige was increasing all around the world. Prime Minister Vajpayee and the NDA campaigned on the slogan of "India Shining." The Vajpayee government seemed assured of returning to power. However, it was not to be. For large segments of the Indian population, particularly those in rural areas, India was not shining, and they were not particularly concerned with international issues. The economic growth that had shone so brightly on the urban middle class had hardly touched the 60 percent of the Indian population who made their living from agriculture. The result was a surprise victory for the Congress Party and its United Progressive Alliance (UPA) partners. The BJP saw its power in Parliament decrease by eighty-eight votes. Conversely, the Congress Party's Lok Sabha delegation increased by eighty-three seats. Congress and its UPA partners were able to form a government with support from the Communists and other left-wing parties.

The question now was whether the new government would proceed along the same lines with the United States that had characterized the Bush-Vajpayee relationship. The answer, which was not long in coming, took the form of a US-India joint statement concerning the Next Steps in Strategic Partnership. On September 19, 2004, the two governments issued a further joint statement in which they announced that they had concluded Phase One of the Next Steps in Strategic Partnership. Phase One included implementation of measures to address proliferation concerns and ensure compliance with US export controls. In turn, the United States had made modifications to US export licensing policies that allowed nonnuclear exports to promote the safety of nuclear facilities and removed certain Indian companies from the Department of Commerce's list of companies with which trade was prohibited for US companies (known as the Entities List).

The 2005 Joint Statement on US-India Strategic Cooperation

The opportunity to take the US-India economic and strategic relationship to a new level was presented by the visit of the new Indian prime minister, Manmohan Singh, to the United States in July 2005. In her March 2005 trip to New Delhi, Secretary of State Condoleezza Rice had pleased her Indian hosts by responding favorably to suggestions that the United States and India should cement their closer relationship by dealing with the nuclear issue. In April 2005 talks in Washington preparatory to the visit of the prime minister, the minister of external affairs, Natwar Singh, and his delegation raised the nuclear issue, and negotiations began in earnest. After intense meetings in which Rice, assisted by Undersecretary for Political Affairs Nicholas Burns, took a leading role, the negotiators agreed to a Joint Statement to be issued by the president and the prime minister.[53]

The Bush administration made a major effort to impress the new UPA government of India with its goodwill and respect. The Singh visit began with full-dress welcoming ceremonies on the South Lawn of the White House on the morning of July 18. The two leaders then went to a bilateral meeting in the Oval Office. At the conclusion of the Oval Office meeting, the Joint Statement was issued. Bush and Singh proceeded to a joint press conference in the East Room. Significantly, the press conference was followed by a meeting with US and Indian business leaders at a CEO Forum, which had been established at the urging of the US ambassador to India, David Mulford. That evening, a formal dinner was held at the White House. The following day, the prime minister addressed a joint session of Congress, and he later met with the India Caucus of the House of Representatives. Press events on July 20 concluded the visit.[54]

The Joint Statement of July 18, 2005, is a seminal document that has guided the emergence of the present US-India strategic relationship. Significantly, there is an acknowledgment in its opening paragraphs of the central role of economic engagement in bringing about the new strategic relationship. After resolving to promote democratic values and combat terrorism, the Joint Statement observes:

> The Prime Minister's visit coincides with the completion of the Next Steps in Strategic Partnership . . . initiative, launched in 2004. The two leaders agree that this provides the basis for expanding bilateral activities and commerce in space, civil nuclear energy and dual-use technology.

As indicated above, the HTCG, founded upon a public-private dialogue involving US and Indian businesses, led to the Next Steps in Strategic Partnership, which in turn provided the basis for the civil nuclear initiative. As if to emphasize the point, the first agreements in the Joint Statement are listed under the heading "For the Economy." This section begins with a pledge to "revitalize the US-India Economic Dialogue," which had been started during the 2000 visit of President Clinton to India. This section leads to the agreement to launch the CEO Forum, which had been foreshadowed by the US-India Commercial Alliance announced during the Brown mission to India a decade earlier. The "For the Economy" section continues with agreements to support and accelerate economic growth and promote the modernization of India's infrastructure. The section concludes with an agreement to launch the US-India Knowledge Initiative on Agriculture, which is discussed below in connection with promotion of a "second green revolution" for India.

The Joint Statement also addressed energy and the environment, democracy and development, nonproliferation and security, high-technology and space. The section on high-technology and space recognizes again the role of the HTCG and the Next Steps in Strategic Partnership. The HTCG is linked to the signing of a science and technology framework agreement, and the Next Steps in Strategic Partnership is linked to the further removal of certain unspecified Indian organizations from the Department of Commerce's Entities List.

For all its concentration on the wide range of issues facing the United States and India, the agreement on civilian nuclear energy far outweighed the rest of the Joint Statement in symbolic value. Accordingly, news coverage was almost exclusively focused on the civilian nuclear aspect of the Joint Statement. This portion of the document expressed the concepts important to India—especially equality between India and the other great powers, which was addressed multiple times. The Joint Statement said, "President Bush . . . stated that as a responsible state with advanced nuclear technology, India should acquire the same benefits and advantages as other such states." And: "The Prime Minister conveyed that for his part, India would reciprocally agree that it would be ready to assume the same responsibilities and practices and acquire the same benefits and advantages as other leading countries with advanced nuclear technology, such as the United States." This language concerning equality created some confusion. The language itself was not limited to civilian nuclear energy, although that was the intent. For example, in the press briefing by Foreign Secretary Shyam Saran on July 18, he was asked:

And I was wondering whether this will enable us [India] to carry on or simulate explosions, and also to go in for mini nukes, because if you are talking of putting us on level with the United States, I'm afraid we'll have to have these two facilities.

Saran responded:

This is not about mini-nukes. This is not about nuclear weapons. As I said, this is about civilian nuclear energy cooperation. So the military aspect is completely outside the ambit of what we're talking about here.

The Joint Statement also addressed the highly symbolic issue of fuel supplies to the GE-built nuclear power plant at Tarapur. According to the statement:

The United States will work with friends and allies to adjust international regimes to enable full civil nuclear energy cooperation and trade with India, *including but not limited to expeditious consideration of fuel supplies for safeguarded nuclear reactors at Tarapur.* (emphasis added)

This verbiage enabled Secretary Saran to say in his press briefing, "Well, fuel for Tarapur is there in black and white." This explicit reference to Tarapur was highly important for the Indian audience.

Through the Joint Statement, the US president took on three obligations: (1) to seek agreement from Congress to adjust US laws and policies to allow civil nuclear energy cooperation with India; (2) to work with the United States' friends and allies to adjust international regimes to enable full civil nuclear energy cooperation and trade with India; and (3) to consult with its partner countries about India's participation in the International Thermonuclear Experimental Reactor program and the Generation IV International Forum.[55]

In return, the prime minister agreed that India would take seven actions: (1) identify and separate civilian and military nuclear facilities and file a declaration regarding its civilian facilities with the International Atomic Energy Agency (IAEA); (2) place its civilian nuclear facilities under IAEA safeguards (the Tarapur facility was already under IAEA safeguards); (3) sign and adhere to an Additional Protocol with respect to its civilian nuclear facilities;[56] (4) continue a unilateral moratorium on nuclear testing; (5) work with the United States for the conclusion of a multilateral Fissile Material Cutoff Treaty; (6) refrain from transfer of enrichment and reprocessing technologies to states that do not have them and support international efforts to limit their spread; (7) ensure that the necessary steps would be taken to secure nuclear materials and technology through comprehensive export control legislation and through harmonization and adherence to Missile Technology Control Regime and Nuclear Suppliers Group guidelines.

Praise and Criticism from around the World

Both praise and criticism poured forth from around the world for this breakthrough in civil nuclear cooperation. In the United States and India, the business communities voiced strong approval. The USIBC issued a press release lauding the joint statement. In India, both FICCI and CII made positive statements.

Indian Americans were particularly vocal in their support for civil nuclear cooperation. This support seemed premised on both economic and personal factors. As noted above, Indian Americans were prominently involved in US-India trade and investment, particularly in high-technology outsourcing. Personally, many Indian Americans looked to the United States' recognition of India's civil nuclear legitimacy and status as ratification of their own dignity and status within the American polity. US-India cooperation on the most powerful of technologies fulfilled their vision of lives that conjoined the land of their birth with their adopted home. Indian Americans had by their own immigration fulfilled their concept of the compatibility of Indian and US values with economic opportunity. US-India civil nuclear cooperation would do the same on an international level.

Criticism came chiefly from the nonproliferation community. In addition to academics of varying kinds, this community is composed chiefly of people who work for nongovernmental organizations. The leading such organization was the Arms Control Association, led by its executive director, Daryl Kimball. Other critical nongovernmental organizations included former senator Sam Nunn's Nuclear Threat Initiative and the Henry L. Stimson Center, cofounded by Michael Krepon. These groups' criticisms were levied not at the underlying principle of cooperation between the United States and India on civil nuclear matters. Rather, their criticism generally was that the agreement should be "improved" by obtaining from the Government of India commitments to additional limitations on India's defense nuclear program. Many of the constraints sought by the critics echoed those that had been sought by the Clinton administration immediately after India's nuclear tests and had been the subject of the discussions between Strobe Talbott and Jaswant Singh.

The Formation of the Coalition for Partnership with India

Representing the leading US traders and investors with India, the USIBC undertook to lead support for the initiative. The president of the USIBC, Ronald S. Somers, had spent some twelve years in India. He first served as a contractor of the US Agency for International Development working on promoting the "fast-track" projects of the Rao government. He later became the manager for the coal-fired Cogentrix project at Mangalore in Karnataka State. And in the final years of his residency in India, he had been the country manager for Unocal Corporation, where he headed a project to bring gas from Bangladesh to India as well as handling the company's other interests. From his experience in India, Somers immediately saw the relationship between the civil nuclear initiative and the interests of US business in India generally. A leader of great enthusiasm and tenacity, he never lost faith that the deal would become a reality.[57]

Maintaining Somers' level of optimism would not always be easy over the next three years of work by the business community in support of the civil nuclear initiative. Not all members of the USIBC could see the connection between their own interests and the initiative. In particular, businesses involved in the prospect of foreign participation in the retail trade and supply lines sourcing from India had difficulty seeing the connection. However, there was strong support from aerospace and defense members, those directly involved in prospective nuclear power trade and investment, financial services members, and a variety of other traders and investors in fields as varied as automobile manufacturing and chemicals. A number of these companies sent representatives on an "Executive Mission" to New Delhi from August 8 to 10, 2005. Led by Somers and the new USIBC chairman, Chip Kaye, the group met with Prime Minister Singh and expressed their support for the deal. In a luncheon address to CII, Kaye made it plain that a main reason for the success of the prime minister's July trip had been growth in the private-sector relationship. Looking forward, Kaye said that "the future of the US-India relationship will be powered by private-sector growth and decisions taken in the boardroom."[58]

Shortly after the July 18, 2005, Joint Statement was released, I was retained to advise and assist the USIBC in its efforts to support the agreement in reaching fruition. We realized that the strength of the business community would be significantly enhanced if we could cooperate with others who shared the USIBC's positive view of the civil nuclear initiative as outlined by Bush and Singh in the Joint Statement. In a paper for Somers, I outlined a "Coalition for Partnership with India" (CPI) that would consist of three basic elements or stakeholders interested in turning the pronouncement into reality. The CPI would be a "three-legged stool," the legs of which were the business community, Indian Americans, and foreign policy experts. This CPI would not be an organization raising funds but would simply serve as a forum to enable like-minded supporters of the initiative to coordinate their support. Retired US Army lieutenant general Dan Christman, senior vice president of the US Chamber of Commerce for international affairs, agreed to chair the CPI. The USIBC would act as secretariat for the CPI, and this secretariat function was placed in my charge. A Web site was set up for the

CPI, and a member of the USIBC's staff, Ted Jones, was assigned to handle its development and other organizational matters. Jones would be a key figure in keeping the CPI running on a day-to-day basis.

After outlining the organization of the CPI, the next step was to identify businesses willing to participate. The immediate past chairman of the USIBC, Frank Wisner, vice chairman of AIG and a former ambassador to India, was instrumental in contacting prospective business supporters. In September 2005, a letter went out from Ambassador Wisner to USIBC members and other companies interested in US-India trade and investment. The response to this letter was significant. Some thirty-five companies indicated their interest in participating in the CPI. From among these companies, a core group of nine companies was recruited: General Electric, Boeing, AIG, Raytheon, Bechtel, Lockheed Martin, Ford, Dow Chemical, and Honeywell. Weekly conference calls were held among the core group. Over the next two years, the core group would expand to include an additional three companies: Textron, Westinghouse, and ITT. Additional strong support also came from J. P. Morgan, AES Corporation, McGraw-Hill, Parsons Brinckerhoff, and Xerox.

With the business component of the CPI in place, attention next turned to the Indian American community. A political difficulty with this community is that many times there is an unwillingness to submit to the leadership of others. Factionalism is carried to an extreme, with many wishing to be the only leader. Therefore, it was especially important to bring together as many responsible leaders of the community as possible at one time. This occurred in October 2005 in a meeting chaired by Christman and attended by a dozen Indian American leaders. By the end of the meeting, there was an agreement to work together as a part of the CPI. By consensus among the Indian American leaders, Swadesh Chatterjee became the principal point of contact between the CPI and various Indian American organizations. Chatterjee was a former president of the Indian American Forum for Political Education (IAFPE), the first nationwide organization to promote political activism by Indian Americans. In addition to IAFPE, Chatterjee was able to pull together the US-India Friendship Council—made up of the American Association of Physicians of Indian Origin, the Asian American Hotel Owners Association, the Alumni of the Indian Institutes of Technology, the Federation of Indian Associations Tri-State Area, and the National Organization of Indian Associations. The US-India Friendship Council functioned closely with the CPI throughout the campaign for passage of the legislation to implement the civil nuclear initiative. The Indian American community was so overwhelmingly in favor of the US-India civil nuclear initiative that there was spontaneous support from the community all over the United States. Thus, in addition to the individuals and organizations of the US-India Friendship Council, many other Indian American organizations and individuals worked to support the effort to pass the legislation necessary for the US-India civil nuclear initiative to become a reality.

The third component of the CPI, foreign policy experts, was necessary to provide a counterweight to the nonproliferation organizations and academics who opposed the initiative. Several people—Wisner; Bill Cohen, former secretary of defense, who headed the strategic consulting company the Cohen Group; and Tom Pickering, also a former ambassador to India, former undersecretary of state for political affairs, and Boeing vice president—were instrumental in attracting other national security experts. Many of these were South Asia regional experts: Karl F. "Rick" Inderfurth was a former assistant secretary of state for South Asia and head of the South Asia Studies Program at George Washington University. Teresita "Tezie" Schaffer headed the South Asia program at the Center for Strategic and International Studies. She and her husband, Howard Schaffer, a professor at Georgetown University, had both served as ambassadors in South Asia; she had been ambassador to Sri Lanka, and he had been ambassador to Bangladesh. Another very important person, especially for his role in organizing a letter from experts endorsing the civil nuclear issue, was Selig "Sig" Harrison, a former journalist and director of the Asia Program at the Center for International Policy. Others who were also instrumental in providing intellectual weight to the effort included Steve Cohen, head of the South Asia program at the Brookings Institution; Walter Andersen, head of a similar program at the School for Advanced International Studies of Johns Hopkins University; and Robert Hathaway, head of the Asia Program at the Woodrow Wilson International Center for Scholars.

The US Congressional Strategy and the Administration's Bill

As the CPI was being put into place, a strategy was outlined for its activities. Two operating decisions made initially were important to this strategy. First, it was recognized that the CPI was supporting the initiative of the George W. Bush administration. The public initiative was not that of the CPI or any of its components. The business community and the increasing economic engagement between the United States and India were fundamental to the inception of the initiative. The political support of the Indian American community was fundamental to the passage of implementing legislation. Foreign policy experts were necessary to provide the intellectual weight to counterbalance the nonproliferation opponents. However, the administration was the moving party, and care was taken not to get ahead of government leadership.   .

Second, even though the CPI had commenced during a Republican administration, its implementation had to be totally bipartisan. The presidency and both houses of Congress were in the hands of Republicans when the initiative was announced in 2005. There were those, particularly major Indian American Republican fund-raisers and some business executives, who argued that the implementing legislation could be passed simply by supporting the administration and the Republican leadership in Congress. However, bipartisanship was necessary for several reasons. The desire was to create trust between the United States and India and bring about a fundamental, permanent change in the two nations' relationships. For this sort of change to be sustainable, it was necessary to gain bipartisan approval that would not be reversed when the parties in control of Congress changed. Perhaps more important, the sixty votes required to overcome a filibuster in the Senate could not be obtained without Democratic support. Also, there were the matters of the thinness of Republican margins in the Senate and House of Representatives and the declining popularity of the Bush presidency. The change of a single senator's party affiliation could change the balance of power in the Senate. Further, the possibility that party majorities could change in the 2006 elections was not remote.

The CPI's strategy for achieving congressional passage of implementing legislation consisted of the basics for a public policy communications program. First, those who should receive the message would be identified. Second, the message for those targeted recipients would be created. Third, there would be selection of the messengers who should deliver the message. Fourth, there would be selection of the media by which the message would be delivered. Fifth, there would be development of the timetable for delivering the message, including how many times it should be delivered.

Because this was a federal legislative communications program, the primary targets of the message would be the members of Congress necessary to pass the legislation. In the broadest sense, that meant obtaining the sixty votes necessary in the Senate to impose cloture on a filibustering senator and a majority in the House. However, the key to the congressional legislative process is the committee system. Unless a bill can get out of committee, in almost all cases it will never receive a vote of the full Senate or House. In this case, the committees with jurisdiction were the Senate Foreign Relations Committee and the House International Relations Committee (in 2006 renamed the House Foreign Affairs Committee). Within the committees, chairs wield exceptional power by virtue of their abilities to set the agenda; their relationships to the leaders of their respective houses; and their abilities, together with the leadership, to reward and punish committee members. In today's Congress, the powers of the committee chairs are wielded in a partisan manner that engenders conflict. Fortunately, in 2005–8 both the Senate Foreign Relations Committee and the House International Relations Committee were among the few committees of Congress that operated in a broadly bipartisan fashion. Their chairs and respective ranking minority members worked exceptionally closely. This meant that the CPI did not have to choose between the chair and the ranking minority member in its advocacy efforts. Rather, advocacy could be pointed at bringing together a consensus between the majority and minority members of the relevant committees.

Thus, the primary targets for delivery of the message were, first, the chairs and ranking minority members of the Senate Foreign Relations Committee and the House International Relations Committee; second, the chairs of the respective subcommittees on South Asia; and third, the members of the committees. The leaderships in both the House and Senate—that is, the speaker, majority leader, and minority leader in the House, and the majority leader and minority leader in the Senate—would become important when and if the bills got out of committee. Other members of Congress, such as those who headed caucuses on India and Indian Americans in the House and the Senate, were also important because of their potential to provide leadership among caucus members.

The development of the message was an important step. Building on the concept of partnership, the message was crafted to show the benefits to the United States. To assist in this effort, the USIBC retained Bruce Fein, an attorney with a number of books to his credit. He had the added advantage of being respected in conservative circles, and particularly in having access to editorial management at conservative publications such as the *Wall Street Journal* and the *Washington Times.*

The deliverers of the message depended upon the recipient. Major authorities in the national security field such as Wisner, Cohen, and Pickering were able to speak one to one with the congressional committee chairs and ranking members to deliver the message. In general contacts with congressional staff, the CPI tried to have teams composed of representatives from each of its three supporting groups. Thus, a typical contact team would have a businessperson, an Indian American, and a national security expert. Within these general categories, particular persons would be chosen, in many cases for their prior relationships with particular members of Congress.

With regard to the media to be used, in most cases this was simply a "leave behind" sheet that capsulated the points made in the meeting. Members of Congress and their staffs were not interested in longer-form materials. There are so many demands on the time of members and staff that written media must be focused and to the point. However, the CPI's Web site (www.strategicpartnership.org) was a key organizational component. The site served as a link to the news and editorial traffic for CPI participants and enabled the CPI to get its press releases and background information to the media. For the wider use of supporters, the CPI published a handbook containing the arguments in support of the initiative that was posted on its Web site. The CPI encouraged and assisted experts in writing editorial commentaries and key advocates in writing letters to Congress. In the later stages of the campaign, there was some advertising done in congressionally oriented publications. Chatterjee's US-India Friendship Council sponsored advertisements, but largely the media used to deliver the message were fact sheets of no more than two pages.

Because this was a congressional advocacy effort, the timeline and opportunities for repetition were largely dictated by the congressional calendar. The beginnings of recesses and the end of the session provided major time structuring for the effort. The first few months of the advocacy effort in 2005 were devoted to developing the message, recruiting companies, and preparing to make contacts. The advocacy effort was to begin in earnest when Congress convened in January 2006.

The Government of India hired two sets of Washington lobbyists to act on its behalf with Congress. The first of these was Barbour, Griffith, and Rogers (BGR). At the time, BGR was an exclusively Republican lobbying operation headed by the former chairman of the Republican National Committee, Haley Barbour. BGR had brought on board former ambassador Blackwill to represent India. Blackwill was assisted primarily by Andrew Parasiliti, a former Republican staff member for the House Committee on International Relations. Later, seeing the importance of Democrats to the passage of authorizing and implementing legislation, the Government of India retained the Venable law firm and the former Democratic senator who was a partner there, Birch Bayh. Graham Wisner, the brother of former US ambassador to India Frank Wisner, and his firm of Patton Boggs were retained to provide lobbying support to the USIBC. Patton Boggs was tasked with organizing meetings with members of Congress and their staffs and with setting up conference calls of the Core Committee of CPI members.

Prerequisites to the Creation of Legislation

However, an immediate problem at the start of the 2006 congressional session was the absence of any legislation to advocate. Before a bill to implement the commitments of the president could be sent to Congress, India had to act on its fundamental undertaking in the July 18, 2005, Joint Statement. This commitment was to separate its military and civilian programs. There were those in the Bush administration who had no problem with India being a nuclear power and being treated as such by the United States. Their thinking was that India should be a counterweight to nuclear China. As the ambassador to India, Robert Blackwill, once said in my presence, "Why wouldn't you want a nuclear-armed India?" But for most US officials, both elected and appointed, the Blackwill approach went too far. Providing support to India's military nuclear program seemed a direct violation of US obligations, particularly its obligations under the Non-Proliferation Treaty. Further, the US political implications in Congress of such an approach were quite negative. It seemed unlikely to many members of Congress that the US electorate would support nuclear aid if it were going to support the Indian military nuclear effort. In fact, the main argument of opponents turned out to be that any cooperation with India on nuclear matters would inevitably aid India's military nuclear program. Thus, if the United States were to provide nuclear assistance to India, it would need to be assured that its assistance was only going to civil nuclear programs. This would require the separation of India's civil and military programs.

The problem here was that sufficient separation of India's civil and military nuclear programs had not been defined in the Joint Statement. The manner and scope of separation thus became a matter for negotiation between the United States and India. Members of Congress made it plain that if the Government of India failed to place a substantial amount of its nuclear power establishment in the civilian category, then they would consider the Indian obligations of separating civilian and military nuclear facilities and programs to be unfulfilled. Negotiations were slow. Separation commitments would have extensive domestic political implications in India. The converse of US opponents' insistence that the agreement provided too little restraint on the Indian military nuclear program was Indian opponents' argument that it provided too much restraint. Having suffered under colonial rule for so long, infringement on the nation's sovereignty is always a potent political issue in India.

When President Bush made his visit to India on March 1 and 2, 2006, the issue of the separation of civilian and military nuclear facilities had still not been resolved. Ron Somers and I were in New Delhi with a USIBC delegation that had been mobilized in support of the president's trip. In addition to the CEO Forum conducting its second formal meeting, the USIBC had organized a day-long program in conjunction with CII and the participation of US and Indian officials. At this meeting, the importance of the nuclear deal was discussed and business support was communicated to the president and the prime minister. This program focused on the broad range of issues facing US-India economic engagement, but the importance of the US-India civil nuclear deal was a dominant theme.

During the course of the meeting, we kept getting messages that the separation issue was still unresolved. We tried, within appropriate limitations, to encourage the government negotiators in their work. However, it was not until late in the afternoon of March 2 that we received information that the United States and India had reached agreement. We were told that this basic issue had not been resolved until President Bush intervened personally to tell the United States' negotiators that he wanted the matter concluded. When the talks were seemingly stalled, Bush basically ordered his subordinates to reach agreement. "The President wants this done" was the formulation reported to the leaders of the US business delegation that went to New Delhi at the time of the visit.

To reach agreement, the US negotiators simply dropped most of their demands for detailed commitments and restraints. The separation agreement simply indicated that India would designate civilian reactors, on which there would be IAEA restraints and inspections ("safeguards"), and those reactors that would be outside the program. Those that were outside the program would be usable in whatever way and for whatever purpose that India desired, including weapons production. This lack of precision on separation was later to be a chief issue in Congress. But for now, Bush had an agreement that enabled him to move forward with the major public event of his Indian mission—an evening speech at the Old Fort in New Delhi. Organized by FICCI, the event had in attendance business and government leaders from all over India as well as our US business delegation. In retrospect, it seems that President Bush was determined that this main public event of the visit would be a success, and for this he needed a "separation agreement" that would enable the initiative to move forward. So it was done, clearing the way for the introduction of legislation that would amend US law to allow trade in civil nuclear technology with India. Although certainly not involved in the negotiations themselves, the private business sector—through FICCI, CII, the USIBC, and the CEO Forum—had provided support in New Delhi for reaching the agreement on separation.

The Introduction of the Administration's Bill

Now legislation could be introduced in the US Congress to meet the obligations President Bush had undertaken in the July 18, 2005, Joint Statement. The prospect and then the fact of the actual introduction of legislation set off furious activity by both the legislation's supporters and opponents. The CPI prepared to swing into action to bring about passage of the legislation. The USIBC hosted a March 10, 2006, briefing for the CPI on the elements of the civilian nuclear initiative and the next steps for its implementation. The chief negotiator and interlocutor for the initiative, the undersecretary of state for political affairs, Nick Burns, gave a report on the president's India trip, the separation agreement, and the status of the initiative. John Rood, special assistant to the president and senior director for counterproliferation, followed with remarks on the nonproliferation benefits of the agreement. The US Chamber of Commerce and the CPI issued a press release citing the launching of a "massive grassroots effort to win congressional approval of a US-India nuclear agreement." On March 15, 2006, leaders of the Indian American community met with Christman, Somers, and me to discuss the strategy outlined above and delineate the tactics for implementing the strategy.

The public face of the struggle between proponents and opponents of the deal was largely seen in the competing statements of endorsement and condemnation by prominent experts and public figures. With the urging and support of the CPI, an open letter to members of Congress put together by the eminent journalist and scholar Selig S. Harrison, director of the Asia Program at the Center for International Policy, obtained the endorsement of twenty-six US foreign policy experts. Not to be outdone, the Federation of American Scientists published a letter to members of Congress signed by thirty-seven winners of the Nobel Prize. In November 2005, Mohammed ElBaradei, head of the IAEA, had endorsed the Indo-US nuclear deal.[59] Now the opponents of the initiative sought a person of equal stature and more US political clout to counter ElBaradei. Early on, I had gone to the Nuclear Threat Initiative to see about the possibility of an endorsement from former senator Sam Nunn. Nunn was the widely respected coauthor of the Nunn-Lugar legislation designed to help control nuclear weapons from the former USSR. At our urging, Undersecretary of State Robert G. Joseph had been sent to visit personally with Nunn. However, it was to no avail. Nunn came out against the agreement in a scathing opinion article.[60] Eventually, we obtained endorsements from such luminaries as Henry Kissinger, Madeleine Albright, Sandy Berger, Frank Carlucci, William S. Cohen, and Rajenda Pachauri. The opposition wound up with endorsements from such equally bright stars as Jimmy Carter, Brent Scowcroft, and Zbigniew Brzezinski.[61] In the final analysis, the battle of the endorsements did not seem to make a great deal of difference. The real determinant seemed to be what actually happened in contacts with members of Congress on the Hill.

The bill the administration sent to Congress was duly introduced by Chairman Richard Lugar in the Senate and Chairman Henry Hyde in the House.[62] The original bill sent to Congress by the administration was a near disaster for the hopes that legislation would pass allowing the initiative to become a reality. Only a few pages long, the legislation had none of the assurances that would enable members concerned about nonproliferation to support it. Neither Lugar nor Hyde showed enthusiasm for the legislation they were introducing. Both noted that their introductions were "by request." This notation is a signal that the sponsors are concerned about what they have been asked to do by the White House and have no personal political stake in the bill they are introducing. Chairman Hyde and ranking minority member Tom Lantos (D-Calif.) were so skeptical of the legislation that they left it to the Senate to work on the legislation in the first instance. The Senate Foreign Relations Committee had held a hearing on the civil nuclear initiative before the introduction of actual legislation. Undersecretaries Burns and Joseph were the chief witnesses. However, with no legislation and no separation agreement in hand at the time, the hearing was very inconclusive.

The House and Senate foreign policy leaders met with the president on his return from India, but with little effect.[63] A better atmosphere was created in the Senate Foreign Relations Committee with the testimony of Secretary of State Rice at a hearing on April 5, 2006. Business, Indian American, and policy expert supporters (the three elements of the CPI) were present in force and prominent in the hearing room. There was widespread interaction between supporters, senators, and staff both before and after Rice testified.

Her testimony was well received. There seemed to be virtual unanimity on the committee in support of the need for closer relations with India. There also seemed to be acceptance of civil nuclear reconciliation as an appropriate vehicle for change. However, the simplistic administration bill still garnered little enthusiasm and little support from either the Republicans or Democrats on the Senate Foreign Relations Committee. The basic difficulty was that the bill said little in the way of how nuclear technology and materials were to be handled once the technology and materials were in Indian hands. The administration contended that these matters could best be handled in the agreement required under Section 123 of the Atomic Energy Act.

After the Rice hearing, the Senate Foreign Relations Committee began rewriting the bill to take into account various nonproliferation concerns of committee members. Although Lugar was the committee chairman, the ranking minority member, Joe Biden (D-Del.), took the lead in this effort, along with his key committee staff members Anthony Blinken, Jonah Blank, and Edward Levine. Biden's leadership made sense because most of the nonproliferation concerns were among Democratic senators. Besides, Lugar was somewhat conflicted by his sense of loyalty to his Republican president. Though Lugar shared concerns about the bill, he apparently did not want to be in the position of confronting the administration with the need to redraft it. Accordingly, the contacts of the CPI, and particularly its Indian American members, with Senator Biden and his staffs, both at the committee and in his office, became more frequent.

On the House side, a similar dynamic unfolded. Chairman Hyde began to defer to ranking minority member Lantos and his staff, led by Robert King, for a rewrite of the administration's bill. Again, the focus was on nonproliferation. The Democratic members of the House were concerned about the perceived inadequacies of the administration's bill in assuring that US-India civil nuclear cooperation would not increase the numbers of nuclear weapons in South Asia. This concern was part of a broader worry that the deal would undercut the international nonproliferation regime and complicate efforts to rein in North Korea and Iran.

Atoms for War?

Concerns about nonproliferation were fed by what appeared to be a coordinated attack from the nongovernmental organizations opposed to the initiative. The premise of this attack was that the whole US-India civil nuclear initiative would enable India to build more bombs than it could build without the initiative. The initiative's opponents argued that India was now constrained in its nuclear weapons program by a lack of uranium. With the United States providing nuclear fuel, India could divert fuel from its existing civil nuclear program to bomb making. A primary source of support for this argument was an article that appeared in an Indian newspaper.[64] This article quoted J. K. Singh, a former additional secretary from the Indian Research and Analysis Wing, which is somewhat similar to the US Central Intelligence Agency. According to Singh, India would have its capacity to produce nuclear weapons increased from between six and ten warheads per year to about fifty warheads. Representative Edward J. Markey, who was leading the opposition in the House of Representatives, circulated this article to all his House colleagues.

The CPI alerted Ashley J. Tellis to the danger to the legislation being created by the Singh claims. Tellis, a leading expert on the Indian nuclear program who had been an adviser to the administration, produced an analysis showing that Singh's perspective was speculation not grounded in fact.[65] According to Tellis, India had shown no intention of wanting to increase its weapons production to the level indicated by Singh, but even if India so desired, available uranium would not be a significant constraint. An article by former secretary of defense William Cohen quoted the Tellis refutation. But the damage had been done. Many members of Congress appeared to be unwilling to act if there was any possibility that legislation would authorize an initiative in violation of the United States' obligations under the Non-Proliferation Treaty. Representative Brad Sherman (D-Calif.) authored an amendment supposedly to prevent this result. However, Sherman's amendment was completely unacceptable to the Indians and would have killed the initiative.

Lantos to the Rescue

Under these circumstances, Lantos came to the rescue with what appeared at the time to be a proposal that would weaken the chances of ultimate passage. He accepted the administration's contention that these nonproliferation matters could indeed be handled in the US-India agreement governing the transfer of nuclear materials and technology under Section 123 of the Atomic Energy Act. However, he was unwilling to leave these issues in the hands of the administration, and he thus proposed that the legislation be divided into two parts. The bill's first part would contain provisions to make the necessary changes to allow civil nuclear trade with India. However, its second part would require approval by Congress separately of the implementing "123 Agreement" before India could take advantage of the legislation. This formulation was embodied in a rewriting of the administration's bill. This revised legislation was introduced in the House by Chairman Hyde on June 26, 2006, as the United States and India Nuclear Cooperation Promotion Act of 2006.[66]

On the Senate side, Lugar and Biden were amenable to the Lantos two-step approach. They continued to work with their respective staffs in drafting legislation that would have bipartisan support in the Senate. In turn, the staffs of both the House and Senate committees were in close contact. Thus, the Senate and House versions of the legislation were moving substantively on convergent paths. At the State Department, it was now clear that the original legislation proposed by the administration was inadequate to the political task of securing the necessary support in Congress. To the credit particularly of Undersecretary Burns and Assistant Secretary of State for Legislative Affairs Jeffrey Bergner, the administration did not challenge the need for substitute legislation and chose to work with the Senate and House committees on drafting legislation that could obtain the needed support. The proponents of the legislation who had joined together in the CPI maintained close contact with Lugar and Biden and with Hyde and Lantos. However, the drafting process took place primarily among the staffs of the House and Senate committees with input from the committees' leaders. The main effort was to come up with legislation that would allay nonproliferation concerns without being so offensive to the Government of India as to kill the deal reached by President Bush and Prime Minister Singh.

By the middle of June 2006, it appeared that Senator Biden was becoming comfortable with the redrafting process. A significant breakthrough came when Biden was willing to provide public advocacy for the enactment of legislation to implement the initiative. Significantly, this initial public advocacy came at the June 22, 2006, annual general meeting of the USIBC. Through the auspices of Swadesh Chatterjee, and thanks in large part to the work of his US-India Friendship Council of Indian American organizations, Biden appeared as the speaker for the closing dinner and gave a strong speech in favor of legislation. His speech was especially powerful because it came after a noon address to the same audience from Vice President Dick Cheney. Cheney had urged passage of the legislation in no uncertain terms in a talk that was uncharacteristically void of partisanship. After Biden's speech, it was plain that the US-India nuclear legislation had strong bipartisan support in the Senate.

Redrafting the Senate bill continued over the Fourth of July recess. Of particular concern to the business community were provisions that dealt with the exporting of enrichment, reprocessing, or heavy water products. Also of concern, because the Indians objected to the intrusiveness of the provision, was a measure that dealt with Indian accountability for nondiversion. Sections 106 and 107 of a new bill dealt with these matters. The new legislation, S 3709, was reported as a replacement for S 2429 on July 20, 2006.

Acting on the Redrafted Bills

With redrafted bills in place in both the House and Senate, the problem became one of time. The year 2006 was a congressional election year, with all the members of the House and a third of the Senate up for election. It was expected that when Congress adjourned for a summer recess on August 3, it would remain in recess until after the elections or, at the very best, return only for the consideration of budget appropriations bills. The House Committee on International Relations had considered amendments and taken a vote on its bill, HR 5682, on June 27, 2006. The bill was reported by a resounding vote of thirty-seven to five. Now, just before the August recess, the House was ready to take up its version of the legislation. The CPI carried on an extensive campaign that included letters from the heads of prominent organizations, op-ed columns, and personal contacts with the staff of the representatives.

On July 26, 2006, the House took up the legislation. Several amendments that would have killed it were offered and defeated. Then came the most significant challenge, in the form of a motion to recommit offered by Representative Edward Markey, the House leader of opposition to the bill. The motion to recommit was so dangerous to passage of the bill because it played upon the virulently anti-Iranian sentiments of the House. The Markey motion to recommit would require the bill to be reported back with instructions to add a new paragraph stating that the president must certify that "India is fully and actively participating in US efforts to dissuade, isolate, and, if necessary, sanction and contain Iran for its efforts to acquire weapons of mass destruction, including a nuclear weapons capability (including the capability to enrich or process nuclear materials), and the means to deliver weapons of mass destruction."[67] The motion to recommit failed by a recorded vote of 192 to 235. This was the high-water mark for opposition in the House.

With passage now assured, the House voted approval of HR 5682 by the overwhelming vote of 359 to 68.

The House legislation was sent to the Senate, but time apparently had run out. The Senate adjourned on August 3 without taking up the legislation. When the Senate came back into session after Labor Day, its business consisted mainly of dealing with contentious appropriations and authorization bills. As always, senators and representatives up for reelection were anxious to return to their states and districts for full-time campaigning. There was no time to deal with the US-India civil nuclear pact and still leave enough time for campaigning. The Senate recessed on September 29, 2006, without taking any action. The supporters of passage of implementing legislation were very concerned that this legislation would not be taken up before the end of the 109th Congress. There was solid support for the legislation in the 109th Congress, but all unpassed legislation dies with the end of a Congress. US-India civil nuclear would have to be reintroduced. No one could predict with certainty the political makeup of the next Congress and how the legislation might fare in a changed legislature.

Passage in the Last Hour of the Last Day

However, there remained one glimmer of hope for passage in the 109th Congress. Not only had there been a failure to act on the civil nuclear legislation, but also there remained ten appropriations bills without any action. Without action on the remaining appropriations, large segments of the government would be unfunded and have to shut down. The only possibility was for a session to be called after the elections. Such sessions are not favored because they include senators and representatives who have been defeated at the polls. Such defeated senators and representatives are often referred to as "lame ducks." Hence, a session that includes them is referred to as a lame duck session. Fortunately for proponents of the US-India civil nuclear deal, Congress's failure to act on many of the basic spending bills that were required to keep the government running offered a chance for consideration of the civil nuclear legislation. By the time Congress had recessed in September, only two of twelve appropriations bills had been acted on. Thus, a lame duck session was a near necessity in 2006. Whether this session would take up major measures in addition to the spending bills remained to be seen.

The wisdom of a bipartisan approach to the legislation was proved when the Democrats won majorities in both houses of Congress in the November elections. Although they would not actually take control until January 2007, the Democrats' position as incoming leaders would have put them in a strong political position to not act on the US-India civil nuclear legislation, if they chose to do so. However, both the incoming majority leader, Senator Harry Reid (D-Nev.) and the incoming chairman of the Senate Foreign Relations Committee, Senator Joseph Biden (D-Del.), were firmly in favor of the legislation. On November 16, 2006, the Senate took up the bill that had been passed by the House of Representatives, HR 5682. On the motion of Chairman Lugar, the Senate struck all the House language and inserted the language of S 3709 in its entirety. As in the House, "killer" amendments were offered. Again, the most serious of these dealt with India's relationship to Iran. Senator Barbara Boxer proposed an amendment requiring the president to determine that India had halted military-to-military contacts with Iran before executing his waiver authority. Business and Indian American supporters of the legislation were in the gallery of the Senate the evening when Boxer offered the amendment. Biden was masterful in beating back the arguments of his fellow Democrats. He pointed out that India did not approve of the US relationship with India's archenemy Pakistan. However, the US relationship with Pakistan did not halt India's willingness to cooperate with the United States. Similarly, Biden argued, disagreements over Iran should not be allowed to bring down this step forward in US-India relations. The Boxer amendment was defeated by a vote of thirty-eight to fifty-nine. The bill then passed the Senate by a vote of eighty-five to twelve.[68]

After the vote, Richard Verma, now an assistant secretary of state for congressional affairs and then an aide to Senator Reid, invited a group of us supporters into Reid's Capitol office. There Reid told us of how, when he was a student, several Indian Americans had befriended him. Reid was grateful for their friendship. As a young man of limited economic means from Searchlight, Nevada, he was particularly appreciative of being included in their meals of rich Indian food. He then showed us a statue of Mahatma Gandhi that had been given to him by those Indian American students and that he kept beside his desk. "Gandhi has a always been an inspiration to me," Reid said simply. It was an emotional moment, especially for the Indian Americans in our group who had worked so hard for passage of the legislation.

Because there were differences between the House and Senate versions of HR 5682, a conference committee was necessary to resolve them. Participants in the CPI continued their lobbying efforts for fear that time would run out before the conference committee could report and the report could be acted upon by both houses of Congress. These concerns were well founded. However, the staffs of the Senate Foreign Relations Committee and the House International Relations Committees, aided by input from the State Department through Assistant Secretary of State for Legislative Affairs Jeffrey Bergner, worked effectively to resolve the differences. The conference committee session approving an agreed-on bill was most unusual. The session was held in public in the hearing room of the House International Relations Committee. With representatives of all segments of the CPI present, the conference committee meeting turned into a tribute for the retiring chairman of the House Foreign Relations Committee, Henry Hyde, who was suffering from an illness that would take his life within a year. In his honor, the legislation had been renamed "The Henry J. Hyde United States–India Peaceful Atomic Energy Cooperation Act of 2006."[69] With the Democrats having won a majority in the 2006 elections, Lantos was on the cusp of becoming the new chairman of the House International Relations Committee, which he and the Democrats were about to take back to its original name of the House Committee on Foreign Affairs. Lantos, perhaps conscious of his own mortality,[70] heaped praise upon Hyde. The House took up the committee report and passed it almost immediately. The final legislative action on the legislation was taken by the Senate early on the morning of December 9, 2006. The Senate adjourned only minutes later.

Enactment of the Implementing Legislation

The signing ceremony for the legislation was held in the East Room of the White House on December 18, 2006. Present in the audience were representatives of the primary constituents of the CPI. In signing the bill into law, President Bush expressly thanked the Indian American community leaders who were present. However, he also made clear the role of economic engagement in bringing about the legislation:

> This bill helps open a new important market for American businesses by paving the way for investment in India's civilian nuclear industry for the first time ever. This new trade will help American companies gain new customers abroad and create new jobs here at home.[71]

The key role that economic engagement and the USIBC had played in producing the Hyde Act was emphasized in an extraordinary letter from

Prime Minister Manmohan Singh to the chairman of the USIBC, Charles "Chip" Kaye, copresident of Warburg Pincus.[72] Prime Minister Singh said:

> I have seen your letter of 8th December in connection with the passage of the legislation in the US Congress relating to the US-India civilian nuclear agreement.
>
> The US-India Business Council has played a stellar role in generating a widespread and deep understanding of the need for greater cooperation between the United States and India and the importance of having bipartisan support for this important legislation. The cooperation that is likely to flow out of this agreement is likely to be beneficial to both countries and, in the long run, can be the basis for meeting the long-term energy requirements for India on a sustainable basis.
>
> I would like to place on record high appreciation for the role played by the US-India Business Council and hope that you would continue to work for greater cooperation between the peoples of our two great democracies.[73]

Negotiating the 123 Agreement

Now the effort to implement the US-India civil nuclear initiative turned to negotiation of an agreement to govern the transfer of civil nuclear goods and technology that would pass political muster both in India and the United States. This 123 Agreement would be key to approval, particularly in India, because Indian law itself did not have to be changed to approve the acceptance of nuclear goods and technology from the United States.

Negotiations for a 123 Agreement centered chiefly on what would happen if India conducted further tests of nuclear devices. This issue involved the so-called right of return as to nuclear materials that had been furnished by the United States to India. India insisted that a primary purpose for the initiative had been to secure the reliability of its nuclear suppliers. Having had experience growing out of retaliation for its 1974 and 1998 tests, India sought a formulation that would not cause an automatic cutoff and return of nuclear materials from the United States. At the same time, India recognized that it must live with the provisions of the US Atomic Energy Act, which were very specific about the impermissibility of the United States continuing trade in nuclear materials with nations that conducted tests and the necessity of obtaining the return of materials provided to any such nations. This issue was addressed through two means in the 123 Agreement: first, ambiguity; and, second, procedural requirements for cutoff and return. Though neither government found these measures completely satisfactory, agreement was reached at the government-to-government level. Some seven months after passage of the Hyde Act, both governments released texts of their 123 Agreement on August 3, 2007.

India's Delays

The release of the text set off a firestorm of criticism and threats from opposition parties in India. The National Democratic Alliance, led by the BJP, took the position that the 123 Agreement unduly restricted India in its nuclear defense program and was an affront to Indian national sovereignty. This position was ironic, in view of the deep involvement of the NDA Vajpayee government in putting into motion the negotiations between the United States and India over civil nuclear cooperation.

More serious to the Singh government from a political perspective was the opposition of the Indian Left Parties, whose support for the United Progressive Alliance government was necessary for the government of Prime Minister Manmohan Singh to maintain its parliamentary majority. The Left Parties decried the 123 Agreement and threatened to withdraw their support if the government went forward with either of the two remaining steps necessary from the Indian side to implement the deal. The first of these steps was obtaining an agreement with the IAEA for "safeguard" inspections of the Indian civil nuclear program. The second was a change in the "Guidelines" of the Nuclear Suppliers Group to allow trade with India by any of its members.

The key leader of the Congress Party, Sonia Gandhi, and many other UPA leaders had no stomach for the loss of their parliamentary majority and the necessity for new elections some two years ahead of the 2009 mandatory term expiration. These leaders rationalized that if the government were unable to sustain its majority in Parliament, the initiative would be dead in any event. Singh, who was prime minister at the behest of Gandhi, agreed not to go forward until a political path could be found that would not bring the UPA government to a premature close.

Indian Business Pitches In

Economic engagement between the United States and India became particularly important from the perspective of Indian politics. Indian organizations that had a significant interest in US-India engagement became even more active in support of the initiative. FICCI and CII went into action both overtly and behind the scenes. Representative of the tack taken by major organizations whose members were deeply involved in US-India trade and investment was an article by Amit Mitra, secretary-general of FICCI, in the *Times of India* challenging "Comrade Prakash Karat," who was the leader of the Communist Party (Marxist) and the Left Parties coalition. According to Mitra, "Whether it is a conspiracy against India or an attachment to an outdated Leninist ideology, sabotaging 123 is tantamount to sabotaging India's emergence as a major power in the global matrix."[74] FICCI formed a "Working Group on Civil Nuclear Energy" that stressed to Indian officials the opportunities for India that would be created by the initiative and the potentially greater synergies between the government and the private sector.[75]

CII also pitched in to help change the political atmosphere for acceptance of the 123 Agreement and the deal generally in India. Some fifteen years earlier, CII had undertaken a process of sponsoring a "Track II" strategic dialogue including US and Indian business, governmental, and academic leaders. Civil nuclear matters were a key part of this dialogue. With approval of the agreement on the line, CII canvassed for support in India across business, government, political parties, and the media. Tarun Das, then CII's secretary-general and later its chief mentor, drove "a single-minded effort to support the government in concluding the civil nuclear agreement."[76]

Prime Minister Singh's Political Deal Moves India Forward

At first, Singh and his colleagues worked to bring about a change in the position of the Left Parties. This approach was unsuccessful. Next, Singh sought allies in Parliament to replace the support of the Left Parties if they should move to bring down the UPA government. Finally, in July 2008, Singh was able to find a group in Parliament willing to supplant the Left Parties. A deal was made with the small Samajwadi Party to support the government on the nuclear issue. This deal gave the UPA just enough votes to survive what the Indians call a "vote of trust," and which in most parliaments is referred to as a "vote of no confidence." This occurred on July 22, 2008, with the government being sustained by a vote of 275 to 256.[77]

Now it was possible for the Government of India to move forward with an IAEA agreement to cover those facilities separated out as civil facilities. India already had an IAEA agreement that covered Tarapur, and the head of the IAEA, Mohammed ElBaradei, was in favor of the US-India initiative. Thus, once India decided to move forward, an IAEA safeguards agreement was not hard to reach, and was accomplished on August 1, 2008.[78] The one hurdle that remained before the US Congress could take up the approval of the 123 Agreement was more difficult. That hurdle was an exemption or waiver for India from the Guidelines of the Nuclear Suppliers Group. Undersecretary of State Bill Burns (who had replaced Nicholas Burns) and Deputy Assistant Secretary of State Evan Feigenbaum led an extraordinary US effort to draft a waiver text and secure pressure on recalcitrant members of the forty-five-member organization. A key event was a September 5, 2008, letter from the Government of India stating its policies on a testing moratorium and no first use of nuclear weapons. A Nuclear Suppliers Group waiver was accomplished on September 6, 2008.[79] Throughout this process, State Department leaders were in constant touch with the US business and Indian American communities.

Congressional Approval

The stage was set for final approval of the 123 Agreement by the US Congress. The support effort by participants in the CPI was reactivated. Again, the effort would be conducted in support of the administration. The private-sector support effort was coordinated from the White House perspective by an aide to Presidential Assistant Karl Rove. Brian McCormick, a special assistant to the president and deputy director of public liaison, was the principal point of contact in this effort. Teams and visitations were activated. These teams contacted key representatives and senators again. There was a virtually spontaneous outpouring from the Indian American community as Indian Americans communicated with senators and representatives with whom they had contacts. In the three years since 2005, the Indian community had grown in activism and sophistication. In the presidential campaigns of both John McCain and Barack Obama, there were many Indian Americans who supported the initiative. Both presidential candidates had voted for the Hyde Act and reiterated their support. National security experts, under the leadership of Selig Harrison, once again contributed an open letter to Congress.

On the House side, it seemed that the question of Indian relations with Iran might once again jeopardize the agreement. As discussed below, the chairman of the House Foreign Affairs Committee, Tom Lantos, had been quite concerned about Indian relations with Iran before his death on February 11, 2008.[80] His successor, Representative Howard L. Berman (D-Calif.), was also concerned about Iran and the security of Israel. His support was essential to waive a thirty-day consideration requirement in order to finish the legislation before the elections recess. Speaker Nancy Pelosi was convinced that the US-India civil nuclear accord was both good policy and good politics, and told the new chairman so. Secretary of State Condoleezza Rice spoke directly with Chairman Berman. Daryl Kimball, executive director of the Arms Control Association, attributed approval in part to "the reluctance of lawmakers facing elections to alienate activists in the Indian American community." According to Kimball, "Nobody wants to be jeopardizing campaign contributions at this point."[81] In the end, Chairman Berman consented to the waiver, held a hearing, and enthusiastically supported the legislation. The bill approving the 123 Agreement passed the House, under expedited procedures requiring a two-thirds majority, by a vote of 298 to 117 on September 27, 2008.[82]

On the Senate side, no senator seemed inclined to exercise the filibuster option. There was some question as to whether Senator Barack Obama, then engaged in a spirited campaign for the presidency, would support the agreement. This concern was based in part on his having voted for a "killer" amendment to the bill that became the Hyde Act. However, Obama had voted for the bill on final passage and continued this support, which was fundamental to receiving the financial and electoral backing of the Indian American community in the campaign. Senator Obama had chosen Senate Foreign Relations Committee chairman Joseph Biden as his vice presidential running mate. Although there was considerable opposition to the US-India civil nuclear agreement among some campaign advisers, Biden was a strong advocate for going forward with the agreement on both political and policy grounds. The South Asia advisory group of the Obama campaign was solidly in favor of the agreement. Two people were particularly eloquent in supporting the agreement: Rick Inderfurth, former assistant secretary of state for South Asia, a professor at George Washington University, and chair of the Obama India Advisory Group; and Bruce Riedel, a former presidential assistant, senior fellow at the Brookings Institution, and candidate Obama's chief South Asia adviser. In the end, Senator Obama opted to continue his support for the US-India civil nuclear agreement and to vote affirmatively on the question of the 123 Agreement. Thus, congressional approval of the 123 Agreement was accomplished with a minimum of debate in the Senate on October 1, 2008.[83]

As it turned out, the approval of the 123 Agreement by Congress was somewhat anticlimactic. All the political elements of the previous victory for the Hyde Act were still intact. With some encouragement from elements of the CPI, Congress basically considered the question of US-India cooperation on civil nuclear matters as old, or finished, business. The opponents of the bill were unable to point out anything in the 123 Agreement that had changed from the basic political calculations that had been instrumental in the passage of the Hyde Act.   •

President Bush signed the legislation approving the 123 Agreement on a bright fall day, October 8, 2008. The president thanked a broadly bipartisan group of senators and representatives for their work in getting the legislation through. As the president said, the legislation represented "more than three years of hard work by a lot of people." As in 2006, the president singled out the Indian American community for credit and recognized that, "for our part, the United States will gain access to a growing market for civilian nuclear technologies and materials that will help American businesses create more jobs for our people here at home."[84] The agreement itself was signed two days later at the State Department by US secretary of state Condoleezza Rice and Indian minister of external affairs Pranab Mukherjee.

The Impact of Approval

The impact of enactment of the Hyde Act and approval of the 123 Agreement on US-India strategic relations is broad and undeniable.[85] There remain a number of steps to commercial realization of US-India civil nuclear cooperation. However, those steps are going forward and, in the process, are fueling a larger, cooperative discussion about energy and the environment. No Obama administration official discusses the US-India relationship without a headline reference to the US-India civil nuclear deal. For example, Secretary of State Hillary Rodham Clinton said in her major address on US-India relations, "The nuclear deal, which was completed through the efforts of former President Bush, removed the final barrier to broader cooperation between us. And that brings us to today. We find ourselves at the beginning of a third era. I'll call it US-India 3.0. The new governments in Washington and New Delhi will build a future together, and we will be discussing the details of that partnership when I visit India next month."[86]

The US Department of Energy is responsible for conducting discussions at a government-to-government level. The United States and India are continuing to hold meetings of the Indo–United States Civil Nuclear Energy Working Group. According to Undersecretary of Energy Dan Poneman, pushing the agreement to operational fruition is one of the Department of Energy's priorities.[87]

With regard to defense security and military matters, the impact is apparent. President Obama and Prime Minister Singh seem to have developed a special bond in dealing with the nexus between terrorism and nuclear weapons.[88] There had been ongoing military-to-military cooperation that began before the successful implementation of the civil nuclear initiative. This cooperation has continued to flourish. Former secretary of defense William Cohen characterized these defense relations as "excellent" in mid-2009,[89] and few would disagree as of this writing. Before the announcement of the initiative on July 18, 2005, not many would have so characterized the relationship.

A major factor in defense cooperation is the interoperability and supply relationships brought about by defense contracting. The good feeling engendered by the civil nuclear relationship was a major factor in causing US-India defense contracting to flourish. Military sales went forward, with awards of a billion-dollar purchase of Lockheed coastal patrol aircraft and an even larger aircraft contract to Boeing. Raytheon continues to sell air traffic control equipment that has military support aspects. Raytheon's equipment was used in the Chandrayaan moon mission. There are numerous additional defense procurements still pending in which US companies are leading contenders. Among these are the multirole combat aircraft procurement, with a value of well over $50 billion.

Shyam Saran, former foreign secretary and later Prime Minister Manmohan Singh's special envoy for nuclear issues and climate change, linked the civil nuclear deal directly to both energy and defense procurements from the United States. He cited the Indian letter of intent for up to 10,000 megawatts of US nuclear power reactors and Indian needs for "force upgradation":

> 10,000 megawatts of nuclear energy may translate into US $150 billion worth of projects, with significant business opportunities and potential collaboration for both Indian and US companies. . . . If India maintains its current level of defense spending to achieve its medium and long-term goals of force upgradation, then a growing part of the expected 10-year acquisition plan of US $120 billion could be reoriented towards the US.[90]

As the US and Indian governments prepared for the November 2010 visit of President Obama to India, the search for a "big idea" to headline the trip was cast largely against the background of the civil nuclear accord. Obama's national security adviser, James Jones, spoke with the prime minister, his national security adviser, the defense minister, and the head of the Indian Air Force about the completion of the nuclear deal, military aircraft purchases, and cooperation on terrorism at the same meetings.[91] On the visit itself, the joint statement by President Obama and Prime Minister Singh contained two paragraphs on the civil nuclear deal and a pledge of support for India's full membership in the Nuclear Suppliers Group.[92] The president's speech to a joint session of Parliament not only announced US support for India becoming a permanent member of the UN Security Council but also referenced joint action to secure vulnerable nuclear materials and support for India's long-espoused goal of a world without nuclear weapons.[93]

On a broader scale, the implementation of the civil nuclear agreement seems to be leading to closer strategic relations across the board. In politics, everything is connected to everything. Thus, the "feel good" factor brought about by the civil nuclear agreement seems to affect the willingness to cooperate on issues as disparate as services outsourcing and international pipelines. In India, there is even talk of India replacing the United Kingdom as the "special relationship" partner of the United States.[94] Tempering this enthusiasm must be the reality that actual civil nuclear trade between the United States and India has not begun as of this writing. There are still obstacles to be overcome on each side, including US export controls and Indian legislation on compensating victims of nuclear accidents. As noted, economic engagement can be negative as well as positive, and failure to fully implement the deal could adversely affect the ability to cooperate strategically.

The Bottom Line

India's nuclear activities have been an issue between the United States and India since not long after Indian independence. For both sides, the nuclear issue became one of deep symbolic significance, impeding engagement and contributing significantly to estrangement between the two democracies. After the Indian reforms of the early 1990s promoted US-India economic engagement, India's "induction" of the nuclear option in 1998 posed a serious obstacle to increasing strategic cooperation. However, economic engagement, coupled with the activism of the Indian American community, was a key driver in the removal of most sanctions and provided the impetus for pushing the US-India civil nuclear initiative to approval in both the

United States and India. Approval of the deal has had a broad influence on the ability of the United States and India to cooperate on matters ranging from defense to energy security.

Thus, the civil nuclear deal's impact so far has been overwhelmingly positive. However, the strategic impact of economic engagement is often mixed. Such is the impact of US services trade with India, particularly as it relates to software and information-technology-enabled services. Let us now turn to a consideration of services outsourcing to India and its impact on US-India strategic relations.

Chapter 3

Services Outsourcing and Economic Development

And yet, even as most American citizens and businesses meet these responsibilities, there are others who are shirking theirs. And many are aided and abetted by a broken tax system, written by well-connected lobbyists on behalf of well-heeled interests and individuals. . . . And it's a tax code that says you should pay lower taxes if you create a job in Bangalore, India than if you create one in Buffalo, New York.

—President Barack Obama, remarks on International Tax Policy Reform,
May 4, 2009

In the fall of 1994, a group met at the Department of Commerce to begin planning for Secretary Ron Brown's trip to India. There was a suggestion that Bangalore be placed on the itinerary.[1] Some questioned the proposal. Why would this relatively small city in southern India be important enough for a stop on a Presidential Business Development Mission? "Because it's the Silicon Valley of India," came the reply. After a bit more discussion, Bangalore went on the notional itinerary. However, few of us fully understood the importance for the United States and India of what was taking place with regard to information technology in India.

That November, I went to India to help prepare for Secretary Brown's India mission. In New Delhi, I was detailed to meet with a group of young computer scientists and entrepreneurs about what they had in mind for the information technology industry in India. These Indians had just organized a group called the National Association of Software and Services Companies (NASSCOM). I must admit that after a day full of meetings with jet lag, and in a warm room in New Delhi, I had difficulty following their excited and detailed presentation. However, I understood enough to know that the plans of my Indian briefers were huge and likely to fundamentally alter US and Indian perceptions of each other. I resolved to keep their presentation firmly in mind when we went to Bangalore to prepare for that part of Brown's Presidential Business Development Mission.

In Bangalore, one of the places we were considering for a Brown stop was the software development facility of Texas Instruments. The Texas Instruments building we visited did not begin to match campuses later created by such American companies as Microsoft, General Electric, and Cisco or by the Indian information technology giants Infosys, Wipro, and Tata Consultancy Services. Nevertheless, by the standards of the day, the Texas Instruments building was impressive—gleaming steel and glass set among the relative chaos of downtown Bangalore. I thought it might make a good stop for the secretary. In the course of meeting with the managing Texas Instruments official in Bangalore, I asked about the impact on US jobs and wages of his company's outsourcing to India. I could see from the New Delhi NASSCOM presentation the possibility of a perception of a significant adverse impact on American workers. Of course, I was concerned that Secretary Brown not be perceived as promoting any such outcome. The Texas Instruments official replied that the operation he ran in Bangalore made Texas Instruments more competitive internationally and therefore able to employ more people at home in the United States at good wages.

My colloquy with the Bangalore Texas Instruments official frames the argument over the impact of outsourcing on jobs and competitiveness that is prominent in both the United States and India. In turn, this argument affects the ability of the United States and India to cooperate on a wide range of strategic issues. For example, in the Indian national elections of 2009, the opposition Bharatiya Janata Party linked the civil nuclear deal to the Obama issue of changing the US tax code to tax the un-repatriated income of US corporations.[2] The argument particularly affects the ability of the United States and India to cooperate on economic growth that benefits the majority of Americans and Indians. India sees as "protectionism" such proposals as those pushed by the Obama administration and includes them as a factor in trade negotiations.[3]

The "Competitiveness" Definition: The Ability to Compete versus the Expansion of Citizen Income

In the United States, there has long been a concern with the ability of the country to compete internationally.[4] The most salient US political aspect of this concern is about the growth of jobs and wages of Americans. There is deep concern that the last decade has seen no job growth and a decline in household income.[5] However, this concern in the United States is not new and is mirrored in India. In 1985, the President's Commission on Industrial Competitiveness defined "competitiveness" as "the degree to which a nation can, under free and fair market conditions, produce goods and services that meet the test of international markets while simultaneously maintaining or expanding the real incomes of its citizens." This definition echoes the parameters of the discussion I was having in Bangalore with the Texas Instruments official and my concerns about the political aspects of a US commerce secretary visiting an Indian outsourcing facility.

When defending outsourcing,[6] business leaders in the United States and India tend to stress that part of the competitiveness definition that speaks of the ability to "produce goods and services that meet the test of international markets." Their argument is that US companies sourcing from those who produce the best quality at the lowest cost enables the US companies to compete internationally. This ability to compete allows them to expand employment and wages in the United States because they have been able to outsource internationally.

However, politicians in both India and the United States are usually most vocal about maintaining jobs and "expanding the real incomes of its citizens." In the US and Indian national elections of 2008 and 2009, this was a refrain of the candidates for president and prime minister. In his presidential campaign, Senator Obama focused on the economic travails of the American middle class. Familiar Obama campaign refrains were "You want to hear about how we're going to attack the challenges facing middle-class families each and every day" and "You need and deserve a president who is going to wake up every day and fight for you, and fight for the middle class and fight to create jobs and grow our economy again."[7] Similarly, in Prime Minister Manmohan Singh's campaign of 2009, a constant theme was "inclusive growth." The Congress Party Manifesto for 2009 contained an entire section headed "Towards Faster and More Inclusive Growth" and promised to present a budget with the "basic objective of returning to faster and more inclusive growth, which is so essential for fulfilling all our social and economic objectives."[8]

Obama's "fighting for the middle class" and Singh's "inclusive growth" were ways of framing "majority prosperity" as a fundamental economic and political issue in a democratic society. The strategic issue of majority prosperity can be described in terms of challenges to the middle class in the United States. In India, where relative poverty is a reality for the majority of the population, inclusiveness or inclusion in national growth is a more apt formulation. Few would characterize a majority of the Indian population as middle class. Regardless of the rhetoric employed, building prosperity that benefits the majority of citizens in both the United States and India is a primary strategic issue confronting the US-India relationship.

The International Complexity of the Production of Both Goods and Services

The "production" aspect of the competitiveness definition cited above (i.e., "produce goods and services that meet the test of international markets") is no longer a purely domestic function with regard to either goods or services. Goods of any complexity "produced" in the United States almost always contain components from outside the country. Increasingly, this is also true of the "services" sold by a US company. In particular, a company in the information technology arena is likely to rely on the work product of those outside the country for the production of a portion of the delivered service. Thus, a US computer software or systems supplier outsourcing to India will argue that outsourcing enables the supplier to "produce . . . services that meet the test of international markets" more efficiently.

Opponents of outsourcing argue that producing services that meet the test of international markets through international outsourcing is at the expense of "expanding or maintaining real incomes of its [US] citizens." Just as parts for goods could be produced in the United States, so could subsidiary services be sourced from US labor. The failure to do so simply sends jobs and wealth overseas—creating jobs in Bangalore not Buffalo, to use Obama's terms.

Thus, the argument in the United States is between those who see international outsourcing of information technology services as enhancing competitiveness and those who see outsourcing as hurting the real incomes of Americans in the middle of the economic spectrum. From the Indian perspective, both parts of the competitiveness definition are promoted by US outsourcing to India. The difference, of course, is that Indians focus on the real incomes of Indians and not Americans. From the Indian perspective, US buyers of India outsourcing services benefit, while the real incomes of Indians are enhanced. The question of expanding or maintaining the real incomes of US citizens is of no particular concern until the question affects an Indian's ability to export Indian services.

If there were agreement that US outsourcing of services to India promoted jobs and the expansion of real incomes in both the United States and India, then outsourcing would be a purely positive factor in promoting strategic cooperation between the two countries. Unfortunately, there is no meeting of the US and Indian minds on this issue. As discussed below, the data and analysis on this subject are mixed and often contradictory. Thus, outsourcing of information technology services from the United States to India has both positive and negative effects on the ability of the United States and India to cooperate on the crucial strategic issue of creating widespread prosperity in both countries.

The Role of Services

In evaluating the impact of outsourcing on the US-India strategic relationship, it is important to appreciate the role of services generally and information-technology-related services particularly in India and the United States and in US-India trade. As a percentage of gross domestic product (GDP), services constituted about 76 percent of the US economy and 54 percent of the Indian economy in 2008. Clearly, any national economic assessments based solely on goods would be misleading for either country.

The role and importance of services trade with India is often underappreciated in the United States. Often the focus is on trade in goods, and India is seen through the same analytic prism as China. This approach is inadequate. For example, in contrasting the Indian and Chinese development experiences, former Morgan Stanley chief economist Stephen Roach has noted the predominant role services growth has played in Indian economic development.[9] During the period from 1990 to 2008, the services share of Indian GDP increased from 40.6 to 53.7 percent.[10] During this period, services accounted for more than 62 percent of GDP growth. As Roach points out, this reliance on services plays to India's strengths in information technology competency, education, and English-language proficiency. The Indian reliance on services for growth is even more remarkable when compared with that of China. In China, the services share of GDP rose from just 31 percent in 1990 to 40.2 percent in 2008.[11] The expansion of China's services economy accounted for some 33 percent of the increase in China's GDP. This means that services occupied about the same place in the Chinese economy of 2008 as they did in the Indian economy of 1990 and contributed about half the growth that services provided in India during the indicated period.

India is the world's leader in information communications technology exports. The World Bank indicates that these exports were approximately $30 billion in 2006. In comparison, China, the second-largest exporter of information communications technology services, exported only about $5.5 billion of such services in 2006.[12] Such exports accounted for about 40 percent of India's total service exports in 2006. From 1998 to 2010, information-technology-enabled services (ITES) grew from about 1.2 to 6.1 percent of Indian GDP and from 4 to 25 percent of total Indian exports.[13] For India to be an indisputable world leader in such a vital export sector, and for such services to play such an important role in GDP and exports, is a source of deep national pride and political importance.

India's ITES sector employs some 2 to 3 million people. With a multiplier for indirect employment, some 10 to 12 million Indians owe their jobs to the sector.[14] Some argue that such a relatively small number in a nation of more than a billion people does not have much effect with regard to Indian majority prosperity.[15] Admittedly, the outsourcing sector alone is unlikely to lift the majority of Indians from poverty. The problems in agriculture and the informal manufacturing and merchant sectors are too great. However, the political impact that ITES outsourcing has had in creating a whole new category of relative prosperity for millions of Indians in less than two decades should not be underestimated. Given the role and growth rate of information technology in modern and modernizing economies, the potential for contributing to the growth of employment and prosperity is substantial.[16] This potential, perhaps as much as present reality, makes the ITES outsourcing sector politically salient, both domestically and internationally.

US-India Engagement in Services and Information-Technology-Enabled Services

The present importance of outsourcing in the US-India economic relationship becomes more apparent when the bilateral data for services generally and information technology services particularly are examined. Unfortunately, this is not easily done. As mentioned above, most discussion of US-India trade is in terms of trade in goods. The reason for this bias is simply that the data for goods trade are so much easier to obtain and so much more reliable than those for services. When goods cross international boundaries, most often a record is created for the purposes of collecting tariffs if for no other reason. It is then a relatively simple matter to compile such data into numbers reflecting bilateral trade in goods. In contrast, services that move internationally often leave no records of their movement. This is especially true with regard to services that move electronically, whether by cable or satellite transmission. In the case of the United States and India, reliance on trade in physical goods tells only about half the story of US-India trade. It does not capture any of the significance of information technology or ITES.

Data on services trade are captured mostly on the basis of sample surveys. Such surveys are notoriously susceptible to the vagaries of the questions asked, the validity of the samples, the thoroughness of polling, and interpretation of the answers. Consequently, both US and Indian observers have lamented the lack of data on services trade and called for improvements.[17] A few examples may be helpful in illustrating the limitations of US-India services data and the misleading impressions left by the reliance on trade in goods and US source services data.

For 2007 (the latest year for which both US-India services and goods trade data were available at the time of writing), US goods exports to India were about $15 billion and imports were about $24 billion, for total trade of about $39 billion.[18] However, US services exports to India were about $9 billion and imports were about $10 billion, for a total of about $19 billion.[19] Thus, total trade in goods and services was about $58 billion, or almost 50 percent higher than indicated by the most frequently cited figures for trade in goods. This has a significance in indicating the importance to the United States and India of the trade relationship. Figure 3.1 indicates the increasing significance over time of adding the US-India services trade to trade in goods in order to reach an accurate assessment of trade between the United States and India.

Even using the total US-India services data from the US government fails to indicate the political importance of the US-India outsourcing relationship. In 2007, US imports of information technology services from India were approximately $4 billion, or some 40 percent of all Indian exports to the United States. As is shown by figure 3.2, which is from US data, the trend line of increase in these outsourcing exports to the United States is extremely steep and upward in direction.

However, US data probably substantially understate the magnitude of Indian information technology service exports to the United States. The Government of India relies basically on NASSCOM in gauging the quantitative impact of India's exports of information technology and ITES to the United States. The NASSCOM figures for 2005 through 2008 are shown in figure 3.3.

Figure 3.1. US-India Total Trade in Goods and Services, 1991–2007 (millions of dollars)

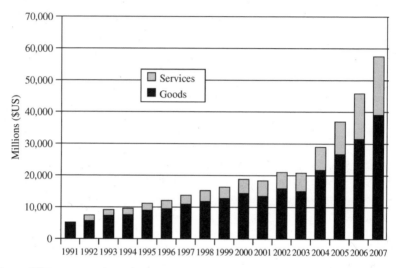

Source: US Department of Commerce.

These figures indicate that the disparity between US government and Government of India data is very great. For 2007, the last year for which both US and Indian data are available as of this writing, the Indian data show information technology service exports some five times greater than the US data. The US Government Accountability Office (GAO) has examined this disparity.[20] The GAO attributes approximately half the discrepancy to the fact that "India counts the earnings of temporary Indian workers residing in the United States as exports to the United States." According to the GAO, "the United States only includes temporary foreign workers who have been in the United States less than one year and who are not on the payrolls of firms in the United States."[21] Arguably, other factors cited by the GAO may indicate that some of the value included in the Indian data as services is included by the United States within numbers for goods or that the US data are more accurate. However, for US political purposes, the earnings of temporary Indian workers residing in the United States are most likely viewed as outsourcing imports by ordinary American citizens. This line of argument would indicate that at least half the Indian outsourcing export figures should be included within the bilateral trade data.

Thus, the US data on information technology and ITES can be increased

Figure 3.2. US Imports of Information Technology Services, 1991–2007 (millions of dollars)

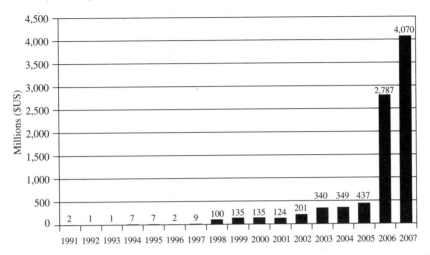

Source: US Department of Commerce.

Figure 3.3. India's Exports to the United States of Information Technology and Information-Technology-Enabled Services, 2005–8 (billions of dollars)

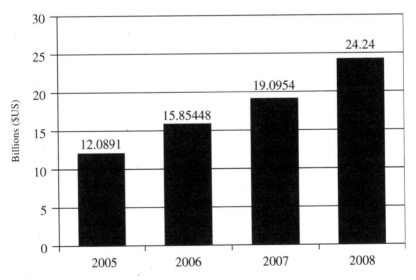

Source: National Association of Software and Services Companies.

by at least half the values shown in the NASSCOM figures. This would mean that for 2007, the US data total should be more than doubled, from approximately $4 billion to more than $8 billion. Such an addition is significant. For example, such an addition for 2007 would increase the figure for total goods and services US trade from $61 billion to more than $65 billion and move the ranking of India as a US trading partner from seventeen to fifteen. If World Bank figures are used, India becomes still more important. The World Bank puts Indian information technology and ITES exports at the full value of the NASSCOM–Government of India figures. This adoption argues for inserting the NASSCOM–Government of India numbers at their full value in US calculations. If this were done, the goods and services US-India trade would be increased by another $15 billion, to approximately $80 billion—about twice the amount of the figure for trade in goods that is usually used by US policymakers in citing the value of US-India trade.

Thus, US-India trade in services generally and in those services particularly considered to be "outsourcing" is much larger than the US data indicate. The data on trade in goods (usually used in US discussions of US-India trade) understate the value of total trade in goods and services by about 50 percent and of trade in outsourcing services by as much as 75 percent. This increased size accounts in part for why the outsourcing issue is more politically salient for both the United States and India than is indicated by the US data.

The Origins of US Political Concerns about Outsourcing to India

Political concerns about outsourcing arose in the United States during the 1990s. However, the relatively small import numbers involved, the prosperity of the times, and widespread job availability in the information technology industry limited its saliency. A relatively small group of US computer professionals complained about being put out of work by younger Indian software engineers and programmers. However, imports of services from India and the movement of jobs and downward pressure on real incomes associated with these imports did not become a significant nationwide political issue until the run-up to the 2004 presidential campaign.

Several factors contributed to Indian outsourcing becoming a national political issue during the years leading up to the 2004 campaign. Indian work on the "Y2K" problem had enhanced the reputation of the Indian software industry for doing reliable, cost-effective work.[22] Richard Celeste, the US ambassador to India at the time of the Y2K effort, characterizes the Y2K experience as the Indian information technology industry's "audition on a global stage."[23] The enhanced reputation gained from this "audition" caused many in the United States to see India as a world-class information technology supplier and competitor for the first time. In 2000–2001 the "dot-com" bubble burst, creating a recession and leaving many US companies with fewer resources to devote to their information technology needs. Many US information companies needed to find less expensive ways to deliver services. Thus, the improved reputation of the Indian industry for quality created by excellent work on the Y2K problem and the need for cheaper services created by the US economic downturn promoted rapidly increasing Indian sales to the United States of information technology and ITES during the first few years of the new century.

By 2004, anxiety about the loss of jobs to cheaper Indian information technology sources was reaching a fever pitch in the United States. Some eighty bills relating to outsourcing had been introduced in more than thirty state legislatures. Most of these bills would restrict the right of state agencies to contract with companies using outsourced foreign labor to perform information technology services. In the US Congress, this approach was taken up in a bill sponsored by Senator Christopher Dodd (D-Conn.) and Senator Tom Daschle (D-S.D.). Representative John J. Duncan (R-Tenn.) offered a bill to prevent information technology outsourcing at the Tennessee Valley Authority. Senator John Kerry (D-Mass.) introduced a bill requiring that those rendering services by telephone from countries outside the United States (e.g., India) disclose the location from which they were working.

In his primary campaign, Kerry used the designation "Benedict Arnold" first for US companies outsourcing work overseas and then for the chief executive officers (CEOs) who ran those companies. In a speech to the Iowa Jefferson Jackson Day Dinner on November 15, 2003, Kerry promised "a real deal that stands up to the powerful interests" by "clos[ing] every loophole for the Benedict Arnold companies that ship jobs overseas." Apparently, Kerry felt that the "Benedict Arnold" line was important to his winning the Iowa contest that was key to his being nominated as the Democratic candidate for president. Upon winning the January 19, 2004, Iowa caucuses, Kerry declared, "We are not going to give one benefit or one reward to any Benedict Arnold company or CEO to take jobs and money overseas and stick you with the bill. That's over." Through the rest of the winter of 2004, the "Benedict Arnold" line of attack was a staple of the Kerry campaign.[24] However, in the spring things began to change.

US Businesses Strike Back at the Critics of Outsourcing

In early March 2004, some two hundred business and trade association representatives convened at the US Chamber of Commerce in Washington to form what was euphemistically named the "Coalition for Economic Growth and American Jobs." At least one Internet critic of outsourcing suggested that the coalition should actually be called "the Coalition Against the Middle Class."[25] The desire to utilize high-quality, less expensive Indian information technology services cut across many areas of US business. US-India economic engagement with regard to information technology brought together companies seeking to exert political influence on the terms of this engagement.

Studies conducted by participants in the Coalition for Economic Growth and American Jobs would help American business choose its words carefully. Using the tools of marketing and political analysis, including focus groups and some limited polling, the coalition crafted a message that fit within both aspects of the President's Commission on Industrial Competition's "competitiveness" definition. The message avoided the term "outsourcing" in favor of "worldwide sourcing," spoke of increasing American competitiveness through "worldwide sourcing," and creating US jobs at good wages. Although there were many entities involved in the coalition, the most active were the American Bankers Association, the Information Technology Association of America, and the US Chamber of Commerce. The American Bankers Association was involved because many of its members relied on offshore outsourcing for handling information systems development and maintenance as well as the processing of records. The Information Technology Association of America (since January 1, 2009, the Technology Association of America) had as members many companies that used offshore outsourcing in the development of their own information technology products. The US Chamber of Commerce had not only banks and technology companies as members but also many companies that were ultimate consumers of Indian information technology services. Because the American Bankers Association was often involved with state regulators, it was put in charge of activities at the state level. The Information Technology

Association of America took the lead with Congress and the administration. The Chamber of Commerce provided coordination and research while teaming with the Business Roundtable on message development.

In India, business leaders began to speak with their government officials about the issue. There was talk about taking the United States to a dispute resolution proceeding at the World Trade Organization. NASSCOM sent a delegation to the United States to oppose anti-outsourcing legislation along with its members' US business colleagues. Interestingly, NASSCOM was rebuffed by the Coalition for Economic Growth and American Jobs. The coalition's leaders told the Indians that their direct and overt involvement would be counterproductive politically. The coalition wished to present a strictly American image to American voters and elected officials. At any rate, the activity by Indian business both in India and in the United States raised the sensitivity of Indian Americans to the anti-outsourcing issue. In a precursor to their activity in support of the US-India civil nuclear initiative, Indian Americans began to get directly involved in opposing the anti-outsourcing campaign. The key activity was communication with operatives in the Kerry campaign to point out how harmful the "Benedict Arnold" line of approach was within the Indian American community. Speaking of a private meeting with Kerry in San Francisco on March 29, 2004, one Indian American Democratic activist said, "So far, the Democratic Party and John Kerry are talking against outsourcing, but we feel this issue is being debated intensely, with input from our group, and we hope to change the prevailing stand by providing more relevant information."[26]

Once Senator Kerry was assured of receiving the Democratic nomination for president, the anti-outsourcing rhetoric of the 2004 presidential campaign virtually ceased. Kerry needed the support of Indian Americans. Indian Americans in 2004 were a growing community of approximately 1.8 million who had the highest per family average income in the United States. The community was overwhelmingly Democratic and contributed to campaigns at a high rate. Shortly after the nomination, the Democratic National Committee formed its first-ever Indian American Council to raise funds and rally support within the Indian American community. That council was active throughout the remainder of the campaign.

Opponents of outsourcing met these business and Indian-American efforts with an outpouring of anti-outsourcing and antiforeigner rhetoric. Leading the charge were the Communication Workers of America (CWA) and the AFL-CIO, with whom the CWA is affiliated. Some CWA locals were particularly active in drawing the relationship between outsourcing, India, and the temporary worker H-1B visas discussed below. The leading television commentator opposing outsourcing was Lou Dobbs of CNN. Using his nightly program, Dobbs was a leading voice for the view that outsourcing weakened the United States in virtually every conceivable way.

From the perspective of President George W. Bush and the Republicans, outsourcing was simply not an issue. In their view, outsourcing was a positive aspect of an international economic system driven by open markets. The *Economic Report of the President 2004* put the matter rather succinctly in the following terms:

> The benefits from new forms of trade, such as in services, are no different from the benefits from traditional trade in goods. Outsourcing of professional services is a prominent example of a new type of trade. The gains from trade that takes place over the Internet or telephone lines are no different than the gains from trade in physical goods transported by ship or plane. When a good or service is produced at lower cost in another country, it makes sense to import it rather than to produce it domestically. This allows the United States to devote its resources to more productive purposes.[27]

When the head of Bush's Council of Economic Advisers, Gregory Mankiw, made the same point in testimony before Congress in the spring of 2004, Kerry and the Democrats tried to take political advantage from Mankiw's statement. The Republican speaker of the House, Dennis Hastert, attempted to ameliorate the political problem by observing that "outsourcing can be a problem for American workers and the American economy."[28] However, as indicated above, Kerry backed off from the issue, especially after the nomination.

The Search for Outsourcing's Economic Reality

When Bush won reelection, outsourcing temporarily was removed as a prominent political issue in the United States. Nevertheless, the anti-outsourcing campaign had built up a certain amount of momentum as a subject for further investigation. With very little good data on the size or impact of outsourcing on the United States, various models produced highly differing results depending on the assumptions used. The Congressional Research Service produced a study that outlined the wide variations in data and estimates of impact.[29] The Department of Commerce was ordered to produce an economic impact assessment. The report took years to finish. When finally complete, the report was described as producing mixed results, but the report itself was never released by the Department of Commerce.[30]

Perhaps the most complete study and analysis of outsourcing in the US-India context of services trade was undertaken by the Brookings Institution. Under the leadership of Lael Brainard, Brookings sponsored seminars and published a compendium of papers on the subject in 2005.[31] Brainard's conclusions are noteworthy in part because she became Obama's undersecretary of the Treasury for international affairs. Her views are presumably continuing to have influence on the Obama administration's policy. The Brookings study concluded that "existing evidence consistently shows that relatively few services and white-collar jobs have been offshored to date."[32] As to the more difficult question of how much of the labor force in the United States is really vulnerable, the study could only conclude that "the answer is difficult to discern from existing data." The study did conclude, "Concerns about the loss of high-value services appear to be overblown in software services, call centers and semiconductor design: the vertical decomposition of these services preserves the highest-value activities in the home market while shedding lower-value processes to overseas providers."[33] The bottom line of the study seemed to be that offshoring was harmful to employment and wages for those who lost their jobs in the United States to the practice, but too economically beneficial in other ways to be eliminated. Thus, according to the study, the way in which to address this problem was to concentrate on "social insurance" to provide compensatory benefits directly to those harmed rather than to inhibit outsourcing. However, in 2005—with George W. Bush sworn in for a second term, both houses of Congress in Republican hands, and the economy improving—the US political wind behind opposition to outsourcing died down. Indian exports of services to the United States continued to soar.

The Political Revival of the Outsourcing Issue

Opposition to outsourcing began to revive in 2006 as Congress considered a comprehensive immigration reform bill. With the November 2006 elections that gave Democrats majorities in both the House and Senate, measures that affected US labor gained new saliency. Ironically, it was a Republican, Senator Charles Grassley (R-Iowa), who teamed with a Democrat,

Senator Dick Durbin (D-Ill.), to bring pressure to bear on visa programs that benefited Indian outsourcing companies. Alleged visa abuses were inserted into the debate over immigration reform by introduction of a bill titled "The H-1B and L-1 Visa Fraud and Abuse Prevention Act of 2007." These alleged abuses centered on actions of Indian information technology services companies.

"H-1B" refers to that subsection of the Immigration and Nationality Act, as amended,[34] that applies to a special category of temporary work visas. This subsection defines a class of aliens coming to the United States temporarily to perform services in a "specialty occupation." "Specialty occupation" is defined elsewhere in the law essentially as requiring "theoretical and practical application of a body of highly specialized knowledge" and a "bachelor's or higher degree."[35] The general theory behind this provision is that such persons are acknowledged as being in short supply in the United States. A certain number of these workers within an annual numerical limitation, which has been 65,000, with an additional 20,000 for foreign nationals who hold master's degrees from US universities in recent years, can be admitted without having to prove that they do not displace American citizen workers. The intending employer files for the visa, which is usually good for three years, extendable to six. "L-1" refers to another section of the Immigration & Nationality Act that defines a temporary visa for intra-company transfers in a managerial, executive, or specialized knowledge capacity.[36] An L-1 visa for managers and executives can be for up to seven years, and, for those having "special knowledge" of the company's product or processes and procedures, for up to five years.[37]

In April 2007, Grassley and Durbin introduced the first bipartisan bill attacking the foundation of the H-1B program and seeking to limit the L-1 program. According to Grassley, "Some employers have abused the H-1B and L-1 temporary work visa programs, using them to bypass qualified American workers. This bill will set up safeguards for American workers, and provide much-needed oversight and enforcement of employers who fail to abide by the law."[38] The major feature of the 2007 Durbin-Grassley bill would reverse the presumption that the United States was in need of a certain number of foreign workers for "specialty occupations." Instead, their bill would require the employer to prove that such a foreign worker was needed. The employer would have to advertise a job opening for thirty days on a Department of Labor Web site. The Department of Labor would also be required to post summaries of all H-1B applications on its Web site. The bill would have prohibited companies from hiring H-1B employees if they already employed more than 50 percent of their workforce as H-1B visa holders and employed more than fifty people.

Although the 2007 Durbin-Grassley bill did not mention Indian companies, it soon became apparent that Indian companies were the main objects of the legislation. In letters to the leading Indian outsourcing companies, Durbin and Grassley accused nine Indian information technology firms of abusing the H-1B visa system and demanded information from them concerning their use of H-1B and L-1 visas.[39] The senators did not stop with letters to the accused companies. They also sent a letter to Emilio T. Gonzales, director of US Citizenship and Immigration Services (USCIS) in the Department of Homeland Security, demanding information and implying violations of law. The senators wrote, "We would like to know how many L visas are approved each year, and what companies use the program. We would also like to know more about the use of the blanket petition for L visa holders, and USCIS's ability to monitor individual visa holders who are allowed entry into the United States on a blanket petition." To emphasize their perspective, the senators closed with an admonition: "We are concerned about the level of fraud monitoring on the H-1B and L visa programs."[40]

Grassley and Durbin made it plain that they intended to attach their bill to the 2007 version of comprehensive immigration reform legislation, designated the "Secure Borders, Economic Opportunity and Immigration Reform Act of 2007,"[41] which was scheduled to be taken up in the Senate in late June. Thus, in their letter to Director Gonzalez, the senators said, "While we anticipate your concerns about providing such information to us by Wednesday, June 20th, we must stress the fact that the US Senate is considering comprehensive legislation that would change immigration policies for years to come. The H-1B and L visa programs must be better understood before further action is taken on this bill."[42] Unfortunately for Grassley and Durbin, and fortunately for those in the United States and India who wanted to keep the H-1B and L-1 visa programs unchanged, the Senate was unable to muster the sixty votes needed to shut off debate on immigration reform, and the Senate leadership had to pull the bill from consideration.

Outsourcing and the 2008 Presidential Campaign

With presidential and congressional campaigns looming, Indian information technology companies got the message that the visa programs on which they relied so heavily were in danger. These companies recognized that questions of outsourcing and visas for Indian service providers could become a salient issue both in Congress and in the presidential campaign of 2008. This time around, unlike in 2004, the Indians were prepared take an active role in the debate. However, Indian information technology and ITES providers heeded what they had learned from the Coalition for Economic Growth and American Jobs. These companies determined that their participation would be through surrogates that presented "an American face." They would emphasize not just the increased efficiency argument but also the contributions that the Indian companies made to US employment and quality of life.

Like the Government of India on the civil nuclear matter, NASSCOM hired former US ambassador to India Robert D. Blackwill as their chief lobbyist. Blackwill served as the coordinator for bringing the resources of Barbour Griffith and Rogers, one of Washington's leading lobbying firms, into play for the Indian information technology companies. Barbour Griffith and Rogers organized some one hundred meetings with congressional staffers and set up a reception on the Hill for NASSCOM executives. A second step was to work through US organizations. According to the then-president of NASSCOM, Kiran Karnik, NASSCOM made "symbolic" donations of from $10,000 to $15,000 to each of the major research organizations with which it worked. These organizations included the Brookings Institution and the Heritage Foundation. NASSCOM also organized a letter-writing campaign from executives of its US customers and used American citizen employees of Indian companies and their subsidiaries to lobby.[43]

With the failure of the immigration bill in 2007, attention had turned to the presidential campaign as the focus of the outsourcing issue. In the spring of 2008, it became plain that the Republicans would be represented by Senator John McCain and the Democrats by Senator Barack Obama. McCain's stance was clear and unequivocal on both visas and outsourcing. McCain said, "The United States should increase the number of visas it grants to skilled Indian workers seeking to come to America. . . . Open trade benefits our economies, and so when voters complain about the 'outsourcing' of jobs to India, I believe we should address their concerns—but by helping them to adapt and compete, not retreat into isolationism and protectionism."[44]

The Obama position was more nuanced but certainly a far cry from the "Benedict Arnold" rhetoric of the Kerry campaign. On H-1B visas, Obama emphasized his view that America needed to improve educational opportunities as the long-term solution to its skills shortage in the information technology field. However, Obama did say,

I will support a temporary increase in the H-1B visa program as a stopgap measure until we can reform our immigration system comprehensively. I support comprehensive immigration reform that includes improvement in our visa programs, including our legal permanent resident visa programs and temporary programs including the H-1B program, to attract some of the world's most talented people to America. We should allow immigrants who earn their degrees in the US to stay, work, and become Americans over time. As part of our comprehensive reform, we should examine our ability to replace a stopgap increase in the number of H-1B visas with an increase in the number of permanent visas we issue to foreign skilled workers.[45]

However, Obama was consistent in his attacks on what he referred to as "tax breaks for companies that are shipping jobs overseas." The tax proposal underlying his campaign rhetoric was not actually aimed at outsourcing as such. Rather, his proposal had to do with a decades-long US international tax policy debate. The central question of this debate was when income earned overseas by US companies or their subsidiaries should be taken into account for purposes of federal corporate income taxation. Most countries tax only the income that is earned within their borders. US corporations are theoretically taxed on their worldwide income, even where earned by a subsidiary. However, under existing US tax law, the income of a US corporation and its subsidiaries earned in a foreign country is generally taxable only when repatriated to the United States.

Because the proposal is aimed at US corporations, Obama's proposal would alter the tax situation of such US companies operating in India as GE, Microsoft, and Oracle. These changes could affect the willingness of these companies to hire overseas if their offshore operations were made less viable by the tax change. However, if the overseas operations remained viable, hiring offshore would continue to be judged simply on its economic merits. Thus, the Obama proposal would probably have little effect on US companies that decided to have their information technology services provided by a subsidiary in Bangalore rather than in Buffalo. With regard to outsourcing to Indian companies providing services from India, the Obama proposal would have nothing to do with such operations. Thus, such Indian outsourcing companies as Wipro, Infosys, and Tata Consultancy Services would be unaffected by the primary international tax change upon which Obama campaigned. Nevertheless, Obama's remarks were widely interpreted by the Indian press as being anti-outsourcing and an example of "continuing to play the anti-outsourcing card."[46]

The Obama proposal to change the time of recognition of US corporate income earned abroad was not the primary protectionist concern of those involved in outsourcing. Rather, the concern was that the new administration, acting with Congress, might take more direct protectionist action. The election of Obama as president along with increased Democratic majorities in the House and Senate provided firm Democratic control of both the executive and legislative branches for the first time in fourteen years. Along with the deepening financial crisis and recession, the election outcomes set the stage for a clash over the outsourcing, H-1B visa, and "buy America" provisions that the Indians saw as symbolic of broader US protectionism. The clash came in the form of a dispute over a provision of the legislation designed to counteract the US financial crisis.

The Outsourcing H-1B Visa Issue during the Early Obama Administration

In one of his first acts as president, Obama submitted a stimulus package of spending designed to inject money into the US economy. The legislation for this effort was introduced in the House of Representatives as the first bill of the 111th Congress (HR 1). Designated the American Recovery and Reinvestment Act of 2009, the bill was basically a supplemental appropriation providing funds for health care, education, clean energy, housing, infrastructure, and other measures designed to stimulate the economy. The measure as enacted had combined spending and revenue effects of approximately $787 billion over the 2009–19 period.[47] Among the many provisions of the legislation were two that had special importance for the US-India economic relationship. Both were protectionist.

One of these protectionist measures dealt with iron, steel, and other construction materials purchased with stimulus funds for use in public buildings and public works. This "buy American" provision required that such funds be used only for US-made materials.[48] This provision occasioned some adverse commentary in India. However, another provision of the stimulus legislation concerning H-1B visas aroused even greater adverse commentary in India. This provision again raised concerns in India that the new administration and the Democratic-controlled US Congress were anti-outsourcing.

The bill as passed by the House made no mention of visas. However, an amendment proposed by Senator Grassley (R-Iowa) with the co-sponsorship of Senator Bernie Sanders (I-Vt.) was added in the Senate to limit the use of H-1B visas. Grassley and Sanders successfully inserted a section titled "Hiring American Workers in Companies Receiving TARP Funding" into HR 1. The measure was given the short title of the "Employ American Workers Act." In essence, the provision prohibits any recipient of funds under the law that established the Troubled Asset Relief Program (TARP)[49] from hiring H-1B visa holders unless that recipient could meet the visa requirements applicable to an "H-1B dependent employer." An H-1B dependent employer must make a filing of several attestations not applicable to the ordinary H-1B visa. The H-1B dependent employer must certify that it has taken good-faith steps to secure US workers using industry-wide standards and offering compensation that is at least as great as compensation offered to nonimmigrants. The employer must also attest that it has offered the job to any US worker of equal or better qualifications and that it will not displace any US worker.

Senator Grassley hailed his success in a press release, stating:

> Hiring American workers for limited available jobs should be a top priority for businesses taking taxpayer money through the TARP bailout program. With the unemployment rate at 7.6 percent, there is no need for companies to hire foreign guest workers through the H-1B program when there are plenty of qualified Americans looking for jobs. Our commonsense amendment simply ensures that recipients of American taxpayer money make American workers their first priority as they look to hire new employees.[50]

As would be expected, the Communication Workers of America union and other US critics of outsourcing were very supportive of the amendment. A posting on a CWA Web site said, "The amendment puts H-1B on par with exorbitant salaries for CEO's who run their companies into the ground, and with the purchasing of cheap foreign steel."[51]

The Indian Reaction

Indian companies and the Government of India reacted quite negatively to the Grassley-Sanders Amendment. Montek Singh Ahluwalia, deputy chairman of India's Planning Commission,[52] said, "This is just irrational protection-ism. It makes no economic sense at all."[53] Because India was about to launch into a national election, the parent body of the opposition Bharatiya Janata Party decided to take a more direct route. The Vishwa Hindu Parishad (VHP, Global Alliance of Hindus) organized a boycott of goods from four-teen US multinational corporations. Although the boycott was of question-able effect, it received considerable press attention. The general secretary of the VHP said, "If these policies hurt Indians abroad, then we have to take steps to hurt American companies in India."[54]

Shortly after passage of the visa restrictions in the stimulus package, NASSCOM and the Confederation of Indian Industries (CII) sent delega-tions to the United States to express their concerns about the legislation and other actions they considered protectionist. The CII delegation was led by the Indian cellular telephone executive Sunil Bharti Mittal and included the chairman of Hindustan Motors Limited, C. K. Birla, and chief executive of-ficer of Hero Honda Motors, Pawan Munjal. The CII delegation met with Secretary of the Treasury Timothy Geithner as well as Lawrence Summers, director of Obama's Council of Economic Advisers. Recognizing the link between economic engagement and strategic concerns, the group also met with Deputy Secretary of State James Steinberg and the special envoy for Afghanistan and Pakistan, Richard Holbrooke.

A first stop for both these delegations was the US-India Business Coun-cil. There the Indians received the full support as well as the advice of the US business community. Warburg Pincus copresident Charles "Chip" Kaye was in Washington to lead this effort. Warburg Pincus is one of the largest private international investors in India. In one deal alone, the company had invested some $400 million in Mittal's company and received $1.4 billion in return. The actions of these Indian business delegations bore fruit almost immediately by prompting the Obama administration's efforts to reach out to the Government of India. There was a growing impression among Indian opinion makers at the time that India was not being given sufficient attention by the new administration. A first public expression of the new Obama ad-ministration's intention to reengage and follow the policies of the Clinton and Bush administrations came when Deputy Secretary of State Steinberg spoke at the Brookings Institution on March 23, 2009. In the speech, he re-iterated the United States' desire to cooperate with India, disavowed pro-tectionist intents, and pledged implementation of the US-India civil nuclear deal. President Obama met with Prime Minister Singh on the margins of the Group of Twenty Conference in London on April 2, 2009, and stressed these same themes.

However, in India the political damage from the H-1B provisions of the US stimulus legislation had been done. The Indian parliamentary election campaigns were being conducted during the March–April 2009 period. The H-1B visa issue was picked up as a theme in these elections. In particular, the Bharatiya Janata Party seized the issue as part of its charge that the United States was unduly influencing the government of Prime Minister Manmohan Singh. The Bharatiya Janata Party argued that the Singh government had failed to prevent the protectionist measures of the US stimulus legislation from becoming law. The Left Parties echoed this line of attack.

The protectionist issue was exacerbated when, in the midst of the Indian national elections, Senators Durbin and Grassley reintroduced their visa legislation as the "H-1B and L-1 Visa Reform Act of 2009." This legislation built on the senators' experiences with their 2007 bill and Grassley's success in amending the stimulus legislation. The major features were again to make the requirements applicable to H-1B dependent employers applicable to all H-1B employers and to tighten the determination requirements for meeting wage standards. The period for determining displacement of a US worker would be extended from 90 to 180 days before and after the filing of an H-1B petition. Perhaps most salient was a restriction on H-1B hiring by employers having more than fifty employees. Such employers would not be able to have more than 50 percent of their workforce made up of H-1B or L-1 visa employees. As of this writing, the Durbin-Grassley legislation has not yet passed but is typical of action prompted by outsourcing that has a continuing ability to affect US-India strategic cooperation.

Another such action was the increasing of the fee for H-1B and L-1 visas that Senator Charles Schumer (D-N.Y.) inserted into the Southwest Border Security Bill. Signed into law by President Obama on August 13, 2010, the measure almost doubled the fee for these visas by increasing it from $2,500 to $4,000 for employers employing more than fifty such visa holders. In his statement issued just before signing the law, President Obama did not mention India and dismissed the measure as "a temporary increase to the fraud prevention and detection fees for some employers seeking high-skilled foreign workers."[55] However, remarks by Senator Schumer identified the leading Indian outsourcing firm Infosys as a "chop shop" deserving to pay higher fees.[56]

The Effect of Outsourcing on US-India Cooperation

US-India economic engagement through outsourcing affects the ability of the United States to work with India, particularly on such strategic issues of economic development as the Doha Round of World Trade Organization (WTO) negotiations. The effect is both positive and negative. Positively, there is little question that the significant trade in information technology, ITES, and business and professional outsourcing provides constituencies in both the United States and India for working together on economic development issues. The companies engaged in outsourcing support such measures as the completion of the Doha Round, the liberalization of foreign investment limitations, and bilateral development initiatives. The negotiating agenda set forth in the 2001 Ministerial Declaration was designated the "Doha Development Agenda" in recognition of the intent for the negotiations to produce a favorable impact on economic development. The WTO Ministerial Meeting convened in Doha in November 2001 set forth a framework for negotiations designed to promote growth and development, emphasizing that "international trade can play a major role in the promotion of economic development and the alleviation of poverty."[57] Both US and Indian firms involved in outsourcing have promoted US-India cooperation in reaching agreement on reducing barriers to trade in services through the Doha Round. This support increases the possibility for a successful conclusion of the round.

Conversely, outsourcing and H-1B issues have created US-India frictions that make it more difficult to conclude the Doha Round. For example, when Senators Grassley and Durbin sent their letters to nine Indian outsourcing companies accusing the companies of visa abuse and demanding information that could be used politically against the companies, the reaction from the minister representing India in the Doha Round negotiations was swift and strong. In a letter to the US trade representative, Susan Schwab, the minister of commerce and industry, Kamal Nath, called the missive "surprising and unwelcome." Minister Nath went on to say, "Such direct intervention by US senators would only create uncertainties in the minds of these companies and undermine business confidence, especially in the current negotiations on services."[58]

The reaction in India to the use of H-1B visa fees to pay for US Southwest border security was swift and adverse. NASSCOM issued a statement attacking the measure as "protectionism and contrary to the Obama administration's repeated pleas to the international community to avoid taking such actions."[59] The NASSCOM statement connected the US action directly to its WTO obligations and promised to take the matter up with Government of India officials. The perceived attack on outsourcing quickly became an agenda item in preparation for the visit of President Obama to India in November 2010. On the trip, Obama distanced himself from his previous rhetoric on outsourcing by dismissing the perceptions of India as " a land of call centers and back offices that cost American jobs." He called such perceptions "old stereotypes."[60]

Economic Engagement and Trade Liberalization

US-India economic engagement through outsourcing also generates support for lowering barriers to trade in services on a bilateral basis. The Pacific Council on International Policy and the Federation of Indian Chambers of Commerce and Industry (FICCI) have proposed a US-India free trade agreement focused on what they refer to as the "innovation economy." Outsourcing is at the heart of the Pacific Council–FICCI proposal. The US-India economic engagement driving the proposal involves the use of computer technology to enhance the provision of technology services. The concept is that tariff- and barrier-free trade between the United States and India in all services related to information technology would enable the United States and India to supply not only their own needs in next-generation information technology services but also the needs of the entire world. The Pacific Council and FICCI base their proposal for a US-India free trade agreement on the success of the United States and India cooperating to achieve the WTO 1997 Information Technology Agreement (ITA).[61]

The ITA was negotiated at the Ministerial Meeting of the WTO in Singapore in December 1996. At the time, Charlene Barshevsky was the acting US trade representative. Barshevsky was (and is again) an able trade attorney from a leading Washington law firm. She sought a public policy success at the Singapore Ministerial Meeting that might lead to her nomination by President Clinton as the US trade representative. She would be filling the vacancy created by Mickey Kantor's becoming secretary of commerce. Private-sector input from many of the companies involved in outsourcing information technology services was to be the fundamental engine for achieving the ITA in Singapore.[62]

From the US side, private-sector input came through the system of private-sector trade advisory committees that advise the president and his US trade representative. There are three levels to this advisory committees system. The President's Advisory Committee for Trade Policy and Negotiations (ACTPN) is at the highest level and chiefly composed of business executives, with a few union and public policy officials. Beneath the ACTPN are policy advisory committees composed of business, agricultural, environmental, and labor representatives with particular policy expertise. However, the most active of the advisory groups are those that operate at the sector and functional levels. Before the Singapore Ministerial Meeting, the Industry Sector Advisory Committee on electronics and information strongly endorsed an ITA. This recommendation was promoted directly to the US trade representative through the ACTPN.[63]

From the Indian side, there were at first mixed feelings about an ITA that would allow information technology goods to enter the country free of duty. There were those in the Confederation of Indian Industries particularly who had thoughts that India should develop its own indigenous capacity for manufacturing computer hardware. Their argument was that the computer hardware industry deserved tariff protection as an "infant industry." However, the members of the Indian outsourcing community were in favor of the ITA. Their reasoning was that the strength of the Indian industry lay in software and services. Importing computer hardware without tariffs made this equipment less expensive and was supportive of delivering information technology services at the lowest cost. Through NASSCOM (which by December 1996 had grown exponentially since I met with its organizers in November 1994) and then through FICCI and CII, a consensus was reached that the ITA would be favorable to the industry sector in which India had its greatest competitive advantage.

At the Singapore Ministerial Meeting, the Indian delegation was officially headed by a reticent commerce minister of state. The leader in fact for India was Tejendra Khanna, the secretary of commerce, and the leading civil servant within the Ministry of Commerce and Industry. Khanna and I had worked together in setting up the US-India Commercial Alliance after the Brown mission. Because I knew Khanna, Barshevsky's deputy Susan Esserman asked me to speak with the Indian delegation and to participate in the negotiations for Indian accession to the ITA. Khanna was a very forward-looking civil servant, later to become chairman of the pharmaceutical company Ranbaxy and then lieutenant governor of the National Capital Territory of Delhi. Khanna was at first very concerned about the effect on a nascent India computer hardware industry of a possible accession by India to the ITA. We discussed with Khanna the fact that India's strength was in software and software-related services and that India's economic development would be most encouraged by computer hardware being imported with no tariffs. After the meeting, Khanna spoke with Indian business leaders, many of whom were leaders in outsourcing as described above, and decided that this line of reasoning had merit.

In the next US-India negotiating session with Barshevsky, the Indians agreed to join the ITA. However, we were informed that internal Government of India clearances could not be obtained by the close of the Singapore Ministerial Meeting. By the terms of the ITA, WTO participants representing 90 percent of world trade would have to notify their acceptance of the ITA by April 1, 1997, for the agreement to become effective. By the closing session, participants representing only 83 percent of world trade had notified their acceptance. However, we all felt that India would live up to its commitment, and we treated the ITA as an achievement. Evidently, President Clinton felt the same way. Just before the closing session, Barshevsky was presented with a bouquet of roses and the information that she had been nominated by the president to become the US trade representative. The Indians did notify their acceptance of the ITA before the April 1, 1997, deadline. Barshevsky was confirmed by the Senate as the US trade representative, and the ITA went into effect.

Indian government and business leaders now generally agree that the ITA has been a positive factor in Indian computer software development, the phenomenal development of the Indian communications industry, and outsourcing generally. The ITA has proven an effective tariff-cutting mechanism. As the only sector-specific WTO agreement,[64] the ITA presently has some seventy participants collectively representing 97 percent of the global information technology trade. Through its Committee of Participants on the Expansion of Trade in Information Technology Products, the ITA's country participants usually hold five formal meetings each year, at which the scope of product coverage has continually expanded. The business and policy interests represented on the Pacific Council and by FICCI justifiably see the ITA as a model for US-India cooperation in developing the "innovation economy."

Thus, US-India economic engagement through outsourcing of services has played and is playing a dual role in the ability of the United States and India to cooperate on the strategic issue of economic development. Outsourcing has served to raise concerns in the United States about job loss and downward pressure on US middle-class wages. The frictions it has created between the United States and India are fundamental to the failure of the United States and India to cooperate on such economic development endeavors as the Doha Round. At the same time, US-India economic engagement in the field of information technology has increased the willingness of the United States and India to work together on such matters as the ITA, which is serving as a model for further bilateral cooperation. Outsourcing is the quintessential generator of what has been referred to above as "feedback loops." In such loops, the political effects on the ability to cooperate point in both positive and negative directions.

The Bottom Line

The category of US-India economic engagement popularly referred to as "outsourcing" is basically trade in information technology services. Because of the difficulty of capturing accurate data for services generally and information technology services specifically, the size and importance of this trade is often understated by US economic analysts. When fully accounted for, these data help to explain the important political impact this economic engagement has on US-India relations. Economic engagement in information technology services has both negative and positive effects on the US-India relationship. Negatively, outsourcing and the related issue of temporary worker visas (chiefly H-1B visas) have been a focal point for US fears about job loss to foreigners and the downward pressure on US wages from foreign competition. The responses of US politicians to these fears and the reactions of Indians to these responses have adversely affected the US-India relationship. Positively, the rapidly increasing size and business importance of the outsourcing relationship has created a community of interest in the United States and India. This community has promoted further cooperation on measures to promote economic growth, such as the ITA. The ITA in turn has served as an exemplar for those advocating the further lowering of trade barriers between the United States and India in order to promote growth. The negative and positive effects of US-India economic engagement through outsourcing continue to play a key role in the ability of the United States and India to cooperate on the strategic issue of economic development through the Doha Round of WTO trade negotiations and other initiatives.

Information technology services outsourcing is the flagship of Indian world-class economic activity. This outsourcing has become a vital component of US business efficiency. Thus, outsourcing is a salient factor driving US-India cooperation in the related field of economic development. However, economic engagement through outsourcing also has effects on strategic cooperation in fields not as obviously related to trade in information technology services. One such linkage is with the fight against terrorists and terrorism. The next chapter presents a case study of that relationship.

Chapter 4

Economic Engagement and Preserving the Peace: The Reaction to Terrorism

In the meantime, this cease-fire is brought to you by GE—and all its friends here in Bangalore.

—Thomas L. Friedman, "India, Pakistan and GE," *New York Times,*
August 11, 2002

On the morning of December 13, 2001, a band of radical Muslim terrorists dressed in Indian police uniforms were admitted past the security barriers and attacked the Indian Parliament in New Delhi. Their plan was no less audacious than that of their brethren who had flown airplanes into the twin towers of New York's World Trade Center and the Pentagon on September 11 of the same year. The New Delhi attackers sought nothing less than to decapitate the Government of India by capturing and killing at Parliament virtually the entire elected leadership of the country. The attack was foiled when a constable spotted the intruders as imposters and raised the alarm, shutting the Parliament Building's gates. In an apparent attempt to ram the gates, the terrorists slammed into a car in the waiting motorcade of the Indian vice president. The terrorists poured out of their car and began firing. In the ensuing gun battle, all five terrorists were killed. One was blown to pieces when a bullet exploded his suicide vest.

The Government of India quickly identified the attackers as members of two terrorist organizations, Lashkar-e-Taiba and Jaish-e-Mohammed. These organizations were based in Pakistan and allegedly aided by the Inter-Services Intelligence agency of the Government of Pakistan. India leveled blame squarely at the Government of Pakistan, while Pakistan denied culpability. Pakistan put its troops on high alert and issued statements citing the dire consequences of any Indian "misadventure."[1] India responded by ordering a general mobilization of its forces and moving troops to the Pakistan border in Punjab and to the Line of Control in Kashmir.

Michael Clark, director of the US-India Business Council, and I were meeting to discuss US-India high-technology cooperation in the days following the attack on Parliament. A constant stream of calls was coming to Clark from US businesses concerned about the situation in India. Most were from companies involved in outsourcing their data management business to India. They recognized the seriousness of the situation and wondered about the security and continuity of the operations that were handling their data. These companies were looking for assurances that the software systems and business processing operations on which they relied would be safe. But who knew what would happen next? We could give the callers no such assurances.

Contemplating Nuclear War on the Subcontinent

I thought back to the US Naval War College exercise that Clark and I had attended in Newport, Rhode Island, two years before. The part of that exercise in which Clark and I participated was focused on the possible consequences of a nuclear war between India and Pakistan. In a hypothetical scenario, a nuclear exchange could kill some 12 million people and destroy major parts of the largest cities in the two countries. The scenario further hypothesized that even with such massive loss of life and structures, the nation of India, with more than a billion people, would continue to function.

No Indians whom I knew thought a nuclear exchange with Pakistan was even remotely likely in 1999. However, for whatever reason, the sponsors of the exercise evidently had in mind the growing tensions that were to erupt in May of that year. India and Pakistan nearly come to full-scale war at that time. General Pervez Musharraf had inserted Pakistani troops across the Line of Control near the small town of Kargil in Kashmir, and the Indians had responded with a fierce defense. The elected prime minister of Pakistan, Nawaz Sharif, later claimed he had not been informed of the operation, although it is plain that at least he had had a general briefing. In any event, full-scale war had been averted, and an uneasy peace restored in large part through the strong intervention of the Bill Clinton administration and an extraordinary meeting between Clinton and Sharif. The Pakistani troops had been pulled back, and, though more than a thousand troops were killed, full-scale war did not occur. However, neither before nor after Kargil had Pakistan subscribed to a "no-first-strike" policy with regard to nuclear weapons.[2] No one really knew what might trigger a first nuclear strike from Pakistan.

For the purposes of the Naval War College exercise, we were asked to contemplate what would happen if the troops were not pulled back from the border and hostilities escalated into a nuclear exchange. It was for other participants to outline other possible consequences in addition to the immediate destruction of life and property. Death and devastation from fallout, holes in the ozone layer of the atmosphere, and the "nuclear winter" from dust clouds were all on the agenda.[3] Our part of the exercise was to discuss potential economic impacts, particularly as they might affect US business interests. Those consequences were serious enough. Massive floods of refugees, disruptions of trade and trade routes, and effects on US company information systems and their investments were considered. The study concluded that even if India emerged largely unaffected by direct war damage, the effects on the Indian economy would be significant. According to the report of the exercise, "investor interest in South Asia would be obliterated."[4]

GE and Its Friends in India

General Electric is the archetypical US-based company investing and operating in and trading with India. An assessment of the effects of an India-Pakistan war on US economic interests might start with the effects on such a company. GE has done business in India since selling and installing a hydroelectric turbine in the Indian state of Madhya Pradesh in 1902. When India moved to open its economy in the early 1990s, GE's chief executive, Jack Welch, was one of the first US business executives to commit his company to taking advantage of the Indian opportunity. A major breakthrough in fulfilling this commitment came in 1993, when Welch appointed Scott Bayman to be chief executive of GE's Indian operations. Both Welch and Bayman were sensitive to the possibilities of furthering GE's interests in India by supporting the US government's interests in reaching out to India through commercial interaction. As was described in chapter 2, Bayman came to Washington in 1994 as we planned for Commerce Secretary Ron Brown's Presidential Business Development Mission to India. Bayman's and GE's input was a major factor in the success of the trip. A large portion of the value of deals announced was in GE-produced power production equipment and airplane engines.

As Bayman later pointed out, GE's original plans to exploit the Indian consumer market through sales of appliances and other electrical goods did not materialize in the way he and Welch had anticipated. According to Bayman, India simply did not have a sufficient number of consumers who could afford the upscale GE products. However, Bayman discovered that India did have highly qualified software engineers and programmers in sufficient numbers to help meet GE's computer systems needs. According to Bayman, the GE plastics business was the first to adopt a formula that highlighted India as a source for its information technology requirements. The plastics business set a target of outsourcing 70 percent of its total information technology needs. Of the amount outsourced, 70 percent was to be outsourced offshore, and of this amount, 70 percent would be done in India. In other words, the GE plastics business would outsource to India more than a third of its information technology needs. At the time, this was a virtually unprecedented commitment to India. To realize its outsourcing goals for plastics, GE first worked in India with Wipro Technologies and its head, Azim Premji. When Bayman showed that those goals could be achieved in India for the plastics business, the next step was to replicate this experience for each of GE's businesses.[5]

By 2000, GE was ready to expand the scope of its information technology and information-technology-enabled services sourcing in India by bringing some of its operations into a GE facility. In September of that year, Welch came to India for the dedication of the John F. Welch Technology Center in Bangalore. Welch was treated like a rock star in India. Crowds gathered wherever he went. I attended a lunch in New Delhi where he spoke after the Bangalore dedication. The Indian press was out in full force, with crowds both inside and outside the venue. Welch's speech on the India opportunity and the need for "speed, stretch, and seamlessness" (GE management principles) was received with great approval. The Welch Center opened with 275 employees operating in 183,000 square feet of space. By May 2002, the facility had increased to 545,000 square feet and 1,525 employees and was continuing to work with Wipro and a variety of other Indian services providers. It was clear from Welch's speech in 2000 that GE had even greater goals in mind for outsourcing to India.[6] By the time of the December 13, 2001, attack on Parliament, GE's experience with outsourcing its information technology and information-technology-enabled services to India was being followed by many other US companies.

American Express, long active in the Indian financial services market, was heavily involved in leveraging the country's information technology resources. It worked chiefly with another Bangalore-based firm, Infosys Technologies. Infosys had been started in 1981 by seven people with an investment of the rupee equivalent of $250. Chief among its founders were N. R. Narayana Murthy and Nandan Nilekani. The first decade and a half were difficult. However, with such customers as American Express, the company began to grow exponentially in the late 1990s. Infosys particularly excelled at the service of business process outsourcing. The call centers that employ thousands of young, educated Indians to provide assistance over the telephone for everything from credit cards to computer malfunctions are the best-known manifestation of this service.

American Express was more than a customer for Infosys; the company was also a business partner. For example, in 2001 American Express formed a team—with Infosys; TIBCO Software of Palo Alto, California; and an investment fund, WestBridge Capital Partners, with offices in Silicon Valley, Bangalore, and Mumbai—to start Workadia, which provides companies with customizable business intranets through browser-accessed hosted Web portals.[7] This venture tied American Express and Infosys together in serving corporations worldwide with services that have come to be known as "cloud computing." In addition to teaming with American Express, Infosys has regularly conducted business with leading US technology companies and has developed strategic alliances with such US-based companies as Hewlett-Packard, IBM, Microsoft, Oracle, and Sun Microsystems.[8]

Thus, at the time of escalating India-Pakistan tensions in 2002, many US businesses were becoming highly reliant on the information technology and information-technology-enabled services of India. Estimates of the percentage of *Fortune* 500 companies doing business with Indian information technology companies ran as high as 60 percent.[9] What these companies wanted most is perhaps summed up by a slogan of India's largest outsourcing company Tata Consultancy Services: "Experience Certainty."[10] The security and assurance of supply of services were the universal denominators for US companies turning to India for outsourcing. In the weeks and months after the terrorist attacks on Parliament, these companies found much about which to be concerned.

The Crisis Grows

In spite of appeals for calm, tensions between India and Pakistan continued to mount. India demanded that Pakistan crack down on the terrorist groups

Lashkar-e-Taiba and Jaish-e-Muhammed. When Pakistan did not act to suit India, India recalled its ambassador. The recall of the ambassador was a highly unusual move, seldom exercised throughout the long history of India-Pakistan crises.[11] India demanded the handing over of twenty terrorist suspects known to be in Pakistan.[12] According to the Indian minister of defense, George Fernandes, there would be no pullback until the terrorist suspects were handed over and raids across the border had ended.[13]

The United States and other countries tried to defuse tensions. President George W. Bush announced further actions against financial sources for terrorist organizations located in Pakistan. Secretary of State Colin Powell went to New Delhi. Significant pressure was brought to bear on Musharraf, who by this time had become president of Pakistan in a bloodless coup. On January 12, 2002, Musharraf made a speech about controlling cross-border terrorism and began detentions of some militants. However, these attempts at deescalation were unavailing. India and Pakistan both conducted missile tests near their border. Indian and Pakistan continued to mass troops on the frontier. Both sides made statements about their nuclear weapons being ready for use.[14]

War seemed imminent when, on May 14, a major terrorist attack occurred near Jammu in Kashmir. The attack killed thirty-four Indians and wounded many more. The attack was on the family quarters of an Indian Army post. Consequently, many of the dead were the family members of Indian soldiers.[15] There were assassinations of local Indian leaders in Kashmir. Firing intensified across the Kashmir Line of Control. Hostile statements were issued by leaders in both countries. The Indian Army asked for permission to attack targets inside Pakistan. On May 22, 2002, Prime Minister Atal Bihari Vajpayee visited an army brigade headquarters at Srinagar in Kashmir. He admonished the troops to prepare for a "decisive battle." In words that caught the world's attention, he said, "The enemy has thrown us a challenge by waging a proxy war. We accept it and pledge to give it a crushing defeat."[16]

Departure Notice and Travel Restrictions
Get the Attention of US Business

Perhaps even more important in raising the consciousness of US and Indian businesses about the dangers of war were the actions taken by US ambassador to India Robert Blackwill. After Vajpayee's speech, Blackwill recommended to the State Department the ordering from India of all nonessential

US personnel and the families of other personnel. At first, the State Department was vague about whether there should be such an order. As events progressed, the department authorized, but did not order, "the departure of all US Government personnel in non-emergency positions and family members in India."[17] Blackwill, who was adept at dramatizing a situation, took the authorization as his opportunity to order out of the country for their own safety the "non-emergency" personnel and families. The State Department issued a travel advisory warning US citizens to leave. These actions got the attention of businesses in both the United States and India. Because the crisis had gone on for about six months, many businesses on both sides had become complacent. Vajpayee's speech and Blackwill's order to leave removed that complacency.

In particular, those foreign companies that depended on India for their information technology needs were now fully alert. The kinds of inquiries and questions that had flooded in during the period immediately after the attack on Parliament began to flow again. The assurances that had been given by Indian outsourcing companies in the December–January time frame were no longer sufficient. Outsourcing requires not only unimpeded telecommunications and electronic data flows but also a constant stream of visits and face-to-face exchanges by managers and technicians. As indicated in chapter 3, this is a basic reason that temporary H-1B visas are so important to the business of Indian outsourcing companies. The inflow of customer representatives and their temporary presence in India is equally important. Without these face-to-face contacts between customers and providers, outsourcing does not work. Thus, a travel warning that "strongly urges that American citizens in India depart the country" has a palpable effect beyond overall concerns about data security and assurance of services.[18]

GE's Due Diligence and the India-Pakistan Crisis

In the spring of 2002, General Electric was conducting a "due diligence" exercise as a part of the decisionmaking progress for increasing still further its investment in India. A key player in this exercise was Michael Gadbaw, the GE vice president and senior counsel for international law and policy. Gadbaw remembers particularly the normally full five-star hotels of New Delhi and Bangalore dropping to about a 25 percent occupancy rate as catching his attention. As a part of the due diligence process there was continual interaction between GE and Indian information technology firms at the highest levels. Although there was no effort by GE to encourage contact with the Indian government, questions and concerns were relayed to Indian executives as a part of the ongoing interaction between GE and Indian industry.[19]

Vivek Paul, vice president of Wipro and a former GE India executive, received email messages from American customers who had begun to look at alternative sources for the processing of their data. Because the inquiries had come from America and US-India trade in services was at stake, Paul reached the Government of India through the Indian ambassador to the United States, Lalit Mansingh.[20] The Infosys chief executive, Nandan Nilekani, remembers the Indian outsourcing industry concerns also being transmitted to the Indian government through their trade association, the National Association of Software and Services Companies (NASSCOM).[21] MindSpring president N. Krishnakumar says that the concerns of the Indian information technology service providers were transmitted to the Government of India through the Confederation of Indian Industries trade association.[22] In India, the use of such trade associations to deal with the government on policy issues is often the preferred method of communicating a company's concerns. Another line of communication on the devastating effect of war on the Indian outsourcing industry was opened by the information technology ministers of Karnataka and other Indian states that are centers of offshore information technology. According to Vivek Kulkarni, then the information technology secretary for the Bangalore region, the technology ministers brought to the Government of India's attention "the problems the Indian IT industry might face if there were a war."[23] Thus, the concerns of American business set in motion communications with the Indian government from multiple sources within the Indian outsourcing industry.

The US government intervened forcefully with Musharraf and the Indians. If the situation developed into war, much less nuclear war, the result would be disastrous from a US diplomatic perspective. The United States was involved in an Afghanistan war and needed vigorous help from Pakistan against Al Qaeda militants who had escaped into Pakistan and were using it as a base of operations. Pulling troops from Pakistan's western border, where the United States wanted help in fighting Al Qaeda and the Taliban, to its eastern border to face India certainly would be disastrous for the American effort.

Secretary of State Colin Powell and his deputy, Richard Armitage, conducted an intensive exercise in crisis management. Armitage met with Musharraf in Islamabad. There he extracted pledges against Pakistan-based cross-border terrorism. Flying on to New Delhi, Armitage made the Pakistani pledges public on June 7, 2002.[24] Secretary of Defense Donald Rumsfeld followed up the Armitage mission with a visit to New Delhi on June 12, 2002. Rumsfeld pointed out to officials in New Delhi that India and Pakistan could "get on a track that would be enormously beneficial to them. And our country has an interest in their economic success." Rumsfeld drove the point home: "Even the tension, even the threat of war, makes people making decisions all over the globe say, 'No, that's not where I want to invest right now.'"[25]

The Tensions Subside

On July 20, 2002, the State Department issued a public announcement noting that "tensions have subsided." The announcement further noted that "authorized departure for US government personnel in non-emergency positions and all family members has been lifted." Indian and Pakistani troops on their respective sides of the border and the Line of Control would not pull back to normal positions until October. However, for all practical purposes, the crisis was over.

Analysts of the crisis with State Department backgrounds attribute the outcome that India and Pakistan did not to go to war to the crisis management efforts of the department. Thomas Friedman's characterization, "That cease-fire was brought to us not by General Powell but by General Electric,"[26] is given little credence by such diplomatic analysts. It is much easier to credit the linear sequence of governmental communication than multiple and diffuse business interactions. Some analysts of the 2001–2 crisis attribute the lack of war to the pacifying effect of nuclear weapons.[27]

From the Indian side, no official could afford to admit that international economic engagement had anything to do with the decision not to respond militarily with cross-border force. In the intense democratic politics of India, any such intimation would be likely to bring down a government as a "sell-out" of the national interest. The commitments and assurances from the Pakistanis by way of the Americans was the accepted rationale for the stalemate and movement away from the commencement of open warfare.

Even for those involved in bringing economic factors to bear on moderating the response to terrorism, there is difficulty in delineating the effects of economic engagement. No one wants to be accused of being "soft on terrorism" for economic gain. Even those willing to talk about their experiences in urging moderation on economic grounds are quick to add their willingness to go to war in the face of "outrageous" acts against the nation.[28] Perhaps the importance of economic engagement in moderating conduct is best indicated in this instance by Indian characterizations of the departure order and travel warning. Indian observers of the episode characterized the action as "American coercive diplomacy."[29] A further indication may be the Indian reaction to the even greater provocation to war that occurred in Mumbai some seven years after the December 13, 2001, attack on Parliament.

Reaction to the Mumbai Attack

On the evening of November 26, 2008, a group of ten Pakistani nationals disembarked from a rubber landing craft in the vicinity of Mumbai's Gateway to India and attacked the Taj Mahal and Oberoi hotels, the Leopold Café, and the other targets described in chapter 1. This terrorist attack was much better planned and more sophisticated than the attack on Parliament. At the end of almost three days of hostilities, 169 people had been killed and more than 400 wounded. The siege did not end until November 29, when nine of the ten gunmen were killed and the tenth was taken into custody. As discussed in chapter 1, this attack was a direct strike against symbols of US-India economic engagement and other sites designed to shock both Indian and American sensibilities. It seems likely that the handlers for the Mumbai terrorists wished to promote wider violence between Muslims and non-Muslims and perhaps war between India and Pakistan.

However, again war did not occur. A familiar pattern unfolded, in spite of the horror of the attack. India blamed Pakistan, and the Government of Pakistan denied involvement or culpability of any kind. There were widespread calls for military retaliation. Secretary of State Condoleezza Rice went to India almost immediately. She and Admiral Mike Mullen, chairman of the Joint Chiefs of Staff, then met in Islamabad with the Pakistanis. Rice was followed a week later by Deputy Secretary of State John Negroponte.[30] The US Federal Bureau of Investigation (FBI) was brought in to work with the Indian authorities. Intelligence was shared showing that the terrorists had indeed originated from and been trained in Pakistan. The new director of the US Central Intelligence Agency made his first international trip to India and then continued on to Pakistan.[31] Pressure was brought to bear on

Pakistan, which eventually admitted the terrorists had come from the territory of Pakistan.

US and Indian business interests were intent on maintaining business as usual and, therefore, peace and stability. For example, the US-India Business Council (USIBC) issued a statement saying that the attacks would not affect investor confidence. A USIBC business mission to start on December 8 would go forward as planned. A joint endeavor between the USIBC and the Federation of Indian Chambers of Commerce and Industry (FICCI) would occur as planned in Mumbai in February.[32] FICCI itself would donate Rs 10 million to the families of the security personnel who had died fighting the terrorists. NASSCOM issued a statement pointing out that New York, London, and Madrid had all faced terrorist attacks. The statement went on to acknowledge, for the benefit of both government and private sectors, that the security and continuity of the information technology industry are essential and would be provided from India without interruption: "As an industry that is international and services customers across the globe, we continue operations, uninterrupted, from centers across India and even Mumbai. . . . NASSCOM offices are open and functional and we will proactively communicate with you on the situation. NASSCOM activities and events across the country, including the international events next week, will continue as planned."[33]

Contrasting with business's call for calm and continuity were Indian political voices calling for the immediate punishment of Pakistan. The Bharatiya Janata Party, leader of the National Democratic Alliance opposition coalition, asked the questions, "Should we wait for the next terror attack so that Pakistan can be punished? Does that mean Pakistan would have no cost to pay for what happened on 26/11?"[34] The party's spokesman demanded the resignation of the Manmohan Singh government, saying, "It is a collective culpable negligence of the government. The responsibility should also be collective, and no government has the right to survive after this."[35] Opposition politicians made these statements with an eye toward the upcoming 2009 nationwide elections. In those elections, the opposition tried to make the handling of the Mumbai attacks and the failure to be tougher on Pakistan an issue. However, these issues failed to gain traction. The Singh government was returned to power, the first government to be returned after a full five-year term since India's first prime minister, Jawaharlal Nehru. The fact that business's call for calm and continuity seemed to win out over the fevered opposition demands for military action is itself an indication that, once again, economic engagement was a force for maintaining the uneasy peace between India and Pakistan.

Indian Restraint Leads to Greater US-India Strategic Cooperation

In turn, the restrained approach of India to the terrorist attacks originating in Pakistan led to closer intelligence and homeland security ties between the United States and India. In 2000, just before President Clinton's trip to India, the United States and India had established a Counterterrorism Joint Working Group. After the experiences of 2002 and 2008, the work of this group and US-India interaction on terrorism increased exponentially.

An indication of this closer cooperation was demonstrated in September 2009 by the four-day visit of Indian interior minister Palianappan Chidambaram to the United States. Chidambaram, who had shifted from minister of finance to minister for home affairs shortly after the Mumbai attack, was invited by the US government to make the trip. His first stop was in New York City. There he was briefed at the Joint Terror Task Force Center by representatives of the FBI, the New York Police Department, and the Coast Guard. The briefings covered defending attacks from the sea and making railways secure, all of particular concern from the Mumbai experience.[36] He then went by train to Washington. In Washington, he met first with Homeland Security Secretary Janet Napolitano, Treasury Secretary Timothy Geithner, and Attorney General Eric Holder as well as National Security Adviser James Jones. He then went to Capitol Hill, where he met with the chairs of the Senate and House committees on intelligence, Dianne Feinstein and Silvestre Reyes. Chidambaram concluded his visit by meeting with Secretary of State Hillary Clinton.

As background to these Chidambaram meetings, a fundamental concern was the deplorable state of Indian equipment and systems for deterring terrorists. Months after the Mumbai attack, the Indian police often lacked even the most basic equipment and technology.[37] A major support for strengthening cooperation between the United States and India would be trade in the high-technology goods and services useful for combating international terrorism. India had already made the decision to purchase six C-130J Super Hercules airplanes from Lockheed Martin to transport special forces and their equipment. The delivery of these aircraft would take place in 2011. India was also negotiating to purchase the even larger C-17 Globemaster transport aircraft.[38] Most needed were coastline defenses to frustrate Mumbai-style attacks. In 2005, the United States had leased two P-3C coastal patrol aircraft to India.[39] Now the United States offered to lease twelve helicopters to India.[40] In addition, India agreed to purchase eight P-8I maritime patrol aircraft from Boeing.[41]

However, what Chidambaram most wanted was the kind of technology that was demonstrated to him at the Joint Terror Task Force Center in New York. To a large extent, the Indian Multi-Agency Centre, initiated by Chidambaram, is based on the US model. Subsidiaries of the Multi-Agency Centre are being established in all state capitals. Chidambaram's secretary of border management is procuring perimeter protection equipment. The agency guarding airports, the Central Industrial Security Force, was exploring the acquisition of biometric and other types of access control technology. Chemical-biological-radiological-nuclear personal equipment, at which US companies excel, was being sought. The most ambitious of Chidambaram's projects for which outside technology was being acquired were a Crime and Criminal Tracking Network and Systems and a National Intelligence Grid. These projects draw heavily on US systems, particularly those in use by the FBI. The Indian Crime and Criminal Tracking Network has a budget of some $400 million.[42] The Government of India considers much of its procurement for homeland security to be secret. Therefore, it is difficult to tell with certainty how much is being acquired from which sources. Suffice it to say that the acquisitions from US sources are significant and growing.

Thus, in the aftermath of the November 26, 2008, terrorist attack, there were threats and counterthreats between India and Pakistan, much as in 2001–2. US-India economic engagement was a force for moderation rather than reprisal. The United States intervened not only to help India in the investigation but also to encourage the Government of Pakistan to take action against terrorists operating from Pakistan against India. The restrained approach of India in not going to war has led to closer US-India government and private-sector cooperation on terrorism.

The Bottom Line

The economic engagement that could be sustained with peace was apparently a factor in the decision of the Indian government not to launch cross-border hostilities in response to the 2001 attack on the Indian Parliament and its aftermath. The decision of the US government to send nonessential personnel out of India and to issue a travel advisory asking all nonessential personnel to leave effectively dramatized the economic disruption that would be caused by war. This effectiveness was in large part because there was extensive economic engagement between the United States and India. Business leaders in both countries worked to bring an understanding to government leaders of the wide potential for economic damage inherit in precipitous cross-border action. Thus far, the pattern set in 2002 has held in responses to other terrorist attacks emanating from Pakistan territory. Even after the most spectacular of these attacks, that on Mumbai, the reaction has been remarkably restrained. In both instances, the United States was able to take advantage of this restraint to work with both Pakistan and India to advance US national interests in preserving peace. Not all US-India economic engagement has had such a positive outcome, as can be seen in the following chapter about US-India engagement on the providing of electric power.

Chapter 5

Economic Engagement, Electric Power, and the Environment

I would rather have expensive power than no power.

—N. K. P. Salve, India's minister of power, March 18, 1995

Signing the Protocol . . . imposes no obligations on the United States.

—Vice President Al Gore, Kyoto Protocol Signing Statement,
November 12, 1998

In March 1995, I was in Mumbai at the Taj Hotel when I received notice from our embassy of a request from union minister of power N. K. P. Salve that I meet with him in New Delhi. Such a request was unusual. The protocol- and status-conscious Government of India officials would usually not think it appropriate for a minister to meet with a foreign official of considerably lesser rank. I assumed that Salve was interested in the views of those on my mission about the attractiveness of the Indian electric power projects that his ministry had prepared for foreign direct investment.

After being part of the mission to India of US commerce secretary Ron Brown in January 1995, I had returned in March, leading a team of potential American electric power investors. The business development mission I was leading was a follow-up to the Brown trip and a previous visit by Secretary of Energy Hazel O'Leary. Its purpose was to focus on what appeared to be significant opportunities for US-India economic engagement in the field of electric power.

During the Brown and O'Leary missions, there had been considerable euphoria about the "fast-track" projects being promoted by the Indian central government and advocated by US officials. From the US government

129

perspective, the optimism was not based just on the ability to benefit mutually from power projects. The projects being proposed also had the potential of being cleaner and "greener" than anything previously undertaken in Indian power production. Indeed, several members of my mission were from companies interested in providing the latest US technology for producing energy while reducing emissions. The prospect of uniting power production and environmental protection seemed an ideal combination for promoting the Bill Clinton administration's agenda for sustainable growth.

In our New Delhi meeting, the honorable minister quickly made it plain that foremost on his mind were not the projects my team had just reviewed but the fast-track program and its difficulties. Of particular concern was the Enron project at Dabhol in the minister's home state of Maharashtra. Salve's Congress Party had just suffered a significant defeat in Maharashtra. The Congress Party had lost the state legislature to a coalition of the opposition Bharatiya Janata Party (BJP) and the ethnic-based Shiv Sena organization. In the campaign, a chief line of attack against the Congress-led state government had been the allegedly outrageous cost of power from the Dabhol project. The BJP–Shiv Sena victory meant national political danger for Salve's party.

Salve was convinced that he was right with his program for promoting foreign direct investment (FDI) in the Indian energy sector. He stuck to the mantra referenced above that expensive power was better than no power. He reasoned that the costs of no power in lost economic growth and opportunity more than offset the premium paid over the price of electricity generated at the existing coal-fired plants. Salve was not particularly interested in environmental matters, but I pointed out that the fast-track program had environmental benefits as well. Modern plants would lower the "externality costs" to the environment compared to existing plants burning Indian soft coal laden with a high percentage of unburnable material.[1] My mission had just visited such a Soviet-style plant in the state of Gujarat, where the ash from the fuel was piled high around the plant and covered many hectares. As chair of a US interdepartmental committee promoting environmental technology exports, I was enthusiastic about this line of reasoning.

Minister Salve wanted continued US economic engagement in support of Dabhol and the fast-track initiative. He wanted it understood that he was still backing the program and that it could still produce benefits both for the United States and India. Political developments in Maharashtra would not deter India from the fast-track goals. And he made it plain that he wanted me to help deliver that message both to my superiors at the Department of

Commerce and to the US private sector. Minister Salve wanted the United States to know that fast track was still on track to be a success for all concerned. However, it was not to be.

Stalled US-India Economic Engagement on Power Production and Climate Change

By the time the United States and India reached Kyoto in December 1997 for negotiation of a protocol to the United Nations Framework Convention on Climate Change, the Dabhol project had been renegotiated and the Indian fast-track program was in deep trouble. Likewise, the Clinton administration's initiative to increase US exports of environmental technology and equipment to India was receiving little attention. In November 1998, President Clinton added a largely meaningless US endorsement to the Kyoto Protocol but declined to submit it to Congress in the face of overwhelming opposition. Fast-track and US-India economic engagement on energy and the environment were stalled. In India, the entire concept of a special program to encourage FDI in electricity production was being derided.[2]

US-India economic engagement on electrical power generation, much less the accompanying environmental technology, had been short-circuited. For the 2000 visit of President Clinton to India, there was an attempt to revive engagement on the environment as a major theme of US-India cooperation. However, little was said about power generation, and the environmental talk lacked the crucial element of economic engagement. US-India cooperation on electric power production has never recovered from the failure of the fast-track initiative. US-India economic engagement on environmental technology is being posited anew as a part of efforts to ameliorate climate change but largely remains an unfulfilled concept. Conceptually, some progress was made at the United Nations Climate Change Conference in Copenhagen, which was held December 7–18, 2009. However, in reality the parties simply delayed action and the United States and India are still far apart on energy, the environment, and climate change.

Economic engagement does not always produce positive strategic results. The unsuccessful US-India engagement over electric power is a case in point. As we shall see, there is a relationship between the US-India experience with producing expensive power and the political inability of the United States to assume the international obligations that would make it a full participant in multinational efforts to combat climate change.

The Background to Engagement on Electric Power Production

When the Government of India embarked on a process of economic liberalization in 1991, one of the chief problems it faced was one it still faces: a
lack of electric power. Electricity had been subsidized, stolen, and wasted
for so long in India that it had obtained the status of a "free" good in the
minds of many Indians. For some voters in some states, this was literally
true. For example, farmers in the Punjab basically received electricity for
free, and they still do. The uneconomic pricing of electricity was a national
phenomenon. Almost all electricity was sold through State Electricity
Boards (SEBs). As a result of uneconomic pricing and theft, virtually all the
SEBs were essentially bankrupt and were able to function only because
of subsidies from the central (or federal) government. This system based
on central government subsidies to the SEBs has often been compared to a
"leaky bucket," whereby substantial vested interests have grown up around
the leaks in the system.

Faced with the near bankruptcy of the country and the SEBs, Prime Minister Narasimha Rao, Minister of Finance Manmohan Singh, and Minister
of Power N. K. P. Salve conceived an initiative to attract foreign independent power developers and capital to India. The power sector was for the
first time opened to both private and foreign investment. In May 1992, a
high-level team composed of the Cabinet secretary and secretaries from the
Finance and Power ministries was sent to the United States to visit prospective US investors in the Indian power sector.[3] The lure for this effort was the
promise of fast-track status to approve power projects. Under the fast-track
program, SEBs were exempted for a period of time from the ordinary requirements that government contracts be competitively bid. Projects were
to receive expedited regulatory approval and could be negotiated based
upon memoranda of understanding (MOUs).

Most significantly, approved fast-track projects were to receive "counterguarantees." Under these counterguarantees, the central government would
guarantee the obligations of the SEBs and their state owners and pay the developer of new generating capacity for electricity if an SEB and the state in
which it was located failed to pay as required under their contracts. Because
the SEBs and the states were essentially insolvent, the counterguarantees
were essential to the ability of the fast-track initiative to attract foreign capital. In addition to the Indian team sent to the United States in 1992, the Indian government solicited investors from Europe and around the world. By
the end of 1992, eight MOUs had received approval for the negotiation of

the contracts necessary for their implementation. And many more had been signed and were awaiting approval by the central government.

The Initial Fast-Track Projects

The eight fast-track projects approved for negotiations covered a wide variety of sizes, technologies, and fuels. Five projects involved US companies. The US projects approved for development were:

1. Enron Power Corporation Project at the village of Dabhol, Maharashtra State, 2,500 megawatts in size; as conceived, this project was ultimately to burn liquefied natural gas (LNG).
2. Cogentrix, Inc., and China Light and Power International project at the city of Mangalore, Karnataka State; 1,000 megawatts in size, this project was to be fueled by imported coal.
3. AES Corporation in the Ib Valley of Orissa State; originally 250 megawatts in size and later 500 megawatts as approved, this project was to be fueled by domestic coal from the leading coal-producing area of India.
4. CMS Electric Company near Neyveli in Tamil Nadu State; 250 megawatts in size, this project was to burn the relatively low-quality lignite mined in the area.
5. Spectrum Technologies USA with Jaya Food Industries (India) in Kakinada, Andhra Pradesh State. This 200-megawatt project was to be fueled by natural gas.

In addition to the US projects, three plants promoted by European and Indian power companies were approved for development under the fast-track program. These were:

1. National Power Plc (United Kingdom), near the city of Vishakhapatnam (short name "Vizag") on the coast of Andhra Pradesh State; 1,000 megawatts in size, this project was to burn coal.
2. EDF (France), GEC (United Kingdom) and Ispat Group (India), near the city of Nagpur, Maharashtra State; 1,000 megawatts in size, this project was to be fueled by coal.
3. GVK Power and Infrastructure Limited (India), in the city of Jegurapadu, Andhra Pradesh State; 200 megawatts in size and later expanded to 500 megawatts, this is a combined-cycle power plant burning natural gas.[4]

All these projects were to have the latest in environmental protection technology. They were to be far cleaner in operation than any existing plants in India.

The Troubled Course of the Flagship Enron Dabhol Project

Clearly, the flagship of the fast-track initiative, and by far the largest such project, was the one to be developed by Enron. The later fraud and criminal convictions of officers of the Enron parent corporation in the United States make it difficult to divorce an analysis of what went wrong with regard to the Dabhol project from the spectacular demise of the entire Enron business. However, understanding the impact of the Dabhol fiasco on the US-India relationship makes the effort to understand Dabhol on its own merits necessary.

When the Indian delegation of secretaries was in the United States in the spring of 1992, one of the companies they met with was Enron Corporation. Among the opportunities that the Indians presented to US investors was one for a gas-fired plant in Maharashtra. The vision of the leader of Enron's international operations, Rebecca Mark, was to supply LNG from Qatar to India. This vision was shared at the time by her superior, chief executive officer Kenneth Lay. The initial use for this gas would be a large power plant on the west coast of India. The plant was to be built through FDI of $2 billion to $3 billion.

However, the Enron vision was larger than a single very large power plant and extended to the use of LNG, especially up the west coast of India through industrialized areas of Maharashtra and to the highly industrialized state of Gujarat. The Enron vision meshed closely with the interests of the Indian officials for a gas-fired power plant in Maharashtra. Thus, there was interest on both sides in pursuing the project. The mutual vision of meeting Indian power needs in the western part of India through FDI and gas was paramount. By June 1992, Indian officials had located several possible sites in Maharashtra State and had discussed generally with Enron what the outlines of the project might be. That month, Enron officials and officials of General Electric visited the Ministry of Power in New Delhi for discussion of the fast-track procedure. Fast track was once again presented by the Indian power officials as a method whereby an electrical power FDI project could be initiated on an MOU with a state electricity board rather than by a competitive bidding process. The intent to provide counterguarantees was confirmed.

After discussions in New Delhi, the Enron team went to Mumbai. There, they met with officials of the Maharashtra State Electricity Board (MSEB) and toured prospective sites. The one in which Enron was most interested was near the village of Dabhol on the coast of Maharashtra about 200 kilometers south of Mumbai. Much to the surprise of the MSEB officials and the delight of the Power Ministry officials in New Delhi, Enron indicated that it was ready to proceed by entering into an MOU immediately. After two days of touring and talking and a day of negotiation in Mumbai, MSEB and Enron signed an MOU based on the draft offered by Enron. The MOU recognized the need to set up an approximately 2,000-megawatt plant to be fired by LNG that an operating entity designated as the "Dabhol Power Company" would build, own, and operate. There would be an "electrical power purchase contract" that would run for twenty years and be structured to achieve a price of $0.073 per kilowatt-hour (kWh). This was about Rs 2.34 per unit at the then-prevailing exchange rates, and was later "rounded up" to Rs 2.40, which became fixed in the public mind as the actual price that Dabhol Power Company had represented would be charged the MSEB.[5] The MSEB would pay for the entire theoretical output of the plant at a 90 percent load factor whether it actually took the output or not (a so-called take-or-pay provision). There were stiff penalties to be assessed for failure to complete the project on schedule or meet the 90 percent load factor. "Dabhol Power Company" turned out to be a joint venture, with Enron owning 80 percent of the equity and General Electric and Bechtel Corporation owning 10 percent each.[6]

The MOU was criticized by both the World Bank and the Indian Central Electricity Authority shortly after it was signed.[7] The most salient criticisms had to do with price and the take-or-pay aspects of the document. The Ministry of Power officials did not seem particularly concerned about these criticisms. The assumption of the person most responsible on the Indian side, Minister Salve, was that Maharashtra and India had a persistent and ongoing base load deficit that carried great opportunity costs for the state and nation. The further assumption was that MSEB customers would gladly pay for electricity at an increased price in order to help bridge the electricity deficit and the power interruptions it caused. Salve's preference for expensive electric power over no power was based on these assumptions. The assumption concerning deficits and opportunity costs was not mere speculation.

National figures showed a base shortfall of about 10 percent, with a peak shortage of about twice that much. The minister viewed the Enron endeavor as just part of the larger fast-track initiative designed to meet national shortages on an expedited basis. The important point was to get India moving as fast as possible toward meeting the deficits. The assumption about willingness to pay was far more speculative. Strangely for a Maharashtra politician schooled in the sensitivities of voters, Minister Salve did not seem particularly concerned about the level of discontent that could be fueled by increases in power charges to consumers.[8]

Contract Approvals and Negotiation

Regardless of the merits of the MOU, even the deal's most virulent critics conceded that "the MOU was not a legally binding document."[9] Whatever the validity of the project, it would not be determined by the MOU but by the deal as it was actually worked out. Though the MOU did not determine the deal, it did set the United States, US private-sector companies, and India on a path of attempting to build an agreement, regulatory regime, and financing mechanisms while determining actual costs and pricing—basically all at the same time. This endeavor has been likened to attempting to fly an airplane while it is under construction.

The next step in the fast-track process was to get approval from the Foreign Investment Promotion Board (FIPB). Two months after signing the MOU, Enron submitted an application to the FIPB for approval of its investment. Formerly called the Foreign Investment Approval Board, the FIPB is designed to protect India from FDI that might compromise the nation's independence or otherwise have an impact on the national interest. Basically, it is a holdover from the immediate postindependence era, when India was particularly concerned about the reimposition of Western colonialism through economic means. The issue of "economic imperialism" is still salient in India. The issue is regularly invoked as a part of a nationalist political appeal and by those on the left side of the political spectrum. In the Enron case, the FIPB recommended that the project be split into two phases. Enron agreed to this bifurcation. Phase I was approved as a 740-megawatt plant fueled by naphtha. Phase II was to be an LNG project of approximately 1,500 megawatts. After completion of phase II, the entire plant would be operated on LNG. The Dabhol plant facilities would include a 2-mile-long gas-offloading dock for LNG from Qatar and a regasification facility.

With FIPB approval, Enron and the MSEB, with the supervision of the

Ministry of Power, turned to the negotiation of a power purchase agreement (PPA). Though the MOU was not legally binding, the PPA certainly would be and would be the fundamental legal basis for the entire project. At the same time it was negotiating the PPA, Enron attempted to line up financing and begin the process of getting the some 150 regulatory approvals that still would be needed even under the fast-track procedure.

The Ministry of Finance wrote the World Bank for an assessment of the project. The response from the World Bank was a significant setback. In a letter from the director of the Bank's India Country Department to Montek Singh Ahluwalia, then secretary to the Department of Economic Affairs of the Ministry of Finance and now deputy chairman of the Planning Commission, the Bank found that the project was "not economically viable, and thus could not be financed by the World Bank."[10] This finding was based on the assessment that the project was too large and that LNG would be too expensive for the MSEB to be able to pay for all the electricity to which it would be obligated.

However, in its letter, the World Bank gave an opening for Enron to argue the shortsightedness of the Bank. The Bank advised that the MSEB should be opting for "the least-cost sequence for Maharashtra power development" and that "local coal and gas are the preferred choices for base load generation." In reality, India did not have at that time "local gas" sufficient for a major power project. Resigning India to "local coal," Enron argued, simply meant that India would continue with the environmentally harmful projects that were causing massive pollution problems throughout the subcontinent. The local coal option was simply a continued use of a model that had failed to meet Indian needs for the "new era" of Indian economic development. Further, the "local coal" favored by the Bank was not local to Maharashtra. Most of the Indian coal deposits were on the other side of the country. Much of this coal was in Orissa, where the World Bank was already deeply involved in an effort to reform the system for supplying electricity. Enron and its supporters basically argued that the Bank's assessment failed to take into account the massive growth in prosperity that many were forecasting for India. This growth in prosperity would further fuel demand and the ability to pay for electricity. This growth would make the project viable. According to Enron, the Bank's assessment simply reflected a typical bureaucratic approach that failed to recognize the opportunity presented by India.

These arguments, together with Enron's projections to buttress them, appealed to governmental officials in both the United States and India. They also appealed to an array of private financiers who wanted to be aggressive about the opportunity supposedly offered by Indian economic growth. However, the potential financial backers would make no commitments until the PPA and the guarantees of the MSEB and the counterguarantee of the Government of India were in place. These financiers would then be able to make an assessment of whether there would be sufficient safeguards along with sufficient returns to justify the risks of financing a huge modern power plant in India.

The PPA between the Dabhol Power Company and the MSEB was negotiated over a period of some eighteen months and concluded on December 8, 1993. Negotiation of a long-term PPA of the type used internationally in independent power production deals was a new experience for the Indian authorities. The Indian pattern was usually for a "cost plus" arrangement, whereby the producer was paid a fixed return of 16 percent plus incentive fees, and cost overruns would be passed on to the state electricity board. Under the Dabhol PPA, the Dabhol Power Company was to assume risks in the capital costs of the project as well as guarantee on-time delivery of the plant and the plant's output and efficiency. However, the PPA legally placed the risks of currency fluctuation, price of fuel, fixed costs, fluctuations in demand, and changes in tariffs and taxes on the MSEB.[11] The basic mechanism for allocating these burdens to the MSEB and ultimately to the governments of Maharashtra and India was the tariff structure of the PPA.

With regard to the risks of currency fluctuation, these were essentially eliminated for Enron and its partners by denominating all payments under the tariff structure in dollars. The tariff itself was divided into two parts. The first of these was a "capacity charge" that included amounts calculated on the fixed costs of the project, including capital repayment, fixed operation and maintenance, and insurance. There was also an undefined quantity of rebate provision in the event that there was a supplier default on Enron's contract for LNG. The amounts applicable to these fixed charges were then related to the capacity of the plant based upon a yearly test for "rated plant capacity." The second part of the tariff structure was an "energy charge." The major component of the energy charge included a fuel charge. Also included in the energy charge were charges for variable operation and maintenance as well as a fee for special operations. As envisaged under the MOU, the tariff under the PPA was a take-or-pay arrangement, whereby the MSEB had to pay the tariff applicable to the rated output of the plant whether or not the electricity was taken by the MSEB. The tariff was set to guarantee an internal rate of return of about 18 percent. However, critics charged that the actual internal rate of return was more likely about 28 percent.[12]

The obligations undertaken by the Dabhol Power Company essentially related to building the plant and producing electricity. Under the PPA, plant construction was assured within thirty-three months. There were guarantees against shortfall in capacity and plant availability. For good measure, Dabhol Power Company also guaranteed the "heat rate" for the plant, a key indicator of plant efficiency. In what turned out to be an extremely important provision, the resolution of disputes under the PPA was to be by international arbitration in London.

The Counterguarantee Imbroglio

With the signing of the PPA, the major remaining legal piece for moving the project forward was a counterguarantee from the Government of India. This obligation was denominated "counterguarantee" because it was to make up for, or "counter," any default of the State of Maharashtra, which had itself guaranteed the obligations of the MSEB as a part of the PPA. The Ministry of Finance was responsible for issuing the counterguarantee.

The Ministry of Finance had been part of the fast-track initiative from the very beginning. Finance sent one of its secretaries on the initial 1992 mission that had worked to recruit US and European investors in the power sector. However, the Enron initiative had encountered more and more political opposition as the project had materialized, and the Finance Ministry became increasingly wary of the counterguarantee. The conclusion of the PPA itself had unleashed a barrage from the opposition parties that indicated they were going to make a major issue of the agreement. In addition to Indian political ramifications, the Finance Ministry also was concerned about the international obligations of the government. With limited foreign currency reserves, the ministry began to have reservations about the program and the debts that a counterguarantee might cause India to assume. On a mission by US secretary of energy Hazel O'Leary in July 1994, a primary thrust of her talks was to get the Government of India to sign the counterguarantees not just for Dabhol but also for all the fast-track projects. This policy thrust was supported by the Department of Commerce and generally by the Clinton administration.

Potential public and private financial backers in both the United States and India took the position that a counterguarantee was essential to their providing funds. Both the US Export-Import Bank and the Overseas Private Investment Corporation (OPIC) made it known they were prepared to back the Dabhol project if it obtained a counterguarantee. Likewise, a consortium of banks led by the Bank of America and ABN Amro Bank NV were ready to proceed if there was a counterguarantee. These facts were relayed to the Government of India and potential Indian lenders. Support for the project was taken up by its potential Indian financers. Particularly, the Industrial Development Bank of India was active in pushing the project indirectly with its government. The Dabhol Power Company counterguarantee was signed September 9, 1994. The signing of the Government of India's counterguarantee by Manmohan Singh, the minister of finance, enabled Enron to put in place the financing. Secretary Brown, with the presence of Enron chairman Ken Lay, oversaw the signing of the Ex-Im Bank and OPIC obligations in New Delhi in January 1995. Commitments for approximately $650 million of debt and $276 of equity were in place by March 1995.

Thus, in early 1995 it appeared that the Dabhol Enron project was prepared to move forward. The movement on this flagship project for US-India economic engagement seemed to be producing further US-India cooperation across the board. Other fast-track projects started to move. Delegations of potential investors and suppliers came from the United States. There was a strong emphasis on the export of US clean energy technologies along with the FDI in Indian power projects. The US interagency Trade Promotion Coordinating Committee set up a Working Group on Environmental Technology Exports.[13] This group had strong US intragovernmental support from the Environmental Protection Agency, the Department of Energy, and the office of Vice President Al Gore. Discussions moved ahead with the Tata Energy Research Institute (now called simply the Energy and Resources Institute) and its director-general, Rajendra K. Pachauri.[14] Climate change was not yet a salient public issue, but the subject of producing energy without undue harm to the environment was very much under discussion. The quest to alleviate Indian energy needs by building a gas-trading relationship with states of the Persian Gulf was in progress. Thus, it appeared that US-India economic engagement through Dabhol and other fast-track projects was having a major positive impact on US-India cooperation on the issue of energy and the environment. However, a political storm was now raging in Maharashtra.

The Winds of Political Change in Maharashtra

In December 1992 and January 1993, Hindu-Muslim rioting took place in Mumbai. The rioting ostensibly began with Muslim protests over the destruction of the Babri Masjid (mosque) in the town of Ayodhya, Uttar Pradesh. In later stages of this rioting, Hindu mobs killed hundreds of Muslims.[15] Then, on March 12, 1993, thirteen bombs were set off in Mumbai killing hundreds more, mostly Hindus. These bombs were alleged to have been planted under the direction of the city's Muslim underworld leader, Dawood Ibrahim, with the help of Pakistan. The bombings were said to have been done in retaliation for the earlier slaughter of Muslims. Shiv Sena activists were widely alleged to have been involved in promoting mob violence, although leaders of the party denied this role and no significant convictions have been obtained.[16] Whatever the actual facts of Shiv Sena involvement, the riots thrust the party into an even more prominent political role based on its perceived actions and its insistence on the supremacy of the Marathi ethnic group in Maharashtra.[17]

Further rioting occurred in 1994, but on a smaller scale. As the rioting abated, Shiv Sena needed to add an economic component to its anti-Muslim, pro-Marathi ethnic group platform if it was to spread its power by democratic means in the coming state elections. An economic issue was necessary if Shiv Sena was to bring down the Congress Party government of Maharastra, then led by Chief Minister Sharad Pawar. For statewide electoral success, it would not be enough to concentrate simply on animosity toward groups perceived to be denying the native Maharashtra ethnic group, the Marathis, their proper place in the state. Shiv Sena found that economic component to their political platform in opposing Enron and the Dabhol power project.

For the 1995 Maharashtra elections, Shiv Sena joined in an election alliance with the Bharatiya Janata Party. In addition to ethnic and religious statements, a foremost Shiv Sena rallying cry was to "push Enron into the Arabian Sea."[18] BJP campaigners were more content to talk about Gandhi's concept of *swadeshi* (loosely translated as "self-reliance") as it applied to power rather than to imply violence. A major thrust of the BJP–Shiv Sena campaign was that Enron had bribed Pawar. The only support adduced for this charge was a report that an Enron official had testified before the Appropriations Committee of the US House of Representatives that Enron had spent some $20 million on the "education and project development process."[19] To many Indians familiar with the corruption that is so prevalent in India, the linkage of this statement to corruption had credibility. In fact, Enron was taken to court in India twenty-four times on allegations that included fraud and corruption. None of these court actions was successful.[20]

Dabohl in Peril

The Maharashtra State elections were held February 9–12, 1995. The BJP–Shiv Sena coalition won a resounding victory. The new state government was sworn in during March and immediately prepared to make good on BJP–Shiv Sena threats to terminate the Dabhol project. The new government chose to proceed through a Cabinet Sub-Committee Review of the project as well as by filing a civil suit in the Mumbai High Court. Both the report of the Review Sub-Committee and the complaint in the civil suit roundly condemned the project and the previous government while calling for a repudiation and cancellation of the project. As soon as the report was finished, the Government of Maharashtra on August 4, 1995, issued a stop-work order to the Dabhol Power Company.

Enron responded to the stop-work order with a notice that it would pursue arbitration in London for damages of at least $300 million. More important, this legal position was supported by a campaign of both governmental and nongovernmental dimensions. From a US government perspective, it appeared that the stop-work order was simply politically based upon a change in the Maharashtra State government. No evidence had been adduced of fraud or corruption. The international component of Enron was working with the administration around the world on cleaner, gas-burning projects that would entail US job-creating exports. Contrary to the analysis of the World Bank, the Ex-Im Bank, and OPIC, an examination of the project indicated that it was financially sound. Advocacy by the Clinton administration was intense. In May, Prime Minister Rao had lost his reelection bid. After a brief stint by the leader of the BJP, Atal Bihari Vajpayee, H. D. Deve Gowda became prime minister. Gowda was familiar with the fast-track initiative from the time he had served as chief minister of Karnataka. President Clinton himself spoke with Gowda about the Dabhol project. Gowda assured Clinton of his support but indicated that this was chiefly a matter for the State of Maharashtra. Clinton's ambassador to India, Frank Wisner, spoke with Indian government officials about the need to establish and maintain Indian international credibility as a respecter of contractual rights.

Enron supplemented this US governmental effort with a vigorous public relations campaign in India. It ran full-page advertisements in Indian newspapers concerning the project. Behind the scenes, it worked with opinion makers to put its position forward. It used the figure of Rs 2.40 per kWh as the cost of electricity from the Dabhol Power Company. But it neglected to point out that this was a price based on certain initial assumptions about cost. It deemphasized the point that the tariff structure was so elastic that the actual price over time could be many times higher than the Rs 2.40 per kWh that was fixed in the public mind. It also refused to recognize that this would be an initial presumed cost to the MSEB without the charges for expenses that the MSEB would have for the transmission and delivery of the electricity. The figure of Rs 2.40 per kWh under no circumstance would be the delivered price to the consumer. However, the Enron campaign was so effective that by the fall of 1996 a poll indicated that some 80 percent of people in Maharashtra and 60 percent of those in India as a whole favored restarting the project.[21]

The Project Resumes

By November 1995, the leader of Shiv Sena, Bal Thackery, was ready to deal. The head of Enron's international operations, Rebecca Mark. met with Thackery in Mumbai. After the meeting, Thackery announced, to the astonishment of many, that Enron had met nearly all his conditions and thus the agreements with the Dabhol Power Company would be renegotiated. The key point of the renegotiation was a purported reduction in the price of the power from the project by 22.5 percent. This theoretical reduction was claimed by expanding the size of the project to 2,450 megawatts and making Phase II a binding part of the contract. There were no changes to the obligations for Phase I, other than an expansion in size and a switch in fuel to be used initially from distillate oil to naphtha. Essentially, by combining Phase I with Phase II and expanding the size of the project, Enron was able to spread costs over a greater theoretical output to achieve "savings." The Government of Maharashtra was brought in to the project with an option to purchase 30 percent of the equity in Dabhol Power Company. In early January 1996, the Government of Maharashtra announced agreement on the terms of the revised contracts, and in February documents were signed to put the new deal in place. Both the Government of Maharashtra lawsuit and the demand for arbitration were withdrawn. Public interest litigation was dismissed. Construction resumed.[22]

However, the troubles with the project were far from over. Protests at the construction site had been common since its inception. In 1997, with construction having resumed, these protests turned violent. These protests and police response fueled attention to the project from outside India. Nongovernmental organizations from throughout the world protested violations of human rights and environmental degradation.

In spite of the protests, both construction under Phase I and the financing of Phase II went forward. Now dozens of financing institutions were becoming involved from across India and throughout the world. In addition to the Industrial Development Bank of India, the Ex-Im Bank and OPIC in the United States, the Export-Import Bank of Japan and Japan's Ministry of International Trade and Industry, and Belgium's Office Nationale du Ducroire were all involved in financing Phase II. The LNG gas supply situation seemed under control, with Enron having secured twenty-year contracts to buy gas from Oman and Abu Dhabi.[23] Enron was committing itself to as many as ten more power projects in India and the sale of gas for other uses.

By the middle of 1997 (when I left the Department of Commerce), the Clinton administration considered the Dabhol project a qualified success in bringing FDI to India, particularly in the vital sector of energy and electric power. The widespread participation in the project from throughout the world, but led by US involvement, seemed to auger well for economic engagement as a path to greater strategic cooperation on energy and the environment. The greatest concern was not the Dabhol project as such. Rather, there was deeper concern about the effect Dabhol's political difficulties would have on other fast-track projects and the needed FDI in India. In the private sector, I continued to work on the policy aspects of the Indian fast-track projects as a senior adviser to the US-India Business Council. Over the next few years, Dabhol and the other fast-track projects faced difficulties that eventually destroyed the entire initiative.

The Indian Political Wheel Spins Again

In May 1999, Phase I of Dabhol was completed and began to generate electricity. The price of electricity for the MSEB was much higher than anticipated. Virtually all the variables that had placed most risks on the MSEB combined to produce bills that were considerably higher than the Rs 2.40 per kWh that had been fixed in the minds of many Indians. The price of fuel had gone up, demand had dropped, and the rupee had fallen against the dollar. Slower economic growth and the perennial budget problems of the MSEB caused it to take only 10 to 60 percent of the electricity for which it was obligated to pay under the take-or-pay provisions of the PPA.[24] Thus, the actual invoiced cost per unit of electricity taken by MSEB was more than double Rs 2.40 per kWh.[25] Enron argued for the right to sell electricity to other state electricity boards. The offer was to reduce the burden on the MSEB to the extent it could sell its electricity elsewhere, but the legal changes necessary to sell electricity across state lines were not forthcoming.

As noted above, a coalition led by the BJP had come to power in March 1998. In October 1999, the wheel of Maharashtra State politics turned again. This time the BJP–Shiv Sena coalition lost its state legislative assembly majority and a coalition led by the Congress Party came to power. Now the political situation between Maharashtra and the central government was reversed from that of 1995. Now the Congress Party prevailed in the state with a BJP coalition at the center. Even though a Congress-led government had brought the Dabhol project into being, the new Congress-led Maharashtra state government of 1999 roundly criticized its predecessors for the renegotiation of the Dabhol contract and its conduct of relations with Enron. In early 2001, the MSEB simply stopped paying its bills. In March, Enron invoked the Government of India's counterguarantee.[26] The following month, Enron again invoked arbitration.

The End of the Line

The impasse of 2001 would be different than the one that had occurred in 1995–96. Rebecca Mark and her associates were gone from Enron, having lost out in a power struggle. In part, this struggle was over whether the future of the company lay with projects internationally like Dabhol, in which the company would actually own and operate assets, or whether it would be a trading company moving energy and other commodities without operating anything. Mark was the foremost advocate to Chairman Lay of the strategy of promoting actual ownership and operation (a strategy dubbed "big iron" by its detractors). Jeffrey Skilling was the advocate of the trading model. By the end of 2000, Mark was forced out. Enron now turned to the trading model as its focus. Although the accounting practices that caused the downfall of Enron had started earlier, the company now became fully immersed in what were later adjudicated as fraudulent and deceptive trading practices. Enron's upper managers were in a desperate effort to raise money and save themselves. Little or no executive attention was being paid to resolving the latest difficulty with the MSEB. In September 2001, Lay tried to sell Enron's stake in the Dabhol Power Company to the Government of India. But the government was not buying. In December 2001, Enron went into bankruptcy, from which it never recovered. The George W. Bush administration at first continued the Clinton policy of advocacy for the project. However, when massive losses came to light along with evidence of illegal conduct in trading, support ended.

The Dabhol project collapsed. Recriminations and losses from the collapse spread throughout the world. Eventually, the project passed into Indian hands with no US participation. Regardless of the facts, the perception in India was that Enron had committed a giant fraud on India. There are those in the United States who share that view. However, others in the US business and finance worlds point to the London arbitration award in favor of Enron and the decision of a US arbitration panel chaired by retired US federal judge Charles Renfrew. In that September 2003 proceeding, the panel held that the Government of India, the Maharashtra State Electricity Board, and the Government of Maharashtra had violated their obligations "for political reasons and without any legal justification."[27] The Maharashtra deficit in power continued to grow. By 2008, Maharashtra had a base load shortage of 19 percent and a peak power shortage of 27 percent.[28]

The Similar Fates of the Other Fast-Track Projects

Similar fates awaited the rest of the fast-track projects. Those involving the US companies Cogentrix, CMS, and AES were uniformly unsuccessful. Cogentrix pulled out after lengthy "public interest litigation" filed against it had stopped the project. CMS and its partner, ABB, after extensive problems receiving payments from the Tamil Nadu State Electricity Board, sold out their interest to an Indian company in 2003. Although AES has continued to do work with the Orissa Power Generation Company, its fast-track 250-megawatt project never materialized.

Cogentrix

The experience of Cogentrix is particularly instructive with regard to the interrelationship between economic engagement and strategic cooperation. In line with the Clinton administration's policy of advocating on behalf of US companies involved in the fast-track program, Secretary Brown intervened with the Government of Karnataka in January 1995 to get the project moving after it had become stalled for internal state political reasons. Cogentrix was a North Carolina–based electric power project developer. Like Enron, it had been solicited by the Government of India for a project that the Ministry of Power deemed in need of FDI and the technical and skill transfers that come with FDI. In 1993, Cogentrix received approval from the Foreign Investment Promotion Board to proceed with development of a plant in the coastal city of Mangalore. The project quickly ran into political trouble with the ruling Congress Party state government in Karnataka.

As in the Enron situation, changes of state government played a significant role in the history of the project. By the time the Brown mission arrived in January 1995,[29] leadership of the state government in Karnataka had changed hands. Deve Gowda, a veteran state politician of the Janata Dal Party, had become chief minister. In the discussions with Brown, Gowda said that he would support the project and allow it to go forward.

The project then became an intensely partisan political issue in Karnataka. The environmental community was aroused to oppose the project. Although the projected plant was to burn coal, the fuel would be imported coal that was cleaner burning than Indian coal. Further, Cogentrix intended to use the latest US environmental technology. This technology not only would provide exports for the United States but also would make the plant far cleaner than any coal-burning plant then existing in India.

Public interest litigation was filed accusing Cogentrix of cost padding, kickbacks, and bribery. Unfortunately for Cogentrix and the project, Gowda had his sights set on politics at the national level rather than shepherding development projects in Karnataka. In May 1996, he ran for the Lok Sabha as leader of the Janata Dal Party and was elected. When Atal Bihari Vajpayee could only maintain a parliamentary majority for less than two weeks, Gowda was able to put together a United Front coalition that made him prime minister. Although Gowda's successor as chief minister was also from the Janata Dal Party, he did not have a personal commitment to the Cogentrix project. The litigation continued with a lower court order that halted work. An appeal to the Supreme Court sat with no action.

With Vajpayee regaining the prime minister's office in March 1998, his new minister of power, P. Rangarajan Kumaramangalam, expressed no interest in assisting the project.. Kumaramangalam simply recommended that Cogentrix do a better job of "PR."[30] Cogentrix became increasingly disenchanted with India as a place to do business. On December 9, 1999, Cogentrix announced it was pulling out of India. At this point, the Vajpayee government became concerned about the effects of the pullout on FDI. Evidently this concern was transmitted to the Supreme Court of India in an informal manner. Four days after the announcement from Cogentrix that it was pulling out of the project, the Indian Supreme Court overturned the ruling of the lower court and cleared the project to move ahead.[31] However, the ruling was too late. Cogentrix had had enough, and it left India.

CMS Electric Company

In comparison with both the Enron and Cogentrix projects, the CMS Electric Company fast-track project at Neyveli, Tamil Nadu, seemed to offer greater possibilities of economic success. CMS had as its chief asset Consumers Energy, an electric power utility serving more than half the people of the State of Michigan. With the interest in independent power production created by deregulation in the United States, CMS sought to move into the international arena through projects in India. The foremost of these was to be a project in Tamil Nadu based upon locally mined lignite coal. Thus, unlike the Enron and Cogentrix projects, which were to use imported fuel, CMS hoped to avoid the price of electricity problems that plagued the other two projects. Also, at 250 megawatts, the plant was to be far smaller than either Dabhol or Mangalore and, therefore, less susceptible to fluctuations in demand from its customer, the Tamil Nadu State Electricity Board (TNSEB). Environmentally, the project was less attractive because of its contemplated fuel. However, in seeking support from the US government, CMS represented that it would bring advanced technology to the environmental problems of burning the lower-quality coal.

Progress on the CMS Neyveli project was much slower than that of the other fast-track projects. In part this was because of a later start, and in part because the promoters were waiting to learn from the experiences of the other fast-track projects. CMS received its Government of India counterguarantee in August 1998. Financing was achieved about a year later, and the project started to produce and sell electricity to the TNSEB in late 2000. In spite of the promising economic aspects of the project, CMS immediately ran into payment problems with the TNSEB. Again, the state electricity board claimed that the electricity was too expensive. But unlike its Maharashtra counterpart, the TNSEB did not simply stop paying but provided partial and late payments as a routine matter. By 2003, CMS had decided to leave India and, indeed, the international market as a whole. In 2007, CMS finally sold its interest in CMS Neyveli and left the country.

AES Corporation

As indicated above, the US power company AES Corporation was approved for a fast-track project in the Ib Valley of Orissa. The project received its counterguarantee in December 1999 after having reached its power purchase agreement. The project had been expanded to 500 megawatts from the original 250 megawatts by the time the counterguarantee was issued. However, in August 2000, the Orissa State government informed AES that it would be unable to buy power from the project. Although AES looked for other customers, they were not forthcoming, and the project died.[32] In a project backed by the World Bank, AES continued to operate and own a minority stake in the primary power generation facility for the State of Orissa. This project has been plagued with disputes over the price of power AES supplies to the state-owned transmission company, Gridco. The Orissa state electricity regulator took over AES's distribution business in 2002. AES also has had plans for other endeavors in India. Ironically, when AES sought clearance from the Foreign Investment Promotion Board for a project in the State of Chhattisgarh in 2006, the State of Orissa opposed approval on the grounds that AES had not brought its Ib Valley fast-track project to fruition.

Spectrum Technologies USA

The Spectrum Technologies USA's gas-fired 208-megawatt project in Andhra Pradesh went into production in 1998 after achieving financial closure in May 1996. This project was originally promoted by an Indian American, Mohan Rao, who was extensively involved in his native state of Andhra Pradesh. The project was undertaken in collaboration with the government-owned National Thermal Power Corporation of India and was taken over by a relative of Rao before it came on line. Thus, it appears that this project dropped out of the fast-track program and became simply a National Thermal Power Corporation project with private Indian participation.[33]

The Aftermath of Fast Track

One purpose of the fast-track initiative was to encourage FDI in India from the United States and other countries. The success of the fast-track projects was planned to stimulate FDI for a wide range of Indian infrastructure projects in need of capital. The United States was already the leading foreign direct investor in India at the time of commencement of the fast-track projects. Thus, the United States was deemed particularly important to India's efforts to attract FDI. The failure of the fast-track initiative, in which the governments of the United States and India put so much time and effort, operated as a constraint rather than an incentive to FDI both in electrical power and across the board. During the period 2003–6, total FDI in the power and oil refinery sector amounted to less than $600 million. India's difficulty in obtaining significant total FDI is readily apparent from a comparison of Indian and Chinese FDI. During the period 2000–2005, FDI into China was annually about ten times the FDI into India.[34] Even if differences between India and China in accounting for FDI are taken into account, China still has a significant lead in FDI on an annual basis.[35]

The Government of India recognized that with the failure of the fast-track initiative, there was an even more acute need for electric power in the country. The BJP-led National Democratic Alliance government of 1999–2004 pressed ahead with structural reforms. Under the leadership of Power Minister Suresh Prabhu, the government produced the Electricity Act of 2003, which provided a badly needed legal framework for a modern electric power system. However, Prabhu was removed from office at the behest of his erstwhile political patron, who was concerned that Prabhu was too honest and had not used his office to produce sufficient funds for the Shiv Sena Party.

The lack of progress in actually creating additional electric power was probably a factor in the defeat of the National Democratic Alliance at the polls in 2004. The new United Progressive Alliance government took note of this and in 2006 launched a new initiative to provide "power to all" by the end of the Eleventh Five-Year Plan in 2012. To meet this goal, the new government pledged to add 100,000 megawatts of capacity. The chief mechanism for adding this capacity was to be a new Ultra Mega Power Projects initiative. This program was conceived as an improved version of the fast-track or "megapower" projects. These projects would be 4,000 megawatts each, about twice the size of Dabhol. Each plant would serve several states. The Ultra Mega projects would avoid charges of favoritism or corruption by being awarded on a competitively bid basis. There would be long-term take-or-pay power purchase contracts, as with the fast-track projects. However, the competitive bidding for the projects would be on the basis of the tariffs that would be charged for the electricity. With tariffs locked in at a supposedly low, competitively bid level, the difficulties of state electricity boards not being able or willing to pay for electricity could be avoided.

Thus, the government reasoned that the Ultra Mega projects will produce inexpensive, plentiful power. The gigantic size of the plants will achieve economies of scale. These economies of scale, combined with the burning of relatively cheap coal and competition based on tariff rates, should produce plants that provide power at a low cost. However, ensuring that 100,000 megawatts of capacity will be added to achieve "power to all" by 2012 will require building twenty-five 4,000-megawatt plants.

Financing remains the key to increasing Indian generation capacity. The designation of the Power Finance Corporation, a company owned by the Government of India, to be the "nodal" or lead agency for the Ultra Mega projects emphasizes this key role of financing. The counterguarantees were to be the mechanism for attracting international financing for the fast-track and megapower projects of the 1990s. The Ultra Mega scheme has no counterguarantee component. Instead it relies on a payment security mechanism consisting of three parts. The build, own, and operate plant developers will receive a revolving letter of credit by distribution licensees. The customer distribution utilities will establish escrow accounts in which the developer would have an irrevocable claim on receivables assigned to the escrow accounts. In the event of default the generators will be able to sell directly to high tariff customers or distribution customers other than the customer signing the power purchase agreement.[36]

When the Indian minister of power came to the United States in 2007 seeking US participants in the Ultra Mega Power Projects, he was disappointed to find a lack of interest in his proposals. The reason, of course, was obvious. The negative feelings engendered on both sides by the experiences associated with the economic engagement growing out of the fast-track projects made it unlikely that US companies and financiers would be willing to take on new projects in India.

The initial experience with the Ultra Mega Power Projects shows that international private-sector participation in the financing and development of the plants is not meeting expectations. Most of these projects are being developed and financed domestically. Of the first four projects awarded, three went to a single Indian firm.[37] Reliance Power Ltd., a company of the Reliance–Anil Dhirubhai Ambani Group, had conducted an initial public offering in India in early 2008. The funds from this offering were the chief source of financing for the Ultra Mega Power Projects awarded to Reliance Power. The project not awarded to Reliance Power went to the Tata-promoted Coastal Gujarat Power Limited. This project sought and obtained some $800 million in financing assistance from the International Finance Corporation, the private-sector entity of the World Bank. The rest of the financing for the Tata plant apparently comes primarily from Indian domestic sources.

Although the Tata plant is to be fired by imported coal, the International Finance Corporation participated on the theory that the "supercritical" technology of the plant would cause a reduction in greenhouse gas emissions in comparison with a coal plant using conventional technology.[38] However, the basic fact is that the Tata plant and the other three initial Ultra Mega projects will be coal burning. Two will be at domestic pithead sites and two at coastal locations to burn imported coal. Currently, an additional ten sites have been identified.[39] An additional award was made to Reliance as of the end of 2009. Of the additional sites identified, most will be for coal-fired plants.[40]

Further US-India Efforts on Electric Energy and the Environment

As indicated above, part of the reason for US government involvement in advocating for US-India cooperation on the fast-track projects was to introduce to India technology that would ameliorate the environmental effects of power production. The concept was that technologies that would fight pollution as the "footprint of inefficiency" would grow the market for exports of US environmental technology. The success of environmental technology in power production would in turn lead to Indian interest and similar technology in manufacturing and transportation. The difficulties of US-India collaboration in power production over the fast-track efforts frustrated this strategy. The United States and India were not able to develop a body of Indian and American business and economic professionals with extensive interaction that might have served as a bridge for ameliorating differences on fundamental issues facing the electrical power industry. The lack of US company participation in the Ultra Mega Power Projects initiative exacerbated this problem. Without such interaction, Indian officials have tended to fall back on traditional, statist approaches to resolving problems associated with supplying electrical power in India.

India continues to struggle with the concept of market-driven solutions to the environmental issues associated with power production. For example, with regard to "clean technology," there is an Indian view that such technology should be transferred to India without charge. In the United States, the transfer of clean technology and the associated goods and services are subject to the same market-driven pricing policies that are applicable to intellectual property generally. Likewise, there are markedly different views on the proper balance between the cost of electric power and environmental protection. These differences in approach are fundamental to US-India difficulties in cooperating on such problems as climate change. These differences spring from India's socialist past, its relative poverty, and its conviction that the developed countries are the basic cause of worldwide environmental problems. Knowledge as a "common heritage of all mankind" is an article of faith for many on the left in India. Because India is so determined to achieve "inclusive growth" for the hundreds of millions of Indians living below the poverty line, there is a reluctance to undertake any expenditures for commitments that might be seen as hampering economic growth. It follows from the conviction that the developed countries grew wealthy by polluting the environment that the "polluter pays" concept should be applied to technology transfer to India. In other words, such developed countries as the United States should pay for the environmental technology to be used in India.

Successful economic engagement engenders forces that are positive politically in meeting shared problems. Unsuccessful economic engagement creates the opposite dynamic. The failed fast-track program created this negative dynamic. US-India relations on strategic environmental matters continue to be the worse for the experience. By 1997, US-India economic engagement on energy should have been producing some shared experience that could have been drawn on at Kyoto. In fact, there was little or no interaction between the United States and India at Kyoto or before on the issues of climate change. What little interaction there was consisted simply of India telling the United States that it would not submit to binding limitations on its climate change emissions. The US Congress would not accede to this position, and the Clinton administration had little in the way of shared US-India economic engagement to bridge this gap.

The Kyoto Protocol imposed no obligations on developing countries, and the United States likewise accepted no obligations. When the United States signed the protocol on November 12, 1998, both Vice President Gore and everyone else associated with the signing knew that it was purely symbolic. The event was a mere shadow of what Gore and other environmentalists had hoped for. As Gore noted in his signing statement, "Signing the Protocol . . . imposes no obligations on the United States."[41] In reality, the political fate of the protocol had been sealed, insofar as the United States was concerned, the previous year. On July 25, 1997, the US Senate passed the Byrd-Hagel Resolution (S 98) by the astounding vote of ninety-five to zero. This resolution said that it was the sense of the Senate that the United States should not be a party to any protocol that did not include binding targets and time-tables for developing countries as well as industrial nations. The Byrd-Hagel Resolution was aimed squarely at India and China. These two countries had established firm positions that they should not be subject to any such targets or timetables. Because the Senate must approve any treaty for it to become effective, the protocol was essentially "dead on arrival," with only the symbolism of signing to provide any US support to the effort.

The Clinton Administration's Efforts

Just a few years earlier, it had seemed to many of us in the Clinton administration that a US-India economic relationship on energy and the environment could be forged that would support cooperation rather than confrontation at Kyoto. This belief was based in part on the perception that US and Indian economic interests in this area of power production were complementary. India had great energy requirements, along with a manifest need to improve its air quality. The United States had some of the leading technologies in both energy and the environment. Because pollution is an indicator of inefficiency, at the Department of Commerce we believed that the United States and India had a common interest in seeing India move toward greater efficiency for both economic environmental reasons. We reasoned that energy and environmental technology exports from the United States could serve to build a US-India community of interest for green energy, which would build support for agreement on common approaches to lessening air pollution. A mechanism for this effort was to be the previously mentioned Trade Promotion Coordinating Committee (TPCC). This interagency group had been established by statute in 1992 and was a favorite initiative of Democratic members of the Senate Banking Committee (which has jurisdiction over export promotion). Chaired by the secretary of commerce, the TPCC had representatives from each agency involved in international trade, including the Department of Energy and the Environmental Protection Agency.

The Environmental Trade Working Group of the TPCC coordinated industry efforts to export US environmental technologies, goods, and services with support from the Department of Commerce, the Department of Energy, the Environmental Protection Agency, and other agencies of the US government. As this group quickly found out, the sale of environmental technology products was intimately bound up with trade and investment in the underlying energy market. There was little interest from the Indian side in the sale or licensing of environmental technology as such. In spite of enthusiasm generated around Secretary Brown's mission, US-India economic engagement around energy was in the doldrums by the time of the Byrd-Hagel Resolution. There was virtually no US-India economic engagement on energy to support US-India cooperation on the Kyoto Protocol. In 1998, the Indian bomb testing took place, and US investment in India slowed to a crawl. Ironically, the resulting sanctions stopped the flow of US financial support for Indian purchases of US clean technology and some programs of the US Agency for International Development regarding the environment.

In the run-up to President Clinton's March 2000 visit, the administration was determined to restart cooperation with India on the environmental front. Both the president and the vice president believed that India could be brought around to a position closer to that of the Clinton administration on environmental issues, including the Kyoto Protocol. The first step in this process was a visit by Secretary of Energy Bill Richardson to India in October 1999. The discussions Richardson had with Minister of External Affairs Jaswant Singh on energy and the environment paralleled those of Deputy Secretary of State Strobe Talbott and Minister Singh on nuclear matters. The result of the Richardson-Singh discussions was a "Joint Statement on Cooperation in Energy and Related Environmental Aspects." The two "largest democracies" noted their willingness to cooperate on both conventional and renewable energy projects. However, the bulk of the Joint Statement was devoted to what India and the United States might do together "to advance the goal of protecting the people of the world from the threat of climate change, while promoting economic growth." The UN Framework Convention on Climate Change (UNFCCC) and the Kyoto Protocol were identified for cooperative efforts. The development of "international rules and procedures for the Kyoto Mechanisms, including the Clean Development Mechanism" was singled out for "working closely together." The Richardson-Singh Joint Statement was a start, or "restart," of US-India attention to Kyoto, energy, and the environment.[42]

On the 2000 Clinton visit itself, there was a major effort to make the environment an important theme. The president used a visit to the Taj Mahal to remind Indians how vulnerable they were to the adverse affects of air pollution. He said, "A constant effort is required to save the Taj Mahal from human environmental degradation—what some scientists call 'marble cancer.' I can't help wondering that if a stone can get cancer, what kind of damage can this pollution do to children?" President Clinton then moved directly to the perils of climate change and to US-India cooperation on the Kyoto Protocol. In conclusion, he said:

And while we work to cooperate between our nations, we must also remember our obligations to realize the promise of the landmark Kyoto Protocol on climate change. For if we act wisely, this agreement can help both the developed and the developing nations to harness the power of the market to build a clean energy future. We must complete the work done in Kyoto so that the United States and other nations can ratify the protocol and it can enter into force.[43]

Clinton announced the resumption of technical assistance from the Department of Energy and the Environmental Protection Agency, along with $200 million in financing for clean energy projects through the US Export-Import Bank and the US Agency for International Development's projects on efficient and clean energy totaling $95 million. Although these programs were rather modest compared with the magnitude of the issue, they were symbolically important. These programs had been stopped or prohibited under the Glenn Amendment sanctions regime (see chapter 2). The announcement was a reminder that the US policy of the sanctions for nuclear testing was at an end and that the United States wished to resume economic engagement for the protection of the environment.

Perhaps most important, Clinton announced an effort to revive private-sector company engagement in the efforts to promote clean energy and ameliorate climate change. According to the president, the US Energy Association and the Confederation of Indian Industries would work in conjunction with the two governments on these issues.[44]

Vice President Gore took up the theme of environmental cooperation when Prime Minister Vajpayee made his reciprocal visit to Washington in September 2000. At a luncheon for the prime minister at the State Department, Gore stressed the need to cooperate on the "inconvenient truth" of climate change. However, there was little enthusiasm shown from either the prime minister or his delegation for work on this issue. The Indian Embassy distributed a background paper that basically reiterated the position that India's only obligations were to receive money and technology in support of its domestic goals to create clean energy.[45] There was basically no US-India business engagement to support reaching accommodation on these issues. The supposed interaction of the US Energy Administration and the Confederation of Indian Industries in creating the private-sector support announced by Clinton in March had not materialized. The Clinton administration's attempt to reengage with India on the environment was too little and too late to have any appreciable results during its tenure.

The George W. Bush Administration's Efforts

With the defeat of Gore by George W. Bush in the presidential election of 2000, the hoped-for US-India cooperation on climate change, championed by the vice president in September, died along with the prospects for any significant participation of the United States in resolving the Kyoto Protocol issues. In one of its first steps, the George W. Bush administration "withdrew" the United States altogether from the protocol. The only action that had been taken by the United States was to affix a symbolic signature to the protocol. Presumably, what was meant by "withdrawal" was that even that symbolic gesture was null and void.[46] The practical effect of the Bush action was to limit US participation in the subsequent Conferences of the Parties to the UNFCCC to mere observation for the remainder of the Bush administration.

President Bush made it plain that one of his objections to the Kyoto Protocol was that it did not require India to take any action. In June 2001, Bush announced a "US Climate Change Initiative." In doing so, he enumerated his reasons for opposing the protocol and included the statement, "India and Germany are among the top emitters, yet India was also exempt from Kyoto."[47]

However, the Bush administration did continue to push US-India joint action in the development of clean energy technology. In biennial forums established during the 2000 Clinton visit, the State Department and the Ministry of External Affairs held bilateral talks on global issues. In the 2002 and 2003 sessions of this Global Issues Forum, cooperation on the development of clean energy technology was featured prominently. In the historic July 18, 2005, Joint Statement that announced the civil nuclear initiative (see chapter 2), there was also a section on "For Energy and the Environment." This section continued a US-India Energy Dialogue and said that India and the United States were committed "to developing and deploying cleaner, more efficient, affordable and diversified energy technologies." This approach was in accordance with the domestically oriented, voluntary approach that President Bush had announced as the policy of his administration on February 14, 2002. Through the end of the Bush administration, the United States and India conducted meetings of the US-India Energy Dialogue. These were government-to-government meetings with associated industry sessions.

Late in the Bush administration, US and India trade associations began to take up the possibility for greater US-India economic engagement on the subject of clean energy. The Confederation of Indian Industries and the US-India Business Council formed a "Green India" initiative that held a conference in Washington in October 2008. US commerce secretary Carlos Gutierrez picked up the emphasis on clean energy. In addition to advocating rapid expansion in civilian nuclear technology, Gutierrez spoke of the opportunities for "sales" of "other clean energy technologies such as wind energy, solar, and biomass" as presenting "opportunities that will yield even more business together."[48] Another Green India conference was held in Delhi the following year with the same themes. At last, there were the first glimmerings of economic engagement that might support US-India inter-action on climate change. However, these activities were not nearly enough to sustain the ambitious political plans of the Obama administration for cli-mate change amelioration.

The Obama Administration's Efforts

Barack Obama was elected on a platform that included a commitment to return to the international climate change process and institute a "cap-and-trade" program for the United States. Shortly after his election, the president-elect wrote to Prime Minister Singh saying that he wanted the United States to work with India on climate change. Both the United States and India appointed special envoys for the subject. For the United States, Washington lawyer Todd Stern was appointed, while India looked to one of its veteran diplomats, Shyam Saran. Obama wanted a forum of both developed and de-veloping countries that would bring the major national players to the table and yet be small enough to produce real progress. On April 27 and 28, 2009, President Obama launched the Major Economies Forum on Energy and Cli-mate.[49] Among the seventeen economies participating, India was prominent in that meeting. However, little progress was made in reconciling the posi-tions of India with those of the United States.

The parties to the UNFCCC set up an ambitious schedule for attempting to reach agreement on a successor to the Kyoto Protocol at Copenhagen in December 2009. A meeting in Bonn on June 1–12, 2009, was to simplify and rationalize a draft but failed to do so. The July meeting of Group of Eight nations in L'Aquila, Italy, offered an opportunity for the Major Economies Forum on Energy and Climate Change to discuss environmental and climate change issues. The seventeen economies of the forum met in a July 9 session cochaired by Obama and Italian prime minister Silvio Berlusconi. However, the Chinese president, Hu Jintao, cut short his participation and left for home to deal with unrest in the western part of China. Without China, the talks were handicapped, to say the least. The forum issued a rather nebu-lous statement.[50] Even this mild measure attracted criticism in India be-cause it referred to a recognition of "the scientific view that the increase in global average temperature above pre-industrial levels ought not to exceed 2 degrees C."[51] The group agreed to meet again at the time of the annual meeting of the UN General Assembly in September. Discussions were also planned for the Group of Twenty (G-20) Summit in Pittsburgh on September 24 and 25.

UN secretary-general Ban Ki-moon assumed leadership of the Major Economies Forum on Energy and Climate Change meeting scheduled for September 22, 2009, in conjunction with the UN General Assembly's annual meeting in New York. Ban styled the session as a "Summit on Climate Change" and opened it to all UN members. The meeting was attended by representatives of some one hundred nations. An Indian, R. K. Pachauri, the chair of the Intergovernmental Panel on Climate Change, spoke after Ban and was followed by Obama. An Indian girl who was thirteen years of age was chosen to speak on behalf of the world's young people.[52] These speeches were followed by roundtables. At the end of the UN meeting, it looked as if the parties were headed toward individual commitments rather than global standards.[53]

Both India and China received favorable commentary based on their willingness to set internal goals. China was particularly praised for Hu Jintao's remarks in linking the cutting of carbon dioxide to gross domestic product (GDP). This was a departure from the previous Chinese and Indian approach of linking such measures to population. Neither the Chinese nor Indian remarks provided any actual numbers.

The climate change portion of the Pittsburgh meetings of the G-20 again was amorphous and vague. For example, the Leaders' Statement issued at the end of the meeting said that the parties "will spare no effort to reach agreement in Copenhagen."[54] Prime Minister Singh's statement on the meeting simply noted, "The G-20 have called for a successful outcome of the UNFCCC at Copenhagen." The most notable development at the Pittsburgh G-20 from an environmental perspective was consideration of the proposal Obama had made at the United Nations for governments to phase out subsidies for fossil fuels. The Leaders' Statement pledged "to phase out and rationalize over the medium term inefficient fossil fuel subsidies while providing targeted support for the poorest."[55] The Indian prime minister's statement said nothing about this pledge. In view of India's numerous subsidies to fossil fuels, the press in India noted this pledge as "one area of concern for India."[56] In defense, a member of the prime minister's delegation said that the G-20 statement applied only to "inefficient" subsidies.[57] The implication was that Indian fossil fuel subsidies were "efficient" and therefore would largely be undisturbed. This clearly was not the meaning ascribed to the resolution by the Americans pushing the proposal.

In reality, neither the September 2009 UN meeting nor the G-20 meeting that dealt with climate change accomplished much. India was waiting to see what the United States would offer. Obama was constrained by the inaction of the US Senate, which had refused to take up climate change legislation but gave strong signals of sticking to its previous position requiring agreed-on cuts from India and China. Realistically, the president had no legislative base upon which to act. Further technical meetings were to be held in October, with a report due by November 15, 2009.

Work in Congress on climate change legislation had begun in the House of Representatives. In June 2009, the House passed a comprehensive clean energy bill. This bill, the "American Clean Energy and Security Act" (ACES),[58] contained global warming provisions compatible with the approach of the Kyoto Protocol. These provisions included a cap-and-trade system and authorization of some funds for the prevention of tropical deforestation and clean technology transfer.

The ACES legislation as passed by the House also included strong protectionist measures. The bill provided allowances to cover the increased costs of "energy intensive, trade-exposed industries," which were specifically designed to cover such sectors as iron, steel, cement, and paper. The legislation also provided for a tariff (creatively called a "border adjustment") for countries that did not join a multilateral agreement. This provision obviously was aimed at India and similar developing countries.

With the fight over health care reform taking much of the Senate's time, it delayed action on ACES at least until after a vote on the highly contested health care legislation. The members of the coalition of organizations supporting ACES seemed determined to build political support for Senate action and were largely silent on issues that would cause difficulties with India and other major developing countries. These supporters mounted a campaign emphasizing the positive aspects of ACES for major US companies.[59] However, these efforts were to no avail. With health care legislation still pending, the Senate had failed to act on ACES by the time of the Copenhagen meeting.

In the run-up to Copenhagen, the Government of India was determined to be seen as a responsible global player. Indian officials had been stung by charges after Kyoto that they were acting in a shortsighted or selfish manner.

However, Indian officials were also acutely aware of the Indian public's political sensitivity to any international action that might be seen as other nations imposing their will on India. India was determined that its position be understood and undertook a vigorous program of public diplomacy to that end. India was at pains to explain why it would not accept outside limitations on its own emissions of greenhouse gases. Indian envoys stressed that under the UNFCCC adopted at Rio de Janeiro in 1992, the developed countries were committed to providing both technology and capital to the developing world to fight climate change. India's argument was that the developed countries had not met these obligations. Particularly prominent in the Indian argument was the fact that the United States produced some 20 tons of carbon dioxide per capita, in contrast to India's 1 ton per capita.[60]

When the coalition government led by the Congress Party was returned to power in the spring of 2009, international leadership on the climate change issue passed to the new minister of the environment, Jairam Ramesh. The appointment of Ramesh and investment of his position with international leadership responsibilities showed that the government wanted to make sure that the issue was handled with intelligence and political sensitivity. Ramesh had been the chief economic adviser to the Congress Party as secretary of its Economic Affairs Division. He was usually an adept politician. In one of his early actions as minister, he obtained a high profile by confronting Hillary Clinton with the parameters of the Indian position on her first visit to India as US secretary of state in July 2009. However, shortly after Clinton's trip to India, the United States and China signed in Washington a memorandum of understanding on climate change, energy, and the environment and announced a large solar initiative.[61] India was now doubly concerned about its international image. It did not want to be perceived in its traditional role of deal breaker, and it was concerned that China was getting ahead of India on the issue of climate change.

Not to be outdone by the Chinese, Ramesh continued his high-profile style with a September 2009 announcement in London that a "breakthrough" had been achieved by India's willingness to impose upon itself numeric limitations. The London announcement appeared to be an exaggeration, because all that India was willing to commit was setting energy efficiency or per capita "targets" that would be nonbinding and unverifiable. Earlier, India had committed to not emitting more greenhouse gases than the Western countries on a per capita basis. However, because India's per capita emissions were so much lower than those of Western countries, this commitment was rather meaningless. Ramesh told an American audience in New York not to expect "miracles" at Copenhagen and emphasized the desirability of technological cooperation financed by the developed countries.

At the UN climate summit organized by the UN secretary-general before the UN General Assembly's annual meeting in September 2009, Indian minister of external affairs S. M. Krishna played the leading role in stating his country's position that climate change activity not be a brake on its development. However, Ramesh was determined to maintain leadership on the issue. China had received more favorable international coverage than India. Much of this coverage was based on President Hu's speech that seemed to indicate China's willingness to consider limitations based on greenhouse gas emissions per unit of GDP, a relationship known as "carbon intensity." Hu's statement was read by some as contrary to the Indian position that equity required that the analysis take place only on the basis of greenhouse gas emissions per capita, a relationship referred to as "carbon efficiency."

Ramesh moved to reassert his leadership position internally within the Indian government. For October, Ramesh organized a meeting in New Delhi for the purposes of showing India-China solidarity on climate change. He also wrote a supposedly secret note to Prime Minister Singh in which he advocated Indian flexibility on the Kyoto Protocol. Ramesh suggested moving from the so-called Group of Seventy-Seven developing nations to the G-20 group of major economies as the vehicle for advancing the Indian position. Unfortunately for Ramesh, the document was leaked to the press. Opponents of the government immediately attempted to link Ramesh's comments to the influence of the United States. This influence was widely decried by the opposition as another example, along with the civil nuclear deal, of the Singh government being too close to the United States for India's good.[62] The uproar created by Ramesh's letter diminished the effect of the memorandum of understanding he signed on behalf of India with the Chinese stating that "developed countries should take the lead in and continue to reduce their greenhouse gas emissions and providing financial resources, technology transfer, and capacity building support to developing countries."[63]

It fell to the prime minister to quiet the controversy created by Ramesh's letter. Singh did this in an address to a conference in New Delhi on climate change and the development and transfer of technology. In his October 22, 2009, address Singh confirmed the orthodoxies of India's international position on climate change. Thus, as Singh prepared for a visit to the United States in late November 2009, India was firm in the positions to which it had clung since the 1992 meeting of the UNFCCC in Rio de Janeiro. The essential positions of India were:

1. India cannot and will not compromise on development, meaning that it would accept no limitations that would harm its GDP growth rate.
2. India is not the cause of the climate change problem. The major cause is the accumulated stock of greenhouse gases in the atmosphere, mainly the result of carbon-based industrial activity in developed countries over the past two centuries.
3. Equating greenhouse gas emissions across nations on a per capita basis is the only just and fair basis for a long-term global arrangement on climate change that is truly equitable. On that basis, India's carbon dioxide emissions are only 1.1 tons compared to over 20 tons for the United States and in excess of 10 tons for most countries that belong to the Organization for Economic Cooperation and Development.
4. India needs technology transfer and adaptation assistance that must be financed by the developed countries. Unless this assistance is forthcoming, as Indian GDP rises, its energy use and total emissions will rise.
5. India is doing its part to keep its emissions footprint within levels that are sustainable and equitable. On its own and not subject to international agreements, India will focus on achieving time-bound outcomes related to the energy efficiency of its economy, the share of renewables in its fuel mix, and several other sector-specific initiatives.

These objectives are reflected in India's National Action Plan on climate change, which contains eight National Missions focusing on both mitigation and adaptation.[64]

India did not want to move at Copenhagen unless there was solid reason to believe that it would benefit economically. India sought financing from the developed world for its efforts to combat climate change. At the same time, India did not want to be seen as a stumbling block or as having ceded major developing-country leadership to China. For its part, the United States wanted to move back to a cooperative leadership position on climate change and produce results that could have a significant effect. However, again the reality was that without congressional action, the United States could not make any binding commitments.

Back home after the Copenhagen meeting culminated with the Copenhagen Accord, Ramesh portrayed the accord as a triumph for India in maintaining the "two-track" process that India saw embodied in the first Rio de Janeiro UN climate change meeting and continuing with Kyoto and then Bali. Basically, the two tracks were (1) developing-country cooperation through the receipt of resources from the developed countries in return for implementation of climate change mitigating actions, and (2) the developed countries' commitment to binding reductions in emissions. "UNFCCC will continue to proceed in two tracks as set out in the Bali Road Map," Ramesh told the upper house of the Indian Parliament, the Rajya Sabha.[65] He further represented the "Copenhagen Green Climate Fund" funding as "approaching" $30 billion during 2010–12 and $100 billion a year by 2020 as an achievement favorable to India. The statement by the prime minister that India would cut "emission intensity of our GDP growth by around 20 percent by 2020 in comparison to 2005"[66] was portrayed simply as a unilateral action undertaken as "moving on the road" to a goal "to the benefit of our own people.[67] Even though China had made a statement of cutting its emissions intensity approximately twice that of India, Ramesh was able to represent the Indian achievements as being in the leadership vanguard through joint action of the so-called BASIC countries—Brazil, South Africa, India, and China. Thus, the Singh government was able to claim with plausibility that it had met all its negotiating goals at Copenhagen. India had not moved significantly. What movement it had made was in return for a pledge of significant funds. Yet India was in the forefront of the negotiations and had not been portrayed as an impediment to the outcome.

Ramesh spoke in his address to the Rajya Sabha of the BASIC countries' interaction with President Obama. From his perspective, Obama characterized the Copenhagen Accord as "a meaningful and unprecedented breakthrough."[68] By this, he apparently meant the provision in the accord for India and the other BASIC countries to list the "mitigation actions" that they intended to take and to report on them. Perhaps the "breakthrough" was actually just that the United States was again interacting with India and other countries in the UN climate change process. As far as producing any results that would have a significant effect on climate change, the commitments for any such achievements had simply been deferred for a year. The prospects for progress dimmed even further as preparatory talks for the December 2010 meeting of the Parties to the UNFCCC in Cancún turned rancorous. Poor nations outside the BASIC grouping objected to even including the Copenhagen Accord in the agenda for Cancún.[69] The inability of the United States and India to agree on a common approach to climate change, while not unique to the US-India relationship, was a continuing factor in the deferral.

Economic Engagement to Support
Cooperation on Climate Change

Missing from the US-India dialogue on climate change at Copenhagen was sufficient support from relevant bilateral economic engagement. As the US-India conversation on the environment and climate change continues, there is a need to find the sort of support that greater US-India economic engagement on electric power might have provided. India and the United States needed further economic engagement to support the sort of deal that would have allowed the United States and India to participate in a Copenhagen Accord as a successor to the Kyoto Protocol. Such engagement can still be built; its basics can be US-India public-private electrical energy projects that involve clean energy technologies. There is increasing interest by US firms in the Indian renewables and clean energy technology markets. Several renewable and clean energy projects might have provided support for a binding deal at Copenhagen. Such projects can still provide support for further US-India cooperation on energy and the environment, including climate change. The following are examples of such projects.

In the summer of 2001, Bill Clinton made his first trip to India after having finished his term as president. The trip was made in conjunction with the American India Foundation and its activities in supporting earthquake relief in the desert areas of Kutch in Gujarat State. In addition to the startling human need created by the earthquake, two other factors were apparent to some of us who accompanied Clinton on that trip. The first was the obvious factor of abundant sunlight, and the second was the strategic location next to the Pakistan border. In the nearby salt marsh flats of the Rann of Kutch, in 1965 India and Pakistan had fought in a brief but sharp encounter as a prelude to their second war over Kashmir.

On September 8, 2009, the Clinton Climate Initiative, a program of the William J. Clinton Foundation, signed a preliminary agreement with the Government of Gujarat to promote a 3,000-megawatt solar plant. According to Ira Magaziner, who signed the agreement on behalf of the foundation, Gujarat had acted to set up the project while others only talked about renewable energy. The Gujarat project was one of four being promoted by Clinton, the others being in California, South Africa, and Australia.[70] The foundation's role in the project was to help bring manufacturers and power generators into the project as well as provide access to international financing. According to a State of Gujarat official, contracts valued at $10 billion are to be awarded. The project is said to be the world's largest, outranking a planned

2,000-megawatt Chinese facility to be built by US First Solar Inc. The Gujarat project is to fit within the Government of India's announced National Solar Mission, which envisages having 20,000 megawatts of solar capacity by 2020. India receives some 5,000 trillion kWh of solar energy a year while having just 2,100 megawatts of installed solar capacity.[71] Because of both where it is and what it does, this Kutch project has significant strategic implications.

General Electric also has a clean energy project that exemplifies the sort of economic engagement that can build support for US-India cooperation on climate change. General Electric, the world's second-largest manufacturer of wind turbines, announced plans in 2008 for setting up a new wind generator plant in South India. This project fits into India's wind energy initiatives.

India has shown significant interest in public-private cooperation to increase wind energy production. India has put into place an accelerated depreciation benefit of 80 percent, together with other tax incentives, for the construction of wind energy facilities. The result has been a boom in wind power construction and installation. India has risen rapidly through the international ranks to become the fourth-largest wind energy country on the basis of installed capacity. The tax-driven nature of the Indian wind power program has received criticism for being oriented toward construction rather than the actual production of power. One such critic has argued that while the country has more than 8,700 megawatts of installed wind power capacity, this capacity only operates with an average plant load of 15 percent. This means that the wind plants are putting out only about one-seventh of the electric power they are capable of producing.[72] In any case, India's rapid rise in installed capacity has also produced a local Indian corporation, Suzlon, that is ranked fifth in the world in wind-turbine manufacturing. Suzlon now has operations in twenty-one countries, including the United States. There is a major Suzlon operation in Pipestone, Minnesota.[73]

Presumably, the new General Electric plant for wind turbines in South India will be intimately involved in the development of Indian clean energy projects. At present, fifteen of these projects are listed for India, ranging in size from 4 to more than 50 megawatts.[74] Typical of these projects is a 12-megawatt wind farm located in the village of Radhapuram in Tamil Nadu State at the tip of the Indian subcontinent. This project is to supply electricity for factories that produce thermomechanically treated bar steel and stainless steel and components. Throughout the states of Maharashtra, Karnataka, Tamil Nadu, and Andhra Pradesh, there are similar projects. With two of the world's leading turbine manufacturers and a common commitment from the United States and India to the Clean Development Mechanism of the Kyoto Protocol (see below), US-India economic engagement in wind energy offers significant opportunities to support strategic cooperation on the environment.

US-India civil nuclear cooperation is discussed in chapter 2 of this book. As noted there, economic engagement on this subject has a strong environmental dimension. This engagement can make a difference in promoting closer cooperation not only on strategic security issues but also in the area of climate change.

US-India economic engagement in the production of cleaner power from coal remains fundamental to providing an economic basis for US-India cooperation on climate change. India relies on coal for more than half its electricity, and it is likely to remain dependent on this fuel in the immediate future. The lack of US-India engagement in the Ultra Mega Power Projects was discussed above. With the increase in the domestic production of natural gas, US-India cooperation in converting from coal to gas may take place in spite of the Enron Dabhol debacle. However, for the immediate future, US-India engagement on coal is essential.

The US FutureGen Project would seem to hold promise for the sort of public-private partnership that may provide a basis for US-India economic engagement in the field of cleaner coal. When President George W. Bush announced this carbon capture storage scheme, India was the first international partner for the project. After the Bush administration canceled the project (the estimated costs rose, and Texas was not chosen as the site for the project), India maintained its willingness to continue participating with the United States in carbon sequestration projects. The Obama administration has now revived the FutureGen project, which is to be conducted at an Illinois location. The FutureGen Industrial Alliance, Inc., a nonprofit industrial consortium composed of more than twenty of the largest coal producers and users in the world, is the corporate vehicle for the project. The alliance plans to invest some $400 million in the project, and the Obama administration has pledged about $1 billion in economic stimulus funds. A new cooperative agreement was signed between the US Department of Energy and the alliance in September 2009. India is an active member of the Carbon Sequestration Leadership Forum sponsored by the Department of Energy. Thus, the FutureGen project, combined with US private companies' participation in Indian coal-fired power projects, seems promising. Such participation can be the sort of economic engagement on "cleaner coal" that could support greater cooperation from India on the environment.

US-India economic engagement on carbon capture and storage must be in more than research and development. As India's power minister, Sushil-kumar Shinde, warned, "We are willing to be participants in any research and development on Carbon Capture and Storage, but unless the commercial viability of the technology is fully established and its safety features amply proved, it would just not be appropriate for India to take up such a project even at the demonstration level."[75] As usual, India is worried about the cost. Shinde has said, "I understand that Carbon Capture and Storage will double the cost of generation and that would definitely be difficult to accept for developing nations."[76]

A related cleaner coal technology project has been offered by General Electric for US-India engagement. GE is a leader in integrated gasification combined-cycle (IGCC) technology. The IGCC technology takes heavy fuels, such as coal and heavy oils; cleans them; and converts them into fuel for gas turbines. GE has supplied turbines for most of the world's operating IGCC plants. GE has worked with Bechtel to develop a standardized commercial offering for optimized IGCC plants, that is, IGCC plants that work as efficiently as theoretically possible to remove greenhouse gases. The technology has several benefits. It uses less water, produces fewer emissions, and has the potential to remove mercury and carbon dioxide at a lower cost than conventional plants. The IGCC technology is presently being used for a plant in the State of Andhra Pradesh. Thus, increased economic engagement involving this cleaner coal technology seems imminently feasible.

The Kyoto Protocol itself has a means to promote US-India economic engagement on projects supportive of further US-India environmental cooperation. The Clean Development Mechanism (CDM), which is defined in Article 12 of the protocol, provides that a party undertaking greenhouse gas reduction commitments may obtain help in meeting those commitments by entering into agreements for common development projects with developing countries that have no such commitments. United Nations examples of common development projects in India would be a rural electrification solar energy installation or the replacement of existing boilers with those that are more energy efficient. A CDM Executive Board oversees a process whereby projects are vetted for their compliance with the requirement that a CDM project provide a reduction in emissions that would not have occurred but for the project. A Designated National Authority must approve the project in the developing country. The UNFCCC must also approve the project.

In the case of India, the Designated National Authority is an interagency body denominated the National Clean Development Mechanism Authority, which is composed of six ministries and agencies plus the Planning Commission. The ministries designated are External Affairs, Finance, Power, and Nonconventional Energy Sources. The agencies are the Department of Industrial Policy and Promotion in the Ministry of Commerce and Industry and the Department of Climate Change in the Ministry of Environment and Forests. The secretary in the Ministry of Environment and Forests is the chairperson, and one of his colleagues from the ministry is a "member-secretary." Projects are assessed for their contributions to social, economic, environmental, and technological well-being. Projects must also meet two "additionality" requirements. The first of these is specified in the Kyoto Protocol to require reductions in greenhouse gas emissions over a baseline that would have occurred without the project. India specifies that these additional reductions must be "measurable and long term." In addition to the reduction additionality, India specifies that the credits achieved by the projects must not be paid for out of "official development assistance," that is, foreign aid. This last additionality assures that projects are bringing funds to India over and above those secured from foreign aid, on the theory that India would receive those funds in any event.[77]

India has been the most active of all developing countries in the CDM program. When it first commenced participation, it led in applications to the UNFCCC.[78] Now its expertise is sufficient for it to offer the lessons of its experience to other participants in the South Asia Association for Regional Cooperation.[79] As of May 1, 2009, India had registered 448 projects. The leading category of registrations was for biomass projects (30 percent), followed by wind (19 percent), waste gas and heat utilization (14 percent), hydroelectric power (12 percent), and energy efficiency (11 percent).

The Bottom Line

The failure of the Dabhol project and other fast-track initiatives was more than a commercial disaster. This failure set back the cause of US-India economic engagement on energy and the environment across the board. Such engagement is one of the few instruments of statecraft available to the United States in bridging the gulf between it and India on such issues as climate change. However, there still are available opportunities for greater US-India bilateral cooperation on renewable energy and cleaner coal technologies. A public-private approach focused on these opportunities is ideally suited to both countries. The Obama administration is determined to make renewable and cleaner energy technology and production one of its signature issues. The government of Manmohan Singh has a similar interest. During the first term of the United Progressive Alliance–led Parliament, India became one of the few countries in the world to establish a Ministry of New and Renewable Energies. This approach presents bureaucratic challenges as the Ministry of Power vies for power with the new ministry. However, the establishment of the Ministry of New and Renewable Energies certainly shows India's determination to make progress in this field.

India repeatedly has demonstrated its interest in the CDMs of the Kyoto Protocol. Thus far, no program has been developed that will bring these US and Indian interests together to build support for a US-India accommodation on climate change. Many Indian leaders now realize that India cannot simply demand that the United States and other developed economies send money and technology to India for India to use as it sees fit. Likewise, many US officials, including members of Congress, feel that America cannot defer action on climate change indefinitely by insisting that India accept restrictions similar to those that will be imposed on the developed nations. Engagement in these sorts of projects should be a part of the US strategy to develop cooperation with India. This means that India and the United States should work together on establishing the profiles for energy plants that will be attractive to private-sector investment for generation. The original fast-tract projects did not work. The Ultra Mega projects did not attract significant US interest. A third generation of electric power generation, transmission, and distribution projects should be jointly identified and advocated by the US and Indian governments.

No deal was reached at Copenhagen, in large part because the US president and Congress made little progress in reaching an agreement on the basics of a climate change bill before the meeting. Congressional "deniers" of the relationship between human action and global warming continued to oppose significant actions to fight climate change. Indian leaders took refuge in their perception that India is the "greenest" major economy in the world and that environmental limitations would hurt the nation's growth prospects. Because the Kyoto Protocol does not expire until 2012, the temptation to delay action was just too great at Copenhagen. That dynamic of delay will probably continue, at least until immediately before the deadline date. The next steps in strategic cooperation on the issue of global climate change will require greater US-India cooperation—which would have been forthcoming if India and the United States had been able to engage economically over a program to produce cleaner energy at the time of fast track. Greater cooperation on environmental matters can still be fostered by a rejuvenated program of economic engagement through the sorts of renewable and cleaner energy projects outlined above. Such a program cannot be a success without strong governmental and private-sector involvement.

As indicated above and as discussed below, productive public-private involvement requires that economic engagement be included as an element of US strategic planning. An example of the need for such planning in the security arena involves US-India interaction on the issue of the Iran-Pakistan-India pipeline. We turn now to a consideration of that episode.

Chapter 6

Energy and Defense Security: The Iran Pipeline Example

I am realistic enough to realize there are many risks because, considering all the uncertainties of the situation there in Iran, I don't know if any international consortium of bankers would probably underwrite this. But we are in a state of preliminary negotiations, and the background of this is we desperately need the supply of gas that Iran has.

—Prime Minister Manmohan Singh, July 19, 2005, *Washington Post*

If India goes ahead with a pipeline to Iran I will block the civil nuclear deal. I can and I will. It is just that simple. India must decide.

—Representative Tom Lantos, chairman, Foreign Affairs Committee, US House of Representatives, November 15, 2007

Washington is a dreary city in the late fall. The beauty of the autumn leaves is gone. The cold and damp of winter are setting in, and the cherry blossoms of spring are but a distant hope. However, it is often one of the few times when work gets done in the capital city. Congress is in town. The president is attending to business, and the phalanx of journalists, lawyers, lobbyists, and interest groups involved in the process of making policy and laws are everywhere. All are rushing to accomplish something before the holiday recesses and, in 2007, the coming election year.

Swadesh Chatterjee, chairman of the US-India Friendship Council, and I, on behalf of the US-India Business Council, felt ourselves fortunate to have gotten an audience with Representative Tom Lantos, chairman of the House Foreign Affairs Committee. The hopes for the US-India civil nuclear deal seemed as dreary as the Washington weather. Although the 123 Agree-

172

ment had been reached with India to govern major points in conducting US-India trade in nuclear technology, the deal had become mired in Indian politics. The deal would not come to fruition if the Indian Parliament could not be persuaded to back it. Even if the prime minister could extract approval from Parliament, other major steps still had to be taken. Agreements with the International Atomic Energy Agency and the Nuclear Suppliers Group would still have to be reached before the matter could be brought back to the US Congress for final approval.

Although the prospects for any immediate action seemed dim, Chatterjee and I were making the rounds of major supporters in Congress to see whether the coalition of Democratic and Republican representatives and senators who had pushed the Hyde Act to passage in 2006 (see chapter 2) was still in place in case the initiative should be approved in India and action would become possible in Congress in 2008. Thus far, the signs were good. Those who had supported the deal in the past seemed to view the matter as settled business and appeared ready to move forward for final approval should the opportunity arise. However, we were in for a shock from the chairman.

We were shown into the chairman's office. Lantos greeted us from the couch, where he sat next to a small white dog. As the silver-haired chairman, the only survivor of a Nazi concentration camp to ever serve in Congress, stroked his pet with obvious affection, he asked, "What can I do for you gentlemen?" I remember thinking that this meeting was not starting well. The chairman knew both Chatterjee and me from the 2005–6 campaign to pass the legislation making possible US-India civil nuclear relations. He knew Chatterjee particularly well as a leader among Indian Americans who had been strong supporters of the chairman in the last election cycle. My uneasy feeling was confirmed when Lantos responded to our entreaties concerning the continued importance of US-India friendship and positive approval of the deal should the opportunity arise in the coming year.

Lantos explained his love of India and his long association with Indians. However, it was not India that was primarily on his mind but Iran. He said he understood India's historical ties with Iran and its predecessor Persian states. He respected India's sovereignty and right to make its own foreign policy decisions. He also understood India's energy needs. He said he did not object to India's relationship with Iran. However, he did object in the strongest possible terms to India's taking any action that would strengthen the present government of Iran.

Chairman Lantos then made the statement quoted above with regard to the proposed Iran-Pakistan-India gas pipeline. He was adamant that such interaction with Iran was unacceptable to him. He pointed out his legislation to strengthen US sanctions on supporting the Iranian petroleum industry in any way, saying "This sanctions charade must stop." His reference was to the relative ineffectiveness in his mind of the administration's enforcement of the existing Iranian sanctions legislation.

Before this meeting with Chairman Lantos, I had thought that the issue of India-Iran relations over energy had been put to rest insofar as the civil nuclear deal was concerned. I should have known not to underestimate the symbolic importance of the proposed pipeline from Iran to India. This symbol was as important to India as it was to the United States. However, in terms of economic engagement over energy, the issue is far from merely symbolic.

India's Oil and Natural Gas Needs

Oil and its derivatives account for some 30 percent of India's total energy consumption.[1] Although India has made commitments to nonpetroleum fuels, petroleum products still continue to account for the overwhelming majority of fuels used in India's transportation sector.[2] India is dependent on imports for some 70 percent of its oil. The gap between consumption and domestic production continues to grow. This increase not only is due to consumption but also indicates declining domestic oil production. Indian crude oil production for its fiscal year 2008–9 was almost 2 percent lower than for the previous year. Though India is presently the seventh-largest net importer of oil, the US Department of Energy expects it to become the fourth-largest importer by 2025. Nearly 75 percent of India's crude oil imports originate in the states bordering on the Persian Gulf.

Oil is not only important for India in satisfying domestic needs. India takes pride in its increasing refinery capacity. Private refining for export has particular domestic political salience, with such huge projects as those undertaken by Reliance Industries Ltd. receiving considerable political attention. There is national pride that the largest refinery complex in the world is at the Reliance Jamnagar site in the State of Gujarat. Thanks to the business of importing oil and exporting the refined products, in 2008–9 India exported more petroleum products than it imported. Exports in 2008–9 were approximately 37 million metric tons, while imports amounted to approximately 18 million metric tons.[3]

To some extent, natural gas can be used as substitute to meet India's dependence on oil, and it is of increasing importance to India in its own right.

In the 2008–9 fiscal year, gas made up about 8 percent of India's energy consumption, of which about 25 percent was imported.[4] As with oil, growth is the most salient aspect of India's gas consumption, which is expected to rise 4.2 percent a year during the period 2006–30.[5] Although domestic discoveries in the Bay of Bengal are adding considerably to Indian production of natural gas, imports are expected to play a prominent role into the foreseeable future. Presently, all natural gas being imported into the country comes in as liquefied natural gas (LNG), of which Qatar is presently the largest source. LNG and the facilities necessary for reception and regasification are expensive. A pipeline is considerably more efficient and less expensive as a delivery mechanism. Thus, a pipeline effectively lowers the cost of the gas.

India is acutely aware of its dependence on foreign oil and natural gas. Fluctuations in price are a major political concern for any Indian government. The prices of all types of petroleum and gas fuels are strictly controlled and heavily subsidized. Any increase in the price of fuel is a major political event in India. Alternatively, the failure to raise prices to meet market costs results in the central government taking on an increased subsidy burden. Thus, India, like other economies dependent on energy imports, wishes to assure itself of adequate supplies at the lowest possible prices.

Given its historic reluctance to embrace market solutions with regard to oil and gas, India has turned to a number of government-driven strategies to ameliorate its petroleum difficulties. Observing the policy of its neighbor China, India has embarked upon an "equity oil and gas" program as one such strategy. This strategy entails government-owned Indian companies acquiring various rights in oil and natural gas production around the world. India's concern is not so much that oil and gas will become unavailable as it is that the price will rise in an unacceptable manner. There is a particular concern that the price rises of recent years have been based in large part on speculation rather than supply and demand. In response to these concerns, India has expressed interest in going beyond a policy of acquiring oil and gas properties to the creation of a consortium of Asian consuming nations that would act as an alternative to present marketing arrangements.

India's "Equity Oil and Gas" Ambitions

Oil and Natural Gas Corporation Ltd. (ONGC) is India's leading petroleum production company. Predominantly state-owned, its subsidary, ONGC Videsh Ltd. (OVL), is charged with implementing the government's equity oil and gas policy, whereby India competes with the oil and gas production companies of other nations. Where the competing companies are owned by other nations, the competition produces a direct international contest for the best and cheapest sources of supply. India has not been notably successful in this competition. In particular, India has often been bested by the state-owned companies of China. India has sought to ameliorate this competition by signing memoranda with China for cooperation in the overseas production of oil and gas.[6] In reality, these attempts to lessen competition have had little effect. Indeed, the entire equity oil and gas policy has had little discernible effect on supply or prices in India. Nevertheless, ONGC Videsh, and by derivation its corporate parent, the Ministry of Petroleum, and the national government itself, all take pride in acquisition and production agreements that stretch from Russia through the Middle East and Africa and even to Latin America.[7] Iran is particularly a country of OVL interest for such agreements. China's involvement with oil and gas in Iran seems a spur to Indian involvement. Indian oil and gas officials do not want to be bested by China—in Iran or anywhere else.

The United States' Oil and Natural Gas Needs

The profile of the United States' dependence on foreign sources of petroleum is somewhat similar to India's. The United States is dependent on oil and its derivatives for about 40 percent of its energy and most of the energy used in transportation. The United States imports about 66 percent of the crude oil processed in its refineries. About 57 percent of the petroleum, meaning both crude oil and refined products like gasoline, consumed by the United States is from foreign sources. However, unlike India, almost half of US petroleum imports come from the Western Hemisphere. About 16 percent of the crude oil imported into the United States is from the Persian Gulf countries. Nevertheless, Persian Gulf oil is more important to the United States than the percentage of imports from that region would indicate. Because the Persian Gulf countries account for about 30 percent of the world's oil production capacity,[8] any significant disruption of that production would have an immediate adverse impact on the price of oil worldwide. For the United States and India, the sharp increase in prices brought about by a disruption in the supply of Persian Gulf oil could be catastrophic.

The United States imports about 15 percent of the natural gas it consumes. Almost all this gas is presently delivered by pipelines. Canada and

Mexico are the leading sources. Shipments of LNG to the United States are relatively small, having varied between 1 and 3 percent during the period 2004–9. The United States sources most of its imported LNG from the Caribbean. With the rising prices of domestically produced gas and gas imported from Canada by pipeline, LNG imports are expected to increase. India's chief supplier of LNG, Qatar, is projected to also become a more important supplier to the United States.

The Effect of Foreign Oil and Natural Gas Interests on US-India Relations

Although India is sometimes criticized for attempting to emulate China and its "equity oil and gas" strategy, privately owned US oil and natural gas companies pursue a similar approach rather than simply relying on international markets. Although US oil companies do not have reserve holdings of a size approaching those of the national oil and gas companies in the nations belonging to the Organization of the Petroleum Exporting Countries, US companies have significant equity holdings both domestically and internationally. Eight of the top fifty oil companies by reserve holdings are US companies. By way of comparison, no Indian companies are in the top fifty companies by amount of reserves.[9] Theoretically, Indian competition with US companies for equity oil and gas could be a factor in causing friction between the United States and India. In reality, the Indian effort is relatively so small that the possible irritation from this particular program has overall been of little importance to the relationship. However, as we shall see, with regard to Iran, the Indian fascination with equity oil and gas is of more significance to the US-India relationship.

The similarities between the United States and India with regard to their petroleum and natural gas profiles provide more cooperative than competitive aspects to their worldwide strategic perspectives. Both nations are concerned about protecting the stability of their foreign sources and lines of supply. This concern extends to worldwide stability and the protection of transportation routes—particularly for the Persian Gulf region generally, where both countries have strong vested energy interests. For this reason, both India and the United States tend to view US-India cooperation as valuable in promoting stability in the Persian Gulf region. This policy of strategic cooperation extends to protection of the means of transporting oil and gas through the Straits of Hormuz (between the Persian Gulf and the Indian

Ocean), along the shipping routes of the Indian Ocean, and through the Straits of Malacca (between the Indian Ocean and the South China Sea). US cooperation with India in maintaining the security of the straits and the Indian Ocean sea lanes has been ongoing for more than a decade. In 2007, the United States, India, Japan, and Australia conducted a large-scale naval exercise dubbed Malabar 07. The United States contributed seventeen ships to this effort, including a nuclear-powered aircraft carrier and a nuclear-powered submarine. India contributed seven ships, including its aircraft carrier and a helicopter launch vessel.[10]

This naval cooperation continues. In May 2009, the navies of the United States, India, and Japan jointly maneuvered off Okinawa.[11] Joint action between the United States and India on piracy is now commonplace. Thus, common economic factors play a significant role in promoting strategic cooperation and ameliorating friction between the United States and India about both the global and Middle Eastern energy scenarios. However, with regard to Iran, these commonalities on the Persian Gulf generally do not dispose of differences in strategic policy.

Like India, the United States also has indirect Iranian economic interests that militate against a complete stoppage of trade with Iran in the oil and gas sector. The stoppage of Iranian oil exports itself would have worldwide price effects simply by constricting supply.[12] Because Iran is the world's fourth-largest exporter of crude oil, and given that petroleum products are fungible, there have been allegations that stopping Iran's oil exports would affect US companies directly. Because of the difficulty in tracing the raw material that goes into refined products, there may be petroleum derived from Iranian oil that is being used in the United States in spite of the legal constraints discussed below.[13]

Further, several of the United States' closest allies import significant amounts of Iranian oil. Japan, South Korea, and Taiwan are leading Iranian oil customers.[14] Pakistan, upon which the United States is heavily dependent for assistance in the war on Islamic extremists, imports oil from Iran and continues to pursue a joint gas pipeline project with Iran.[15] US interference with these exports would have adverse effects on US relations with these countries.

Some US products of importance to the Iranian energy industry were sold in Iran through foreign-owned dealerships, such as the Swiss business that sells Caterpillar equipment in Tehran. Among foreign subsidiaries of US companies identified in the recent past as doing indirect business in Iran are those that have been connected to Foster Wheeler, Natco Group, Overseas Shipholding Group, UOP (a Honeywell subsidiary), Itron, Fluor, Flow-serve, Parker Drilling, Vantage Energy Services, and Weatherford.[16]

In spite of these common interests, there are significant US-India economic engagement asymmetries when it comes to Iran. Iran is responsible for about 16 percent of India's crude oil imports, while the United States presently imports none directly from Iran. Iran is India's second-leading source of crude oil.[17] From an Indian perspective, there is no feasible alternative to this energy supply. India's state-owned oil companies—ONGC Videsh, Ltd., Indian Oil Corporation Limited, and Oil India Limited—hold an interest in the Farsi Offshore Block in the Persian Gulf, where a development plan is in progress.[18] Indian companies obtained contracts for the development of a free trade zone port at the Iranian town of Chabahar on the Gulf of Oman. Indian companies also have been developing rail and road connections to the Chabahar port.[19] Of the forty-one firms the US Government Accountability Office identified in March 2010 as having commercial activity in the Iranian oil, gas, and petrochemical sectors, five were listed as located in India and a sixth, Hinduja, has its major activities in India. This was the largest number of such firms for any single country.[20] Reliance Industries was shipping significant amounts of gasoline to Iran. However, it claims to have stopped importation from Iran and says that all its exports of gasoline now go to the United States.[21] The chief incentives to this change in the course of action by Reliance seem to be the attraction of the US market and the roughly $900 million in US Export-Import Bank guarantees that it secured for its Gujarat refinery complex.

The foregoing is the economic and energy context in which the controversy between the United States and India over the Iran-Pakistan-India pipeline should be understood. Superficially, the project would seem economically viable because India's energy needs are so acute and Iran's natural gas supplies are so abundant and relatively close at hand. There are more similarities than differences in the US and Indian perspectives on the international sourcing of oil and natural gas generally. However, there is a basic US-India tension between the economic similarities in US and Indian oil and gas importation interests and differences over Iran as an important source. Economic engagement between the United States and India over the issue of oil and gas is largely indirect. The United States and India do not directly collaborate on oil and gas sourcing, and competition on this issue is rather insignificant. However, the indirect nature of the context makes economic engagement no less important as a part of the United States' and India's strategic considerations concerning the Iran-Pakistan-India pipeline.

Let us now examine this pipeline controversy itself for lessons in the importance of economic engagement to the status of this iconic issue.

The Historic Roots and Checkered Progress of the Proposed Iran-Pakistan-India Pipeline

The Iran-Pakistan-India (IPI) pipeline was proposed after the Iranian revolution and US hostage crisis of 1979 but well in advance of the US-Iran conflict over the Iranian nuclear program. Ali Shams Ardekani, an Iranian energy economist who had served as deputy foreign minister, teamed with Rajendra K. Pachauri to make the initial proposal in 1989.[22] India was the focus of the consumption end of the project from the very first. Ardekani initially envisaged the project as transmitting natural gas to "the Indian subcontinent not just from Iran but included sourcing from Qatar and even Turkmenistan as well."[23] Ardekani thought of the IPI pipeline chiefly in terms of the economic benefits of the piped gas over more expensive LNG. Foreshadowing his later fame in regard to the Nobel Prize, Pachauri emphasized the environmental benefits as well as the potential for promoting peace in the region. Such a pipeline would be a means to augment Indian energy supplies with a fuel that was cleaner than coal and oil. When confronted with the India-Pakistan hostility issue, Pachauri noted that the gas pipeline from the former Soviet Union to Western Europe was negotiated at the height of the Cold War and was a force for stability.[24]

However, more than twenty years after the IPI gas pipeline was first proposed, the project has yet to be commenced. More important, India's participation now seems highly unlikely. India did not attend Iran-Pakistan talks on the project in 2008, and it did not enter into a revised pricing formula that Iran and Pakistan signed in January 2009.[25] Significantly, the Indian government's present five-year plan, which extends through 2012, does not project any gas from the IPI pipeline. What are the factors that have militated against Indian participation in the IPI pipeline project?

The United States' Experience with Sanctions and India's Behavior

In its efforts to change the behavior of Iran with regard to its nuclear program, the United States has resorted to sanctions that increasingly affect the economic interests of such "third-party" nations as India. As discussed below, these sanctions are the sort of "negative economic engagement" actions that are seen as an alternative to military action. It remains to be seen whether these sanctions will have an effect generally on the conduct of India vis-à-vis Iran. However, thus far, sanctions have apparently not been a significant factor affecting Indian participation in the IPI project.

In part, this lack of effect may be a reflection of the general ineffectiveness of sanctions. Many have questioned the effectiveness of sanctions.[26] This general criticism applies directly to Iranian sanctions. The US Government Accountability Office has deemed the impact of sanctions in furthering US objectives regarding Iran as "unclear."[27] The uncertain effect of sanctions with regard to Iran does not come from a lack of experience with such measures. Sanctions were a part of the Jimmy Carter administration's response to seizure of American hostages at the time of the Iranian Revolution in 1979. With the return of the hostages, the sanctions were removed. However, a ban on imports of Iranian goods and services was reinstated in October 1987 by executive order. The effect on the behavior of the Iranian government was minimal.

In 1995, Iran opened its oil and natural gas industry to foreign investment. The US administration and Congress seized on this development as presenting an opportunity to bring further economic pressure on Iran. On May 6, 1995, President Bill Clinton issued Executive Order 12959 banning US companies from trading with or investing in Iran. The forerunner of the present Iran Sanctions Act (ISA; then called the Iran Libya Sanctions Act) was signed into law on August 5, 1996. The crux of the ISA was to require the president to impose at least two of a list of seven sanctions on any foreign company that invests more than $20 million in one year in Iran's energy sector. The intent was to deny Iran the resources to develop a nuclear program as well as for supporting organizations like Hezbollah, Hamas, and the Palestine Islamic Jihad. These entities had been named terrorist organizations and operated chiefly against the US ally Israel.

In terms of actual consequences, the ISA historically has been ineffective. The reasons for this ineffectiveness started with the terms of the statute itself. Although the latest amendments to the ISA attempt to address the ambiguity issue, the ISA's terms and wording are unclear. The ISA speaks in terms of investments "in" Iran. Whether building portions of a pipeline outside Iran or even to the Iranian border would be covered was an open question. As discussed below, this issue has apparently not been resolved by the most recent amendments to the ISA.

The ISA was obviously aimed at non-US companies, because US companies were prohibited already at the time of enactment from such transactions through executive order. Thus, the ISA faced immediate attacks as being extraterritorial. The initial test case involved the investment of approximately $2 billion over the lifetime of a project to develop phases of the South Pars natural gas field. The chief investor was Total SA of France, which signed an investment contract in 1997 that involved partners including Gazprom of Russia and Petronas of Malaysia. This initial attempt to use the ISA to sanction foreign firms foundered on a combination of factors. First, the European Union (EU) threatened to take the United States to a dispute resolution proceeding before the World Trade Organization (WTO). Under WTO rules and precedents, the US case was weak. WTO treaty obligations simply provide very little room for the imposition of extraterritorial sanctions for political purposes. Second, the EU pledged to cooperate more closely with the United States in pursuing the proliferation of weapons of mass destruction and terrorists. The end result was that President Clinton granted a "national interest" waiver under section 9(c) of the ISA and the project went forward.[28]

In the late 1990s, Turkey and Iran collaborated on the construction of a pipeline to ship natural gas from Iran to Turkey. Gas has flowed through this pipeline since 2001. When the US government initially considered whether the pipeline to Turkey should trigger sanctions, the government assumed that the pipeline was to carry only Turkmenistan gas. This was an obvious ruse to allow no action against the American NATO ally Turkey. A similar pipeline to Armenia was also built and is in use. The Armenian pipeline was ignored, evidently in part because the amount involved was not deemed consequential.

Proponents of the ISA's effectiveness could point to several instances in which projects have been deterred or withdrawn under threat of sanction. Among these were prospective investments by such major investors as Royal Dutch Shell and Repsol. However, a significant number of such deals have gone forward. From 1999 through 2007, these investments amounted to approximately $30 billion in oil and gas field development and refinery upgrades. They included contracts with companies from France, Italy, Canada, Norway, Sweden, South Korea, Japan, Brazil, China, and Malaysia.[29]

Indian officials looking at the US history on enforcement of sanctions with regard to Total SA and for gas pipelines with Turkey and Armenia were apparently unimpressed by the US sanctions regime as it might apply to the IPI pipeline. Indeed, there seemed to be a sense that the ISA effort was "halfhearted" and riddled with "loopholes."[30]

In 2010, the US Congress attempted to correct what it saw as deficiencies in the coverage and enforcement of sanctions against Iran. On June 28, 2010,

Congress sent to the president the "Comprehensive Iran Sanctions, Accountability and Divestment Act of 2010." This legislation was signed into law on July 1, 2010. Not surprisingly, this extension and revision of the Iran Sanctions Act did not address the Iran-Pakistan-India pipeline directly. The 2010 act increased the number of sanctions that could be applied under the ISA from six to nine, lowered the dollar amounts for triggering sanctions, and virtually required the president to impose at least three sanctions on a company contravening the act. However, the legislation did not solve the ambiguities as to whether India (and Pakistan) would contravene the act by participating in the IPI pipeline.[31] Successive administrations have interpreted the ISA definition of "investment" to include participation in the construction of energy routes to Iran. However, no US official has stated outright that participation in the IPI pipeline would invoke sanctions.[32]

Multilaterally, concern over Iran's nuclear program has led the United States to seek and obtain multiple UN Security Council resolutions imposing sanctions. The first three of these sanctions resolutions were chiefly pointed directly at Iran's possible development of nuclear weapons. The sanctions included prohibitions on the transfer to Iran of nuclear, missile, and dual-use items that could be used for weapons development. Also included were the freezing of assets of forty named Iranian persons and entities allegedly connected with Iran's nuclear program. The resolutions called on states not to export arms to Iran, and to inspect cargoes carried by Iranian air and ocean shipping if there are indications that they carry prohibited cargo. None of these actions by the UN Security Council would affect the IPI pipeline.[33]

The United States sought and obtained on June 9, 2010, a fourth UN sanctions resolution to press Iran to change its nuclear development conduct. This resolution continued the sanctions focus on connection to the Iranian nuclear development and military activities. Although provisions were added authorizing states to impose sanctions on Iranian shipping and financial services, these services would have to be connected to the specified targets of the resolution. Nowhere was there any indication that the resolution envisaged nonnuclear and nonmilitary activities such as gas pipelines to be within the subject matter of the resolution. Therefore, the sanctions adopted by the UN Security Council were not instrumental in India's reluctance to proceed with the IPI pipeline.[34]

Thus, it has not been sanctions, either unilaterally or multilaterally, or the threat of sanctions that have thus far kept India from going forward with the pipeline.

The Effect of the US-India Civil Nuclear Initiative on India's Participation

As was discussed in chapter 2, Chairman Howard L. Berman (D-Calif.), after due consideration and apparent consultation with the House of Representatives leadership, did not link approval of the 123 Agreement to India's not proceeding with the IPI pipeline. Had he done so, the deal would have been killed as a political matter in India. As was explained, the US-India civil nuclear deal was highly contentious in the Indian Parliament. The long delay in India's bringing the initiative forward and the narrowness of the United Progressive Alliance government's majority on the "vote of trust" were evidence of the deal's precarious political state in Parliament. Any linkage by the House of Representatives between the initiative and the IPI pipeline would certainly have sunk the measure in India. As a domestic political matter, no Indian government can admit that the United States influences, much less decides, any aspect of Indian foreign policy toward Iran. This is especially true when the vital national interest of energy supply is involved.

The key economic objective of the US-India civil nuclear initiative is the same as that for the IPI pipeline. Both projects are designed primarily to enhance the energy available to India. In the prime minister's public briefing paper advocating approval of the US-India 123 Agreement, the electrical power to be produced from nuclear energy was highlighted as the basic reason for approval.[35] India's initial goal stated at the time of consideration of the US-India 123 Agreement was 20,000 megawatts of nuclear power, to be achieved by 2020. This goal has been increased to 40,000 megawatts by 2020, and Prime Minister Manmohan Singh has stated that India could produce 470,000 megawatts of nuclear power by 2050.[36] This goal may seem inflated, given that India in 2009 was producing only 3,800 megawatts of power from nuclear energy. However, if the International Atomic Energy Agency's upper estimates for Indian growth in nuclear power through 2030 are projected forward to 2050, India would achieve the goal indicated by the prime minister.[37]

Although it is highly unlikely that the rate of growth projected through 2030 could be sustained for another twenty years, these ambitious goals and targets show the great impact that the opening to nuclear energy is having on Indian leaders' thinking on energy sources. To a large extent, the achievement of targets in the vicinity of those indicated by the prime minister can be a substitute for risky projects like the IPI pipeline. The convergence of purpose is a salient factor in increasing the impact of an economic incentive to strategic cooperation.

The civil nuclear deal probably played a role in India's reluctance to proceed with the IPI pipeline during the period 2005–8. However, the influence of the deal has been favorable from a US perspective, largely because of the initiative's positive economic and political factors rather than from fear of the United States refusing to proceed if India became an active participant in the project.

Other Economic Factors in India's Failure to Proceed

Economic factors have played the most important role in driving India's decisions on the IPI pipeline project. The assurance and security of natural gas supplies are among the strongest factors attracting India to the project. The pipeline as originally conceived would cross the Pakistani province of Balochistan to get to India. For ethnic reasons, Balochistan has been in a condition of near revolt against the central government of Pakistan for years. Although this unrest has not received the US news coverage of the fight against the Pakistani Taliban, it is a significant threat to the security of Pakistan. The ability of the central government to guarantee supplies through a pipeline across Balochistan is extremely doubtful. Even when the pipeline would enter the provinces of Sindh and Punjab, the proven ability of Islamic extremists to disrupt infrastructure in those areas further impinges upon the assurance and security of supply. The track records of both Pakistan and Iran in meeting international commitments likewise cannot be encouraging to India as it looks at the assurance of supply and security factors.

More fundamentally, price has militated against Indian participation in the IPI pipeline. Famous for their harsh and erratic negotiating tactics, the Iranians initially offered natural gas at the price of $8.00 per million British thermal units (Btu). Both the Indians and the Pakistanis refused to pay more than $4.25 per million Btu.[38] India's costs for producing natural gas varied between $4.20 and $5.73 per million Btu.[39] In addition to the price from Iran, India would have to pay approximately $1.20 per million Btu in transportation costs and transit fees for wheeling the gas through Pakistan. This would make the natural gas from Iran the most costly on the Indian market.[40] Iran and Pakistan reached an agreement on a "pricing formula" in mid-2009 that pegged the price of the gas to a percentage of oil prices. However, it was unclear whether the pricing agreement would hold in the face of volatile oil prices.

Questions of assurance of supply and pricing fundamentally affect the question of financing. As quoted above, Prime Minister Singh raised financing as a basic impediment to the project immediately after the summit meeting with President George W. Bush that produced the Joint Statement of July 18, 2005. The total cost of the project is estimated at more than $7.5 billion. Pakistan estimates its share of the costs at about $1.25 billion, to be financed on a "public-private partnership basis."[41] However, the reality seems to be that financing will not come from private sources, given the uncertainties involved. In the past, Pakistan has said that it has received assurances from the Asian Development Bank that it is prepared to offer financing.[42] Russia has indicated support for the project. Apparently this support is, in part, based upon a theory that the diversion of Iranian gas to the east would prevent competition with Russian gas in the European market. If Iranian gas were shipped to Europe, it would present considerable price competition for the Russian gas. China has also expressed an interest in financing the project.[43] But none of these potential governmental sources of financing had actually offered funds as of this writing.

The Bottom Line

The case of the Iran-Pakistan-India pipeline illustrates several aspects of the relationship between economic engagement and strategic cooperation. These include the centrality of energy, the relative ineffectiveness of sanctions, and the importance of economic incentives.

Energy is a primary strategic driver in the twenty-first century. The United States and India both are bound to oil and natural gas in order to achieve their national goals. Because these resources are distributed unequally on a national geographical basis, cooperation and competition for them must be a prominent part of both US and Indian strategic conceptualizations. The strategic importance of energy is not simply a matter of competing for a finite supply of oil and gas. The commonality of US and Indian energy interests offers more opportunities for cooperation than for competitive friction. In the case of the Iran-Pakistan-India pipeline, the economic engagement issues have been handled unsystematically. Both nations would be well served by a more systematic approach to the relationship between energy and their abilities to cooperate on such strategic issues as Iran. Energy is now never collateral for strategic considerations. The United States and India have an energy dialogue. However, this dialogue focuses on technology and is insufficiently integrated into the two nations' foreign policy considerations. US-India cooperation on energy should be reexamined by each country from a strategic perspective. This reexamination should result in a more complete integration of the energy sector into the strategic plans and actions of both parties.

The US-India experience with the IPI pipeline illustrates the deficiencies of reliance on sanctions to affect the behavior of a nation on important strategic issues. The Iran Sanctions Act and threats based upon it were little more than an irritant in US-India engagement over the IPI pipeline. The Government Accountability Office observed that the effects of the Iran Sanctions Act were unclear even after study. No government effort has been made to judge the overall effectiveness of the ISA sanctions and threatened sanctions in the US-India context. Such an assessment should be fundamental. If the sanctions' effects are unclear, they offer little more than a hope of effectiveness rather than a useful tool of foreign policy.

The economic benefits of incentives, such as those embodied in the US-India civil nuclear initiative, are far more effective than sanctions in achieving cooperation. From his perspective of seeking to bring pressure on Iran, Chairman Lantos was perceptive in focusing on the relationship between the IPI pipeline and the civil nuclear legislation. However, his threats to hold the legislation hostage to Indian action on the pipeline were counterproductive. Fortunately, his successor as chairman of the House Foreign Affairs Committee, the House leadership, and the Bush administration took a broader view. The relationship of the civil nuclear legislation to the IPI pipeline was viewed and handled in the fuller context of US-India economic engagement over energy. When such incentives can be cast as alternatives to a disfavored course of action, they are particularly effective.

The example of the interrelationship between Iran and the Indian company Reliance Industries is instructive. Reliance pulled back from sending refined gasoline to Iran because of economic factors that involved the United States. One of these was the considerable amount of loan guarantees afforded by the US Export-Import Bank. A more important incentive was the US market as a place to sell its refined products. In dealing with India, the United States is likely to be most successful in promoting the US view of desired behavior by tailoring positive economic incentives that relate to India's interests. The lessons from the IPI pipeline case are of more than bilateral significance. The broader application of these observations will be discussed in the concluding chapter of this book. The IPI pipeline case also shows how US-India strategic issues most often involve many other national actors. Let us now turn to a case concerning the impact of US-India economic engagement on the ability of the United States and India to cooperate on strategic issues in a multilateral setting.

Chapter 7

Economic Engagement and Multilateralism: Meeting the Financial Meltdown

I think he [Prime Minister Manmohan Singh] is a very wise and decent man, and has done a wonderful job in guiding India, even prior to being prime minister, along a path of extraordinary economic growth that is a marvel, I think, for all the world.

—President Barack Obama, London, April 2, 2009

November 30, 1999, was the first day of the Ministerial Conference of the World Trade Organization (WTO) in Seattle. Although it was a beautiful day, things were already getting ugly. A small army of protesters had gathered. The protesters made no secret of their intention to wreak havoc in Seattle. I had been at the WTO Ministerial in Singapore in 1996, but the atmosphere in Seattle was nothing like the purposeful order that had prevailed only three years earlier.

Except for a few speeches, nothing much happens on the first day of a ministerial. Thus, the US-India Business Council had picked this day for a luncheon meeting of US and Indian business leaders. The luncheon had taken place at a restaurant overlooking the waters of Puget Sound. There had been lively conversation about tariffs and trade barriers. The event seemed to auger well for US-India cooperation and a productive conference. However, it was not to be.

Amit Mitra, secretary-general of the Federation of Indian Chambers of Commerce and Industry, and I were walking back from the luncheon to the ministerial conference center when we began to encounter crowds of protesters. There were shouts and the sound of breaking glass. The crowds became thicker, and it was more and more difficult to make our way up the hill the remaining three blocks to the conference center. Up ahead, we could see police drawn up in a defensive line to keep protesters from the center. The crowd was taunting the police. A protester picked up a metal newspaper stand and tossed it through a shop window. When the people in the crowd saw that there was no reaction from the police to this vandalism, they became more restive and started to break more windows and overturn anything that was not nailed down.

Suddenly, Mitra and I were surrounded by a group of earnest young people. They encircled us, linked arms, and began to move us forcibly away from our destination. Thinking quickly, Mitra shouted at our captors, "Have you no respect for foreign guests? Especially when we are here to protest the actions of the American administration as much as you are?" "Where are you from?" shouted one of the crowd. "I am from India," replied Mitra. "Well, I guess you're okay. We can let you go. But what about this other guy?" said the ringleader, gesturing at me. "Oh, he's Canadian, and the Canadians are protesting too," rejoined Mitra. Proud of my American citizenship, I nonetheless did not challenge Mitra's assertion before my American captors. So they let us both go.

As soon as we were released, I noticed a security officer beckoning to me through the partially opened door to an otherwise-shuttered establishment. Mitra and I quickly made our way to the opening. Once we were inside, the door was locked behind us. We thanked the guard for giving us shelter from the mob. The guard told us that if we made our way to the back of the building, we would find the entrance to a tunnel that went under the street and came up behind the police lines. We did so, and thus made our way to the conference center and the site of the opening plenary.

In his opening address, WTO director-general Mike Moore famously said, "This conference is doomed—doomed to succeed."[1] As it turned out, Moore was only half right. The conference was doomed. The Indian minister of commerce and industry, Murasoli Maran, made it plain from the very first that India was there to defend its notion of a limited WTO. According to Maran, "Our assessment has all along been that the Uruguay Round Agreements have not served all the membership well. There are critical gaps that need to be urgently addressed. Asymmetries and inequities in several of the agreements including those related to antidumping, subsidies, intellectual property, trade-related investment measures, and the nonrealization of expected benefits from agreements such as textiles and agriculture during implementation had been a matter of great concern."[2] India was particularly vociferous in its opposition to any form of investment and competition policy being included in the WTO. There was no cooperation between the United States and India at the Seattle Ministerial. As the United States sought to expand the agenda for the WTO, India pressed hard to prevent any such expansion. In the end, nothing was accomplished in Seattle. This outcome could not have been foretold at the founding of the WTO just six years earlier.

The United States and India in the Completion of the World Trade Organization

When I arrived at the Department of Commerce in the early fall of 1993, negotiations for the establishment of the WTO were in their final stage. The bureau I was to head, Trade Development, was heavily involved in supporting the US trade representative, Mickey Kantor, in these negotiations, as were other parts of Commerce's International Trade Administration. A hallmark of Bill Clinton's presidency was his willingness, as a "new" Democrat, to embrace international trade. Perhaps the greatest symbol of this willingness was Clinton's taking the Uruguay Round of multilateral trade negotiations to fruition. These negotiations began in 1986 under the administration of Ronald Reagan. The negotiations were pursued with vigor during the administration of George H. W. Bush as part of the Republican agenda to promote freer trade around the world. Thus, the Uruguay Round was basically a Republican initiative, or at least an initiative begun and carried close to conclusion by Republican administrations. However, new Democrat Bill Clinton saw the conclusion of the negotiations and establishment of the WTO as essential to the economic growth on which he had promised to focus in the 1992 campaign.

From the vantage point of a neophyte at the Department of Commerce in 1993, it seemed that the obstreperous negativity I had associated with India's position on trade was a thing of the past. The United States had difficulty with India when it came to intellectual property rights,[3] but it seemed that India was prepared to go forward in accordance with the philosophy that had led to the opening of its economy in 1991. In fact, this impression was apparently not far from reality. The leaders of the Government of India understood that its liberalizing economic reforms would be supported by a liberal world trading order. The government of Prime Minister Narasimha Rao believed that by fully participating in the Uruguay Round and the WTO, India could help assure a world trading order that served its interests.[4]

For its part, the US government did not appear to pay much attention to

India. The United States' WTO negotiators were concerned that, in the final analysis, India be willing to join the Uruguay Round–WTO consensus. However, to many it seemed that the Indian economy was still too small and its growth was too slow to have an impact on US interests. The Indian image still was one of poverty and international aid. Perhaps this contributed to the situation in which the United States and other developed countries let India and other developing countries resort to the process of "dirty tariffication." By this process, India bound its tariff rates at levels significantly higher than its applied rates. Because India's tariffs were bound at such high rates, the Rao government was able to make the case to its domestic critics that the Uruguay Round Agreement actually had little effect on India's ability to set tariffs as it pleased. Further, India was a leader in negotiating a full range of exceptions, or "flexibilities," for developing countries. These provisions would provide India with maximum freedom in regard to market access and production subsidies.[5] The Uruguay Round negotiations culminated in an agreement to create the World Trade Organization, signed at Marrakech on April 15, 1994, with an effective date of January 1, 1995.

US-India WTO Cooperation after the Founding

As indicated in chapter 3, India played a constructive role in Singapore at the 1996 Ministerial. The Information Technology Agreement, which removed tariffs from a variety of goods connected with information technology, could not have been secured without India's participation. By 1999, however, US-India progress on multilateral cooperation on trade had been set back substantially. It is no coincidence that this setback coincided with the 1998–2001 period, when the United States imposed sanctions for nuclear testing and its foreign direct investment in India entered a phase of decline. The economic crisis affecting Southeast Asia was also a factor.[6]

The Fourth Ministerial Conference of the WTO convened in Doha in November 2001. Foreign direct investment in India had been trending up again when the world economy received the blow of uncertainty from the terrorist attacks of September 11, 2001. India was on the defensive concerning foreign trade. This defensive WTO posture had been seen as a favorable domestic political factor for the Bharatiya Janata Party and its National Democratic Alliance in securing a victory in the national elections of September 1999. The hard-line stance of the commerce minister, Murasoli Maran, seemingly had been approved by many Indian voters. His conduct at Seattle was widely interpreted in India as a victory in resisting foreign trade pressures. The bad feeling engendered by the fiasco in Seattle still had not dissipated by the time of the Doha Ministerial Meeting. Under these circumstances, cooperation between the United States and India on the issue of multilateral trade liberalism was not great.

Minister Maran led the Indian delegation to the WTO Ministerial meeting in Doha with the same determination to restrict the WTO agenda that his government believed had been successful at Seattle. The Indian delegation came to Doha to press the United States and the West on (1) "implementation," (2) the carried-over agenda from the Singapore Ministerial, and (3) intellectual property.

A major theme of India was that the developed countries still had not implemented provisions of the Uruguay Round Agreement.[7] About a hundred such implementation issues had been identified by India and other developing countries. Although these issues involved an array of disparate matters, the common refrain was the failure of the developed countries to give "special and differentiated" treatment to the developing countries. For example, the developing countries were to be given "balance of payment" exceptions to certain tariff obligations. How this would work had not been defined. India led the effort to force the Doha negotiations to address these implementation issues as a prerequisite for moving to a further round of trade liberalization negotiations. The position of the United States and other developing countries was that these issues were generally subsidiary legal or technical topics and could be resolved in the course of WTO operations or through the WTO dispute resolution mechanisms. India, however, confronted the issues directly and made addressing them a prerequisite of proceeding. The result was that more than forty of the implementation issues were settled at or before the Doha conference, a special decision was issued on implementation-related issues and concerns, and a paragraph on implementation was added to the main Doha Ministerial Declaration.[8]

At Doha, Maran made it explicit that India opposed the consideration of a group of issues that had first been raised at the Singapore Ministerial in 1996. These issues included treatment of foreign investment, competition policy, and transparency in government procurement. Maran used his time at the plenary session to remind participants that the WTO was not a "global government" and should not attempt to address issues that were not directly a part of trade.[9] India counted it a success when these issues were kept out of the negotiations and listed only for clarification as to the scope and definition of the issues.

The third major area of concentration by the Indian delegation to Doha was on the effort to obtain a declaration on the Agreement on Trade-Related Aspects of Intellectual Property Rights (TRIPS). India sought to clarify the flexibilities of the TRIPS Agreement in such a manner as to hold down the cost of patented drugs. These flexibilities would be helpful to India's impoverished hundreds of millions as well as to Indian generic drug manufacturers. As discussed in chapter 9, this effort was successful.

The George W. Bush administration came to office in January 2001 with the determination to improve on the Clinton trade record and to reverse the debacle in Seattle. However, with the events of September 11, 2001, there was very little Bush administration attention left for any subjects other than initiation of the war on terrorism. The United States had little success in cooperating with India in the run-up to the Doha Ministerial Conference. The main agenda item for the United States was simply to initiate another round of negotiations for liberalization. On specific items of most concern to the administration, the United States lost to India and the developing nations at every turn. The attempt by the United States to keep the TRIPS Agreement from being diluted was unsuccessful. The United States wanted to include negotiations on labor standards, but it was unsuccessful in doing so. Likewise, the United States' interest in excluding discussion of antidumping regimes resulted only in antidumping being featured prominently in the Doha Declaration.

US-India Confrontation in the Doha Round Negotiations

Finally, India did agree at Doha to launch a new round of WTO negotiations. This concurrence was achieved by packaging twenty-one subjects as the Doha Development Agenda. The Ministerial Declaration said:

> International trade can play a major role in the promotion of economic development and the alleviation of poverty. We recognize the need for all our peoples to benefit from the increased opportunities and welfare gains that the multilateral trading system generates. The majority of WTO members are developing countries. We seek to place their needs and interests at the heart of the Work Programme adopted in this Declaration.[10]

Although this focus was flattering to India's interests, the Indian government remained skeptical about moving toward freer trade under the WTO's aegis. For its part, the United States wanted to move ahead, but only if negotiations were able to produce significantly enhanced market access for US products. The US position was that no deal was better than a cosmetic enhancement that produced little of real value to American business. Although US-India economic engagement was growing rapidly, there did not seem to be the impetus on either the US or Indian side to tie this bilateral growth into progress on the Doha Development Agenda. During the next seven years, a succession of US trade representatives would come to understand the importance of bridging the negotiating gap by bringing US-India economic engagement into juxtaposition with negotiating objectives. However, they would be unable to leverage this understanding into a deal with India.

Robert Zoellick was the US trade representative at the September 2003 WTO Ministerial in Cancún. The ministerial had been called to assess progress on the Doha Development Agenda. Particularly, there were hopes of breaking what had become an impasse in the agricultural negotiations over the level of subsidies and market access. Zoellick charged into the negotiations determined to bring about agreement by dent of intellect, activity, and overwhelming advocacy for the logic of the US position. The result was another debacle on the order of the failed Seattle Ministerial. According to Zoellick, the division that brought failure at Cancún was "between the can-do and the won't do." He singled out India for special disapproval as one of the "won't do" nations, saying "India's bound agricultural tariff is 112 percent" and chastising Brazil for turning to India instead of working with the United States on farm subsidies and agricultural tariffs.[11] As for the Government of India, it apparently had no regrets. When former commerce minister Maran died in November 2003, his successor, Arun Jaitly, was among those praising him for crafting the Indian position at Seattle and Doha, and giving Maran credit for Indian intransigence at Cancún.[12]

Although Zoellick tried hard, he never developed any rapport with his Indian interlocutors and made little progress in connecting US-India bilateral economic engagement with the broader multilateral negotiations. There was great hope for a more cooperative relationship when a member of the US House of Representatives, Robert Portman, became US trade representative in March 2005. In late 2004, India had changed governments, with a surprising win by the Congress Party–led United Progressive Alliance. The original architect for the opening of the Indian economy, Manmohan Singh, had become prime minister. A personable politician from Madhya Pradesh, Kamal Nath, was appointed minister of commerce and industry, and therefore India's chief trade negotiator. With two new trade negotiators and a government in Delhi headed by the father of Indian economic reforms, there seemed to be reason for optimism. Hopefully, the United States and India would resume the cooperation that had enabled the formation of the WTO in 1994 and the successful Singapore Ministerial in 1996. This optimism seemed to be justified at the Hong Kong Ministerial in December 2005. At the end of the conference, the ministers agreed on a declaration that "puts the Round back on track." The declaration expressed the resolve "to conclude the negotiations launched successfully in 2001."[13] However, it was not to be, in large part because the United States and India could not find common ground.

In early 2006, I met with Minister Nath at an event in Chicago sponsored by the Federation of Indian Chambers of Commerce and Industry. He had a firm grasp of the tariff issue I was there to discuss with him. However, rather than discuss my issue, he wanted to talk more about the WTO Doha Round, and particularly the issue of agricultural subsidies. He said that he very much wanted to make a "deal" with the United States, but that he was frustrated by the lack of progress on agricultural subsidies. He said that he understood perfectly well why such subsidies had such a strong political constituency in the United States. When I started to demur, Nath interrupted. He said that he understood the relationship between the US Senate and the wealthy farmers of the state we were in, Illinois, and the other states of the Midwest. He wanted me to know that when he spoke of protecting the farmers of India there was no equivalence to the farmers of the United States. With the Indian farmers, he felt that protection was literally a matter of life and death for the hundreds of millions who barely eked out a living from the land. In his view, US farmers were prosperous, and a lessening of what he considered protective subsidies would affect them only marginally. He said he understood that in the US Senate, farmers had a disproportionate political impact because farm states were crucial to the supermajority of senators necessary to pass legislation.

Nath told me of the "$1 deal" he had offered to US trade representative Portman. When I expressed puzzlement at what such a deal might be, Nath said that he offered that if the Congress would cut US agricultural subsidies by even $1, he would concede everything else Portman sought in the Doha Round negotiations. Of course, Nath was being facetious to make his point. Nevertheless, Minister Nath took hope from the fact that Portman had been an elected politician, as was Nath. He hoped a deal could be made with Portman.

Nath is a politician to the core. He had ambitions to be chief minister of the state of Madhya Pradesh, and perhaps later prime minister. He needed a deal that would make him a hero to the farmers of India. He hoped that he might get one from US trade representative Portman at the summer 2006 "modalities" meeting of the WTO ministers and heads of delegations in Geneva. However, in April 2006, President Bush made Portman the head of the Office of Management and Budget. Nath was left to negotiate with Portman's deputy, Susan Schwab, who later was confirmed as US trade representative. Nath and Schwab had very different personalities. Even though Schwab had been around Washington for some time, she had never been an elected politician. She was a policy expert who was not shy about demonstrating her expertise. Nath and Schwab had none of the camaraderie experienced by Nath and Portman.

Along with other factors, Nath apparently took this removal of Portman from the US trade representative post as a sign that the Bush administration was not serious about making the kind of deal that Nath felt he and India had to have. Other factors that Nath may have considered were the lack of pressure from either the Indian or US business communities to make a deal. There were numerous US-India economic issues about which the respective business communities were concerned. However, little attention was paid to the Doha Round as a mechanism for resolving these issues. This was a time of good feeling about the growing strategic relationship between the United States and India. However, in neither country was the WTO or the concept of "free trade" politically advantageous. In the landmark July 18, 2005, Joint Statement between Bush and Singh, there was no mention of the Doha Round, the WTO, or any other multilateral entity.

Thus, it came as no surprise that the June–July 2006 modalities meetings and the 2008 meetings in Geneva to produce a Doha work program were unsuccessful. Nath waited until after the July 22, 2008, US-India civil nuclear trust vote in the Indian Parliament before going to Geneva. Having survived the trust vote, the United Progressive Alliance government was now plainly looking to the 2009 India elections. In his opening statement in Geneva, Nath said:

> My Government now has a renewed mandate to deliver on development issues to the people of India. I trust the decisions that we arrive at in the WTO in the next few days will enable me to deliver on that mandate.[14]

Nath's comments on a Special Safeguard Mechanism (SSM) for agricultural imports into developing countries foreshadowed the impasse that would bring down the 2008 mini-ministerial meeting:

We are not at all happy about [the reaction to] the SSM proposal. All manner of objections are being raised to our right to safeguard the livelihood concerns of hundreds of millions. Are we expected to stand by, see a surge in imports and do nothing? Do we give developed countries the unfettered right to continue subsidizing and then dumping those subsidies on cost jeopardizing lives of billions? The position of developed countries is utterly self-righteous: they have enjoyed their SSG[15] (and want to continue it) but our SSM must be subject to all sorts of shackles and restraints. This self-righteousness will not do. If it means no deal, so be it.[16]

There was no deal. The perception that the United States and India were unable to cooperate in a multilateral setting began to grow. However, a new economic crisis was to show that economic engagement could be fundamental to US-India cooperation in other multinational settings.

US-India Cooperation in Reforming the G-20 to Meet the Meltdown

Nath had spoken in Geneva in 2008 of "meeting in the rather grim context of a number of crises in various parts of the word."[17] His reference was to the economic difficulties that had begun with a subprime real estate mortgage lending collapse in the United States and had progressed into a worldwide crisis that threatened a full-scale international economic meltdown. The inability to make progress on trade issues at the WTO was a part of the problem. However, the WTO and the other worldwide post–World War II multilateral institutions, the International Monetary Fund and the World Bank, seemed incapable of meeting the international aspects of the meltdown on their own.[18] Clearly, nations acting in isolation were also incapable of restoring international economic confidence. India and the United States, as two leading nations from the developing and developed worlds, needed to work together to resolve the crises of which Nath spoke. Because the WTO and the other multilateral institutions seemed incapable of action, the United States and India led the turn to a little-used mechanism known as the Group of Twenty, or G-20.[19]

The G-20 had been formed in response to developing countries' anger surrounding the inadequacy of the traditional grouping of rich countries, the G-7 (the United States, the United Kingdom, Japan, France, Germany, Italy, and Canada) or G-8 (these seven most developed large economies, plus Russia) to deal with the Asian monetary crisis of 1997. Of particular concern to the developing countries was the misallocation of power at the International Monetary Fund.[20] There was a deep well of developing-economy resentment at the IMF and the rich countries that run it. This resentment was prompted in large part by G-7 countries imposing through the IMF stringent economic prescriptions on developing countries when the G-7 countries refused to follow those same prescriptions.

India was a leader in the movement to crack the stranglehold of the G-7 countries on international monetary policy. India pushed for the establishment of the so-called Group of 22 announced by President Clinton at the Asia-Pacific Economic Cooperation forum's meeting in Vancouver in November 1997. The avowed purpose of the Group of 22 was to bring together the finance ministers and central bankers of the G-7 with those from fifteen of the leading emerging market economies "to advance the reform of the global financial system." Meetings of the Group of 22 took place in Washington in April and October 1998 and in an enlarged format with representatives from thirty-three nations in March and April 1999. From the very first, the G-20 and its precursors were involved in an examination of the stability of the international financial system and effective functioning of global capital markets. The Group of 22 became the G-20[21] when the finance ministers and central bank governors met in Berlin in December 1999 and institutionalized the group by establishing a chair with a two-year term and a secretariat.[22]

In the search for a vehicle to further international coordination in response to the financial services meltdown of 2008, the Bush administration seized upon the G-20 as a useful vehicle. Other leading economic nations agreed. Bush called for a meeting of the heads of state and heads of government of the G-20 nations to take place in Washington on November 14 and 15, 2008. The choice of the G-20 was not altogether obvious. Before the summit in 2008, G-20 representatives at the highest levels had been limited to finance ministers and central bankers. The Washington G-20 Summit was the first to involve heads of states and heads of governments. Before Washington, the G-20 had been chiefly in the business of advising the IMF and World Bank. From the November 2008 meeting onward, the G-20 would become something quite different.

US and Indian international businesses and their trade associations were instrumental in pushing their respective governments to move forward internationally with an organization that was wider than the G-7 or G-8 but not so unwieldy as the United Nations, International Monetary Fund, World Bank, or WTO. India business viewed the G-7 as a "rich man's club." US business understood that the economic crisis could not be met without the participation of rising economic powerhouses like India, China, and Brazil.

Upon the announcement of the 2008 G-20 meeting, the national chambers of commerce of the G-20 countries issued a declaration calling on the summit participants to "restructure the global financial system, restore the confidence in financial markets and alleviate as much as possible the effects of the financial crisis on the real economy."[23] The Federation of Indian Chambers of Commerce was particularly active during the run-up to the 2008 summit. The federation urged the G-20 leaders meeting in Washington to come up with a global economic road map to protect the real economy, rebuild confidence in financial institutions, and support the business and investment capacity of small entrepreneurs.

Having agitated for more than a decade on the subject of moving away from a developed-nations approach, India took the lead at the Washington Summit in driving home the need for using the G-20 to meet the crisis and reform the system. Prime Minister Singh told the heads of state and government assembled in Washington:

I would like to emphasise the importance of broad-based multilateral approaches to our efforts. Bodies such as the G-7 are no longer sufficient to meet the demands of the day. We need to ensure that any new architecture we design is genuinely multilateral with adequate representation from countries reflecting changes in economic realities.[24]

India also insisted that the actions of the G-20 should be, in part, a mechanism for restructuring the IMF. Specifically with regard to the IMF, Prime Minister Singh admonished:

The International Monetary Fund is the logical body to perform the task of multilateral surveillance of macroeconomic imbalances and their relationship to financial stability. However, it is relevant to ask whether its systems and procedures are adequate to the task. Over the years, the Fund has become marginal to the task of policy analysis and consultations on macroeconomic imbalances and related policies in the major countries. That task is now performed in other forums, though it is questionable whether it is being performed well. I believe we need a comprehensive review of the procedures of the IMF leading to recommendations on governance reform which would enable the Fund to perform the role of macroeconomic policy coordination.

Prime Minister Singh called for "alternative modalities" to achieve a "more legitimate representation" that would "reflect the current and prospective economic realities." He further insisted that the two bodies dealing with regulatory issues, the Basel Committee on Banking Supervision and the Financial Stability Forum, which had been limited to G-7 representatives, have a broader representation, including India. He then called for other major steps in addition to reform of the architecture of institutions dealing with global financial matters: (1) a coordinated fiscal stimulus, (2) an increase in IMF resources, (3) the establishment of additional funds worth $50 billion at the World Bank and regional banks for infrastructure development, (4) increased export credit finance, and (5) specific steps to help developing countries through the crisis.

From their bilateral state visits in 2005 and 2006 and their continual work together on the civil nuclear initiative through the signing of the 123 Agreement in October 2008, President Bush, Prime Minister Singh, and their ministers had spent much time building the US-India relationship. Thus it was not surprising that the approach of President Bush, although more general, was compatible with that of Prime Minister Singh. The evening before the summit, President Bush said:

We will focus on key, five objectives: understanding the causes of the global crisis; reviewing the effectiveness of our responses thus far; identifying principles for reforming our financial and regulatory systems; launching a specific action plan to implement those principles; and reaffirming our conviction that free market principles offer the surest path to lasting prosperity.[25]

On the Indian point of reforming the governance of the IMF, President Bush agreed that "both the IMF and World Bank should modernize their governance structures."

After the meeting, President Bush took credit for selecting a forum that would include India and other major emerging economies: "And obviously I decided that we ought to have the G-20 nations, as opposed to the G-8 or the G-13."[26] The statement from the G-20, in which India concurred, basically took the Bush approach of outlining principles. The "common principles" set forth in the final statement were (1) strengthening transparency and accountability, (2) enhancing sound regulation, (3) promoting integrity in financial markets, (4) reinforcing international cooperation, and (5) reforming international financial institutions. The statement also outlined "immediate" and "medium-term" actions. These actions were generally cast in the form of what "should" be done and were not of a binding nature. The one binding agreement had to do with the rejection of protectionism:

We will refrain from raising new barriers to investment or to trade in goods and services, imposing new export restrictions, or implementing World Trade Organization (WTO)–inconsistent measures to stimulate exports.[27]

This promise was quickly broken by both the United States and India. A few days after the November G-20 Summit, India raised its tariffs on iron, steel, and soybeans.[28] In January, the United States enacted a "buy America" provision for steel and a limitation on the use of temporary visas. At the behest of US steelmakers and unions, Section 1605 was added to the American Recovery and Reinvestment Act of 2009 (Stimulus Act). This provision required that no funds made available under the Stimulus Act could be used for "a project for the construction, alteration, maintenance, or repair of a public building or public work unless all of the iron, steel, and manufactured goods used in the project are produced in the United States." Section 1611 of that same act prohibited the use of H-1B visas to hire workers for any bank or other organization receiving funds under the Emergency Economic Stabilization Act of 2008.

Next Steps at the G-20

President Barack Obama and his administration got off to a somewhat shaky start with regard to relations with India. In part, this was a result of traditional Indian sensitivity to the protocols and perceptions of esteem, and in part it was because of matters of substance. Some Indian commentators saw the failure of Obama and Singh to talk until more than a week after the election as a slight to India. The significance of the delay was supposedly augmented by the fact that president-elect Obama and Pakistani president Asif Ali Zardari spoke just a few days after Obama's election.[29] Some of these same commentators were also concerned by Obama's offhand remarks to a reporter that a "special envoy" on Kashmir might be appointed and that this envoy might be President Clinton. The Government of India strongly objected when there were suggestions that Richard Holbrooke might have as part of his "special envoy" portfolio India as well as Afghanistan and Pakistan. India was supportive of the Obama administration's shift of attention from Iraq to Afghanistan and Pakistan. However, the inclusion of India with Pakistan and Afghanistan in a special envoy's portfolio signaled to India the possibility of the United States linking its treatment of India to Pakistani interests. After years of effort to "de-hyphenate" US policies toward India and Pakistan, this linkage was unacceptable. With significant lobbying by the Indian Embassy, the description of Holbrooke's portfolio was limited to "Af/Pak," that is, the conflict between the US and Islamic radicals having operations from the territories of Afghanistan and Pakistan.

Minister Manmohan Singh and the new US president, Barack Obama, met for the first time at the Summit of G-20 Leaders in London on April 2, 2009. It is significant that this first meeting should take place in a setting where the chief topic was economic cooperation. Attempts to formulate a coordinated response to an international financial meltdown showed the key role played by economic engagement as the engine of political issues. It was not the many defense security issues that prompted a consideration of economic matters at the April 2 meeting. Rather, it was the need to act on the most significant economic crisis since the Great Depression that led to the first Obama-Singh discussions about terrorism, peace with Pakistan, and an array of other strategic issues.

The Role of Business

Both US and Indian business interests saw the April 2, 2009, G-20 meeting in London as an opportunity for the United States and India to improve the relationship between India and the new Obama administration by focusing on economic issues. India shared the United States' view that economic stimulus was required to meet the challenge of the meltdown. At a March 4, 2009, meeting in Washington sponsored by the US-India Business Council and the Asia Society, common action to meet the financial crisis was the unifying theme. On behalf of US business, former US ambassador to India Frank Wisner called on leaders of the two nations to take full advantage of the London G-20 to coordinate their approaches to the world financial system.

In India, Prime Minister Singh met with the top business leaders to get their views on how best to utilize the London G-20 meeting. Singh reviewed the current economic situation and then sought views on India's stand at the G-20 summit for a way out of the global crisis. The list of both private and public officials attending the consultation with Singh indicated the importance of economic issues as a driver of Indian foreign policy. The meeting was attended by Tata Group head Ratan Tata, Aditya Birla Group chairman Kumar Mangalam Birla, ICICI Bank managing director and CEO K. V. Kamath, Essar Group's Shashi Ruia, and Harsh Pati Singhania, president of the Federation of Indian Chambers of Commerce and Industry. Other prominent businessmen included Assocham president Sajjan Jindal, R. P. Goenka of the Goenka Group, Adi Godrej of the Godrej Group, Sunil Kant Munjal of the Hero Group, Baba Kalyani of Bharat Forge, and Confederation of Indian Industries chief mentor Tarun Das. From the government side, Planning Commission deputy chairman Montek Singh Ahluwalia, Reserve Bank of India governor D. Subbarao, and Cabinet secretary K. M. Chandrasekhar also attended the meeting. The meeting lasted two and a half hours, with an emphasis on inclusive growth and how India might become an engine of growth for the world economy.[30]

Indian private-sector representatives also advised Singh that India should use the G-20 to ensure that economic protectionism among the rich nations did not raise barriers to trade. This theme was echoed in a joint declaration of chambers of commerce of the G-20 nations, including the US Chamber of Commerce and the Federation of Indian Chambers of Commerce and Industry. Their statement acknowledged the linkage between the G-20 and the WTO. According to the G-20 chambers of commerce, business interests were looking to the G-20 to invigorate the WTO Doha Round and prevent "falling to the temptation of protectionism," which "would not only restrict trade in goods and services, but also distort the global economy, hindering rather than helping the recovery." The coalition of chambers continued with a plea that the WTO "must continue to play its role as global governor of the multilateral trading system."[31]

Stimulus to Meet the Meltdown

Before the April 2009 G-20 Summit, President Obama and his administration pushed hard for a commitment at the G-20 on increasing stimulus measures. Although the Germans and the French resisted these calls, Prime Minister Singh made it clear that India was in favor of such countercyclical moves. According to Singh, "We are now seeing a contraction that has overshot and contracyclical stimulus is therefore necessary in all countries." He continued, "I hope the summit will give a clear signal that we are willing to act in a coordinated, or at least in a credible concerted manner, to ensure that the downslide in minimized." At the April 2, 2009, G-20 Summit, the Germans and French would not relent in their antistimulus position. President Obama was reduced to emphasizing what had already been done in the way of stimulus while moving on to less contentious matters. The G-20 at London emphasized regulatory reform and additional resources made available to the IMF, the World Bank, and the multilateral development banks. The funds made available by G-20 members to these multilateral financial institutions were said to constitute an additional $1.1 trillion program. The Indians were delighted to view this program as a "massive provision of $1.1 trillion for emerging market economies." In its statement at the end of the London conference, India took note of the seats that India had gained at the Financial Stability Forum and on the Basel Committee on Banking Supervision, two key standard-setting bodies. India also welcomed the commitment to reform governance of the IMF and the other international financial institutions and looked forward to the implementation of this pledge at the next meeting of the leaders of the G-20 to be held in September 2009.

Convergence between the United States and India on the business of the April 2, 2009, G-20 summit supported the very positive comments of Obama and Singh about each other. Both leaders stressed their discussions on counterterrorism. Prime Minister Singh noted "a significant convergence of views and approaches in this regard." Significantly, Singh thanked President Obama "for all he has done in the US Senate and outside in the past few years to make possible the transformation of India-US relations, and to bring to fruition our civil nuclear initiative."[32]

The fruits of US-India economic engagement in bringing about cooperation in meeting the meltdown became apparent at the September 24–25, 2009, G-20 Summit in Pittsburgh. The choice of Pittsburgh as the venue for the summit was in itself a harbinger for the US-India cooperation that was fundamental to the outcome. Pittsburgh had grown from a small trading post at the junction of two rivers to make a third in the midst of large coal and iron ore deposits. From this fortunate site rose one of the world's premier manufacturing complexes for iron, steel, and products made of these metals. However, the conditions that had made Pittsburgh wealthy as a manufacturing center for metals had disappeared. In part this was because of change in demand and in part because of competition from lower-cost nations. Under the onslaught of economic change and international competition, the industries that had made Pittsburgh great declined. Then, in the early 1980s, Pittsburgh's leaders made a conscious decision to try to resurrect their economy through "high technology"—the very same software, information technology, and information-technology-enabled services that had transformed Bangalore, Hyderabad, Pune, and other Indian cities. Replacing the manufacturing of metal and its derivatives in Pittsburgh were the same sorts of information technology services that were an engine of India's growth.

The federally funded Software Engineering Institute (SEI) at Carnegie Mellon University is just one example of the economic interaction between the software industries of India and of the United States facilitated by activity in Pittsburgh. SEI formulates and supervises a system for evaluating systems and software engineering production throughout the world. Enterprises involved in systems and software engineering may obtain evaluations according to the SEI Capability Maturity Model Integration for Systems Engineering and Software Engineering at levels that run from I to V. There are only eighty software centers in the world with level V ratings, and sixty of these are in India. The drive for quality assurance in accordance with the Pittsburgh-based SEI is widely credited with transforming the Indian information technology industry.[33]

Virtually all the economic points advocated by India in talks with the United States before the Pittsburgh G-20 Summit were adopted in the Leaders' Statement issued at the end of the meeting. Perhaps most important for India and the other developing countries was the decision to replace the G-8 with the G-20 as the premier forum for international economic cooperation. This was a move that had been advocated by Obama, and it coincided with India's interests. Related to this move, recognizing the growing importance particularly of India, China, and Brazil, was the decision to increase the IMF quota shares for the developing countries by at least 5 percent. In his press conference, Prime Minister Singh had said, "It is a compromise figure. Our demand was for 7 percent, and we got 5 percent."[34]

At Pittsburgh, the G-20 leaders agreed that there would be no premature withdrawal of stimulus measures. Countries like Germany and France that feared the inflationary effects of continued stimulus still opposed more stimulus. However, this time, unlike in London the previous year, the United States and India led the way in approving continued stimulus measures to improve the prospects that there would be no relapse into recession. It seemed particularly satisfying to Prime Minister Singh that a new process of "peer review" had been adopted as a part of the framework for discussing global macroeconomic balances.[35] India took great pride in the role that it played at the Pittsburgh meeting. Indians, ever attuned to protocol, took special note that Singh had been seated next to Obama at the main session of the meeting.[36]

Thus, US-India economic engagement had helped produce cooperation · between the United States and India at the G-20 on meeting the challenges of the world financial services meltdown. In turn, US-India cooperation at the G-20 was causing the United States to work more closely with India on global financial matters in such multilateral organizations as the IMF, the World Bank, the Financial Stability Forum, and the Basel Committee on Banking Supervision.

However, it remained to be seen whether the impetus of US-India cooperation at the G-20 would affect how the United States and India worked to resolve the impasse at the WTO. Signs from the G-20 meeting in Pittsburgh indicated that there could be a positive impact. There were new trade ministers in both India and the United States. The brilliant but obdurate Kamal Nath had been replaced by the amiable Anand Sharma as minister of commerce and industry. The policy-oriented Susan Schwab had been replaced by a personable former mayor of Dallas, Ron Kirk, as US trade representative. The change to Sharma at the behest of Prime Minister Singh seemed designed to signal the possibility of closer US-India cooperation at the WTO. Singh was determined that India not be seen as the stumbling block to agreement on trade as well as environmental matters. Indeed, at a September meeting of WTO negotiators in Delhi just before the Pittsburgh G-20, progress seemed to have been made. In Pittsburgh, Prime Minister Singh noted the New Delhi mini-ministerial meeting of the WTO earlier in September and reported to his countrymen that India's role "in reviving the process of negotiations was appreciated."

Although the process of WTO negotiations on the Doha Round has been revived, the process has yet to produce the kind of cooperative spirit evident at the Pittsburgh G-20 meeting. The meeting of WTO ministers in late November and early December 2009 failed to achieve any breakthrough. Although the world economy is no longer in free fall, the sort of growing economic engagement necessary to produce agreement has not resumed. Many citizens of the United States and India are experiencing increased hardship in the form of unemployment or reduced wages and benefits. Under these circumstances, international economic engagement is viewed with distrust and anxiety. The prospect of increased foreign competition is feared.

In his November 2010 visit to India, President Obama made a valiant effort to reignite the optimism concerning US-India economic engagement as a producer of jobs and prosperity for both sides. From my position as a member of the US business delegation and as participant on panels of nationwide television commentators, Obama's efforts were well received by India. This good feeling was carried forward officially as Obama and Singh carried forward their cooperation at the meeting of the G-20 in Seoul. However, the Seoul meeting was dominated by the failure of the group as a whole to make progress on the issues of currency valuation and fiscal stimulus. The positive and negative aspects of President Obama's visit to Asia at the end of 2010 were a further demonstration of the importance of policy planning for economic engagement as an engine for strategic cooperation.

The Bottom Line

The liberalization of the Indian economy and US-India economic engagement drove an initial phase of cooperation between the United States and India in founding and operating the multilateral World Trade Organization. A prominent example of US-India cooperation during this initial phase was the creation of the WTO Information Technology Agreement. This agreement was supported successfully by businesses engaged in US-India information technology trade and investment. The Information Technology Agreement virtually eliminated tariffs on trade in many categories of hardware associated with information technology. The elimination of these tariffs, in turn, promoted further economic engagement between the United States and India in information technology and information-technology-enabled services.

A combination of bilateral and global factors combined to make the 1999 Seattle WTO Ministerial meeting a significant setback for multilateral cooperation on trade and investment. Coming at a time of US sanctions against India for the testing of nuclear devices, the Seattle multilateral setback was both a reflection of and driven in part by a lack of US-India cooperation.

Although India was persuaded in 2001 to participate in the WTO Doha Round, this participation came to be marked by confrontation between the United States and India. The hallmark of this confrontation was disagreement over agricultural subsidy and access issues. Because there has been relatively little US-India economic engagement in the agricultural sector during the focus period of this study (1991–2010), there has been insufficient push from the private sector to resolve the fundamental agricultural issues.

However, the broader US-India economic engagement of the study period, resulting in intensified strategic cooperation during the last decade, has driven considerable US-India cooperation in meeting the financial services meltdown of 2007–8 and the resultant economic retrenchment. The most salient aspect of this US-India cooperation has been in the reformation of the G-20. The United States and India have cooperated closely in this forum to promote policies supporting economic growth. The United States and India have also cooperated through the G-20 to create a more inclusive international system. This cooperation is reflected particularly in the ongoing reform of the International Monetary Fund, the World Bank, and other multilateral economic institutions.

Against the background of confrontation at the WTO over agricultural issues but cooperation on other matters, let us now examine the case of the strategic issue of food security. In particular, this case involves the circumstances of US-India agricultural economic engagement that produced the first green revolution and the changed circumstances that have frustrated the production of a second green revolution.

Chapter 8

Economic Engagement and Food Security: Green Revolutions

The green revolution has been a team effort and much of the credit for its spectacular development must go to Indian officials, organizations, scientists and farmers. However, to you, Dr. Swaminathan, a great deal of the credit must go for first recognizing the potential value of the Mexican dwarfs. Had this not occurred, it is quite possible that there would not have been a green revolution in Asia.

—Norman Borlaug, acceptance speech for the Nobel Peace Prize,
Oslo, December 10, 1970

In January 1965, two groups of Americans passed each other in the early morning chill of a winter's day in New Delhi. The first group was composed of US Foreign Agricultural Service officials headed to the US Embassy and then to meet their Indian counterparts about Public Law (PL) 480 shipments of US grain to India. The second group was composed of Rockefeller Foundation employees going to meet Indian scientists and agricultural experts for another day of work on "the Green Revolution." Both groups joked among themselves about how they were off to "save India."[1]

The group of US officials was dealing with the PL 480 issue at a crucial time. The US Congress had passed the Agricultural Trade and Development and Assistance Act of 1954 as Public Law 480 of the 83rd Congress. The act was signed into law by President Dwight D. Eisenhower in that year. President John F. Kennedy renamed the initiative the "Food for Peace Program" under legislation passed in 1961. PL 480 quickly became the major tool for economic engagement between the United States and India. By 1965, PL 480 had become the largest single US international aid program and India had become the largest single recipient country.

210

The act as amended consists of several different titles; the most relevant for purposes of US-India relations are Titles I and II. Title I pertains to concessional credit food aid. Under this title, sales of grain (chiefly wheat) were made to India under full-term (up to thirty years with a seven-year grace period) credit arrangements in Indian rupees. Title II is a grant program that provides for the donation of US agricultural commodities by the US government to meet humanitarian needs. Under the program, shipments of commodities will not be made unless there are adequate handling and storage facilities and the distribution will not interfere with domestic production and marketing. In the early 1960s, there had been some questions about India on both the facilities and interference counts. However, those questions had been resolved in India's favor.[2]

From the start, PL 480 shipments made a significant impact on the ability of India to feed its people. The shipments, particularly of wheat, were fundamental, with some 12 million tons being shipped in the first five years (1954–59) of the program. Significantly, most of the proceeds of the sale in rupees of commodities was recycled for Indian development. During the initial five years of operation, rupees equivalent to $350 million of the some $1.3 billion in rupees received from India under the PL 480 program went directly to Indian development projects as grants. These projects included river valley power and irrigation, agricultural education, and loans to farmers.[3] Thus, approximately 20 percent of the proceeds continued as direct grants for the life of the program. Another 60 percent of proceeds went to the Government of India as economic development loans, and another 5 percent or so was loaned to private enterprises. These general ratios applied throughout the life of the program.[4]

In January 1965, the US agricultural officials headed to work at the Embassy in New Delhi and with their Government of India counterparts were operating on the assumption that the US PL 480 program would continue on a modest, upward trend. However, three factors were about to change the program and Indian agriculture. The first factor was President Lyndon B. Johnson, who in January 1965 was being sworn in for a full term, and his actions to condition the PL 480 program with regard to India. The second and related factor was the advent of the "green revolution," upon which the Rockefeller Foundation experts were working. And the third factor was that India was about to experience some of the worst droughts in its history. These factors led first to a gigantic expansion of the program and then to its termination, all within seven years.

The Rockefeller Foundation employees going to work on that January day in 1965 were disciples of Norman Borlaug. Back in 1944, Borlaug had been a PhD microbiologist on the staff of the du Pont de Nemours Foundation in charge of research on agricultural bactericides and fungicides when he accepted a new position to organize and direct the Cooperative Wheat Research and Production Program in Mexico, a joint undertaking of the Rockefeller Foundation and the Government of Mexico. After decades of intense research, Borlaug found a high-yielding, disease-resistant wheat with truly revolutionary implications. Similar progress was made with rice at another Rockefeller Foundation project, the International Rice Institute, founded with the Government of the Philippines in 1960. Together with the Rockefeller Foundation, Borlaug moved to transfer the technology stemming from these breakthroughs to those countries most in need of greater agricultural production. The main thrust of this initiative was to put new cereal strains into modernized production in India and approximately two dozen other developing countries. The Rockefeller group on the way to work in that early morning New Delhi chill of 1965 was working to make that vision a reality.

Neither the US government officials nor the Rockefeller Foundation employees going to work in January 1965 would by any means "save India." However, their contributions would be instrumental in the unfolding of one of the most dramatic episodes in US-India economic engagement. As will be seen, the strategic consequences of this episode in US-India economic relations were enormous and are still unfolding.

The Outsized Political Importance of Agriculture in the United States and India

Anything having to do with agriculture, farmers, and food is of high political importance in both India and the United States. Because food is a common denominator, this is understandable for any democracy. All human beings must eat. Those with a vote are going to vote for candidates and programs that see that the majority of citizens are well fed. The Nobel Prize–winning economist Amartya Sen has famously written that no democracy has ever presided over a famine. He and others attribute this fact to the reality that a democratic government must respond to the basic human need for food to stay in power. Thus, even though India has more malnourished citizens than any other nation on Earth, it also has one of the world's largest public feeding programs and a system designed to enable poor people to buy food. The agricultural program of the United States and the massive subsidies that sustain it supply large quantities of relatively high-quality food at low prices to the US consumer. Perhaps because of the success of this program, the US agricultural system is not usually associated politically in urban areas with its ability to provide food relatively cheaply. More often, the issue is associated with its effects on farmers and their livelihood. However, if the US agricultural system failed to meet the democratic expectation of providing sufficient food at affordable prices, the political pressure from consumers for change would be enormous and similar to pressures that are routine in the Indian system.

On the production side of agricultural politics, farmers have political power in both countries that goes far beyond their involvement in the supply chain of food for the consumer. In India, that power is easily understood within the dynamic of democracy. Today the number of Indians dependent on agriculture for their incomes is just under 60 percent.[5] In 1965, more than 75 percent of the Indian population was dependent on agriculture for a living. Adding to the electoral impact of these numbers is the fact that in India the electoral participation rate tends to be higher as socioeconomic status declines. In India, as in most nations, the socioeconomic status of farmers is on the lower end of the scale. Hence, those involved in agricultural production tend to vote in greater percentages than the urbanized consumer classes. This gives those who make their living from the land even more political importance than their majority numbers indicate. In addition, Indians, like Americans, tend to have a romanticized view of the farmer that makes farmers' welfare politically potent even among those not directly involved in agriculture. Perhaps springing in part from the ethos of Mohandas Gandhi, the rural poor are given a prominent image as the repository of Indian basic values. This increases the political saliency of issues that affect farmers and increases their political stature.

In the United States, the basis for the significant political power of the farm community is less obvious than in India, where sheer numbers can produce electoral majorities. Only about 1.5 percent of all those employed in the United States in 2008 worked in agricultural pursuits.[6] The primary reasons for the outsized political power of farmers in the United States lie with the US constitutional system and more especially with the formation and operation of the US Senate.

Constitutionally, the president of the United States is not elected directly but through the Electoral College, where each state receives a portion of its votes based upon its representation in Congress. The Senate is, of course, organized on the principle of equal representation for each of the states. The two electoral votes per state given for Senate representation enhances the Electoral College power of voters in states with smaller populations. Many of these less populous states have a higher proportion of their voters involved in agriculture than do the more populous states. For example, in America's most-populous state, California, with some 37 million people, only about 800,000 (2 percent) live in rural areas. In America's least-populous state, Wyoming, with a population just over half a million, 400,000 (80 percent) live in rural areas. Similarly, New York, with a population of almost 20 million, only has about 1.5 million (7 percent) living in rural areas, while Iowa, with a population of just over 3 million, has a rural population of some 1.3 million (43 percent).[7] Although those employed in agriculture are a minority even in states that are significantly rural, agriculture is often the driving economic force in such states.[8] Thus, a politically ignorable minority in most states, the farm vote becomes crucial in a number of Midwestern and Southern states. Farmers in these states are able to exercise more presidential electoral power than their fellow citizens in more populous, generally urbanized states. Adding to this presidential electoral power of farmers is the US system for selecting presidential candidates. The farm state of Iowa holds the earliest selection of delegates to the Democratic and Republican presidential nominating conventions. As it was with Barack Obama, Iowa is often key to obtaining a nomination to run for president.

The constitutional position of the Senate itself is fundamental to the political power of agriculture in the United States. The peculiar US constitutional system of checks and balances requires Senate approval in order for the executive branch to act in many areas. The Constitution requires Senate approval of treaties and many presidential appointments. The Senate is necessary to any act of Congress and has a far more independent role in legislation than the upper houses of most parliamentary democracies. The Senate Rules of Procedure further enhance the power of states where farmers are important politically. The Senate rule on filibustering—the possibility of talking legislation to death by unlimited debate—is fundamental in this regard. The Senate rule on filibustering requires a supermajority of sixty votes for cloture, or the closing of debate. This requirement makes every state's senators crucial on most votes. Few measures can attract sixty votes in the Senate without the inclusion of senators from states where farmers are a critical voting interest. Thus, the farm vote is given outsized political power in the US Senate both by the allocation of equal votes by state and the rule requiring the supermajority needed to end unlimited debate. In India, conversely, the upper house of the legislature, the Rajya Sabha, has very little power, so there is no equivalent mechanism to the Senate. However, as in India, the image of the family farm and the yeoman farmer as repositories of American values has strong political appeal. From the time of Thomas Jefferson and his declamations on the value of the yeoman farmer, this portrayal of agricultural workers has produced political dividends for the agricultural sector.

The political power of the US and Indian agricultural communities had significant political effects on both the PL 480 and the green revolution programs. Vice versa, the PL 480 and green revolution programs deeply affected these communities. American farmers and their trade associations were dealing with huge surpluses in the early 1950s. The PL 480 mechanism seemed an ideal way to dispose of these surpluses. In addition to the need for food for the general populace, Indian farmers and agricultural scientists were pleading for new technology to improve yields and incomes.

US Public Law 480 and the Green Revolution

During the period from 1955 through 1972, economic engagement between the United States and India in the form of the PL 480 program and the green revolution fundamentally affected US-India relations and the abilities of the two countries to cooperate on strategic matters. As indicated above, the crucial year was 1965. In the summer of that year, the monsoon failed. Indian grain production plunged from 89 to 72 million tons, and requests for assistance that had been running around 4 million tons a year went up accordingly. Indian farmers and the public clamored for assistance. When President Johnson had first come to power after the assassination of President John F. Kennedy in 1963, he had allowed the PL 480 program to grow in response to India's requests. But now another force of nature, President Johnson in micromanagement mode, intervened. He could see that the upward spiral of assistance to India was becoming unsustainable with the US Congress in spite of overwhelming support from the farm states. Thus, without consulting with members of his staff, he ordered a review of PL 480 with a view to getting the Indians to "clean up their act." He wanted a plan for India to develop its own "food security," its ability to feed itself. He then wanted an agreement for India to implement the plan in exchange for massive food aid. One of the chief components of this plan and the agreement was for India, in effect, to implement the green revolution.[9]

Johnson got his agreement with India when the US secretary of agriculture, Orville Freeman, met with his counterpart, the Indian minister of food and agriculture, Chidambaram Subramaniam, in Rome at a meeting of the Food and Agriculture Organization of the United Nations. This meeting took place in late November 1965, with Freeman under strict orders from Johnson to "trade hard" to secure a written document setting forth Indian commitments on agricultural reform. The agreement was to cover India's Fourth Five-Year Plan, which ran from April 1, 1966, to March 31, 1971, in line with the Government of India's fiscal years. Freeman and Subramaniam signed the agreement on November 25, and it was transmitted to Johnson in Texas with an "Eyes Only" designation, meaning that it was to be seen only by the president and kept in the utmost secrecy.[10]

The first provision of the agreement was that India would double its investment in agriculture during the fourth plan period as compared to the previous five-year plan. This doubling of investment would result in the expenditure of the rupee equivalent of some $5 billion. Indian agricultural investment during the first year of the plan was to be increased at least by 40 percent, "even though the emergency might require cutbacks in other areas of investment." The agreement specified Indian budget mechanisms that were so fundamental that they were virtually constitutional in nature. According to the document, "It was agreed that new instrumentalities such as the agricultural production board, a committee of Cabinet members and other key officials chaired by the food and agriculture minister and vested with the authority to make binding decisions on matters of agricultural production, will be used to achieve the necessary allocation of resources to Indian agriculture." Thus, India would be ceding to bilateral agreement with the United States not only overall actions but also the internal governmental processes by which those actions would be accomplished.

The November 25, 1965, agreement also laid out in considerable detail India's commitment to specifics for implementing the green revolution. The agreement prescribed that "32 million acres of the most productive land farmed by the more efficient farmers will be designated for a crash production program with a target of 25 million tons of additional food grains by 1970 on this selected acreage." The new imported varieties of seed were specified by origin, designating the improved varieties from the Rockefeller-sponsored institutions in Mexico for wheat and the Philippines for rice. New irrigation techniques were specified. There was to be a transition from "traditional flow method to control maximum irrigation" and the development of "minor irrigation sources to attain a water balance for multiple cropping."

The United States was the chief source of imported fertilizer, and the agreement saw that the interests of US exporters of fertilizer were addressed.

The agreement specified that shortfalls in specified targets for the use of fertilizer would be made up of imports "at world market prices." As for fertilizer manufacturing in India, the agreement set forth both private participation and foreign direct investment requirements. According to the agreement, "a Cabinet-level committee, now chaired by the Prime Minister, will make a continuing effort to see that bureaucratic procedures do not hinder or discourage private foreign investment in fertilizer production and distribution." Driving the point home, there was to be no tie-in between credit for purchasing fertilizer and its origin. The agreement said plainly that "farmers will be given credit regardless of where they buy their fertilizer."

Although the PL 480 legislation contained provisions designed to see that the program did not adversely affect the livelihood of Indian farmers, it was not designed to prescribe the financial mechanisms for an agricultural production system. The agreement supplemented PL 480 by setting forth such mechanisms, including provisions dealing with the supply of credit to farmers. The "current system of credit cooperatives" was acknowledged to be inadequate. The Indian government was to "systematically review and test alternative credit possibilities." A listing of alternatives for review and testing was provided including credit subsidies, and an "all-Indian agricultural credit organization" was specified.[11]

Thus, the Rome Agreement of 1965 was an extraordinary document by any political measure. The commitments concerning Indian expenditures and budgeting alone were demeaning and probably violated the Indian Constitution. A minister of the Government of India was committing his government to certain levels of expenditures with regard to agriculture, even if this required cutbacks in other programs. For a sovereign democracy to agree to such a bargain where the budget was the chief prerogative of Parliament seemed to violate not only Indian sovereignty but also the principles of Indian governance. However, the extraordinary nature of the agreement did not stop there. The commitments concerning the details of agricultural production were like those usually dealt with by domestic legislation rather than being designated by an international agreement. Had the agreement become public knowledge in India, the political backlash would have been considerable. No wonder the document was held in secrecy for a number of years.[12]

After the agreement was reached in Rome, Johnson let the PL 480 commodities flow freely for a period of time. However, a leader with a will as strong as Johnson's was about to take the stage in India. Prime Minister Lal Badhur Shastri, while in Tashkent for a peace conference with Pakistan, died of a heart attack in January 1966. Indira Gandhi, the daughter of India's first prime minister, Jawaharlal Nehru, became prime minister. At first, Gandhi was content for India to proceed with the Rome Agreement. In a visit to Washington in March 1966, she even agreed to go further with economic reform, including a devaluation of the rupee. However, these further measures were not well received in India, and she grew disenchanted with Washington's economic pronouncements for India. In 1966, Johnson again tightened the reins on food aid to India and repeatedly called for stricter implementation of the points agreed to in Rome.

Prime Minister Gandhi was not pleased by Johnson's pressure tactics for reforming the Indian agricultural system. The very idea that any nation should try to dictate to India concerning its own methods of production and distribution was anathema to Gandhi. In her view, India's sovereignty was once again being challenged by Western outsiders. This was what the fight for independence had been about. In the view of Indian nationalists, India was not in desperate straits for food because of anything India had done or not done. Rather, this was the cruel legacy of a British imperial master that had deliberately and systematically stolen the wealth of India and imposed hunger and poverty on one of the great nations of the Earth. Nevertheless, India was desperate. Gandhi pushed forward on reforms. But she would do the American president one better. The Government of India would use every means at its disposal to enable India to become self-sufficient in food. Food security was as important a priority as any other aspect of national security. For good measure, Gandhi began to criticize the United States on other international security fronts, including its conduct of the Vietnam War.

Gandhi had apparently found a more willing collaborator and one less likely to offend Indian sensibilities with the inauguration of Richard Nixon in 1969. When Nixon became president, he sought to distinguish his approach to India on the question of PL 480 assistance from that of President Johnson. Nixon did not want the Government of India to think that he was continuing "the Johnson policy of keeping them on a short leash."[13] Prime Minister Gandhi agreed completely, but she still wanted independence from US assistance as soon as possible. She asked the Indian collaborator of Borlaug, M. S. Swaminathan of the Indian Agricultural Research Institute, how India could be free of imports. According to Swaminathan, "Indira was a strong nationalist. . . . She wanted an independent foreign policy, and food was a political weapon." The reforms and technology injections envisaged by Borlaug and Swaminathan and insisted on by Johnson were put into action. Agricultural Minister C. Subramaniam and Secretary Siva Raman succeeded in getting the Government of India to import 18,000 tons of high-yielding varieties of wheat seed that had been developed by Borlaug in Mexico. In 1970, Borlaug was awarded the Nobel Peace Prize for his work. In his acceptance speech, he praised Swaminathan and the other Indians involved for their part in creating the green revolution. Swaminathan received the Ramon Magsaysay Award for Community Leadership in 1971, and he later received the World Food Prize.

By 1972, India had nearly doubled its harvest of wheat compared with 1968. Both food aid and US-India economic interaction on the subject of agriculture declined steadily in 1970 and 1971. In 1972, Gandhi halted Indian participation in the PL 480 program. The United States and India were now at loggerheads on a number of strategic issues. Beginning at the time Johnson had established the "short rein" policy, India had become more and more critical of the United States over the Vietnam War. Kissinger went to China with the aid of Pakistan in 1971, and the Indians signed an Indo-Soviet Friendship Treaty weeks later. In the 1971 war between India and Pakistan over the establishment of East Pakistan as the independent nation of Bangladesh, the United States ordered the aircraft carrier *Eisenhower* into the Bay of Bengal in support of Pakistan.[14]

During the most intensive phase of US-India economic engagement over the green revolution (1965–67), the interaction seemed to produce positive benefits in the overall relationship. US governmental and nongovernmental officials developed a common bond as they labored together to solve common problems. For the political community at large in India, the interaction made it more difficult to paint the United States as the neo-imperialist successor to the British as the despoiler of India. This interaction in implementing a green revolution seemed to fit more neatly with the image of the United States established while Franklin D. Roosevelt was president. Roosevelt had been a strong supporter of India's aspirations for independence.

Engagement after Indian Withdrawal from the PL 480 Program

However, as India became more self-sufficient, Indian criticism of PL 480 grew. In retrospect, the program was criticized as hurting Indian wheat farmers, causing inflation, and basically existing just to allow the United States to dispose of surpluses.[15] The green revolution itself began to attract criticism from commentators in both the United States and India.[16] Particularly, those on the left and environmentalists were increasingly critical of the modern agricultural technology and practices initiated under the green revolution. Much of this criticism echoed concerns that were expressed internationally about modern farming techniques. As details of the US reform demands and the Rome Agreement became more widely known, concerns about infringement on Indian sovereignty were incorporated into this criticism. The Bhopal tragedy of December 1984—when the leakage of methyl isocyanate used in making the pesticide Sevin at a Union Carbide plant killed thousands and disabled many more—which was concomitant with the government's policies for "the complete Indianization of all foreign companies," was significant not only in its impact on victims but also for its effect in hampering engagement in providing the agricultural input insecticide.[17] The result was basically a withdrawal of India from engagement with the United States and the rest of the world on agricultural matters. Though India would make periodic purchases of essential commodities and inputs such as fertilizers, the emphasis was on Indian self-sufficiency. Although the economic reforms of the 1990s were important to India's manufacturing and service sectors, they left agriculture virtually untouched.

A Second Green Revolution?

As Borlaug had foreseen, India, in the first decade of the twenty-first century, was again confronted with the question of food security.[18] The population was again straining the food supply. The issue again began to affect the ability of the United States and India to cooperate strategically. In 2005, Prime Minister Manmohan Singh called for a "second green revolution." The same US-India July 18, 2005, Joint Statement that had announced civil nuclear cooperation contained a passage on agriculture. According to this statement, President Bush and Prime Minister Singh agreed to "launch a US-India Knowledge Initiative on Agriculture focused on promoting teaching, research, service and commercial linkages." When the two leaders met again in New Delhi on March 2, 2006, they reported that they had:

Sought to expand cooperation in agriculture by:
  1. Launching the Knowledge Initiative on Agriculture with a three-year financial commitment to link our universities, technical institutions, and business to support agricultural education, joint research, and capacity building projects including in the area of biotechnology.
  2. Endorsing an agreed work plan to promote bilateral trade in agriculture through agreements that lay out a path to open the US market to

Indian mangoes, recognize India as having authority to certify shipments of Indian products to the United States meet USDA [US Department of Agriculture] organic standards, and provide for discussions on current regulations affecting trade in fresh fruits and vegetables, poultry and dairy, and almonds.

The United States and India proceeded to launch a three-year program on agriculture. The launching of the initiative was accompanied by considerable nostalgia for the first green revolution. At long last, India gave personal, official recognition to Borlaug, awarding him the Padma Vibhushan, India's second-highest civilian award, in January 2006 for his work on the green revolution some forty years earlier. The US-India Knowledge Initiative on Agriculture was consciously modeled on the first green revolution, even naming Borlaug and Swaminathan as "honorary advisors." When Borlaug died on September 12, 2009, at the age of ninety-five, the Indian tributes to him were effusive. Prime Minister Singh and Minister of Agriculture Pawar both offered statements of condolence. Singh said, "At a time in the sixties when the country was facing the spectre of severe food shortages, the introduction of Dr. Borlaug's high-yielding varieties of seeds set in motion a technological revolution in Indian agriculture that led eventually to the country achieving self-sufficiency in food grains. The green revolution lifted the spirits of the Indian people and gave them new hope and confidence in their ability to tackle the country's daunting economic challenges."[19] Pawar added, "Father of the green revolution, Norman Borlaug is credited with what he himself described as a temporary success in man's war against hunger and deprivation. . . . As India moves toward the second green revolution, his enduring vision will be a source of inspiration and sustenance for all of us."[20]

The United States committed $24 million to the Agricultural Knowledge Initiative over the three-year period 2006–8.[21] India committed a similar amount. However, it was difficult to tell whether either country's commitment was simply an expenditure that it would have made in any event. Much of the US money was encompassed within existing programs of the US Agency for International Development (USAID), including "Partnerships for Innovation and Knowledge in Agriculture," which essentially entail technology transfer. Other such USAID projects include a Michigan State University–Tamil Nadu Agricultural University horticulture project and a similar program led by the University of Wisconsin–Madison. Other US universities have been involved in biotechnology, water management, and university capacity building under the initiative. However, the cost of all the US projects put together is dwarfed by the amounts spent during the first green revolution. The amounts committed do not even compare favorably with the approximately $210 million World Bank project focused on on agriculture innovation and sustainability that was commenced in 2006.[22]

The Obama Administration and Food Security

Hunger and food security have been adopted by the Obama administration as a "signature issue" in foreign policy. During Hillary Clinton's first trip to India as secretary of state, both she and the Indian minister of agriculture, Sharad Pawar, spoke of the US-India agricultural collaboration "over more than 50 years." As Secretary Clinton pointed out, this collaboration had produced results enabling India to feed 20 percent of the world's people even though it had only 5 percent of the world's arable land.[23] However, past achievements will not feed a growing Indian population during the next fifty years.

Presumably, the Obama administration will carry forward the food security issue with India. However, how this will be done and what it will achieve are unclear. Like Bush's effort, Obama again seems to be trying to copy the approach of the first green revolution.

At the July 2009 Group of Eight (G-8) Summit in L'Aquila, Italy, to which leaders from some twenty-eight other countries were invited, the Obama administration presented a "food security initiative." This initiative laid out five principles: (1) stronger coordination among donors supplying assistance to developed countries in the areas of food and agriculture, (2) support for comprehensive strategies, (3) investment through country-owned plans, (4) leveraging effective multilateral institutions, and (5) sustained commitments.[24] The Obama administration's international food security initiative thus is evidently designed to supplement developed-country assistance for emergency food aid and nutrition programs with assistance for sustainable agricultural development. Such a shift in emphasis from food aid to agricultural development assistance has long been advocated by many in the international assistance community. For example, the director-general of the Food and Agricultural Organization of the United Nations, Jacques Diouf, from Senegal has noted, "This is what the FAO has been preaching for years without success."[25]

The major drivers behind the food security initiative at the G-8 and G-20 meetings in 2009 were the Bill & Melinda Gates Foundation and the Rockefeller Foundation. However, the primary agricultural focus of these organizations—and, in turn, of President Obama—is not India or even Asia. Their focus is on recreating the Indian green revolution experience in Africa. In 2006, the Gates Foundation started the Alliance for a Green Revolution in Africa—AGRA—even the acronym for the initiative had a decidedly Indian flavor. The Rockefeller Foundation, building on its decades of experience in this field, became a partner in AGRA. The United Kingdom's Department for International Development, the UK counterpart to USAID, also became a core donor.[26] Obama has made explicit his desire to use the Indian green revolution experience as a template for agricultural development in Africa. In an interview before his trip to Ghana in July 2009, he responded to a question on development assistance as follows:

> Now, I also think, on the ground, in many of these countries, how we think about not high-tech stuff but low-tech technologies to, for example, improve food production is vitally important. I'm still frustrated over the fact that the green revolution that we introduced in India in the '60s we haven't yet introduced into Africa in 2009.[27]

The Obama food security initiative seems unlikely to contribute to the US-India economic interchange necessary to promote strategic cooperation with India on food security if this initiative is directed at Africa. On September 26, 2009, Secretary of State Clinton attempted to broaden the initiative's perspective when she cohosted with UN secretary-general Ban Ki-moon a meeting on food security during the annual meeting of the UN General Assembly. Clinton emphasized the five principles indicated above.[28] However, the meeting led with testimony from the president of Rwanda, and the Government of India seemed to take little interest in the meeting.

While President Obama was in India in November 2010, he attended an exhibition of agriculture technology in Mumbai. In the Obama-Singh joint statement, the two leaders gave a new name to a second green revolution—the "evergreen revolution." However, the emphasis still was on technology as the leaders expressed their commitment "to work together to develop, test, and replicate transformative technologies to extend food security as part of an Evergreen Revolution."[29]

Why No Second Green Revolution from US-India Engagement?

The George W. Bush administration's Agricultural Knowledge Initiative achieved very little, and certainly nothing like the breakthroughs in production that were the result of the first green revolution. Unless adjustments are made, the Obama administration's vastly expanded multilateral effort seems equally unlikely to achieve either a second green revolution in India or a first green revolution in Africa.

There are several reasons for this likely ineffectiveness. The world system of agricultural development has changed since 1965. No longer is it possible for scientifically oriented nongovernmental organizations supported by governments and receptive farm communities to effect the sort of broad systemic change that brings about phenomenal increases in production. Today the research and development function lies to a far greater degree with private companies. The private sector is relatively more important than the sort of public and semipublic organizations that fueled agricultural knowledge creation in the past. The Indian side of the Agricultural Knowledge Initiative belatedly recognized this when India added both the Federation of Indian Chambers of Commerce and Industry and the Confederation of Indian Industries to its Indian board members. Thus, the United States and India had private-sector members on the Board of the US-India Agricultural Knowledge Initiative. However, the initiative was basically a government-to-government endeavor. In New Delhi in 2007, the chief economic theoretician of the Congress Party and then–minister of state for commerce and industry told a group of visiting US business executives that private enterprise basically "has nothing to do with" the Agricultural Knowledge Initiative.[30]

The relationship between the United States and India is now fundamentally different than it was in 1965. There is no ability of the United States to play a superior role through food commodity and technological resources as there was in 1965. An agreement such as that of November 25, 1965, between Freeman and Subrimaniam is unthinkable. Now the relationship is basically that of equals. In the agricultural areas, the United States and India have not taken advantage of the opportunity to forge a new partnership of equality. The standoff between the United States and India in the Doha Round of the World Trade Organization trade negotiations is an example of the failure to forge a partnership focused on the higher goal of a second green revolution. India is determined to pursue the protection of its agricultural market, while the United States is just as determined to defend its massive agricultural subsidy program.

Trade disputes between the United States and India inhibit bilateral agricultural economic engagement. And this lack of engagement adversely affects the strategic cooperation necessary for effective promotion by the United States and India of a second green revolution. Without significant US agricultural trade with India, there is unlikely to be support in the US Congress for the programs necessary for rapid advances in Indian agriculture.

The Impediment of US-India Agricultural Trade Disputes

Bilateral trade disputes relevant to agriculture are a significant impediment to forging the partnership of equality necessary to support a second green revolution. For example, since the demise of the PL 480 program with India, disputes over US commercial exports of grain to India have inhibited the relationship. Tariff levels have been important, but also fundamental have been phytosanitary disputes. Chief among these has been the dispute over weed seeds in US grain.

Indian wheat farmers have long complained about the introduction of foreign weeds on the subcontinent. The problem of invasive species of weeds is common throughout the world. However, for many Indian wheat farmers, it is an article of faith that their invasive weeds originated with US shipments of PL 480 wheat or with the seeds for the new varieties of more productive wheat that originated from the research of Borlaug and were imported as fundamental to the creation of the green revolution in India.

In response to political pressure, in 2003 the Ministry of Agriculture issued a directive titled "Plant Quarantine (Regulation of Import into India) Order, 2003," which set new and stricter requirements for allowable weed seeds in grain imports. At the time the order was issued, it had little significance for US exporters. India was self-sufficient in wheat, and there appeared to be no opportunity for sales to India. However, because of a poor harvest in 2005, India decided to import wheat in 2006. An international tender for a relatively small amount of wheat was issued in February of that year. When the wheat procured proved inadequate, another tender was issued in April. The United States complained that its wheat-exporting companies were, in effect, excluded from competition by the stringent weed seed requirements. US agricultural officials pointed out that the standards set by US regulations were accepted by 110 countries around the world. For example, India was the only country known to have listed the weed *bromus secalinus,* or "rye brome," as a quarantined weed in grain for consumption.[31] The United States asked for a relaxation of the standards. Pursuant to this request, the standards were relaxed somewhat on a temporary basis to promote competition on the tender, but the basic restriction remained.[32] Those in the US industry believed that it would be uneconomic to change their methods of cleaning grain to accommodate India and that India's demands were without scientific basis.

The outcry from Indian farm organizations and scientists against any relaxation of the weed standard, along with continued pressure from the United States for removal of the restriction, resulted in the Government of India appointing an "Empowered Group of Ministers" (EGOM) to resolve the matter. The EGOM in turn appointed the secretaries of their ministries to report recommendations. Bilateral discussions were held in Washington at the US Department of Agriculture's Animal and Plant Inspection Service and the Federal Grain Inspection Service. US grain industry service representatives conducted the Indian delegation on a site visit to wheat export and inspection facilities in Portland, Oregon.[33]

However, the US effort was to no avail. On June 7, 2007, the US Embassy in New Delhi announced that no agreement had been reached.[34] In July the Committee of Secretaries recommended that the 2003 standards not be changed, and in September the EGOM formally accepted the report. In India the decision was cited as a laudable example of India being able to stand up to US pressure. A chart was provided by the Ministry of Agriculture showing the exact number (21,074,429) of weed seeds detected in imported wheat in 2006–7.[35] The decision of the Government of India was met with cynicism and disbelief by both US public and private officials involved in the controversy. The US Embassy suggested that India's import inspection process was unreliable. Because wheat from other countries was still being imported, the United States called upon the Government of India "to conduct independent tests of imported wheat arriving in Indian ports to verify that these standards are truly being met."[36] US Wheat Associates suggested sarcastically, "To allay any concern about the possible spread of 'exotic' weed seeds, perhaps the Indian government could use the high premiums they now pay in just one year to invest in cleaning facilities at their port to meet their own uniquely restrictive standards and allow future wheat imports at competitive prices."[37] Corruption in the form of payments to the grain inspectors and/or their superiors was suspected. The theory was that US exporters, constrained by the US Foreign Corrupt Practices Act, would not pay the bribes that were surmised to be routine for non-US exporters.

Thus, Indian phytosanitary norms applicable to weed seeds serve as of this writing to exclude US wheat from the Indian market. When world demand is high and prices are elevated, the ability of US wheat growers to export to India has little effect on their total exports. This changes with increased Indian demand and US supplies of wheat. In any event, the weed seed issue is illustrative of controversies that make US-India agricultural economic engagement more difficult.

A somewhat more positive example is the controversy over the importation of Indian mangoes into the United States. From 1990 to 2007, the United States prohibited imports of Indian mangoes over concerns about the spread of the mango stone weevil to the United States. After extensive negotiations, an irradiation facility was established at the Bhaba Atomic Research Center in Maharashtra State to irradiate mangoes for shipment to the United States. This facility was approved by the US Department of Agriculture in April 2007.[38] Some 160 tons of the fruit were processed through this facility for shipment during 2007. Significant increases in exports to the United States in 2008 and 2009 were expected. Because of difficulty in operating the irradiation facility, the global economic decline, and poor crop conditions, these increases did not occur.[39] However, economic engagement with regard to exporting mangoes has already enabled the United States and India to cooperate on other trade matters. Particularly, an initial step toward the importation of Harley Davidson motorcycles into India has been linked with the progress on mangoes.[40] More important, the experience with mangoes has led to further US-India agreement on the importation to the United States of litchi fruit.[41]

The wheat weed seed and mango episodes show that failure to address regulatory nontariff barriers to trade has an adverse affect but that a successful approach to these barriers promotes the economic interaction that leads to further cooperation. Perhaps the two episodes also indicate that the United States places more emphasis on legal reasoning and scientific proof than deal making as a method to resolve such issues.

The Role of Indian Agricultural and Food Regulations

India has been slow to allow the market to work throughout the food supply chain. A plethora of controls are maintained in the name of protecting both the urban poor and economically disadvantaged farmers. The state-owned buying and storage firms as well as the price-controlled retail establishments are a significant holdover from the days of India as a semisocialist, or "mixed-economy," state. India purports to have an agricultural system that is largely driven by private enterprise and markets. But the reality is much different. The Essential Commodities Act provides a strong mechanism for controlling prices and markets. The Indian Public Distribution System, ostensibly targeted at providing food to the economically disadvantaged and the prevention of famine, acts as a significant governor on the whole agricultural and food distribution system. The Food Corporation of India provides not just a safety net for poor people but also a stranglehold on the entire agricultural and food distribution system. The system of State Food and Civil Supplies Corporations and wholesale dealers that distribute to Fair Price Shops and ultimately to consumers and ration card holders is now more of a factor in agricultural production than technical inputs.[42]

The 2006–9 experience of India with regard to sugar is illustrative of the regulatory barriers to the creation of a second green revolution. The experience shows the difficulty of significantly increasing production while attempting to calibrate all economic aspects of production and distribution for protective political purposes. In 2006, sugar prices rose rapidly. Instead of attempting measures to bring about long-term increases in supply to meet demand, the Indian government banned exports of sugar. Toward the end of 2006, sugar prices began to fall rapidly. In 2007, prices continued to fall, and by 2008 they were so low that many farmers did not even bother to harvest their crops. Many that did sold the sugarcane for use as fuel in power generation. Many sugarcane farmers switched to other crops. In 2009, prices surged ahead, and the government again intervened. Through intervention in the export market, quotas on sales by sugar mills, and the setting of minimum prices for farmers, the government seeks to fine-tune the system not to increase supply but to meet political objectives for producers and processors. For instance, in 2009, with national elections looming, the government required the factories to sell 10 percent of their output at below-market prices to aid the poor and banned futures trading in sugar.[43]

India would like to use the forces of the market to ameliorate its food production and processing problems. However, for political reasons, the government cannot bring itself to fully open the distribution system to the forces of the market and international participation. The country's production and processing issues cannot be resolved unless the distribution system is liberalized by further opening food retailing. Utilization of retail market demand and the funds retailing generates are necessary to stimulate the innovation and investment necessary to modernize the food supply chain. The lack of income from retail inhibits every stage of the supply chain upstream from retailing. Without full realization of the market potential at the retail or consumer level, wholesalers cannot afford the warehousing and transportation necessary for a modern storage and movement of agricultural products. Without full realization at the wholesaler level, funds are not generated for adequate storage and processing by the initial buyers of agricultural production, and farmers cannot be paid prices for their production at levels necessary to make them prosperous.

Thus far, Indian reforms in retailing of food have been painfully slow and inadequate. An obvious and often-stated reason for this situation is the political concern for the 40 to 50 million people employed in the small retail operations that sell groceries. Threatening these small retail operations through increased competition from modern food retailers has proven to be hazardous, particularly outside major metropolitan areas. In 2007, protests broke out in several of the smaller Indian cities against "Reliance Fresh," a food distribution venture of the giant Reliance Industries. These protests were against Reliance for attempting to enter the fresh fruits and vegetables business. The protests were violent in several cities. In India's most populous state, Uttar Pradesh, the chief minister ordered all the Reliance Fresh stores shut down.[44] In West Bengal, similar protests were run by produce traders unhappy with the large retailers Metro Cash and Carry, RPG, and the Future Group for buying direct from farmers.

Official reaction to the prospect of foreign investment in the retailing of food has also been negative. Foreign direct investment would supply both needed capital and expertise. Several US companies are interested in food retailing in India. Most notable among these companies is Wal-Mart. However, India refuses to allow any foreign investment in multibrand retailing. A compromise approach followed by India is to allow foreign investment at the wholesale level in stores that supply small retailers. In India, such operations are called "cash and carry." This has been the route followed by Wal-Mart, together with an Indian partner. Thus, Wal-Mart has entered into an equal partnership arrangement with Bharti Enterprises called Bharti-Walmart. The first store owned by Bharti Wal-Mart in the city of Amritsar was delayed for fear of violence. However, the Amritsar store is now considered a success, and Bharti-Walmart has plans to open an additional fifteen stores over three years with an investment in each of up to $7 million.[45]

Other international distributors—such as Tesco of the United Kingdom and Carrefour of France—are attempting to utilize the Bharti-Walmart model. However, in the summer of 2009 a parliamentary standing committee on commerce issued a report titled "Foreign and Domestic Investment in Retail Sector." The report recommends a complete ban on "domestic corporate heavyweights and foreign retailers from entering into retail trade in grocery, fruits and vegetables." Further, the committee recommended a ban on the issuance of any further licenses for the cash-and-carry wholesale business.[46]

The recommendations of the committee are not likely to be put into law for domestic Indian corporations. However, the recommendations have continued to add fuel to the political controversy over opening up retail food sales. And this controversy has continued to inhibit the use of market mechanisms for reforming the agricultural system.

The Role of Changing Methods for the Supply of Agricultural Inputs

Changes to methods of supplying basic agricultural inputs seeds, fertilizer, and pesticides also make the model for producing the first green revolution inapplicable to producing a second green revolution. Perhaps the most publicly salient aspect of the first green revolution was the introduction and use of improved varieties of wheat and rice seeds. As noted above, these varieties were developed in a strong public-private partnership and furnished on a highly subsidized basis from the work of research and development entities financed in large part by nonprofit foundations. Though such entities continue to play a role, the research, development, production, and furnishing of improved varieties of seeds is now driven internationally by private enterprise on a for-profit basis. The new generation of seeds from entities operating on such a basis has been remarkably effective but highly controversial. In US-India agricultural engagement, the most prominent example of changed circumstances for the furnishing of seeds has been the role of Monsanto in India.

Monsanto, headquartered in Missouri, is one of the world's largest seed companies, with sales in 2009 of some $11.7 billion and net income of $2.1 billion. In the late 1990s, Monsanto "reinvented" itself by divesting itself of its commercial chemicals business to focus on biotechnology and particularly genetically modified plant varieties.[47] During this period, it made acquisitions in India that positioned the company to be a major factor in the supply of modern seed varieties in India. This engagement with India was controversial from the start, with demonstrations fueled by the worldwide protests against genetically modified seeds. In 2002, Monsanto introduced cotton seeds designed to be resistant to certain pests.

This and subsequent activities of Monsanto have been protested on two basic premises. First is the premise that genetically modified plants are inherently harmful to the environment and health. Genetically modified cotton seeds have been a success for Monsanto, with some 80 percent of all cotton production in India using such seeds and production having doubled from 2002 to 2008.[48] However, Monsanto's attempts to introduce genetically modified seeds in the food sector have been thwarted. Most recently, the Government of India has rejected Monsanto's introduction of genetically modified eggplant or, in Hindi, *brinjal*.[49] Given the cultural importance of food and diet in India, protests founded on the health implications of food have political impact.

Second, but more important politically, is the premise that genetically modified seeds are economically harmful to the small farmer. Small farmers for millennia have used seeds saved from the previous crop for the next season's planting. Such seeds are often traded among farmers. Because non-varietals hybrid or genetically modified plants such as cotton do not produce seeds capable of reproduction, farmers using these seeds must purchase new seeds each year. Where varietal seeds are capable of reproduction, the ancient practices are deemed violations of intellectual property rights when applied to proprietary seeds. Thus, there are those who say that the use of Monsanto's seeds contributes to the economic hardship of small farmers by constraining the ancient cycle of obtaining seeds for new planting from the crop of the previous season. Further, there are claims that the sale of such seeds causes farmer suicides because of their cost and because farmers go into debt to purchase them.[50] In spite of the political difficulties, there are signs that the Government of India seeks ways to obtain and use seeds that are engineered for specific traits.[51]

As indicated above, modern fertilizers played an important role in raising productivity levels during the most intensive periods for implementing the first green revolution. The importation and application of fertilizers was a key part of the 1965 Rome Agreement, in which special protections were provided for US fertilizer exports. Thus, US exports of fertilizers were a part of the rapid increase in agricultural production described as the green revolution in India.

This state of affairs was changed in 1977, when the Indian government adopted a "Retention Price Scheme" at the recommendation of the Fertilizer Prices Committee. Under this scheme, subsidy was not provided to the farmer but to the manufacturers of fertilizer and established for them a fixed margin of profit. To satisfy the farmer vote, fertilizer prices were fixed at levels often below the cost of production. Imports and exports became the sole prerogative of the government. Although there were occasional imports of fertilizers to meet what Indian bureaucrats viewed as shortages, imports in most years were not of the main types of fertilizers used and manufactured in India.

The fertilizer subsidy scheme adopted in 1977 was roundly criticized both in India and the United States on an economic basis. However, the scheme was popular politically, and it was not until 2003 that modest reforms were made by modifying it with regard to the method for payment of the subsidy.[52] This "Group Pricing Scheme" lowered the amount of the subsidy. However, the subsidy largely kept prices lower than world prices, making it uneconomic for US fertilizer manufacturers to compete. In the run-up to the 2009 elections, the Government of India approved new pricing schemes for lowering prices of some types of fertilizers to the farmer.[53] Along with a loan forgiveness program for farmers, this further subsidy to the agricultural sector was thought to have played a major role in the electoral victory secured among farmers by the Congress Party and the United Progressive Alliance in 2009.

In the 2009 United Progressive Alliance government's budget, the fertilizer subsidy reform received prominent attention. In his Budget Speech, Finance Minister Pranab Mukherjee cited both "the declining response of agricultural productivity to increased fertilizer usage" and the need "to ensure balanced application of fertilizers." The government pledged to move "towards a nutrient-based subsidy regime instead of the current product pricing regime." The government indicated that "this unshackling of the fertilizer manufacturing sector is expected to attract fresh investments in this sector." Minister Mukherjee also said, "In due course, it is also intended to move to a system of direct transfer of subsidy to the farmers."[54] These pledges, together with changes in the import regime, could make a substantial difference to US trade and investment in fertilizers. Resumed economic engagement with India in this sector so important to a second green revolution could have a profound impact on the ability of the United States and India to cooperate in this area. In the spring of 2010, the Singh government moved forward with fertilizer subsidy reforms by announcing a "Nutrient Based Subsidy" policy.[55] However, farm politics caused the government to back off from reform with regard to the key fertilizer urea and modify other parts of its program.[56] The result was some progress but not enough to restore US-India economic engagement in the fertilizer sector to the status it enjoyed during the first green revolution.

Pesticides are another key, human-made component of a second green revolution for which circumstances have changed drastically since the first green revolution in India. Because of the profound effect of pests on Indian agricultural productivity at the time of the first green revolution, Indians both inside and outside the agricultural sector welcomed US engagement in the supply and production of pesticides. This is no longer the case. Indian nongovernmental organizations routinely decry the presence of pesticides in food and drinking water. As noted above, the Union Carbide tragedy at Bhopal in December 1984 still casts a pall on US-India economic engagement on pesticides. Controversy still swirls around questions of civil liability and criminal culpability. Protesters worldwide have sought to transfer liability and culpability questions from Union Carbide to the purchaser of this firm's non-Indian assets, Dow Chemical.[57] The possibility of easy US-India economic engagement on the subject of agricultural pesticides is gone.

Much attention has been given to the dissemination to the Indian farmer of knowledge and information. This dissemination, based on a US land grant college–agricultural extension service model, seems to be the basis for much US-India economic engagement through present USAID programs.[58] However, as discussed below, much has changed in this field from the days of the first green revolution. Today, the private sector plays a much more fundamental role, especially through the mechanism of contract farming.

Natural Inputs and the Possibilities for a Second Green Revolution

The situation with regard to the natural inputs necessary for a second green revolution has also changed. India has always been dependent upon the monsoon rains for crop production. Historically, the failure of the monsoon was associated with famine. One strand of the fabric producing the first green revolution was the development of techniques to tap India's once-abundant supply of groundwater. The availability of these techniques was exploited by the subsidization of the electricity necessary to run the pumps bringing groundwater to the surface. Electricity subsidies are paid from state budgets to make up for the differences between fixed fees based on the declared horsepower of pumps and the actual costs of the electricity. As noted above, electricity is virtually free for farmers in some Indian states. In addition, the irrigation systems are themselves subsidized. These subsidies for electricity and irrigation facilities have led to the overexploitation of groundwater.[59] Groundwater is now so depleted that it cannot be counted upon for the increased irrigation necessary to support a vastly expanded harvest.[60]

Once again, the most vulnerable aspect of Indian agricultural production has become the availability of water. The failure of the monsoon has a radical effect on agricultural production. In 2009, this vulnerability was made plain. By the middle of August, the Indian Meteorological Department found that rainfall for the summer monsoon was 29 percent below normal and declared 2009 a drought year. The Reserve Bank of India said that prices were likely to go up. During a single week, on an annualized basis, the prices of cereals were up by 12 percent, beans and peas were up by 18 percent, and fruit and vegetables were up by 18.4 percent.[61] Although, the deputy chairman of the Planning Commission, Montek Singh Ahluwalia, sought to dampen speculation that the below-average monsoon could produce inflation, he admitted that a decrease in growth prospects was likely.[62] The situation was said to be as bad as that in 2002 that was blamed for cutting the growth of gross domestic product from 5.6 to 3.8 percent. For his part, Prime Minister Singh organized an interagency Group of Ministers to plan for dealing with the problem. In this case, the ministers of finance, agriculture, railroads, and petroleum were commissioned to come up with a plan for dealing with the results of the failure of the autumn, or "Kharif," harvest.[63]

The availability of land for the expansion of agricultural production is also a constraint on the creation of a second green revolution. When the first green revolution commenced, there was a considerable amount of fallow land in India that could be put into production with modern techniques. Now there are fewer prospects for adding additional land to food cultivation. In fact, with the increasing salinity caused by overfertilization, the removal of groundwater, and other factors, the amount of land that can sustain agricultural production seems to be shrinking.[64] Perhaps a more important constraint that has become more acute since the first green revolution is the size of landholdings.[65] Since the beginning of the Republic of India, it has been the official policy to limit the size of landholdings and redistribute land above ceiling limitations. With the implementation of this policy and the continuous growth of the farm population, the average size of landholdings has continued to decrease. More than 50 percent of all operational holdings are less than 1 hectare. Less than 4 percent of working farms encompass more than 10 hectares.[66] The smaller farm landholdings become, the more difficult it is to apply the sorts of modern farming techniques that brought the first green revolution.

The increasing prominence and violence of disputes over the conversion of farmland to industrial uses is an indication of how exacerbated the issue of farmland has become. The most prominent of these demonstrations occurred in the villages of Nandigram and Singhur in the State of West Bengal. The Nandigram incident began in 2007, when the Government of West Bengal attempted to secure land for the establishment of a chemical facility for an Indonesian industrial group. The police were called in. Police/protester clashes resulted in the deaths of at least fourteen demonstrators and the injury of scores. A similar situation ensued when Tata sought to establish a production plant for its low-cost Nano car near Singhur. As a result of the demonstrations, Tata pulled out of West Bengal and is manufacturing the Nano at a plant in Gujarat State. Protests and conflict over the taking of agricultural land are now commonplace whenever the government seeks space for a new or expanded special economic zone (SEZ).

A factor feeding this conflict over farmland is the incomplete status of India's land tenure system. Farmers often have not been given title to land promised them under programs for land reform, even though they occupy the land and consider it theirs. The uncertainty of many farmers is increased by the deplorable state of land records, which makes it difficult to actually prove title. Farmers having no title or who are unable to prove title to land have little to lose by embracing violence when the government tries to give land upon which they are working for use in a SEZ. The power of this issue is indicated by the fact that the leader of the pro-farmland, anti-SEZ demonstrations, Mamata Banerjee, was given a prominent Cabinet position in the Singh government that took office in 2009.

Private-Sector Economic Engagement and the Possibilities for a Second Green Revolution

There are signs that US-India private-sector engagement is starting to provide a base that may one day serve to support full US-India cooperation on food security. Several US private-sector agribusinesses have intensified their economic engagement with India since the opening up of the Indian economy. These US-India agribusiness projects can have a major impact on the ability of the United States and India to cooperate on the strategic issue of food security. The following are examples of such projects.

Chief among the US companies operating projects related to increasing agricultural productivity in India is PepsiCo, which has focused initially on projects designed to increase productivity in the Indian State of Punjab. In 1989, PepsiCo launched a project with the Punjab Agriculture University and Punjab Agro Industries Corporation. This program focused on evolving agricultural practices to help Punjab farmers produce internationally competitive products. Accelerating their efforts since economic liberalization, PepsiCo and its partners have used a 27-acre research facility and demonstration station in Punjab to help develop new varieties of plants. Tomato cultivation had been a particular area of success. Working backward from a large tomato-processing plant, PepsiCo used contract farming to bring enough tomatoes to its Zahura plant to keep it running at maximum capacity. In contract farming, the buyer and farmer enter into a contract whereby the buyer supplies all inputs except land and labor. In turn, the seller agrees to provide the buyer with a certain quality and quantity of crops at a time in the future. One of the inputs provided by PepsiCo India was its type of tomato. The results have been that from 1989 through 2009, tomato production in Punjab rose from 28,000 tons to more than 200,000 tons. And the yields of tomatoes have tripled, from 16 to 54 tons per hectare.[67]

Potatoes have been another PepsiCo success story. Under the PepsiCo contract farming scheme, backward integration has taken place to supply Frito-Lay plants in Punjab, West Bengal, and Maharashtra. Pepsico works with more than 10,000 farmers in seven Indian states and plans to triple the number of farmers it worked with in 2009 by 2012. The construction of state-of-the-art storage facilities has progressed with the expansion of the potato operation.[68] The success of Frito-Lay in potato chips has prompted others to enter modern potato processing and expand into such products as French fries, potato flakes, and potato powder. The benefits of modern, or as denominated in India, "organized," potato production include reduction of postharvest losses, an instant food source, and employment generation at higher income levels.[69] PepsiCo has extended its success in tomatoes and potatoes to basmati rice and peanuts. The objective of the peanut endeavor is to transition the PepsiCo Indian portfolio into the production of export-quality, value-added products. In addition to snack peanuts in roasted, salted, flavored, and coated lines, this endeavor is expected to include peanut butter for export.[70]

Another example is ADM, which formed a joint venture with the Tinna Group in 1998. The principal business of the joint venture is the processing of oilseeds into edible oils, animal feeds and feed ingredients, and biodiesel fuels. The joint venture, Tinna Oils & Chemicals Limited, has conducted its own extension service that offers training to farmers in best agricultural practices. There are some twenty Tinna crop development centers staffed by trained agronomists. The program operates a telephone help line to address cultivation issues. Until a few years ago, such a telephone-based service would have made little sense. However, because India has been adding mobile telephones at the rate of some 10 million a month for the past two years, such services are now becoming useful to farmers. The crop development centers also serve as a vehicle for the joint venture to market pesticides, seeds, and fertilizers to farmers. The program distributes cash prizes for achieving high yields. At the present time, Tinna reaches some 50,000 to 100,000 farmers a year.[71]

General Mills offers a food industry model that has the potential for increasing economic engagement in a significant manner. The company conducts its customary retail product sales activities in India with Pillsbury brand flours and mixes. General Mills also supports the food service industry through sales and technical support and training. Most significantly, it exports from India a range of products for sale in the United States, the United Kingdom, the United Arab Emirates, and Singapore. In addition, it combines its production for the Indian and foreign markets with support for its operations worldwide in information technology, information-technology-enabled services, and technical support service. This combination of export, import, and services sourcing is the type of broad-based economic engagement that has an impact on the ability of the United States and India to cooperate. Engagement on this range of activities has a more significant impact than conducting any one or two of these activities alone.

Collectively and individually, the US-India private-sector agricultural endeavors discussed here suffer from the difficulty that they presently are not large enough to make the necessary impact on the Indian system for producing, processing, storing, and distributing food. Such programs are promising and capable of providing a foundation of support for further cooperation on food security. However, the programs are small in comparison with the size of Indian agriculture. Additional means for expanding the base of US-India economic engagement is necessary to harness the potential support for these programs. Such expanded economic engagement can make a difference in whether India is able to meet the challenges of food security that it now faces.

The Need for US and Indian Changes in Approach

The first green revolution was a product of US-India public-private economic engagement. Although Indian sensibilities were offended by some of the political techniques employed by President Johnson to promote reform, the success of the program has borne dividends for decades. These dividends are partly in the form of the ability of the United States and India to cooperate strategically on the issue of food security. Both sides tend to view the contribution of the green revolution in enabling India to feed itself as one of the greatest accomplishments of the US-India engagement. A measure of the esteem in which the United States and India hold their bilateral cooperation on this issue is that the two countries, now faced with another crisis in Indian food security, are looking to their previous path to success as a way to meet the present challenge. This is shown by the inclusion of the Agricultural Knowledge Initiative as a component of the Bush-Singh Joint Statement of July 18, 2005. Although not given the attention accorded the civil nuclear part of that statement, the provisions regarding food security and agriculture were fundamental from the perspective of both parties. Making Borlaug and Swaminathan honorary cochairs of the Agricultural Knowledge Initiative is also indicative of the conscious attempt to pattern the current engagement between United States and India on the issue of food security after the successful first green revolution. However, this pattern is not wholly applicable to present realities. If slavishly followed, it will only lead to disappointment on both sides.

The first green revolution was in large part a product of assistance provided from essentially US sources to India. Although significant contributions to the effort were made by India and Indian scientists and leaders, the basic template for engagement was one of assistance. For the reasons discussed above, the assistance model of the first green revolution is no longer applicable. Likewise, the reliance on governmental and nonprofit interaction is outmoded.

A second green revolution will also require a greater appreciation for the role that Indian economic reform plays in creating revolutionary change in food security. In the first green revolution, interaction between scientists was only one of the actions necessary to make the revolution a success. Though the image of Borlaug and his associates working with Swaminathan and Indian scientists cooperatively to create astounding increases in productivity is attractive, that image obscures the reality of the economic reform steps that were taken. The leadership for change in the Indian system of agricultural economics provided first by Minister Subrimaniam and then–prime minister Indira Gandhi was absolutely essential to the achievement of Indian food security. Whether the impetus for this change was wholly Indian or benefited from the strong-arm tactics of President Johnson is now irrelevant. The essential point is that the needed economic reforms took place.

Nowhere is this more evident than in the reforms that provided agricultural nutrients during the 1965–71 period. Liberalization in both the domestic production and importation of fertilizers was essential. Changes in the economic system for irrigation and the electricity subsidies that supported them were also fundamental. The ability of the central government to target the most productive land and farmers was very supportive of the first green revolution. Unfortunately, economic reforms became ossified, institutionalized, and in many instances changed in ways that made them no longer responsive to evolving economic, environmental, and social needs.

The agricultural economic reforms that were so much a part of the first green revolution largely did not continue to evolve. In fact, the case can be made that after the immediate goal of food sufficiency was obtained, there was politically motivated economic regression. Although the economic reforms that commenced in India in 1991 have continued to evolve in the economy at large, the economic system governing Indian agricultural production and food distribution has not kept pace. To be sure, there have been changes that make the system more responsive. However, overall the economic reforms that have driven increases in prosperity in information technology, manufacturing, and the urban economy have left the agricultural and food system and, hence, farmer prosperity behind.

Systemic economic change for the agricultural production and food distribution sector is now needed as the primary support for a second green revolution. Much of the systematic change that is needed can be facilitated by greater US-India economic engagement. A precursor to developing the US-India economic engagement that can support strategic cooperation in achieving food security is a recognition that food security cannot simply mean self-sufficiency in all aspects of agricultural production and food distribution. Both India and the United States cannot achieve their legitimate goals if agriculture and food remain fenced off from the market disciplines that have increased prosperity in other sectors.

An essential step is for the United States and India to cooperate on the food distribution system that operates in India. Unless the full potential of the Indian retail market for food is realized, there will be insufficient value injected upstream to provide for the transportation, processing, preservation, and storage of the agricultural production necessary for food security. Meeting the food security needs of India requires a holistic and systemic approach throughout the food value chain. Further economic reform must start with the consumer and the retail systems that meet the consumer's needs. The full participation of United States and other foreign retailers will provide needed capital and know-how that will support immediate upgrades to the entire system.

Similarly, the market cannot work to maximum effectiveness in supporting a second green revolution if trade in agricultural production is not liberalized. India needs US markets beyond mangoes, spices, and prepared Indian foods. These markets will not materialize unless the primarily nontariff barriers to their importation become inconsequential to the flow of trade. The United States also needs agricultural markets beyond its borders. There must be ways to protect the poorest of Indian farmers from the diminution of their livelihoods while at the same time meeting the needs for sufficient food at affordable prices. The answer to this conundrum does not lie in simply protecting farmers but also in utilizing the power of the international market.

An immediate goal for using international trade to support a second green revolution must be in the liberalization of trade for the inputs that are necessary for increased production. Here the first and most obvious targets of economic reform are the regimes that control the production and distribution of fertilizer in India. The present system, as Indian leaders realize, is inadequate to the country's needs. This highly regulated, restricted, and subsidized system has outlived its usefulness. A strong argument can be made that this system is now counterproductive to Indian long-term goals. This is particularly true with regard to the fertilizer urea. The system for the production and distribution of urea has been named by many as a major contributor to the sort of environmental degradation that is now making significant amounts of Indian land unproductive. The impact of trade barriers on irrigation inputs is also important. Restraints on the flow of the goods and technology for irrigation need to be removed. Pesticides compatible with enhancement of the environment and human health will remain a needed input to support increased agricultural production for the foreseeable future. There are still tariff and nontariff barriers that inhibit the trade of this needed input.

The political difficulty of achieving further liberalization of the agricultural production and food distribution systems in democracies like India and the United States should not be underestimated. However, any strategy for a second green revolution in India that does not take into account the crucial role of such reforms will not succeed. Liberalization does not mean that either regulation or the welfare of the economically disadvantaged should be abandoned to the whims of the market. Of course, extensive and rigorous regulation will be necessary to protect the health, safety, and welfare of citizens and to see that markets are not subverted by fraud and corruption. Programs to make sure that economically disadvantaged people have food are a necessity. However, these political realities should not mask the needs for systemic reform if a second green revolution is to be achieved in India.

When these basic steps toward liberalization in the markets are taken, there will then be a basis for the sort of technology injection that is fundamental to a second green revolution. The private sector will become more fully involved in both the United States and India. Political support for government-assisted technology transfer and subsidy reform will be increased. For example, the Lugar-Casey Global Food Security Act as of this writing languishes in the US Senate.[72] This bill is specifically designed to launch a "new green revolution." The bill would require the administration to appoint a high-level coordinator to devise and implement "a government-wide food security system." The legislation provides an authorization of $10 billion over five years for foreign agricultural assistance. This assistance is focused on the sort of activity envisaged in the US-India Agricultural Knowledge Initiative. Lugar and Borlaug describe this focus as "special attention to research and outreach, so small farmers can quickly utilize breakthroughs made in the laboratory. Helping small farmers raises rural incomes, thus easing poverty, hunger's chief cause."[73] Similarly the Manmohan Singh government is making a major attempt to reform the fertilizer subsidy scheme. Thus far, that effort has not borne fruit simply because there is not enough support from the private sector. However, the point is larger than any particular piece of legislation proposed in the United States or India. Unless there is extensive private-sector economic engagement supporting legislation necessary for or supportive of a second green revolution, such legislation is unlikely to be achieved.

The Bottom Line

US-India strategic cooperation was successful in achieving the first green revolution. Thus far, the same efforts at strategic cooperation have been unsuccessful in achieving a second green revolution. The lessons for the formulation and conduct of US foreign policy from these experiences with the green revolution are plain. Economic engagement fueled by the interests of the private sector and guided in public-private partnership by government is an essential component for achieving food security. A holistic approach that takes into account all the factors for achieving the goal is necessary. Concentration on a scientific or technical solution is inadequate. The days when the United States could rely on the transfer of superior agricultural technology to India as a major element of its foreign policy are gone. Gone also is a time when the strong-arm tactics of a Johnson could achieve results. The United States simply does not have the leverage it once had in the food security arena. Even if the United States had vast superiority in agricultural technology and food resources, the attempted use of this superiority would be unavailing.

In food security, as in so many other areas, the US government is badly organized to formulate and execute a holistic strategy led by economic engagement. Achieving US-India cooperation in food security requires an inter-agency strategy that encompasses all relevant parts of the government. We shall return to this subject in chapter 10, the conclusion. However, let us first look at the application of many of the factors discussed in this chapter to the issue of health security.

Chapter 9

Economic Engagement and Health Security: The Fight against HIV/AIDS

AIDS is now becoming a major national problem, and we need to tackle this on a war footing. We need to have a mass movement to ensure that this disease is rapidly checked and its growth arrested. We will also ensure that medicines are available to common people at reasonable prices.

—Prime Minister Manmohan Singh, Independence Day Address,
August 15, 2005

Around a conference table in Washington, we were listening to the executive of a major US pharmaceutical company pour out his woes in dealing with the Government of India. The executive was anxious to have his company's patented drug for the treatment of HIV/AIDS accepted for use by the Government of India. The problem was not price or even intellectual property protection. The problem was time. How fast could the acceptance process take place? As I listened to the discussion of the intricacies of the Indian acceptance process, I thought of how far US-India relations on the matters of pharmaceuticals and health had come in less than two decades. I also thought of how far they needed to go to make a significant impact on the major health security issues facing India and the United States.

India Confronts the Challenge of HIV/AIDS

As India confronted the challenge of bankruptcy in 1991, it also faced a new health security issue. HIV/AIDS was becoming a menace too important to ignore. As in most of the world, the initial reaction in India had been to deny

243

the problem. Indians generally view themselves as circumspect and prudent in matters involving sex. The concept of a disease of epic proportions being transmitted sexually by activity largely outside the marriage partnership simply could not be true of the moralistic Indian population. But it was true. Surveys surfacing at this time indicated that India had one of the largest HIV/AIDS problems in the world. To its credit, the new government of Narasimha Rao faced the problem. Under intense public and political skepticism, the government launched the National AIDS Control Program and created the National AIDS Control Organization (NACO) to lead the effort. NACO was a division of the Ministry of Health and Human Resources with completely inadequate resources to fight the epidemic. In addition to promoting prevention, NACO needed to get drugs to treat the substantial number of HIV/AIDS patients. NACO called on both Indian and international drug companies to join the effort. Indian companies were happy to supply large amounts of the needed drugs at low prices. The Indian companies would do this largely by copying drugs invented by the large international pharmaceutical companies. In India, this was perfectly legal at the time.

Not only were the US and other international companies unwilling to help with donated or cut-rate sales of drugs and know-how, but also they viewed the actions of the Indian companies to supply copies of the drugs on which they held US and other foreign patents as theft. Companies that held patents to existing HIV/AIDS drugs and were in a race to develop additional patentable drugs warned that the Indian approach would result in Indians being unable to secure world-class HIV/AIDS treatment.

The Background for US-India Conflict over Intellectual Property Rights in Drugs

The issue was joined over intellectual property rights. Although some US and international drug companies had done business in India for decades, this business was generally limited. Many such companies feared that more extensive involvement would only increase their risks of what they considered intellectual property theft. They feared not only outright copying but also the transfer of know-how that would enable copying in the future. Indian political leaders historically had taken the position that India's lack of substantive or "product" patent protection simply recognized the need to provide life-saving and life-enhancing drugs to a relatively poor population.

Upon becoming an independent nation in 1947, India inherited a colonial health care system and a set of intellectual property laws based on those of the colonial power, the United Kingdom. The first years of independence were in the era before the revolution in pharmaceutical treatments to fight illness in the human body. There simply were not many drugs available. The few rudimentary drugs on the market were as likely to be produced in India as in the former colonial power or elsewhere in the developed world. This changed in the 1950s as the numbers and effectiveness of drugs discovered and developed in the private sector grew at rates previously unknown in human history. Advanced pharmaceuticals were primarily imported from Britain and other countries in the developed West.

Under the inherited colonial law, pharmaceutical inventions were treated in India like other inventions for patent purposes. They were given protection both for the products themselves and for the inventive processes for producing them. There were some limited manufacturing operations started in India by British drug companies and a few private-sector companies of Indian origin. With assistance from the Soviet Union, the Government of India started Hindustan Antibiotics Ltd and Indian Drugs and Pharmaceuticals Ltd with the goal of making India self-sufficient in pharmaceuticals.[1] Indian research and development was carried out almost exclusively by government institutions operating on the Soviet model for scientific research and development.

This situation of foreign drug companies controlling most of the market and strong patent protection began to change in 1970. In that year, Prime Minister Indira Gandhi began to take the country in a more sharply socialist direction than even her father, India's first prime minister, Jawaharlal Nehru. One of the first steps in this swing to the left was the passage of the Indian Patents Act, 1970. The key provision of this act was in its Chapter II: "In the case of inventions claiming substances intended for use, or capable of being used, as . . . medicine or drug, . . . no patent shall be granted in respect of claims for the substances themselves, but claims for the methods or processes of manufacture shall be patentable."[2] The provisions of the new law went into effect in 1972. Immediately, indigenous Indian companies began to take advantage of the law to copy drugs that had been invented and patented outside India. One observer calculates that the share of the Indian national pharmaceutical market controlled by indigenous Indian companies went from 30 percent in 1972 to 77 percent by 2005.[3]

Another measure introduced in 1970 also discouraged foreign pharmaceutical companies from investing or trading with India. In keeping with Prime Minister Gandhi's evolving vision of governmental intervention in the economy, a National Pharmaceutical Pricing Authority was authorized to administer a price control regime. Price controls began with the Drugs Price Control Order, issued pursuant to the Essential Commodities Act, which contained a list of "essential" drugs as to which prices were set. The price control mechanism traditionally operated on bulk drugs and all formulations that were derived from those drugs. However, there was authority to list for price control formulations and combinations where such listing was "in the public interest."[4] Not surprisingly, there were also provisions that allowed the National Pharmaceutical Pricing Authority to exempt from price control drugs discovered in India or produced by a new process or an Indian small-scale industry. Thus, Indian companies would be insulated from foreign competition and yet able to take advantage of foreign patents. With technical skills unequaled in the developing world, Indian pharmaceutical companies thrived under the new regime. Existing Indian pharmaceutical companies expanded, and hundreds of new companies sprang up.

The Development of Major Indian Pharmaceutical Companies Able to Operate Internationally

Typical among the Indian pharmaceutical companies able to take advantage of the removal of patent protection from medicinal products and the discouragement of foreign imports through price controls were Ranbaxy; Chemical, Industrial, and Pharmaceutical Laboratories (CIPLA); Dr. Reddy's Laboratories Ltd.; and Sun Pharmaceuticals Industries, Ltd. These Indian companies went on to become the four largest companies in the Indian pharmaceutical industry and key points of US-India economic interaction. As we shall see, some have begun to assume characteristics of research-based companies not unlike their US counterparts. However, historically, all benefited under the 1970 Indian Patents Act as generic manufacturers legally copying drugs patented outside India.

Ranbaxy started its rise to prominence as a small Indian manufacturer of generic drugs. Started before independence and incorporated in 1961 by the head of a prominent Sikh family from Punjab State, the company was at first little more than a trader in pharmaceutical products. But it changed in character and scope in 1967, when Parvinder Singh returned from the United States with a master's degree from Washington State University and a PhD from the University of Michigan.[5] Soon after the 1970 Patents Act became effective, Ranbaxy raised money through an initial public offering. The proceeds from this offering went to building a chemicals facility in the Punjab for the manufacture of generic drugs. The company's initial success in generics enabled it to build a state-of-the-art facility in Toansa, also in the Punjab. In a major breakthrough, the Toansa facility received approval from the US Food and Drug Administration (FDA) in 1988. This achievement allowed Ranbaxy to enter the US market for generics through a joint marketing agreement with Eli Lilly. The effect of this experience was to play a key role in the development of Ranbaxy and in the movement of India toward integration in the international pharmaceutical system.

CIPLA was founded in 1935 in Mumbai by Khwaja Abdul Hamied. Hamied and CIPLA were important supporters of the drive for Indian independence. The founder's son, Yusuf Hamid, was instrumental in convincing Prime Minister Gandhi to have her government change the patent law in 1970. At the time, CIPLA and ICI Pharmaceuticals were involved in a dispute over CIPLA's admitted copying of the British firm's high blood pressure medicine propanolol, an early beta blocker. According to the younger Hamied, he asked Gandhi in a face-to-face meeting, "Should millions of Indians be denied the use of a lifesaving drug just because the originator doesn't like the color of our skin?"[6] There is no evidence that ICI Pharmaceuticals was trying to enforce its patent on the basis of skin color. Hamied was playing on the Indian sensitivity to the racial discrimination practiced by the former colonial masters. Nevertheless, the remark indicates the potent political dimension to the dispute over patent protection for pharmaceuticals. When the new patent law and price controls went into effect, CIPLA responded with an expanded product line. CIPLA's abilities to manufacture to world-class standards made it a model for other Indian pharmaceutical producers. The company expanded from three to eleven modern plants before the patent law changed in 2005.[7]

Dr. Reddy's Laboratories Ltd. was one of the many Indian companies that came into being after the 1970 Patents Act stripped pharmaceuticals of product patent protection. Unlike most of the newcomers, Dr. Reddy's quickly rose to prominence and claims to be the first indigenous Indian company to achieve sales in excess of $1 billion.[8] When the changes to the patent law became effective in 1972, Dr. Kallam Anjil Reddy was a PhD chemist working for the state-owned Indian Drugs and Pharmaceuticals Limited. Recognizing the opportunity afforded by the new law, Reddy cofounded two startups to make ingredients for drugs that had lost their patent protection in India. The first of these was Uniloids Ltd., founded in 1973 in Hyderabad, capital of Reddy's home state of Andhra Pradesh. The second startup was

Standard Organics Ltd., founded in 1980 to make sulfur-based bulk ingredients. In 1984, Reddy took his share from the sale of Standard Organics and started Dr. Reddy's Laboratories. An initial public offering provided the funds to establish facilities for making first ibuprofen and then a generic copy of a drug patented by Merck, norfloxacin, and then the antibiotic ciprofloxacin.[9]

The founder of Sun Pharmaceutical Industries, Ltd., Dilip S. Shanghvi, also saw the opportunity afforded by the change in the patent law. In 1983, as a recent commerce graduate of Calcutta University, Shangvi started Sun in Calcutta (now named Kolkata) with just five products on the strength of his family's investment. A public offering in 1994 raised money for plant construction and acquisitions. Shanghvi recognized that Calcutta, surrounding West Bengal State, and the hinterland of Bihar State were not the best base for a growing company. So in 1997, Sun moved its base of operations to Mumbai and began a rapid climb up the size rankings of Indian companies.

Although each of these companies—Ranbaxy, Dr. Reddy's, CIPLA, and Sun Pharma—was primarily a generic company and owed its prosperity to the ability to copy drugs patented elsewhere, together they would play an important, if complicated, role in the progress of India toward integration in the world system for the production and distribution of pharmaceuticals. This role was different from the obstructionist approach taken by the many hundreds of smaller Indian pharmaceutical companies, which were generally adamantly against any changes that would give product patent protection to pharmaceuticals. The larger Indian companies, because of their engagement with the world system on a scale that blunted the tendency to follow only their short-term interests, took a more nuanced approach to the question of change in the patent law that would make it possible for the Government of India to move forward with an agenda to make India a major international economic factor.

India, the Founding of the World Trade Organization, and TRIPS

As a part of its 1991 reforms, the Rao government saw the need for India to participate more fully in the world economy across the board. It was obvious to the finance minister, Manmohan Singh, that in order to fulfill this vision, India would have to join the new World Trade Organization (WTO). Rao agreed. The major nations of the world had been engaged since 1986 in an effort to create from the General Agreement on Tariffs and Trade (GATT) a comprehensive "World Trade Organization." India was one of the twenty-three original members of GATT. However, the role of India since GATT's founding in 1947 often had been antithetical to the spirit of the organization in seeking to create ever-wider markets operating with minimum government control. Indeed, when negotiations for the revision of GATT and the formation of the WTO began in 1982, India led the fight against another round of multilateral trade negotiations to break down barriers and open international trade still further. When the GATT ministers finally met in Punta del Este, Uruguay, in 1986, India vehemently opposed having intellectual property included in the negotiations. But after the United States agreed that services issues could be negotiated separately, India allowed intellectual property rights to be discussed in the context of the negotiations. India continued to oppose the United States on substantive international protections for intellectual property.[10]

Under Rao, with the advice of Singh, India started to play a less obstructionist role on the issue of intellectual property rights. Rao and Singh understood that a sine qua non of reaching a successful Uruguay Round conclusion would be the negotiation of the Agreement on the Trade-Related Aspects of Intellectual Property Rights, referred to as the TRIPS Agreement. If India wanted to be member and leading participant in the new WTO, it would have to find a way to accept the TRIPS Agreement.

The Rao government undertook to fashion a domestic political way for India to be able to enter into such an agreement. For all the reasons indicated above, this would be a monumental political task. This agreement would almost certainly require both product and process protection for pharmaceuticals. It was virtually an article of Indian political faith that the ability to avoid product patents was necessary to meet even partially the needs for medicines of the hundreds of millions of Indians who lived in poverty. TRIPS compliance would make illegal the kind of copying that NACO was relying upon to provide the treatments for HIV/AIDS patients. In the almost two decades of operating without product patent protection, significant economic interests had been built up throughout the country. As indicated above, the copying of drugs patented outside India had been a mainstay in the growth of the Indian industry. However, because of pressure from US and other international pharmaceutical companies, the United States and other developed countries were adamant that the TRIPS Agreement be a prerequisite for India or any other nation joining the WTO.

US-India Economic Engagement in the
Pharmaceutical Sector before TRIPS

To square the circle for India, the government turned to the largest Indian pharmaceutical companies. By this time, these companies were beginning to see their futures as tied to the international market. Thus, they saw that there was a necessity to expand their generic business while following the dream of developing original drugs that had hopes of becoming the next "blockbuster." Each major company was now involved in significant international dealings. And several of these dealings were with multinational pharmaceutical companies that had ambitions of their own for operations in India.

Eli Lilly is consistently ranked among the top twenty pharmaceutical companies worldwide. Founded in 1876 in Indiana, the company is known not only for its research and development of widely used and often controversial drugs but also for its active stands on political issues. Both former president George H. W. Bush and the disgraced former chairman of Enron, Kenneth Lay, have served on its Board of Directors. Recently, the company has been involved in controversy for both its off-label marketing, for which it was fined more than $1 billion,[11] and its working with Dutch authorities to stop shipments of Indian generic drugs through Europe, as will be discussed below. However, in the early 1990s, when the negotiations for the establishment of the WTO and the TRIPS Agreement were taking place, Eli Lilly was interested in supplementing its patent-based business with a more robust generics business. Randy Tobias, formerly at AT&T, had arrived as the head of international business at Lilly with a strong belief in the potential of India. Under Tobias' prodding, the company became interested in taking advantage of India's growing technological prowess and price advantages for research. In Parvinder Singh of Ranbaxy, Tobias found a colleague receptive to his ideas for transforming Eli Lilly into a more internationally oriented company.[12]

Parvinder Singh had become managing director of Ranbaxy in 1982 and had taken over full control from his father, Bhai Mohan Singh, as chairman and chief executive officer (CEO) in 1993. Unlike his father, who had acquired the company in exchange for a debt owed by the Indian cofounders, Parvinder Singh had an international outlook and affinity from the outset of his career. His US education and role in the creation of the first manufacturing plant in India certified by the FDA have been noted above. In 1992, Eli Lilly and Ranbaxy entered into a joint marketing agreement. Ranbaxy would market Eli Lilly products in India, and Eli Lilly would do the same for Ranbaxy products in the United States. The following year, the two companies entered into a joint venture that would also involve the conduct of clinical trials in India.[13] Together with the modern research facility Ranbaxy opened at Gurgoan outside Delhi in 1994, the Eli Lilly relationship sent Ranbaxy well on its way to becoming an international research-based pharmaceutical company.

These developments gave a powerful signal to the governments of both the United States and India on the issue of pharmaceuticals and intellectual property. Parvinder Singh was very well connected politically, as were the leaders of Eli Lilly. Singh served on a number of governmental committees and commissions, including the Prime Minister's Council on Trade and Industry.[14] Singh worked particularly through the Confederation of Indian Industries on trade policy and was great friends with Omkar Kanwar, who was in the leadership of the Federation of Indian Chambers of Commerce and Industry. Eli Lilly long took a leadership role in the Pharmaceutical Research and Manufacturers of America and the US Chamber of Commerce. The message from the Ranbaxy–Eli Lilly relationship was that it was in the interests of both the US and Indian major pharmaceutical companies that there be an agreement on TRIPS that would allow India to become a member of the WTO and give the products of its companies most-favored-nation tariff treatment.

Another powerful signal was sent by Dr. Reddy's. In 1992, Reddy astonished the Indian pharmaceuticals industry by declaring that the future of his company, and by extension the Indian industry, lay in becoming innovators and not just copiers of drugs patented elsewhere. In that year, Reddy established a research foundation. By the end of the following year, Dr. Reddy's had a research and development division that was operational. Dr. Reddy's also was moving on the generics front to establish operations to produce generics that were legal in the United States and other jurisdictions that followed a product patent system. Reddy concentrated on drugs whose patents had expired or had been abandoned that could legally be produced without a license from the inventor. In 1994, Dr. Reddy's opened a facility in New Jersey to legally exploit the US market. Like Parvinder Singh, Reddy was well connected in India. He served on numerous boards and commissions, and his views gave backing to those in the Government of India who wished to find a way forward for the TRIPS Agreement.

The other two major Indian pharmaceutical companies discussed above —CIPLA, the third largest in India, and Sun Pharmaceuticals, the fourth largest—at the time of the negotiation of TRIPS were also making statements about the importance of research to India and the Indian pharmaceutical sector. CIPLA opposed TRIPS from the start and still does. However, CIPLA let it be known that it too was interested in making off-patent drugs that could be sold legally in the United States and Europe. These are generic drugs that are legal in the so-called regulated markets, that is, markets that have a product patent system for pharmaceuticals. CIPLA later hardened its position against product patent protection and was a strong advocate for copying patented drugs to make them available anywhere in the world. However, CIPLA and its head, Y. K. Hamied, have a maverick political reputation in India. Their political influence was not comparable to that of Ranbaxy and Dr. Reddy's during the time of the negotiation of TRIPS and India's accession to the WTO.

Sun Pharma established its own research center in 1993 and was planning for its first plant to produce active pharmaceutical ingredients for the international market. This plant opened at Panoli in 1995 and was quickly followed by the acquisition of an additional plant from Knoll Pharmaceutical, which later became a subsidiary of the major US drug firm Abbott.[15]

In addition to Eli Lilly, other international pharmaceutical companies had also been doing business in India for years. GlaxoSmithKline, the second-largest pharmaceutical company in the world, is of mixed British and American heritage. Its predecessor companies, Glaxo Wellcome and Smith Kline Beecham, were both active in India long before the decisions on agreeing to TRIPS. The Glaxo side of the company entered colonial India in 1925, having inaugurated its first pharmaceutical product the year before. Smith Kline was started at Philadelphia in the nineteenth century. Smith Kline remained a US company until acquiring the Beecham Group in 1989 and moving its headquarters to England. Glaxo has always had a strong presence in the United States, its largest market and a major research, development, and production site. Thus, GlaxoSmithKline and its predecessor organizations have always had strong relations with the governments of both the United States and the United Kingdom as well as India. These contacts were exercised both directly and through trade associations to which it belonged in the negotiations over the establishment of the WTO and the TRIPS Agreement. Similarly, other major US pharmaceutical companies also played a role. Pfizer, Abbott, Merck, Wyeth, and Parke Davis were already manufacturing in India at the time of the TRIPS negotiations. Although these operations were largely for unpatented products, their presence in India and involvement with US and Indian trade associations and governments was a leavening factor in the TRIPS negotiations.

When I arrived at the Department of Commerce in 1993, the Office of the US Trade Representative (USTR) was deeply involved in attempting to bring the Uruguay Round of multilateral trade negotiations to a successful conclusion. The bureau I headed, Trade Development, had within it industry desks, several of which focused in part on health and medical products and supported the USTR. Lobbyists for the various pharmaceutical manufacturers and their trade association were quite active in making sure that the issue of intellectual property and particularly patent protection for drugs was near the top of the agenda for dealing with India. This priority had been established during the George H. W. Bush administration but was adopted by the Bill Clinton administration with little debate. When Secretary of Commerce Ron Brown and Undersecretary for International Trade Jeffrey Garten formulated the "Big Emerging Markets" strategy for the top ten emerging markets, health was selected as one of the "Big Emerging Sectors" upon which we would focus our trade development efforts. Consequently, as we dealt with India in 1993 and 1994, Indian acceptance of a TRIPS Agreement with strong patent protection was one of the items we attempted to promote. Although India was portrayed as the heart of international pharmaceutical piracy, there was a general understanding that Ranbaxy and Dr. Reddy's particularly had interests in common with the US industry.[16]

On April 15, 1994, the deal establishing TRIPS was entered into as a part of the agreement reached at Marrakech.[17] By signing the agreement, India committed itself, with regard to pharmaceuticals, to (1) the reestablishment of product patents; (2) extending the term of the patent from seventeen to twenty years from the date of filing; (3) the obligation to grant the patentee exclusive rights of "making, using, offering for sale, selling, or importing" the patented invention; (4) a switch of the burden of proof in cases of alleged process patent infringement from the patent holder to the infringer; and (5) during the Indian ten-year transition period, the right to file patent applications ("mail box rule") and receive "exclusive marketing rights" under certain conditions. India obtained (1) the ability to join the WTO; (2) the ability to make limited exceptions to the exclusive rights conferred on the patent holder; (3) the right to provide for compulsory licensing under certain conditions; (4) recognition of the needs for flexibility and the right to adopt measures "to protect public health and nutrition"; (5) noninterference with the doctrine that the first sale exhausts the control over price and place of sale, thus enabling parallel imports; and (6) a delay in the time period for implementation until January 1, 2005, subject to certain provisions.[18] Both sides got immediate most-favored-nation and national treatment for their exports.

Thus, in reality the major players in the Indian pharmaceutical industry had worked with the Government of India to find a way to realize their ambitions of taking advantage of the US generic market while also moving toward becoming international research and development companies. In a sense, the TRIPS Agreement laid the foundation for their entering the international arena as research-based, or "innovator," pharmaceutical companies. The economic engagement of these leading Indian companies with key players in the US and international markets provided an unofficial channel for information flows and compromise. The key to Indian participation in TRIPS, and thus admission to the WTO, lay in achieving sufficient conditions, or "flexibilities," to protect Indian companies' and national interests. The Indian companies obtained delay sufficient to adjust to the next stage of development for the Indian pharmaceutical industry. With the support of Indian drug companies, the Government of India negotiated for various exceptions that would make it possible for these companies to still carry on a large business based upon the copying of drugs developed by US and other international pharmaceutical companies. When negotiations were concluded successfully, India had secured its basic objectives. Conversely, US pharmaceutical companies appeared to have secured interim rights and their basic objective of eventually providing patent protection in India for their products.

Confrontations between the US and Indian Drug Companies over HIV/AIDS in South Africa and TRIPS

From the perspective of the United States and American-based research pharmaceutical companies, after TRIPS it seemed that India, the United States, and their respective major firms would cooperate on health security issues, including HIV/AIDS, based on the US view of intellectual property rights as they applied to pharmaceuticals. The US government, at the instance of the large pharmaceutical companies, constantly advocated that India was obligated to adopt statutes and rules that mirrored US patent laws and should do so without delay. Because the Indian understanding of the details of their obligations differed from those of the US companies, the US and other multinational pharmaceutical companies often took a confrontational approach to India on the questions of patent law. However, by the time the Indians enacted statutes to become "TRIPS compliant," effective January 1, 2005, political and economic factors had interacted to bring about a relationship between the United States and India in the fight against HIV/AIDS different from that which had been envisaged by the United States and its companies upon the signing of the TRIPS Agreement.

In 1998, thirty US and other international pharmaceutical companies reached the apogee (or perhaps nadir, depending on your point of view) in their policy of confronting the Indian manufacturers of HIV/AIDS drugs and their customers over patent rights. These international companies sued the Nelson Mandela government of South Africa. Although the suit was nominally against South Africa, the main target of the action was in fact the generic drug companies of India and India's interpretation of TRIPS requirements. At issue were amendments to South Africa's Medicines and Related Substances Act. These amendments, passed in 1997, provided for compulsory licensing, parallel importation, and other measures that largely embodied Indian views of TRIPS "flexibilities."

As noted above, these "flexibilities" were included in the TRIPS Agreement at the insistence of India and other developing countries. However, they are left largely undefined. For example, Article 27 recognizes the existence of an exclusion for patentability "to protect . . . life or health." With regard to compulsory licensing, Article 31 of TRIPS refers to the situation "Where the law of Member allows for other use of the subject matter of a patent without the authorization of the right holder." The article then goes on to list fifteen provisions that "shall be respected." Similarly, for parallel importation—that is, the importation of unlicensed patented products from a foreign supplier—TRIPS basically recognizes this right in an obtuse way by providing in Article 6 that nothing in the agreement shall be used to address the issue of the exhaustion of the intellectual property rights by the first sale of the product.

In the face of an HIV/AIDS epidemic, South Africa was essentially trying to enact the TRIPS "flexibilities" into law. The international research-based drug companies attacked the amendments as being incompatible with the Constitution of South Africa and the TRIPS Agreement. The constitutional attacks were mounted chiefly on the principles that too much power had been placed in the hands of the minister of health to make key determinations concerning "conditions," "circumstances," "requirements for therapeutic equivalence," and "benefits of substitution." The companies also alleged that the amendments to South African law took their property without provision for compensation. With regard to TRIPS compatibility, the suit alleged that the amendments were in conflict with the provisions of TRIPS Article 27 as to the equal treatment of imported or locally produced products. The applicants alleged that the amendments "discriminate in favour of imported medicines to the detriment of the manufacturers of local products."[19] The "foreign manufacturers" targeted by this allegation were chiefly the generic manufacturers of India. South Africa manufactures significant amounts of the HIV/AIDS medicines it uses through the South African subsidiaries of major international pharmaceutical companies. However, the allegation of discrimination against South African manufacturers and in favor of foreign manufacturers indicates that the amendments were aimed squarely at the importation of unlicensed drugs from India for use in the South African fight against HIV/AIDS.

The drug companies sought a preliminary injunction, or "interim interdict," against posting the notice that would put the amendments into effect.[20] The purpose of the injunction would be to maintain the status quo pending the outcome of a trial on the case. The drug companies won this preliminary injunction. However, the interim interdict would prove to be a Pyrrhic victory.

The community of activists and nongovernmental organizations saw the lawsuit against South Africa as the perfect opportunity to defeat the research-based, multinational pharmaceutical companies on the issues of patent law protection and pricing for HIV/AIDS drugs. Initial leadership in this effort came from a group of thirty-five AIDS activists who met in New York in 1999. Among these were representatives of the New York, Philadelphia, and Paris chapters of the nongovernmental organization ACT UP.[21] ACT UP was already famous for its media-attracting tactics in attacking those they believed responsible for denying HIV/AIDS drugs to the poor. Street theater involving large amounts of blood was considered ACT UP's forte. Doctors Without Borders, the Ralph Nader Consumer Project on Technology, and a variety of trade unions were to be a part of the coalition aiming to use the South African suit as the battleground for changing patent law protection and the pricing of HIV/AIDS drugs. The pressure on pricing that could be derived from the Indian generic manufacturers generally and CIPLA in particular were to be key in the coalition's strategy. But first the coalition needed a target of opportunity that would attract media attention. The coalition found that ideal target of opportunity in the vice president of the United States, who was running for president—Al Gore.

When I was serving as assistant secretary of commerce, strong Clinton administration support for intellectual property rights was accepted as policy across the board. At the same time, the administration's position was clearly to take aggressive steps to counter HIV/AIDS around the world. For this latter purpose, Vice President Gore took the lead. We at the Department of Commerce and our colleagues in export promotion at the USTR and the Department of State were aware of protests from activists about the costs of HIV/AIDS drugs. However, the linkage between the policy of strong intellectual property protection and harm to the fight against HIV/AIDS was not made within the government. The Indian and other generic companies were simply outliers in the world system. In 1998, the USTR put South Africa on the "Special 301 watch list"—a list of countries designated for special monitoring and possible unilateral action by the United States for perceived violations of intellectual property rights—in part because of the Amendments to the Medicines Act. At the 1999 WTO Ministerial Meeting in Seattle, the United States' position on TRIPS was that it should not even be discussed, much less reopened.

Gore was an ideal target and point of attack for the activists fighting the patent issue in South Africa. He had served as a cochair of the US–South Africa Binational Commission. At meetings of the Binational Commission, advocacy of the US drug companies' position on the amendments to the South African Medicines Act was routine. More important, Gore was running for president, with all the press coverage that entails. As his campaign was starting to heat up in 1999, a memorandum went from the Department of State to Congress, titled "US government Efforts to Negotiate the Repeal, Termination, or Withdrawal of Article 15(c) of the South African Medicines and Related Substances Act of 1965." The report called Article 15(c) "inconsistent with South Africa's obligations and commitments under the WTO Agreement on Trade-Related Aspects of Intellectual Property Rights (TRIPS)."[22]

The State Department memorandum inflamed the HIV/AIDS activist community and served as a tool for recruiting protestors to disrupt meetings, perform acts of civil disobedience, and otherwise harm the Gore campaign. In June, the activists began their protests. The results were immediate. Newspaper coverage was intense and mostly hostile to the pharmaceutical companies. The head of the Congressional Black Caucus, Representative James Clyburn (D-S.C.), wrote Gore about trade policy toward South Africa. Gore wrote back, saying that he supported South Africa engaging in parallel importation and compulsory licensing so long as they were TRIPS compliant.[23] Thus, cracks were beginning to show in the Clinton administration's support for the US drug companies' interpretation of patent protection for HIV/AIDS drugs.

The pressure began to affect the drug company plaintiffs in the litigation. The first sign of unease within the litigating coalition of pharmaceutical companies came in August 1999, when Bristol-Myers Squibb announced that it would donate $100 million to help South Africa and other African nations develop strategies to fight HIV/AIDS. A more potent indication came in May 2000, when five US and other international companies—Bristol-Myers Squibb, Merck, Glaxo-Wellcome, Hoffmann–La Roche, and Boehringer Ingelheim—were said to have agreed with a United Nations agency to cut drug prices to fight AIDS in Africa. The announcement proved to be an exaggeration, but it set the stage for other offers as the innovator pharmaceutical companies sought to fight the effectiveness of the political protests.

By 2001, it was clear that the litigating companies were fighting a losing battle. The suit was widely seen as overreaching by the international companies in the face of a terrible epidemic of human suffering and death. In March 2001, Merck and Bristol-Myers Squibb offered to cut their prices. They were followed by an offer from Abbott. However, in the face of lower offers from CIPLA and other Indian generic manufacturers, these price offers seemed hollow. CIPLA offered to sell versions of the triple-therapy antiretroviral drug, normally costing thousands of dollars for an individual's annual treatments, to nongovernmental organizations for $350 per year, and another Indian generic manufacturer, Hetero, offered $347.[24] CIPLA asked South Africa for permission to sell inexpensive copycat versions of eight anti-HIV drugs—one to be priced at a mere five cents a tablet. According to Ralph Nader's Consumer Project on Technology, "We had a quote from a generic company for 22 cents a day for ddI."[25] AIDS activists and nongovernmental organizations kept up the pressure. Doctors Without Borders claimed a petition with some 250,000 signers asking that the drug companies drop their lawsuit. The Congress of South African Trade Unions organized protest meetings.[26]

It now became plain to the plaintiffs that whether or not they won the case as a matter of law, they would lose badly in the court of worldwide public opinion. This loss would likely redound to the detriment of the plaintiffs in the form of new laws weakening the ability of the companies to protect their patents. On April 21, 2001, the plaintiffs withdrew their lawsuit. The international drug companies portrayed the outcome as a settlement that had resolved the situation. In reality, the case was a public relations debacle, out of which the major pharmaceutical companies had achieved nothing.

The continued offers of the Indian generic manufacturers for ever lower prices were major factors in virtually all the major drug companies offering African nations "special pricing mechanisms." These mechanisms from the research-based companies in response to pricing pressure from the Indian manufacturers caused the price of HIV/AIDS drugs for South Africa to fall dramatically. The prices in South Africa of antiretrovirals fell by about 90 percent.[27]

However, as the research-based major pharmaceutical companies had long pointed out, dropping the prices of HIV/AIDS drugs did not solve the problem of HIV/AIDS in South Africa—or, for that matter, India. The delivery of drugs was still inadequate, as was the entire system for prevention, diagnosis, and treatment. Plainly, more was required. The fight against HIV/AIDS and for health security could be furthered by US-India cooperation. But this cooperation would become optimal only if there was sufficient economic engagement between the United States and India to provide the impetus for cooperation. The private sector, in the form of both business and charitable organizations in partnership with government, would be necessary to bring this about.

US-India Commercial Engagement over Pharmaceuticals Increases

During the run-up to the effective date (January 1, 2005) of the Indian patent law amendment providing product patent protection, US and other international pharmaceutical companies began a rapid increase in the scope and number of commercial deals with Indian manufacturers. Although the policy and legal departments of the US companies might be decrying the Indian manufacturers, their commercial officials were making deals with the same companies being attacked on a policy basis. The tipping point in this process probably came in the form of a 2003 agreement between GlaxoSmithKline and Ranbaxy. Under this deal, GlaxoSmithKline turned over to Ranbaxy substances thought to have medicinal value if properly developed. If made commercially viable, Ranbaxy would receive a share of the intellectual property rights and the royalties flowing from them.

The trend toward more US-India deals in the health sector was abetted by the emergence of US-India pharmaceutical outsourcing. This outsourcing was similar to that which had swept the US-India information technology field. The factors of increased quality at lower prices were proving powerful incentives in the field of health, just as they had in information technology. Bristol-Myers Squibb, one of the first to break from the phalanx of international major companies in the South African case, was also one of the first to enter into a research-based partnership in India. Bristol-Myers Squibb joined with Biocon in Bangalore for a venture that includes a research facility for 400 scientists.[28] Similarly, Eli Lilly, Ranbaxy's original partner in India, teamed with Suven Life Sciences in Hyderabad. The object of this agreement was the development of drugs for brain diseases. Forest Labs of New York began work with Aurigene of Bangalore. Jubilant Biosys, also of Bangalore, had drug discovery partnerships that include several United States–based pharmaceutical companies. Pirimal Life Sciences, based in Mumbai, concluded research agreements with Merck and Eli Lilly.[29] Thus, US-India collaborations grew common, with most major United States–based pharmaceutical companies entering into agreements with Indian companies.

The Role of Nongovernmental Organizations in Economic Engagement over HIV/AIDS

The activities of nongovernmental organizations played an even greater role in changing US-India strategic cooperation on HIV/AIDS. The activities of the William J. Clinton Foundation provide a leading example. In 2001, former president Clinton started an organization that would become the primary vehicle for his postpresidential public activities. The William J. Clinton Foundation was built using much the same approach that had brought Clinton success in politics and which was a keystone of his administration. This approach was to forge partnerships between the private sector and governmental entities, with himself at the nexus between public and private activities. These partnerships were fueled by a prodigious fund-raising capacity.

One of the first initiatives of the Clinton Foundation was to assist in the fight against HIV/AIDS. As president, late in his administration, Clinton had turned from full support of the intellectual property rights of the United States–based research and development pharmaceutical companies to a much more nuanced position. As a consummate politician, he saw and understood the uproar created in response to the 1999 South African lawsuit and the protests of the activists. On his India trip in March 2000, Clinton and Prime Minister Atal Bihari Vajpayee had issued a United States–India Joint Leadership Statement on HIV/AIDS in which they committed themselves to development of new technologies including a vaccine.[30] In May 2000, Clinton issued an executive order that bound the United States not to "seek through negotiation or otherwise the revocation or revision of any intellectual property law or policy of a beneficiary Sub-Saharan African country . . . that regulates HIV/AIDS pharmaceuticals or medical technologies." A condition of this noninterference order was provision of intellectual property protection consistent with TRIPS.[31] However, his executive order marked a basic change in the Clinton administration's position on the question of balancing intellectual property rights and the needs of HIV/AIDS patients in countries most affected by AIDS. Clinton carried this approach forward into the work of his foundation.

Clinton noted that the major drug companies were particularly vulnerable on the question of pricing. He understood the role that Indian manufacturers had played in bringing about price concessions. Thus, his first thrust in bringing down the costs of HIV/AIDS drugs was to go to the Indian manufacturers in an effort to get them to lower prices even further. In October 2003, after about a year of negotiation, the Clinton Foundation struck deals with the major Indian companies involved in producing HIV/AIDS drugs, CIPLA, Ranbaxy, and Matrix Laboratories. A similar deal was struck with the South African manufacturer Aspen Pharmacare. Combinations of three drugs would be provided in about a dozen countries in Southern Africa and the Caribbean, where the foundation was trying to establish countrywide health care, treatment, and prevention programs. On the leading combination, the price per patient per year would be lowered from about $255 to $132.[32]

In 2006, the Clinton Foundation announced further pricing agreements with CIPLA, Ranbaxy, and Strides Arcolab to offer the antiretroviral efavirenz for $240 per patient per year. CIPLA also agreed to offer another antiretroviral, abacavir, for $447 per year. (These were price reductions of about 90 percent from the original retail pricing.) These companies would rely on a supply of active ingredients from the Indian supplier Matrix Laboratories.[33] In 2008, the Clinton Foundation worked with the British Department for International Development (DFID) to provide support for Indian generic drug manufacturers. DFID announced a grant of £9 million to provide technical assistance to Indian generic manufacturers. This assistance would be to help in producing and registering generic antiretroviral drugs and in negotiating discounted price contracts for these drugs.[34]

By 2009, the Clinton Foundation's HIV/AIDS program would claim that 2 million people were benefiting from medicines purchased under its Clinton Health Access Initiative (CHAI) agreements in seventy countries that represented more than 92 percent of people living with AIDS globally.[35] Appropriately, the acronym for this effort—CHAI—is the Hindi word for tea. The connection between Indian drug companies and CHAI has been fundamental to its success. The activities of CHAI have influenced US pharmaceutical companies to work with India on a cooperative pricing basis.

In 1994, I attended a breakfast for CEOs with Secretary Brown at the Department of Commerce. The purpose of the breakfast meeting was to get CEOs' views on trade issues facing the United States. I had just returned from a trip to the West Coast that included a visit to the Redmond, Washington, headquarters of Microsoft. My small Department of Commerce delegation had visited various midlevel Microsoft officials to discuss how we might work with them to further the United States' interest in foreign markets. To my disappointment, the attitude of the Microsoft officials was basically against public-private cooperation to further common interests. The attitude rather was that Microsoft knew what was best. The government could then follow their directions in the limited area of intellectual property rights, and Microsoft would handle other matters on its own. Bill Gates was present at that breakfast back at the Department of Commerce. His attitude and comments indicated that what my delegation experienced in Redmond was a reflection of his outlook. However, the Gates outlook on working with governments obviously changed. Perhaps spurred by antitrust difficulties, Microsoft, and presumably Gates, came to understand the value of working more closely with government on public policy issues. This was reflected not only in the intensive government and public relations activities of Microsoft, but also in the operation of the charitable foundation started by Gates and his wife, Melinda.

In 2003, the Bill & Melinda Gates Foundation launched in India a $258 million, five-year program designated Avahan ("call to action" in Hindi). One of the factors that attracted Bill Gates to this program was the opportunity to work directly with the Indian National AIDS Control Organization. The Gates Foundation's interaction with NACO was a major factor in changing the dynamic between the United States and India in attacking HIV/AIDS. Unlike the Clinton Foundation with its program, the Gates Foundation began its cooperative HIV/AIDS activities with an emphasis on prevention rather than treatment. The Gates concept was to concentrate on prevention among the most at-risk populations in the Indian states where HIV/AIDS was most prevalent. The fruits of this experience would then be used to build an HIV prevention model. This model could then be transferred to others, chiefly NACO, for replication and use in prevention throughout the country. Finally, information gained from the effort would be disseminated throughout the world.

In 2009, the Gates Foundation increased its commitment to Avahan by an additional $80 million, to bring its total support to $338 million. Gates met personally with the Indian secretary for health and family welfare to discuss how the model prevention programs developed by the Gates Foundation could be sustained over time.[36] The foundation also became active on the drug supply side of the HIV/AIDS effort. In 2006, Brazil, Chile, France, Norway, and the United Kingdom created an international drug purchasing facility, UNITAID, to concentrate on HIV/AIDS, malaria, and tuberculosis. These countries agreed to levy a tax on airline tickets to finance the effort. UNITAID was launched in September of that year at the opening session of the United Nations General Assembly. The Bill & Melinda Gates Foundation contributed significantly to UNITAID and has a seat on its Executive Board.[37]

The Effects of Legal Engagement

Civil legal engagement is an aspect of economic engagement. Legal engagement concerning the Indian patent law that went into effect as of January 1, 2005, has served both to support and hinder the ability of the United States and India to cooperate on the strategic issue of health security. The basic change of extending product patent protection to pharmaceuticals enabled the United States and India to move forward not just within the multilateral context of the WTO but also bilaterally and in the private sector. After January 1, 2005, developments in India further blunted the characterization of Indian companies as drug pirates, facilitating further US-India cooperation in the private sector.

India moved with deliberate speed to set up a bureaucracy and judicial system to give reality to its new role as a member of the international pharmaceutical patent community. However, the Indian law itself and its evident provisions for protecting many of the Indian pharmaceutical firms' interests as manufacturers and suppliers of generic drugs created impediments to further US-India economic engagement. Under TRIPS, Indian manufacture of a drug patented overseas should have been limited to drugs patented before the effective date of TRIPS (January 1, 1995) or whose patents had expired (off patent). However, the Indian Patents Act, 2005, allowed copying producers to continue the production of drugs patented between 1995 and 2005 if an Indian firm had made a "significant" investment in such a drug and paid the patent holder a "reasonable" royalty. In practice, this has meant that virtually all Indian generic firms copying drugs patented before 2005 have been allowed to continue producing the drugs.[38] Although challenges to this part of the law did not result in litigation, the disputes over this provision had an immediate chilling effect on the willingness of US research-based companies to accept that India was meeting its obligations under TRIPS.

The major research-based multinational pharmaceutical companies have complained about other portions of the Indian patent law not being compliant with TRIPS. In 2007, Novartis challenged the failure of the Indian patent authority to grant a patent to a modified form of its leukemia drug Gleevac. At issue was Section 3(d) of the Indian 2005 patent law, which requires "enhancement of known efficacy" as a condition of patentability. The law provides that the following shall not be patentable:

The mere discovery of a new form of a known substance which does not result in the enhancement of the known efficacy of that substance or the mere discovery of any new property or new use for a known substance or of the mere use of a known process, machine or apparatus unless such known process results in a new product or employs at least one new reactant.

The official explanation in the law makes the provision even more restrictive:

For the purposes of this clause, salts, esters, ethers, polymorphs, metabolites, pure form, particle size, isomers, mixtures of isomers, complexes, metabolites, pure form, particle size, isomers, mixtures of isomers, complexes, combinations and other derivatives of known substances shall be considered to be the same substance, unless they differ significantly in properties with regard to efficacy.

Section 3(d) has been interpreted by the Indian authorities to prohibit the granting of an Indian patent for "incremental innovation" that fails to change the efficacy of the drug. The purpose of this provision is to prohibit patent holders from lengthening the period of patent protection through the "evergreening" of a patented drug. The Indian court upheld the finding of the Indian Patent Office that Gleevac did not differ significantly in properties with regard to efficacy from a previously patented substance. In other words, to meet the efficacy test, an applicant would have to show a different effect from that of a previously patented drug. The court refused to rule that the failure to grant the patent was a violation of India's obligations under TRIPS. Novartis did not appeal. Similar analyses caused the Indian Patent Office to reject applications by the US drug companies Gilead Sciences for Tenofovir and Tibotec Pharmaceuticals (a subsidiary of Johnson & Johnson) for Darunavir. Both these drugs are used in HIV/AIDS therapy.[39] With Tenofovir, the Indian case for patenting was harmed when the US Patent and Trademark Office revoked several patents on Tenofovir.[40]

The international research-based pharmaceutical companies have roundly condemned Section 3(d) and the decisions flowing from this provision of the Indian patent law. These companies now seek "harmonization" to create an international regime under which all national laws are the same. Presumably, "harmonization" could work to bring about the elimination of the Indian Section 3(d). Harmonization through the WTO is being resisted by India and Indian pharmaceutical companies. In view of WTO actions over the past decade, it is unlikely that any "harmonization" process will materially affect the WTO's compulsory licensing and parallel importation regime for HIV/AIDS, tuberculosis, and malaria. The political forces against any such result are simply too strong.

At the WTO, actions concerning the scope of patent protection have continued to evolve in a manner favorable to the Indian industry. The commencement of the Doha Round of WTO negotiations in 2001 saw the ministers of member countries adopt a "Declaration on the TRIPS Agreement and Public Health," which clarified the flexibilities in the original TRIPS Agreement both in regard to compulsory licensing and parallel importation. The clarification made it plain that these flexibilities were quite broad and placed considerable discretion in the member countries for their implementation. The declaration also instructed the Council for TRIPS to find an "expeditious solution" to the problem of least-developed nations being able to take advantage of compulsory licensing from such countries as India. This was accomplished by delaying the obligations of least-developed countries to have pharmaceutical patents until 2016 and the granting in 2003 of a "waiver" of the requirement that authorization of a compulsory license could only be predominantly for the supply of a domestic market. This waiver is to be made permanent under a 2005 decision that says it will become permanent as an amendment to TRIPS upon the acceptances of two-thirds of the WTO members. Both the United States and India have accepted.[41] Acceptance by two-thirds seems assured.

The net effect of Indian patent law developments and the movement of

WTO actions over the past fifteen years is that India is no longer considered completely outside the mainstream of intellectual property protection with regard to pharmaceuticals. US-India economic engagement in the private sector, including both for-profit companies and foundations, has been an engine for these developments. US-India economic engagement in the pharmaceutical sector ameliorated hostility in both US and Indian government attitudes toward pharmaceutical patent protection. US-India conflicts over patent protection for pharmaceuticals was a facet of that economic engagement but did not alter the movement toward greater conversion in the governing legal and regulatory schemes.

The Effect of US-India Governmental Engagement on the Fight against HIV/AIDS

Economic engagement in the pharmaceutical sector has affected and been affected by bilateral government-to-government economic cooperation on the key health security issue of HIV/AIDS. The US government, through the US Agency for International Development (USAID), initiated an HIV/AIDS assistance program that worked with the Indian National AIDS Control Organization from its beginning. Initially, cooperation was on a modest scale and mainly followed the traditional assistance paradigm. In 1992, USAID cooperated with NACO to launch the AIDS Prevention and Control Project in Tamil Nadu. This program concentrated on decreasing risky behavior and increasing condom use among high-risk groups. A similar AVERT program was launched in Maharashtra in 1999.[42] For the period 1997–2007, USAID funded an Implementing AIDS Prevention and Care (IMPACT) project to support NACO's strategic plan. The major focus of the IMPACT project was on capacity building for the Government of India, nongovernmental organizations, and the private sector.[43]

As noted above, President Clinton, during his visit to India in March 2000, attempted to move US-India interaction from simply a USAID support initiative to a broader cooperative approach. The US-India joint leadership statement on AIDS/HIV was issued in connection with his stop in Hyderabad at a high-technology facility to emphasize cooperation on high technology. The approach was to involve "public, academic, business and nongovernmental sectors." The leaders noted that "India and the United States are home to some of the world's finest scientists and facilities." They went on to say, "We intend to expand collaborative research in HIV/AIDS prevention. We are applying our nations' substantial public health expertise and scientific capacities to fight the global pandemic." This was an important shift in the approach to US-India cooperation—from assistance to collaboration. However, in 2000 the Clinton administration was drawing to a close. Significantly, the George W. Bush administration put this wider approach into action.

Although unwilling to give credit to the Clinton administration for virtually anything involved with India,[44] Ambassador Robert D. Blackwill confirmed this broader approach in a 2002 visit to the Indian Government Hospital of Thoracic Medicine. Speaking in the Indian State of Tamil Nadu, he called attention to the efforts of the US Centers for Disease Control and Prevention (CDC) to develop an HIV/AIDS information system in partnership with an Indian information technology company. In meetings with the Tamil Nadu chief minister, Blackwill emphasized the role of the CDC and the National Institutes of Health in cooperating with India to fight HIV/AIDS.[45]

In 2003, US involvement in the fight against AIDS received a major boost with the announcement by the Bush administration of the President's Emergency Plan for AIDS Relief (PEPFAR). PEPFAR pledged $15 billion over five years to fight HIV/AIDS. Although this program was aimed chiefly at African countries, some $20 million to $30 million of the money was available immediately to augment existing programs in India. Additional funds were made available to India from PEPFAR as it developed. In 2007, USAID, NACO, and the State of Karnataka launched the Samastha Initiative with funding of $22 million from PEPFAR over a five-year period.[46] Perhaps as important as the monetary assistance in enhancing US-India health security cooperation, CIPLA and Ranbaxy both received FDA approvals for various antiretroviral drugs. These approvals made drugs from these Indian companies eligible for purchase by entities receiving USAID funds. And these purchases under programs receiving USAID funds further legitimatized the use of Indian companies' drugs along with those manufactured by US companies. NACO thus was able to purchase both Indian and US drugs for its programs using USAID funds. Related corporate cooperation included the launching of a public-private partnership to fight HIV/AIDS in the form of the establishment of an Indo-US Corporate Fund that had been announced in the Joint Statement of President Bush and Prime Minister Manmohan Singh July 18, 2005. Leading in this effort were ICICI Bank and the Confederation of Indian Industries.[47]

The role of the US Department of Health and Human Services agencies grew exponentially after the broad-based reengagement signaled by Clinton's 2000 visit and carried forward on a grander scale through the Bush administration's emphasis on India as a strategic partner. The number of FDA-approved manufacturing sites in India went from 75 in 2005 to 175 in 2008, making India the country with by far the largest number of FDA-approved facilities outside the United States. The FDA is opening full-time offices in Delhi and Mumbai.[48] The progress made by the Indian industry in gaining international legitimacy was affected negatively (although justifiably) by actions of the FDA in November 2008, when it banned the importation of drugs from two Ranbaxy plants because of falsified data concerning shelf-life tests and other measures. The FDA later halted review of drug applications from one of the sites.[49] The CDC was a primary user of PEPFAR money. National Institutes of Health (NIH) projects in India went from 17 to 67 between 1998 and 2003. These NIH projects tripled again by 2008, to 190. Typical of NIH's involvement in India was a Vaccine Action Program undertaken in cooperation with India's Department of Biotechnology. NIH also collaborated with the Indian Council of Medical Research to advance epidemiological, prevention, and operational research on HIV/AIDS.

Thus, with regard to cooperation between the United States and India on the leading health security issue of HIV/AIDS, economic engagement and intergovernmental engagement have operated in the sort of "feedback loops" discussed in chapters 1 and 3. Economic engagement in the pharmaceutical sector both affected and was affected by governmental engagement. Even activities that seem intergovernmental in nature can be viewed as economic engagement that promotes, in turn, greater governmental cooperation. US government aid to India's NACO program is an example of US-India cooperation in health security that has stimulated the involvement of the US private sector as a resource for the program. Early USAID funding of NACO— together with commercial deals, legal cases, and foundation philanthropy —promoted still greater cooperation through USAID. These types of economic engagement work together to provide an impetus for further cooperation in fighting HIV/AIDS.

The Bottom Line

Trade and investment with India by US pharmaceutical companies, the development and international activities of Indian pharmaceutical companies, business deals between US and Indian companies, the activities of private organizations like the Gates and Clinton foundations, and legal developments in the courts and at the WTO all are aspects of US-India economic engagement. This engagement has on balance facilitated increasing cooperation between the United States and India on the strategic issue of health security, as exemplified by the fight against HIV/AIDS. Progress has never been in a straight upward line. Nevertheless, the general trend is upward toward integration and cooperation. India's movement from international outlier to a key cooperator in meeting world health security issues is manifest.

The Government of India now routinely cooperates with the US government intensely at a quantitatively significant level in the fight against HIV/AIDS. The present degree of US-India governmental cooperation in this field of health security would have been impossible without the economic engagement discussed in this chapter. From these experiences in US-India economic engagement can be drawn observations concerning the conduct of US foreign policy.

Chapter 10

Conclusion:
Where Do We Go from Here?

At the outset of this book, three questions were posed about the relationship between economic engagement and strategic cooperation. These descriptive, normative, and prescriptive questions were:

- What is the impact of economic engagement on strategic relations?
- What should be the impact of economic engagement on strategic relations?
- What, if anything, should the US government do to make the impact of economic engagement work more fully to the benefit of the US national interest?

The Importance of US-India Economic Engagement,
1991–2010, for US Foreign Policy

The case studies, or episodes, discussed herein are intended to provide information and insights helpful in responding to these three questions. Admittedly, these case studies are taken from a single bilateral relationship and for a limited period of time. However, for both the United States and India, the US-India relationship is likely to be the most important over the duration of the twenty-first century. The focus period, 1991–2010, was one of formative change that is continuing. Thus, the US-India bilateral relationship during this period and the cases drawn from the period should be instructive for the formation and conduct of US foreign policy.

As the world's two largest democracies, the United States and India are home to more than a fifth of all the people on Earth. Their economies are the first- and fourth-largest in the world on a purchasing power parity basis.

270

The US and Indian economies are both now run in large part in accordance with the principles of free enterprise and the rule of law. In large part because of India's youthful and dynamic population, many analysts predict that its economy will continue to grow at substantial rates longer than other major developing nations. The United States and India are both nuclear powers with, respectively, the world's most powerful and third-largest militaries. With so many indications of importance and commonality, the significance of the two countries' relationship is manifest. US foreign policy should be built from the center out. That is to say, US policy must be successful in engaging with America's important democratic friends before it can be successful with nondemocratic actual or potential adversaries. Taken together, these factors indicate that the US-India relationship surpasses in importance even the US-China relationship.

The case studies are from the focus period 1991 through 2010. This was the period from the commencement of the fundamental Indian economic reforms in 1991 through the cementing of a multifaceted US-India strategic relationship in 2010. This was the era of greatest change for the Republic of India and in the US-India relationship. Because these changes were so fundamental and enjoy such widespread support in both democracies, they are likely to endure. US foreign policy now must deal with an age of transition from the Eurocentric focus of the last two centuries to take special account of the rise of Asian nations. The United States, as the leading Western nation, and India, as a rising Asian nation, moved from estrangement to engagement on many fronts during the years 1991–2010.

The cases from the US-India relationship during 1991–2010 are thus doubly important as guides to the planning and conduct of US foreign policy in the remainder of the twenty-first century. This double importance occurs because of both the political and temporal context from which they are taken. Their political and temporal context should make these cases widely instructive for the conduct of US foreign policy. They may be just as instructive for India.

What Is the Impact of Economic Engagement on Strategic Relations?

At the outset, I set forth the thesis that US-India economic engagement is the engine of US-India strategic cooperation. The economies of the two countries are central to their respective abilities to act on the international scene. However, the focus of the present inquiry goes beyond the question of the impact of economic size, prosperity, and vitality on countries' abilities to act in international strategic matters. The intent in presenting the several case studies of this book has been to examine the influence of the bilateral economic engagement. The characterization of economic engagement as an "engine" is, of course, a simplification. The question of causation is never adequately answered by specifying a single cause. Rather, the cases studied herein imply that economic engagement has a profound effect upon the ability of the United States and India to cooperate strategically.

The thesis of economic engagement as the engine of strategic cooperation certainly does not apply unaltered to all international relations at all times. The nations of Europe before World War I were engaged economically across a wide spectrum of activities. But this economic engagement did not promote cooperation on strategic issues sufficient to prevent war. Similarly, economic engagement between the United States and Japan before World War II was insufficient to promote the requisite strategic cooperation. In this book, the characterization of US-India economic engagement as the engine of US-India strategic cooperation focuses on the dynamic of economic interaction that influences what happens at the electorate and official levels of two democracies. The observations from the cases under review here will need to be adapted to fit different countries at different times.

The directional arrows of economic engagement influence do not point in only one direction. Rather, the studies of this book indicate that influence flows in "feedback loops" between US-India economic engagement and the electorates, between the electorates and officials, and between officials and economic engagement. Nevertheless, the cases I have discussed justify the characterization of economic engagement as the engine that keeps these feedback loops of influence flowing.

The US-India civil nuclear initiative is the iconic case for studying the effect of economic engagement on strategic cooperation. In this case, economic engagement set in motion a major change in strategic cooperation. The Indian economic reforms that started in 1991 opened India to US trade and investment in a manner unprecedented in the history of the Republic of India. Many of the political and cultural factors that are commonly cited as reasons for predisposing the United States and India to be "natural allies" were present from the beginning of the Republic of India. Before 1991, both the United States and India were democracies. Both used English as a common language of nationwide business and government. Both subscribed to the rule of law and common concepts of civil liberties. To a certain extent, both even had a common adversary in China. And yet, in the term applied by Dennis Kux, India and the United States were "estranged democracies."[1] The missing factor necessary to set in motion the breakdown of estrangement was economic engagement. With economic liberalization, US-India trade and investment grew at an impressive rate from the very start of the reforms. With this growth in economic engagement, commonalities in government, language, law, and international security interests began to work synergistically to produce an entirely different milieu for cooperation on strategic issues.[2] Economic engagement opened a new path for US-India governmental interaction. Attitudes changed among both US and Indian officials. These officials saw economic benefits to their respective countries from this engagement. With attitudes moving from estrangement toward friendship, the pace of US-India economic engagement quickened, and vested interests in further improvement of the relationship grew. In the United States, these interests in further improvement coalesced in the business, Indian American, and policy communities. Thus, when the officials of the George W. Bush administration reached the stage of wanting to remove the chief impediment to better US-India relations—confrontation over Indian nuclear policy—the business, Indian American, and policy communities combined to make this legislatively possible.

The success in achieving legislative approval of the civil nuclear initiative in both countries is now leading to direct US-India cooperation on energy. Perhaps less directly but just as important, the initiative's success is having an impact on US-India cooperation across the board. But it is the initiative's impact with regard to security issues that makes it particularly salient as the leading case study. Through the US-India civil nuclear initiative, India has been brought more fully within the system for controlling nuclear proliferation. Bilaterally, India and the United States are cooperating more fully than ever on the nuclear issue. This cooperation is seen at multilateral bodies like the International Atomic Energy Agency and the Nuclear Suppliers Group. The cooperation between the United States and India on interdiction and strengthening their nonproliferation regimes is at an all-time high. Further, the engagement in defense procurement and the resulting improvements in military interoperability simply would not have been possible without the restoration of trust engendered by the success of the US-India civil nuclear initiative.

The engagement of the United States and India on nuclear energy can also be seen as a significant factor in India's reluctance to move forward on the Iran-Pakistan-India pipeline. The influence of this factor should not be attributed to any threat to withhold civil nuclear cooperation or concerns about sanctions. Rather, common US-India economic concerns about energy, its security, and its reliability are far more important than negative approaches. Economic engagement works best to further US foreign policy goals when leveraged positively. US-India engagement on civil nuclear energy had the advantage relative to the pipeline that the engagement was a positive incentive to cooperation in the same general sector that encompasses the pipeline proposal. The civil nuclear initiative and the pipeline are both primarily concerned with the energy that India needs. The cooperation between the United States and India on energy proved conducive to addressing US concerns about the pipeline.

US-India outsourcing is also a primary example of economic engagement between the two countries. Because outsourcing is obviously closely related to the strategic issue of economic development, it has a manifest impact on the ability of the United States and India to cooperate on this issue. And this impact is strong and direct. The increase in size of US-India trade figures when services outsourcing is added to the numbers for trade goods indicates its impact quantitatively. The analysis given in this book shows how fundamental engagement on this issue is for many companies in expanding their trade with and investment in India beyond information technology. Conversely, outsourcing has been a driving force for Indian investments in the United States that help build prosperity in this country. The saliency of the outsourcing issues in both US presidential and Indian parliamentary elections is a chief indicator of its strong impact on domestic politics in both nations. This political impact, in turn, affects the ability of the two countries' governments to cooperate strategically. As noted, this effect is both positive and negative. US-India outsourcing adds to the buildup of commercial interests that supports closer cooperation. However, the concerns that are aroused within the United States about the displacement of workers detract from the ability to cooperate. Likewise, the controversies over limitations on temporary work visas and "buy American" restrictions lessen the willingness of Indian officials to collaborate on economic issues.

The case concerning Indian moderation in the face of terrorist attacks shows the impact of economic engagement on one of the most serious US foreign policy concerns—the prevention of war, especially nuclear war, between India and Pakistan. This book has shown that economic engagement, generally considered to be unconnected with questions of war and peace, can have an ameliorating effect on the propensity to meet violence with violence. The need to protect the viability of the outsourcing model was a factor in defusing a situation that could have led to nuclear war in 2002. The framework for India considering its course of action in 2002 was still applicable in the face of the Mumbai attacks in 2008. Although politicians and diplomats give themselves credit for preserving the peace, the roots of accommodation may be found partially in the need to preserve the fruits of economic engagement. In this case, economic engagement promoted US-India cooperation in preserving peace. This cooperation in turn has led to greater strategic cooperation between the United States and India in the prevention of terrorism.

Perhaps the most pertinent example of the negative effects that can arise from economic engagement gone awry is that of Dabhol Enron and the other electric power fast-track projects. Instead of engendering trust and confidence between the United States and India, the demise of this initiative did exactly the opposite. The disastrous outcome of this program caused recriminations and doubts throughout the electrical energy infrastructure sectors in both the United States and India and throughout the world. The inability of India to marshal the capital, technology, know-how, and matériel to rectify its chronic electric power shortages can be attributed in no small part to the failure of US-India cooperation on the fast-track projects.

More important, the failure of Dabhol Enron and fast-track projects has had a tremendous opportunity cost. This initiative and its outgrowths were to serve as a primary vehicle for bringing about US-India cooperation on environmentally friendly technology. The introduction and development of "green technology" was set back significantly by the problems associated with Dabhol Enron and fast track. Had this initiative been successful, the United States and India would have moved forward in a much more cooperative manner on the amelioration of the harmful effects to the environment from power generation. In turn, this cooperation would have provided a body of shared experiences and expectations that could have gone far to promote greater cooperation on the issue of climate change. Without this body of shared experiences and expectations, a valuable bridge to US-India cooperation on climate change was lost. Even today, one of the best hopes for an engine that will promote further US-India cooperation on climate change is a revival of joint projects introducing and developing green technology.

The case study concerning food security concerns two "green revolutions." The first of these occurred successfully in the 1960s. The second one has been promoted over the last decade but has yet to occur. The economic engagement that took place through the Public Law 480 program policy prescriptions, US aid, and the Rockefeller Foundation was suited for the context of the 1960s and was the engine for success of the first green revolution. Policy prescriptions and transfers of technology, know-how, and resources have proven inadequate to promote the cooperation needed for a second green revolution. The changed circumstances of the last decade make this type of economic engagement that worked in the 1960s ineffective with regard to the food security issues of the twenty-first century. The assistance model that worked to bring about the first green revolution is no longer applicable. Yet economic engagement in the form of assistance still has a catalytic role to play. However, under present circumstances, such assistance can never again be the sort of economic engagement that will be the engine of strategic cooperation on food security. US-India strategic cooperation to produce a second green revolution will require much more than a concentration on inputs and technical innovation to increase agricultural yields.

US-India economic engagement can still be the key to creating a second green revolution in India if adapted to present circumstances. However, current government-led initiatives will not be the engine for successful achievement of a second green revolution. Efforts to produce a second revolution need the involvement of private-sector entities across the board and on a scale previously unknown in India's attempts to deal with food security. US-based private-sector entities can be instrumental in this effort. Instead of being avoided as inimical to the public interest, intellectual property rights should be used to leverage progress in technology. Using market principles and allowing foreign involvement in food distribution at all levels, including retail, are fundamental to releasing the growth in food and agriculture necessary to achieve food security for the twenty-first century. India's poor people must be fed. However, the best interests of the economically deprived population are not served by current restrictions that prevent the full involvement of private foreign entities in the food processing and distribution chain.

The case study involving the strategic issue of health security and the fight against HIV/AIDS shows that the economic engagement between the US and Indian pharmaceutical sectors has been vital to the effort. Without the changes in intellectual property law and norms driven by this economic engagement, the United States and India could not have come into a full partnership for cooperation on HIV/AIDS and other health security issues. These changes have come not only through Indian patent law but also at the World

Trade Organization (WTO) and in US presidential directives. The study also shows the particular effectiveness over the past decade of foundations and other nongovernmental organizations working in conjunction with governments and generic drug manufacturers to achieve US-India cooperation.

In describing the impact of US-India economic engagement on cooperation in multilateral forums such as the WTO and in meeting the global financial meltdown of 2008–9, the replacement of the Group of Eight (G-8) with the Group of Twenty (G-20) is perhaps the most salient development. For decades, the G-8, preceded by the G-7, was the premier forum for discussion and action that moved the multilateral economic process forward. Economic engagement has been the engine that has moved this activity into the larger forum of the G-20, which includes India as a major player. The G-8 is now basically a historical relic. In the G-20, the United States and India will consult together and with the governments of other nations that have major economies.

What Should Be the Impact of Economic Engagement on Strategic Relations?

The case studies in this book are also useful in formulating a response to the question, "What should be the impact of economic engagement on strategic relations?" David Rothkopf notes that during the first term of the Bill Clinton administration (when we were both at the Commerce Department), some took umbrage at the use of the term "commercial diplomacy." These critics viewed the term as indicating a subordination of national interests on policy issues to the drive for private gain.[3] The more appropriate interpretation is that economic engagement is a powerful force in international relations that can be used positively to advance national interests in diverse fields. The US-India cases of this book show that economic engagement can be either useful or harmful to the attainment of strategic goals, but it will always be a force with which to be reckoned. Being made by humans, economic engagement is not a force of nature but one that can be subject to human intellect and action. Thus, the question becomes what should be the role of government in influencing international economic engagement.

As indicated at the outset, Benn Steil and Robert Litan, in their work on financial statecraft, make a strong case that it is in the political interest of the United States to promote a stable international money and banking system.[4] This US interest is seen as being furthered through the reform of the world's multilateral financial institutions, principally the International Monetary Fund and the World Bank, as well as efforts to promote stability, in their view, through dollarization. Certainly, most observers would agree that the United States has a strong interest in promoting the stability of an international system for money and banking, even if there is dissent from a dollarization initiative. This US interest also extends to promoting an open and just trading system through the WTO and the economic initiatives of the United Nations.

However, the case studies presented here show a larger US interest in economic engagement that extends beyond a concern for macroeconomic stability or even the framework for a rules-based international financial and trading system. US-India economic engagement during the period 1991–2010 shows that this engagement on the microeconomic, or commercial, level can be a valuable tool for furthering the strategic interests of the United States. History indicates that, except as a way to send messages, unilateral sanctions are largely useless and multilateral sanctions are not much better. However, economic engagement should be embraced as a positive tool for furthering strategic interests. Economic engagement of the types discussed in the preceding chapters shows that support for such engagement can have strategic benefits far beyond the immediate economic benefits flowing from the instances of engagement. Viewed in this light, economic engagement should be used by the United States to make an even greater positive impact on strategic cooperation than is now the case. Conversely, the United States has an interest in ameliorating the negative impact of economic engagement that is unsuccessful in promoting long-term interests.

Economic engagement works best to further the strategic interests of the United States when it promotes the interests of both parties to the engagement. The United States and India have large mutual interests to be served by this engagement. Discerning these common interests and then working to increase the positive impact of engagement in furthering them are fundamental to economic statecraft. Where these interests have been discerned by the United States and India and their governments have supported engagement to further them, the benefits have been significant. Similarly, around the world, it will be beneficial for the United States to discern such mutual interests and put in place economic engagement programs to support them. Thus, the basic answer to the question of what should be the impact of economic engagement on strategic relations is that it should be positive and even more significant.

What, If Anything, Should the US Government Do to Make the Impact of Economic Engagement Work More Fully to the Benefit of the US National Interest?

An initial response to this third, prescriptive question is that the US government should improve its ability to make economic engagement work more fully to the benefit of the US national interest. In this regard, the following are suggestions drawn from the case studies of this book and the author's observations about the US-India relationship.

An economic engagement plan should be an integral part of the plan for furthering US interests on every strategic issue and international relationship of importance to the United States. Considerable progress has been made in this regard during the past two decades. As Laura Tyson and others have observed, military security, national security, and economic security are all part of the same system.[5] This observation should be a principal operating assumption requiring that all strategic planning identify the salient economic aspects of a strategic issue and formulate the manner in which economic levers will be used, in conjunction with other means, to achieve the desired results. Many will contend that this is already being done. However, particularly at the federal departments most heavily charged with carrying out foreign policy—the Department of State and Department of Defense—there is a lack of status and appreciation for the fundamental role that economic engagement should play in addressing strategic issues. This bias can also be observed among the relevant congressional committees and their staffs. Too often, positive economic engagement, especially economic engagement involving the private sector, is perceived as inferior to military/political means for accomplishing a particular foreign policy goal. The question should not be one of inferiority or superiority but what works. Almost always, economic engagement will be most effective when utilized together with other instruments to achieve a particular strategic goal.

To achieve optimum effectiveness from economic engagement, the government must have adequate professional expertise. There is a deficiency throughout the government in career economic and business expertise. In part, this difficulty is due to an insufficient number of professionals employed to provide such expertise as their primary duty. In addition, among political officers, there is often insufficient economic and business expertise to appreciate the need for its full utilization. A related difficulty is the lack of status and appreciation of those who are primarily experts in economics and business. Again, these difficulties are particularly noticeable at the State and Defense departments. Although there is economic and business expertise at these departments, it is most often considered so secondary to the mission that those involved in military/political affairs fail to fully utilize it. This failure to appreciate the fundamental role of economic engagement is paralleled by inadequate status for those who have primary expertise in that field.

At the Department of the Treasury, there is obviously considerable economic expertise. The professional deficit at Treasury is not in economic training or experience. However, at Treasury the concentration is so heavily on macroeconomic issues that there is little expertise or appreciation for economic engagement at a microeconomic or business level. Even on a macroeconomic level, the ability to relate and integrate economic considerations with larger strategic considerations is limited. At the Commerce Department, the situation is somewhat the opposite of that at Treasury. There is plenty of microeconomic and business expertise. Within the Commercial Service, there are many with expertise in markets and export development. Likewise, in the Advocacy Center, professionals with transactional experience and training apply their expertise on a daily basis. The industry desk professionals have economic-sector expertise. At the Market Access and Compliance Bureau, the professional staff has training and experience vital to both bilateral and multilateral issues. However, throughout the International Trade Administration at Commerce, there is a paucity of staff members with macroeconomic expertise. Consequently, the ability to relate export and import issues to broader questions of international economics is limited.

Because economics and business expertise and experience are both limited and unevenly distributed throughout the federal government, it follows that there is a need to be able to call on this expertise wherever it exists. However, the endemic federal government problems of turf protection and empire building continually result in inadequate interagency cooperation in using economic engagement as a tool to pursue strategic goals. The needed expertise for the optimal pursuit of any major strategic objective rarely exists within a single department. Nevertheless, in practice the first endeavor of most departments is to capture as many administration initiatives as possible and then to exclude other departments from their planning and implementation. This approach percolates down through the departments and becomes the modus operandi for the agencies and bureaus. Even where the participation of multiple departments is required by White House or congressional direction, such interagency operation often does not take place. Once it is ordered or determined which department will have lead responsibility, the other departments or agencies rarely provide full support. The sourcing of needed economic engagement expertise from wherever it exists within the government and utilizing it to produce a coherent program seldom occurs.[6]

Interagency integration to fully utilize relevant economic engagement expertise from throughout the government requires strong leadership from the White House and the councils set up to promote this integration. A primary purpose of the National Security Council and the National Economic Council is to promote interagency cooperation. Seamlessness may never be achieved, but a better use of the government's many resources to employ economic engagement as an engine of foreign policy can be achieved. The proverbial "stove piping" on a department-by-department basis needs to be overcome.

During the Bill Clinton administration, I dealt with some senior policymakers who had a disdain for organizational matters. Their bias was in favor of applying human resources to a problem or project, regardless of what was referred to as the "arrangement of the boxes" on an organizational chart. This approach had its merits, but it produced a certain ad hoc quality of decisionmaking with regard to the use of economic engagement. The attitude of these policymakers apparently was based on a conception that a few leaders with sufficient information would make rational decisions based upon a clear definition of goals and an understanding of the available means to achieve them. Graham Allison and Philip Zelikow, in their seminal work on decisionmaking during the Cuban missile crisis, have shown the incompleteness of such an approach.[7] Their "organizational behavior" model draws on extensive social sciences scholarship to demonstrate the importance of supplementing "rational actor" and "governmental politics" models with close attention to the abilities and the proclivities of organizations. Likewise, greater attention should be given to the interoperability of the various agencies that can be used to further the use of economic engagement as an instrument to promote international strategic cooperation. The object should be to produce an effective system for using economic engagement as a tool of statecraft.

The private sector should be an integral part of using economic engagement to further US strategic interests. In a country where capitalism, free enterprise, and markets are the primary means of producing goods and services, any economic engagement component of foreign policy that does not include the private sector will be incomplete and anemic. In most instances, US public international assistance cannot be funded at levels to make an economic impact sufficient to achieve the desired goals. There simply cannot be "Marshall Plans" to meet all important strategic goals. The amounts that are available from the government will be dwarfed by the size of modern trade and investment flows. Where it is available, aid should be viewed as a lever or catalyst to promote the sort of private-sector activity that will advance the interests of both donor and recipient. In many instances, private-sector, nonprofit entities will be the most adept at leveraging assistance to create international partnerships. It is not just private-sector, for-profit entities that need to be involved; private foundations, funds, and nongovernmental organizations should also be integrated into the effort. The government should employ the leveraging and catalytic qualities of these kinds of organizations wherever public and private interests coincide. The same can be said for private business on a broader scale. The economic engagement impact of private, for-profit business can extend far beyond that of government and nonprofit organizations. Private, for-profit economic engagement can lead directly to the production of goods, services, and wealth that promotes or frustrates US goals for international strategic cooperation.

What is good for business is not necessarily good for the United States, or even large segments of Americans. The interests of labor are fundamental to those of the United States. This is also true in India and all democracies. The controversies over jobs, outsourcing, H-1B visas, and "buy American" provisions show that the particular interests affected by different types of engagement must be examined closely to determine the national interest. This examination should take place in accordance with democratic principles requiring benefit to the majority and noninfringement on basic human rights. Large segments of organized labor in both the United States and India do not see international economic engagement as being in their interests. These points of view must be taken into account. Likewise, support for economic engagement in some instances can lead to distortions and even outright corruption. Discerning the appropriate choices to be made so as to make economic engagement work for the strategic interests of the United States—for business as well as labor, and without undue distortions, favoritism, or corruption—is a difficult task. Yet the benefits to the strategic interests of the United States are so important that this task of making appropriate choices with respect to economic engagement should be an integral part of the making and conducting of foreign policy.

The proper integration of private-sector means into achieving international strategic cooperation presents special challenges for the government.

However, these challenges, if properly met, will not prevent the formation of public-private partnerships that advance the national interest.

The first and most difficult challenge is putting in place mechanisms to ensure that governmental resources are not being used for private gain. There are many laws, rules, regulations, and enforcement mechanisms designed to prevent corruption and fraud, but the problem is more subtle than preventing illegal or unethical activity. Citizens and their elected officials must be assured that governmental resources are being properly employed to utilize partnerships with the private sector. Without such assurance, the public will not support public-private interaction, and elected officials, from the president on down, will not embrace the concept. In this regard, the guidelines developed at the Commerce Department for determining the availability of advocacy services and for governing the selection of business delegations to accompany department officials on missions may be instructive. The guidelines require a showing of public benefit through such means as the production of US jobs as a prerequisite to joint action.

A related challenge is to show that such public-private partnerships do not distort competition among US private-sector entities by favoring one competitor over another. In Europe, there are concepts of "chosen instrument" and "national champion" that allow governments to choose one private-sector entity over another to advance national interests in the international arena. Such concepts are not acceptable in the United States, where equality of treatment among competitors is a bedrock principle. Instead, transparency and openness to all similarly situated private-sector entities should be the approach. Where competitive interests are at stake, the support provided must be of a nature that is helpful to all US competitors, or the government must forgo public-private engagement on the issue. Again, the Commerce Department's guidelines for advocacy and participation in departmental missions are an excellent template for formulating government-wide standards.

Also raised as an impediment to government partnering with the private sector on economic engagement issues is the specter of market distortion abroad. The problem is somewhat akin to that of subsidization. Questions of subsidization are subject to the WTO's disciplines. Where government support of economic engagement does not run afoul of these disciplines, such support should be accepted as a legitimate instrument of foreign policy. Governments routinely and acceptably work to promote the economic engagement of companies operating from their national territories. Where there is specific activity that can be seen as furthering particular US private-sector interests over those of a foreign competitor, US governmental involvement usually operates to level the playing field against foreign competition. Thus, the United States should move more fully to involve its private sector as a partner in the use of economic engagement to promote strategic cooperation. The challenges to this involvement can be met by facing the difficulties indicated and by providing for fair and open mechanisms to promote it.

The Bottom Line

Economic engagement is and should be the engine for promoting international cooperation on a wide range of strategic issues. The United States will be well served by recognizing this principle and moving to incorporate economic engagement as a fundamental factor in making and implementing its foreign policy. Economic engagement can be made to work more fully to the benefit of the US national interest through a series of measures. The United States should make economic engagement an explicit and consistent part of planning for each major strategic issue. The government must enhance its professional economic and business capabilities. The president and Congress must require interagency integration and cooperation on economic engagement issues of strategic importance. Public-private partnership should be embraced as an appropriate tool for the promotion of cooperation on strategic issues.

The growth in US-India cooperation on strategic issues from 1991 through 2010 is one of the great bipartisan successes of US foreign policy. Attention to the role of economic engagement in driving this cooperation can provide lessons of lasting importance for the United States, for India, and for all those interested in addressing strategic issues.

Notes

Chapter 1

1. See Raymond E. Vickery Jr., "The Ceylonese Press and the Fall of the Siri-mavo Bandaranaike Government," *South Atlantic Quarterly* 66, no. 3 (Summer 1967): 424–39.

2. John Stuart Mill, *Principles of Political Economy,* book 3. chap 17, sec. 5. See also the discussion by John L. Graham, "Trade Brings Peace," in *War and Reconciliation,* edited by Joseph Runzo and Nancy M. Martin (Cambridge: Cambridge University Press, 2006).

3. Thomas Hobbes, *Leviathan,* 1651.

4. Vladimir I. Lenin, "Socialism and War," in *Lenin: Collected Works* (Peking: Foreign Language Press, 1970), vol. 21, 295–338 (orig. pub. as pamphlet in 1915).

5. Harold D. Lasswell, *Politics: Who Gets What, When, How* (New York: Meridian Books, 1958); See also the leading survey work on political aspects of the international economic system: Joan Edelman Spero and Jeffrey A. Hart, *The Politics of International Economic Relations,* 7th ed. (Belmont, Calif.: Wadsworth Cengage Learning, 2010).

6. Information and diplomacy can also be used to communicate and manipulate messages about national values. Particularly in this era of concern about Islamic fundamentalism, values—including morals, culture, and religion—are elements of foreign policy. Some commentators have concluded that presently there is a lack of appreciation for religion in the conduct of international relations. Among US presidents, Woodrow Wilson, Ronald Reagan, and Jimmy Carter are particularly associated with a values approach to foreign policy. Values have often been cited as fundamental to the US-India relationship. However, values are most often thought of as US interests or properties rather than instruments of US foreign policy.

7. Benn Steil and Robert E. Litan, *Financial Statecraft: The Role of Financial Markets in American Foreign Policy* (New Haven, Conn.: Yale University Press, 2006).

8. See, e.g., Richard N. Haass, *Economic Sanctions and American Diplomacy* (Washington, D.C.: Brookings Institution Press, 1998). This perspective is widened by Richard N. Haass and O'Sullivan, eds., *Honey and Vinegar: Incentives, Sanctions, and Foreign Policy* (Washington, D.C.: Brookings Institution Press, 2000). Nevertheless, the weight of the literature seems on the "vinegar" rather than the "honey."

285

9. See, e.g., Harry Kopp, *Commercial Diplomacy and the National Interest* (Washington, D.C.: American Academy of Diplomacy / Business Council for International Understanding, 2004).

10. David Allen Baldwin, *Economic Statecraft* (Princeton, N.J.: Princeton University Press, 1985).

11. Political economy has attempted to deal with politics and economics as a unified field for centuries. International political economy as a subset of the discipline tends to veer between an analysis of the effects of competing economic theories and the effects of national political systems on international relations. See, e.g., Robert Gilpin, *The Political Economy of International Relations* (Princeton, N.J.: Princeton University Press, 1987); and its successor work, Robert Gilpin, *Global Political Economy: Understanding the International Economic Order* (Princeton, N.J.: Princeton University Press, 2001). However, works of political economy, by and large, do not deal with economic engagement as an instrument of foreign policy.

12. Barack Obama, "Remarks by President Obama and Prime Minister Singh of India during Arrival Ceremony," November 24, 2009, http://www.whitehouse.gov/the-press-office.

13. Barack Obama, "Remarks by the President in Address to the Nation on the Way Forward in Afghanistan and Pakistan," December 1, 2009, http://www.whitehouse.gov/the-press-office.

14. Manmohan Singh, "Prime Minister's Address to the United States–India Business Council," November 23, 2009, http://pmindia.nic.in/visits.htm.

15. Manmohan Singh, "Prime Minister's Address at the Council on Foreign Relations," November 23, 2009, http://pmindia.nic.in/visits.htm.

16. George W. Bush, "The President's News Conference with Prime Minister Singh," July 18, 2005, http://presidency.ucsb.edu/ws/index.php?pid=73910&st=&st1=.

17. Atal Bihari Vajpayee, "Address at the US-India Business Summit," September 15, 2000, http://www.indianembassy.org/indusrel/pm_us_2000/pm_cii_september_15_2000.htm.

18. See P. V. Narasimha Rao, "Address to Joint Meeting of Congress," May 18, 1994, http://www.indianembassy.org/indusrel/india_us/rao_congress_May_18_1994.htm.

19. But see Charles A. Kupchan, *How Enemies Become Friends: The Sources of Stable Peace* (Princeton, N.J.: Princeton University Press, 2010).

20. See Teresita C. Schaffer, *India and the United States in the 21st Century* (Washington, D.C.: CSIS Press, 2009), chap. 2, "The Economic Engine," 18–43.

21. Author's interview with Samuel R. ("Sandy") Berger, July 21, 2009.

22. David Rothkopf, *Running the World: The Inside Story of the National Security Council and the Architects of American Power* (New York: PublicAffairs, 2005), 306. For similar observations, also see Karl F. Inderfurth and Loch K. Johnson, eds., *Fateful Decisions: Inside the National Security Council* (New York: Oxford University Press, 2004); and Ivo H. Daalder and I. M. Destler, *In the Shadow of the Oval Office* (New York: Simon & Schuster, 2009).

23. See Rothkopf, *Running the World,* 315–16.

24. See Stephen P. Cohen, *India Emerging Power* (Washington, D.C.: Brookings Institution Press, 2001); and Walter K. Andersen, "India in 1994: Economics to the Fore," *Asian Survey* 35, no. 2 (1995): 123–39.

25. Richard Nixon, "Memorandum Establishing the Council on International Eco-

nomic Policy," January 19, 1971, in *The American Presidency Project* [online], edited by John T. Woolley and Gerhard Peters (Santa Barbara: University of California, Santa Barbara, n.d.), http://www.presidency.ucsb.edu/ws/?pid=3021.

26. Joseph S. Nye Jr., *Soft Power: The Means to Success in World Politics* (New York: PublicAffairs, 2004), 8.

27. See Craig Cohen, Joseph S. Nye Jr., and Richard Armitage, *A Smarter, More Secure America: Report of the CSIS Commission on Smart Power* (Washington, D.C.: CSIS Press, 2007).

28. Eamon Javers, "A Familiar Face at Treasury," *Politico,* September 23, 2009.

29. Mary Beth Sheridan and Greg Jaffe, "Gates Proposes 3 Funds to Aid Unstable Countries," *Washington Post,* December 24, 2009, 2.

30. Executive Office of the President, "National Security Strategy," May 2010, www.whitehouse.gov/sites/default/files/rss_strategy.gov.

31. Francis Fukuyama, "The End of History?" *The National Interest,* Summer 1989, 3–18; Francis Fukuyama, *The End of History and the Last Man* (New York: Free Press, 1992).

32. See Jim Hoagland, "How We Failed Wei Jengshan," *Washington Post,* December 17, 1995, also published as "Mixed Messages from America Encourage Chinese Rights Abusees" *International Herald Tribune,* December 17, 1995.

33. Note that the controversy over the role BP may have played in the release by Scotland of the Lockerbie bomber Abdel Basset al-Megrahi has revived the criticism that mixing economic engagement with strategic issues runs afoul of national moral imperatives. See John Gapper, "A Fine Line between Bribery and Political Deal-Making," *Financial Times,* July 22, 2010.

34. These internal critics of advocacy must have missed getting a copy of Secretary of State Lawrence Eagleburger's November 30, 1989, proclamation of a "Bill of Rights for Business." See Kopp, *Commercial Diplomacy,* 122.

35. See Charles Ford, "Commercial Diplomacy: The Next Wave," *Foreign Service Journal,* April 2005, 19–30, where Ford argues that the impact of shifting the Foreign Commercial Service out of the Department of State was "to push commercial diplomacy to the margins of our mainstream foreign policy" (p. 23).

36. Ambassador Ashley Wills, former assistant US trade representative for South Asia (2003–6) and deputy chief of mission in New Delhi (1995–2000), observes that the US trade representative is seldom able to participate with effect on interagency strategic issues in spite of being a part of the Executive Office of the President. Author's interview with Ashley Wills, March 8, 2010.

37. For a description of the committees as they existed in 2002, see US General Accounting Office, *International Trade Advisory System Should be Updated to Better Serve US Policy Needs,* GAO-02-876 (Washington, D.C.: US Government Printing Office, 2002); and for updates to the system, see International Trade Administration, "Industry Trade Advisory Committee," http://www.trade.gov/itac/committees/.

38. William J. Clinton, *My Life* (New York: Random House, 2005), 704–5.

39. See Sunil Khilnani, "Bridging Identities: India as a Positive Power?" in *Through a Billion Voices: India's Role in a Multi-Polar World,* edited by Elena Jurado and Priya Shankar (Berlin: Foresight, 2010).

40. See Prime Minister's Office, "Dr. Manmohan Singh Prime Minister of India Personal Profile," 2010, http://pmindia.nic.in/meet.htm.

Chapter 2

1. Ingrid Belton Henik, then policy director for the US-India Business Council, and I were in this meeting together. Outside the Dirksen Building on September 11, 2001, the streets of Washington were in virtual gridlock as vehicles attempted to leave the city. Ingrid and I briefly considered trying to take the Washington Metro back to our respective offices. However, the fear of being stuck below ground caused us to opt for walking westward along E Street. After we had gone a few blocks, a military jet came flying by and explosions were heard in the distance. It seemed that war had come to the United States. Ingrid and I parted company at my wife's office building at 555 13th Street, NW. I went upstairs to an office on the thirteenth floor with a panoramic view out over the Mall and the Washington Monument toward the Pentagon. The Pentagon was on fire. Billows of smoke stained the horizon. Indeed, the United States was at war.

2. See George Perkovich, *India's Nuclear Bomb: The Impact on Global Proliferation* (Berkeley: University of California Press, 2002), 30.

3. See Dennis Kux, *India and the United States: Estranged Democracies, 1941–1991* (Darby, Pa.: Diane Publishing, 1993), 153.

4. "Heavy water," D_2O, is the moderator most used in reactors that breed plutonium, a key component of a nuclear explosive device. Heavy water is used for Canadian reactors, whereas "light water" (regular water, H_2O) is used in US designs to produce electricity and is not useful for producing plutonium. See http://hyperphysics.phy-astr.gsu.edu/Hbase/NucEne/ligwat.html.

5. Perkovich, *India's Nuclear Bomb,* 27.

6. Ibid.

7. I was in India during the years 1964–65 as a student under the Fulbright-Hays Program. The Indians with whom I came in contact were overwhelmingly inclined favorably toward the United States and Americans.

8. Perkovich, *India's Nuclear Bomb,* 57; also see 52, 55–57.

9. *United Nations Treaty Series,* no. 10485, vol. 729, 169–75, http://treaties.un.org/doc/Publication/UNTS/Volume%20729/volume-729-I-10485-English.pdf.

10. 42 U.S.C. 2011 et seq.

11. 22 U.S.C. 3201 et seq.

12. Note that the view that India was entitled to keep its nuclear options open was shared even by Indian politicians who opposed India developing nuclear weapons. Former US ambassador to India Richard Celeste says that in a meeting he attended before his confirmation in 1997, then–prime minister Inder Kumar Gujral told Secretary of State Madeleine Albright that he opposed any limitations on India's rights to develop nuclear weapons, even though he opposed such development. Author's interview with Richard Celeste, March 6, 2010.

13. See http://irmep.org/ila/nukes/glenn/default.asp.

14. 22 U.S.C. 6301 et seq.

15. See Leonard S. Spector, "Status of US Sanctions Imposed on India and Pakistan," James Martin Center for Nonproliferation Studies, 2001, http://cns.miis.edu/research/wtc01/pakind.htm.

16. President Clinton indicated his intention to nominate me as assistant secretary of commerce for trade development, on September 16, 1993. I had my hearing before the Senate Banking Committee on February 28, 1994. However, confirmation was delayed

by Senator Byron Dorgan (D-N.D.), who took me and two other prospective officials of the Clinton administration "hostage" as leverage for his getting US trade representative action on protection from the importation of Canadian hard wheat. The assistant secretary of commerce for trade development has nothing to do with the importation of agricultural commodities. However, I later found that this sort of hostage taking was a routine means for a senator to gain action from the executive branch, even when the president was of one's own party. Holds have now become so widespread and so partisan that confirmation of presidential appointees seems to be grinding to a halt; see, e.g., Senator Richard Shelby (R-Ala.) placing a hold on seventy Obama nominees in January 2010. Because the Department of Commerce was shorthanded for middle management in 1993, I started work as a consultant in September even though I was not able to occupy the office or participate in any business as an assistant secretary. I was not sworn in until April 21, 1994. This sort of delay in the confirmation of nominees is typical at middle levels of a new administration. The inefficiencies of the process have been the subject of reform attempts. See, e.g., Brookings Institution Presidential Appointee Initiative, "Presidential Appointee Initiative Issues Call to Service," June 18, 2003, http://www.brookings.edu/media/NewsReleases/2003/20030618pai.aspx.

17. At Brown's funeral in 1996, Clinton paused in the middle of his National Cathedral eulogy and said, "On a personal note, I want to say to my friend just one last time— Thank you. If it weren't for you, I wouldn't be here." William J. Clinton, "Remarks at the Funeral of Secretary of Commerce Ronald H. Brown," April 10, 1996, in *The American Presidency Project* [online], edited by John T. Woolley and Gerhard Peters (Santa Barbara: University of California, Santa Barbara, n.d.), http://www.presidency.ucsb.edu/ws/?pid=52653.

18. These markets were Argentina, Brazil, China, India, Indonesia, Mexico, Poland, South Africa, South Korea, and Turkey. For a fuller explication of the Big Emerging Markets thesis, see Jeffrey E. Garten, *The Big Ten: The Big Emerging Markets and How They Will Change Our Lives* (New York: Basic Books, 1998) .

19. Author's interview with Samuel R. ("Sandy") Berger, July 21, 2009.

20. Author's interview with Scott Bayman, June 16, 2009.

21. Copps would go on to succeed the author as assistant secretary of commerce for trade development and then to become a commissioner of the Federal Communications Commission.

22. Mottur had served on Clinton's 1992 campaign staff in charge of technology and the high-technology community. See "Remarks and a Question-and-Answer Session with Silicon Graphics Employees in Mountain View, California," February 22, 1993, in *Public Papers of the Presidents, William J. Clinton, 1993,* edited by Office of the Federal Register (Washington, D.C.: US Government Printing Office, 1994), vol. 1, 171–79. Mottur had also been a member of Senator Ted Kennedy's staff and shared his deep affection for Ireland. From this background, he played a significant role in using economic engagement to support the Clinton administration's efforts to bring peace to Northern Ireland. See Bill Clinton, *My Life* (New York: Random House, 2005), 705, 784.

23. Author's interview with Frank Wisner, February 27, 2010. The other two "great divides" in Wisner's view were the legacy of the Cold War (in which many in Washington saw the Indians as siding with the Soviet Union) and the lack of "political transformation" necessary to match the changed status of India as an emerging power.

24. Ibid.

25. P. Chidambaram was later minister of finance in both the United Front Government and that of the United Progressive Alliance beginning in 2004. Since the terrorist attacks of November 2008, Chidambaram has served as minister of home affairs.

26. See Sumit Ganguly, *Asian Survey,* February 1997, 126.

27. Letter from Samuel R. ("Sandy") Berger to the author, January 3, 1998.

28. See Devish Kapur and Pratap Bhanu Mehta, "India in 1998: The Travails of Political Fragmentation," *Asian Survey,* 39, no. 1 (January–February 1999): 163.

29. Perkovich, *India's Nuclear Bomb.* This is the definitive study of the Indian nuclear weapons program through 2000.

30. Apparently, this feeling of having been "let down" was based on statements of Minister of Defense George Fernandes to Secretary of Energy Bill Richardson and Foreign Secretary Krishnan Raghunath to Undersecretary of State for Political Affairs Tom Pickering that implied no testing. See Strobe Talbott, *Engaging India: Diplomacy, Democracy, and the Bomb* (Washington, D.C.: Brookings Institution Press, 2004), 47–48.

31. Berger interview.

32. "Presidential Determination No. 98-22 of May 13, 1998," *Federal Register* 63, no. 97 (May 20, 1998): 27665.

33. See James M. Zimmerman, "US Sanctions against India; Arms Control Act; Impact on Exports" http://library.findlaw.com/1998/May/13/127144.html; and King & Spalding, "Client Alert: US Sanctions Against India," May 15, 1998, http://www.kslaw .com/portal/server.pt?space=KSPublicRedirect&control=KSPublic&RedirectID=38.

34. PL 105-194 (112 Stat. 627).

35. See Trade Development Division, Kansas Department of Commerce, "2007 Kansas Export Statistics," http://www.kansaszommerce.com/LinkClick.aspx?fileticket =IRBS6LHK%2Blk%3D&tabod=216.

36. The Omnibus Consolidated and Emergency Supplemental Appropriations Act of 1999 is PL 105-277 (112 Stat. 2681).

37. See Dianne E. Rennack, "India and Pakistan: Current US Economic Sanctions," Congressional Research Service report for Congress, October 12, 2001.

38. "Presidential Determination No. 2000-4 of October 27, 1999," *Federal Register* 64, no. 215 (November 8, 1999): 60649.

39. Author's interview with Michael T. Clark, February 16, 2010.

40. Talbott, *Engaging India,* 6.

41. See Vivek Wadhwa et al., *America's New Immigrant Entrepreneurs* (Durham, N.C.: School of Engineering, Duke University, 2007).

42. For a comprehensive review of the rollback of the Glenn Amendment sanctions and the role of Indian Americans in that rollback, see Robert M. Hathaway, "Confrontation and Retreat: The US Congress and the South Asian Nuclear Tests," *Arms Control Today,* January–February 2000, 9–10; and "Unfinished Passage: India, Indian Americans and the US Congress," *Washington Quarterly* 24, no. 2 (Spring 2001): 21–34.

43. William J. Clinton, "Remarks by the President to the Indian Joint Session of Parliament," March 22, 2000, http://usinfo.org/wf-archive/2000/000322/epf301.htm.

44. The author was an organizer of these roundtables and the presentations to the secretary and the minister as well as the business delegation for the mission.

45. Clark interview.

46. See Office of the Federal Register, *Public Papers of the Presidents of the United States, Administration of William J. Clinton, 2000* (Washington, D.C.: US Government Printing Office, 2000), 596–98.

47. See James Mann, *Rise of the Vulcans: The History of Bush's War Cabinet* (New York: Penguin, 2004).

48. "Joint Statement between the United States of America and the Republic of India, November 9, 2001," in *2001 Public Papers of the Presidents of the United States, Books I and II,* edited by Office of the Federal Register (Washington, D.C.: US Government Printing Office, 2002), 1396–97.

49. See Kenneth I. Juster, "US-India Relations and High-Technology Trade," 2003, http://www.bis.doc.gov/mews/2003/kennewdelhinov03.htm.

50. Author's interview with Kenneth Juster, June 17, 2009.

51. Because these Indian trade associations are bitter rivals, getting them to work together was an achievement.

52. See Juster, "US-India Relations," 4–7.

53. See the transcript of Foreign Secretary Shyam Saran's press conference of July 18, 2005, in which he acknowledges the role of the meeting between Rice and the Indian minister of external affairs, Natwar Singh, in working out the Joint Statement, at http://www.indianembassy.org/press_release/2005/July/30.htm.

54. See the documents and transcripts concerning the July 18–20, 2005, visit of Prime Minister Singh to the United States collected at http://www.indianembassy.org/press_release/2005/July/21.htm.

55. The Generation IV International Forum is a consortium working to develop reactors that deal more efficiently with waste, safety, competitiveness, and proliferation resistance. See http://www.gen-4.or/GIF/About/faq/faq-definition.htm.

56. The "Additional Protocol" is a series of undertakings by a country agreeing to safeguards that provides access, inspection rights, and state information to make inspections effective in finding the facts about both declared and undeclared nuclear activity. See International Atomic Energy Agency, "IAEA Safeguards Overview: Comprehensive Safeguards Agreements and Additional Protocols," http://www.iaea.org/Publications/Factsheets/English/sg_overview.html.

57. Author's interview with Ronald S. Somers, March 15, 2009.

58. Confederation of Indian Industry, "US Report: August 2005," August 2005.

59. See Aziz Haniffa, "ElBaradei Endorses Indo-US Nuclear Deal," *India Abroad,* November 18, 2005.

60. Sam Nunn, "Nuclear Pig in a Poke," *Wall Street Journal,* May 24, 2006.

61. See http://responsiblenucleartrade.com.

62. The bill was introduced March 16, 2006, in the Senate as S 2429, and in the House as HR 4974.

63. See *Congressional Record,* March 16, 2006, 2321.

64. "India Can Make 50 Nuclear Warheads a Year," *The Hindu,* June 19, 2006.

65. Ashley J. Tellis, "Atoms for War? US-Indian Civilian Nuclear Cooperation and India's Nuclear Arsenal," *Carnegie Endowment Report,* June 2006, http://carnegie endowment.org/files/atomsforwarfinal4.pdf.

66. HR 5682, introduced June 26, 2006.

67. *Congressional Record,* July 26, 2006, H5928.

68. For a comprehensive view of the legislative history through November 22, 2006, see Sharon Squassoni and Jill Marie Parillo, "US-India Nuclear Cooperation: A Side-by-Side Comparison of Current Legislation," Congressional Research Service, November 22, 2006.

69. Chairman Hyde was suffering from a heart condition and could not be present

at the signing ceremony. He would die of complications from heart surgery on November 29, 2007. See Adam Clymer, "Henry J. Hyde, a Power in the House of Representatives, Dies at 83," *New York Times,* November 30, 2007.

70. Representative Lantos would die February 11, 2008, before the completion of the two-step legislative process he had devised for the civil nuclear agreement. See the discussion below.

71. George W. Bush, "Remarks on Signing the Henry J. Hyde Peaceful Atomic Energy Cooperation Act of 2006," *The American Presidency Project,* December 18, 2006, http://www.presidency.ucsb.edu/ws/print.php?pid=24403.

72. As a general rule, prime ministers of India do not write thank-you letters to trade associations—particularly foreign trade associations.

73. Manmohan Singh, letter, December 22, 2006, http://www.contentfirst.com/past/USIBC/The_Way_Forwardfinal_June.pdf.

74. Amit Mitra, "Sabotaging India's Rise," *Times of India,* April 10, 2008.

75. Author's interview with Amit Mitra, February 25, 2010.

76. Author's interview with Tarun Das, March 10, 2010.

77. See Somini Sengupta, "Indian Government Survives Confidence Vote," *New York Times,* July 23, 2008.

78. See "IAEA Board Approves India-Safeguards Agreement," *IAEA.org,* August 1, 2008, http://www.iaea.org/NewsCenter/News/2008/board010808.html.

79. See "Inventory of International Nonproliferation Organizations and Regimes," Center for Nonproliferation Studies, last update, March 5, 2009, http://cns.miis.edu/inventory/pdfs/nsg.pdf.

80. See Marisa Lagos, "Longtime Rep. Tom Lantos Dies of Cancer," *San Francisco Chronicle,* February 12, 2008, http://sfgate.com/cgi-bin/article.cg?f=/c/a/2008/02/12/mnidv09vh.dtl.

81. Paul Richter, "Congress Approves US-India Nuclear Deal," *Los Angeles Times,* October 2, 2008, http://articles.latimes.com/2008/oct/o02/world/fg-usindia2.

82. See HR 7081, "United States–India Nuclear Cooperation Approval and Nonproliferation Enhancement Act, *Congressional Record,* September 27, 2008, H10223.

83. See *Congressional Record,* October 1, 2008, S10291.

84. George W. Bush, "Remarks on Signing the United States–India Nuclear Cooperation Approval and Nonproliferation Enhancement Act," *The American Presidency Project,* http://www.presidency.ucsb.edu/ws/index.php?pid=84528&st=&st1=.

85. As President Bush said in his inimitable style, "It's a big deal." Ibid.

86. See Hillary Rodham Clinton, "Remarks at US-India Business Council's 34th Anniversary Synergies Summit," June 17, 2009, http://www.state.gov/secretary/rm/2009a/06/125033.htm.

87. See "US and India Hold a Second Meeting of the Indo-United States Civil Nuclear Energy Working Group," April 30, 2009, http://www.energy.gov/news2009/7368.htm.

88. See, e.g., David E. Sanger and William J. Broad, "Agenda of Nuclear Talks Leaves Out a New Threat," *New York Times,* April 12, 2010.

89. William S. Cohen, "Remarks at US-India Business Council's 34th Anniversary Synergies Summit," June 17, 2009.

90. Shyam Saran, "Indo-US Civil Nuclear Agreement: Expectations and Consequences," Brookings Institution, March 23, 2009.

91. See Indrani Bagochi, "Search for a 'Big Idea' Ahead of Obama's Visit in Nov.," *Times of India,* July 16, 2010, http://timesofindia.indiatimes.com/articleshow/6173258 .cms.

92. See "Joint Statement by President Obama and Prime Minister Singh of India," November 8, 2010, http://whitehouse.gov//the-press-office/2010/11/08/joint-statement.

93. See "Remarks by the President to the Joint Session of the Indian Parliament in New Delhi," November 8, 2010, http//www.whitehouse.gov/the-press-office/2010/11/ 08/remarks-president.

94. See Pretap Bhanu Mehta, "India Eyes an American Special Relationship," *Financial Times,* July 26, 2010.

Chapter 3

1. Effective November 1, 2006, the Government of Karnataka voted to change the city name "Bangalore" to "Bengaluru." However, the city is still widely called by its old name.

2. See "BJP to Link N-Deal Execution to US Outsourcing Move," *Times of India,* May 6, 2009, http://timesofindia.indiatimes.com/articleshow/msid-4492192,prtpage-1 .cms.

3. See Press Trust of India, "Tax Break Withdrawal Reeks of Protectionism, India Inc to US," *Economic Times,* February 25, 2009, http://economictimes.indiatimes.com/ articleshow/4191288.cms?prtpage=1.

4. For a discussion of the competitiveness debate in the United States, see Kent Hughes, *Building the Next American Century: The Past and Future of Economic Competitiveness* (Washington, D.C., and Baltimore: Woodrow Wilson Center Press and Johns Hopkins University Press, 2005).

5. See Neil Irwin, "Aughts Were a Lost Decade for US Economy, Workers: Period Brought Zero Job Creation, Decline in Household Net Worth," *Washington Post,* January 2, 2010.

6. The term "outsourcing" is used here as it is most often used in US and Indian political commentary, i.e., as a synonym for outsourcing of services from beyond the borders of the United States. Outsourcing from beyond the borders of the United States is more accurately referred to as "offshore outsourcing," or simply "offshoring" where production takes place in a foreign territory but still within the enterprise. Technically, "outsourcing" means the transfer of the production of goods or services for use by an enterprise from within the enterprise to a source outside the enterprise.

7. For a searchable database of Obama speeches referencing the "middle class," see "askSam ebooks & Databases," http://www.asksam.com/books/search2.asp?file +Obama-Speeches.ask&search=Middle+Class&btnSearchEBooks=search.

8. See "Indian National Congress's Lok Sabha Election Manifesto," http://ibnlive .in.com/news/full-text-congress-manifesto-for-general-elections-09/88510-37-65.html.

9. See Stephen S. Roach, "What About Us?" *Global: Daily Economic Comment* (Morgan Stanley, July 2, 2004); and Barry Bosworth and Susan Collins, "Accounting for Growth: Comparing China and India," *Journal of Economic Perspectives* 22, no. 1 (Winter 2008): 45–66.

10. US Central Intelligence Agency, *The World Factbook* (Langley, Va.: US Central Intelligence Agency, 2009), www.cia.gov/library/publication/the-world-factbook/geos/IN.html.

11. Ibid.

12. "India Leads in IT Export: World Bank," *MSN News,* April 23, 2009, http://news.in.msn.com/business/article.aspx?cp-documentid+2993586.

13. NASSCOM, *IT-BPO Sector in India: Strategic Review 2010* (New Delhi: NASSCOM, 2010).

14. Ibid.

15. See, e.g., Dipankar Gupta, *The Caged Phoenix: Can India Fly?* (Washington, D.C., and Stanford, Calif.: Woodrow Wilson Center Press and Stanford University Press, 2009).

16. See T. N. Srinivasan, "Information Technology Enabled Services and India's Growth Prospects," in *Brookings Trade Forum 2005: Offshoring White-Collar Work— The Issues and the Implications,* edited by Susan M. Collins and Lael Brainard (Washington, D.C.: Brookings Institution Press, 2006); and NASSCOM, *Perspective 2020: Transform Business, Transform India* (New Delhi: NASSCOM, 2010). See also Arvind Panagariya, *India: The Emerging Giant* (New York: Oxford University Press, 2008).

17. See, e.g., US Government Accountability Office, *Offshoring of Services: An Overview of the Issues* (Washington, D.C.: US Government Printing Office, 2005), 52, and references cited therein.

18. Bureau of the Census, US Department of Commerce, http://www.census.gov/foreign-trade/balance/c5330.html#2007.

19. Office of the United States Trade Representative, http://www.ustr.gov/countries-regions/south-central-asia/india.

20. US Government Accountability Office, "US and India Data on Offshoring Show Significant Differences," *GAO Highlights,* GAO-06-116, October 2005.

21. Ibid., 3; and on 10: "Those examining trends in offshoring often compare US and Indian data series; however, there are at least five factors that make this comparison difficult and affect the difference between US and Indian data. These factors relate to (1) the treatment of services provided by foreign temporary workers in the United States; (2) the definition of some services, such as computer programs embedded in goods and certain information technology-enabled services; (3) the treatment of transactions between firms in India and the overseas offices of US firms; (4) the reporting of country-specific data on trade in affiliated services; and (5) the sources of data and other methodological differences in the collection of services data." Also see "Frequently Asked Questions," Bureau of Economic Analysis, US Department of Commerce: "A GAO study showed that US data on offshoring of services from India are more than 20 times smaller than India's data. What's the story?" (http://faq.bea.gov/cgi-bin/bea.cfg/php/enduser/std_adp.php?p_faqid=324&p_created=1163013475&p_sid=1uQvY5Xj&p_accessibility=0&p_redirect=&p_lva=&p_sp=cF9zcmNoPTEmcF9zb3J0X2J5PSZwX2dyaWRzb3J0PSZwX3Jvd19jbnQ9Q9MywzJnBfcHJvZHM9JnBfY2F0cz0wJnBfcHY9Jn BfY3Y9JnBfc2VhcmNoX3R5cGU9YW5zd2Vyc2VhcmNoJnBfcGFnZT0xJnBfc2VhcmNoX3RleHQ9ZWFyY2hfdGV4dGRGV4dDlvZmZzaG9yaW5nJn5n&p_li=&p_topview=1).

22. The "Y2K" problem was a concern that because the dates for most twentieth-century computer programs had been written in a format that only used the last two digits of the year designation, programs would not be able to recognize the difference between years beginning "19" from those beginning "20," e.g., unable to tell the year 1900 from

the year 2000. Consequently, programs for automating transactions where a date was required would become inoperable. The task of providing fixes for such programs was widely outsourced to India.

23. Author's interview with Richard Celeste, March 6, 2010.

24. See "Kerry on the Benedict Arnolds," *Washington Times,* May 16, 2004, http://www.washingtontimes.com/news/2004/may/16/20040516-102448-2933r/print/.

25. This was found at http://www.zazona.com/NewArchive/2004-03-03 percent20 Coalition percent20Against percent20the percent20A.

26. Ishani Duttagupta, "Can Kerry win NRI Hearts & Cash? TNN, March 29, 2004, http://economictimes.indiatimes.com/articleshowarchive.cms?msid+587688.

27. Council of Economic Advisers, *Economic Report of the President 2004* (Washington, D.C.: US Government Printing Office, 2004), 25.

28. See Daniel W. Drezner, "The Outsourcing Bogeyman," *Foreign Affairs,* May–June 2004, http://www.foreignaffairs.com/articles/59889/daniel-w-drezner/the-outsourcing -bogeyman.

29. US Government Accountability Office, *Offshoring of Services: An Overview of the Issues,* GAO-06-5, (Washington, D.C.: US Government Printing Office, 2005).

30. See Richard McCormack, "Commerce Department Report on Offshore Outsourcing Finally Sees the Light of Day," *Manufacturing & Technology News,* July 24, 2006.

31. Collins and Brainard, *Brookings Trade Forum 2005.*

32. Ibid., x.

33. Ibid., xi.

34. 8 U.S.C. 1101 (a) (15) (H) (i) (b).

35. 8 U.S.C. 1184 (i) (1).

36. 8 U.S.C. 1101 (a) (15 (L).

37. 9 U.S.C. 1184 (c) (2).

38. Senator Charles Grassley, "Press Release," April 2, 2007: "Grassley and Durbin introduced first bipartisan H-1B, L.-1 visa reform bill to protect American workers" (http://Grassley.senate.gov/news/Article.cfm?customel_dataPageID_1502+10956).

39. This development was duly noted in the Indian press. See Press Trust of India, "US Senators Now Fear Abuse of L Visa, Seek Checks," http://w3.nexis.com/new/ delivery/PrintDoc.do?fromCart=false&dnldFilePath= percent2F.

40. Charles Grassley and Dick Durbin, Letter, June 13, 2007, httb://durban.senate .gov/showRelease.cfm?releaseID=277832.

41. S 1348, 110th Congress, also considered as S 1639.

42. Grassley and Durbin, Letter.

43. Anand Giridharadas, "Lobbying in US, Indian Firms Present an American Face," *New York Times,* September 4, 2007, http://www.nytimes.com/2007/09/04/business/ worldbusiness/04outsource.html?_r=18&sq=Indian percent20Lobbying percent20in percent20US7st=nyp&scp=18&pagewanted=print.

44. John McCain, "McCain on India," *Indian Express,* August 10, 2008.

45. Michael Arrington, "Q&A with Senator Barack Obama on Key Technology Issues," *TechCrunch,* November 26, 2007, http://www.techcrunch.com/2007/11/26qa-with -senator-barack-obama-on-key-technology-issues/.

46. Press Trust of India, "Obama Opposes Outsourcing of Jobs," *Rediff India Abroad,* (February 27, 2008, http://www.rediff.com/money/2008/feb/27bpo.htm.

47. Douglas W. Elmendorf, director, Congressional Budget Office, letter to Nancy

Pelosi, speaker of the House of Representatives, February 13, 2009, http://www.cbo .gov/ftpdocs/99xx/coc9989/hr1confernce.pdf.

48. See Section 1605, Division A, Public Law 111-5. HR 2847 is a fiscal year 2011 appropriations bill providing funding for the Commerce Department, the Justice Department, and other agencies. In the version passed by the House on December 16, 2009, it also contained a $150 billion stimulus component titled "Jobs for Main Street Act." HR 2847 includes the same "buy American" provision as the American Recovery and Reinvestment Act of February 2009, with some additional language on waivers.

49. Emergency Stabilization Act of 2008, Public Law 110-343.

50. Charles Grassley, "Grassley Amendment to Ensure Americans Are Priority in Hiring by TARP Recipients Clears Senate," press release, February 6, 2009, http://grassley .senate.gov/news/Article.cfm?customel_dataPageID_1502=19225.

51. Norm Matloff, "Sanders/Grassley H-1B Amendment Is Great Symbolic Victory," *NumbersUSA*, http://www.cwalocal4250.org/outsourcing/binarydata/Sanders.pdf.

52. The prime minister is the chairman of the Planning Commission. Montek Singh Ahluwalia is one of India's leading economists. His position as chairman of the Planning Commission is somewhat like the head of the Office of Management and Budget in the US system.

53. Mehul Srivastava, "Anger Grows in India over US Visa Rules," *Economic Times*, February 25, 2009, http://economictimes.indiatimes.com/features/Anger-grows-in-India -over-US-visa-rules/articleshow/4189959.cms.

54. Mehul Srivastava, "Anger Grows in India over US Visa Rules," *Business Week*, February 25, 2009, as reprinted in *Economic Times*, http://economictimes.indiatimes .com/articleshow/4189959.cms?prtpage=1.

55. Barack Obama, "Statement by the President on the Passage of the Southwest Border Security Bill," August 12, 2010, http://www.whitehouse.gov/the-press-office/ 2010/08/12/statement-president-passage-southwest-border-security-bill.

56. Narayan Lakshman, "Obama Signs Controversial Border Security Bill into Law," *The Hindu*, August 13, 2010, http://www.thehindu.com/news/international/article 568137.ece.

57. Doha WTO Ministerial Meeting 2001, "Ministerial Declaration," WT/MIN(01)/ DEC/1, November 20, 2001, http://www.wto.org/english/thewto_e/minist_e/mindecl_e .htm.

58. Alan Beattie, "US-India Visa Row Overshadows Doha Talks," *Financial Times*, May 17, 2007, http://www.ft.com/cms/s/1780e47a-0495-11dc-8aed-000b5df10621 .html?nclick_check=1.

59. NASSCOM, "Statement from NASSCOM on Border Security Bill by US," http://www.nasscom.in/Nasscom/templates/NormalPage.aspx?id=59660.

60. Barack Obama, "Remarks by the President to U.S.-India Business Council and Entrepreneurship Summit," November 11, 2008, http://www.whitehouse.gov/the-press -office/2010/11/08/remarks-president-us-india-business-council-and-entrepreneurship- summit.

61. Pacific Council on International Policy and Federation of Indian Chambers of Commerce and Industry, "Charting New Frontiers: Enhancing India-US Cooperation in the Global Innovation Economy," Report of the Joint Task Force of the Pacific Council on International Policy and the Federation of Indian Chambers of Commerce and Industry, June 2009, 21.

62. As the chief representative of the Department of Commerce to the 1996 Ministerial, I observed the powerful impact of US and Indian private-sector engagement on achieving agreement on a major trade initiative.

63. For a description of the committees as they existed in 2002, see US General Accounting Office, *International Trade Advisory System Should be Updated to Better Serve US Policy Needs*, GAO-02-876 (Washington, D.C.: US Government Printing Office, 2002); and for updates to the system, see International Trade Administration, "Industry Trade Advisory Committee," http://www.trade.gov/itac/committees/. Administration of the sector and functional advisory committees was a part of my charge as assistant secretary of commerce, trade development.

64. See the description of the Information Technology Agreement and its workings at "Information Technology Agreement: Introduction," http://www.wto.org/englis/tratop_E/inftec_e/itainto_e.htm.

Chapter 4

1. PBS, "India Blames Pakistan Militant Group for Parliament Attack," *OnlineNews Hour,* December 14, 2001, http://www.pbs.org/newshour/updates/december01/india_12-14.html. The complete quotation is "India will pay heavily if they engage in any misadventure." This quotation is attributed to a Pakistani government spokesman, Major General Rashid Qureshi.

2. See "Nuclear Weapons Doctrine," *GlobalSecurity.org,* http://www.globalsecurity.org/wmd/world/pakistan/doctrine.htm.

3. See Natural Resources Defense Council, "The Consequences of Nuclear Conflict between India and Pakistan," June 4, 2002, http://www.nrdc.org/nuclear/southasia.asp. Also see Michael J. Mills et al., "Massive Global Ozone Loss Predicted Following Regional Nuclear Conflict," *Proceedings of the National Academy of Sciences* 105 (2008): 5307–12; and Ira Helfand, *An Assessment of the Extent of Projected Global Famine Resulting from Limited, Regional Nuclear War* (London: Royal Society of Medicine, 2007), http://www.psr.org/assets/pdfs/an-assessment -of-the-extent.pdf.

4. Paul D. Taylor and Andres Vaart, "Economic Security Exercise South Asia Proliferation Project," sponsored by the United States Naval War College, March 1999, 11.

5. Author's interview with Scott Bayman, June 26, 2009.

6. General Electric Web site, http://www.ge.com/research/grc_3_3_11.html. By April 2009, the Welch Center alone was to grow to 1,153,000 square feet with some 4,200 employees.

7. See "American Express, TIBCO Software, Infosys and WetBridge Create New Company, Workadia L.L.C," TIBCO press release, June 5, 2001, http://www.tibco.com/company/news/releases/2001/press377.jsp.

8. For a list of Infosys' strategic partners, http://www.infosys.com/about/alliances/default.asp.

9. See David Jacobs and Joel Yudken, *The Internet, Organizational Change, and Labor: The Challenge of Virtualization* (New York: Routledge, 2003).

10. Tata Consultancy Services Web site, www.tcs.com/homepage/Pages/default.aspx.

11. Celia W. Dugger, "India Recalls Envoy to Pakistan over Attack on Parliament," *New York Times,* December 21, 2001.

12. Associated Press, "India Releases Suspects List," *Los Angeles Times,* January 12, 2002.

13. Michael R. Gordon, "India Presses Its Conditions for Pullback from Border," *New York Times,* January 18, 2002.

14. See Polly Nyak and Michael Krepon, *US Crisis Management in South Asia's Twin Peaks Crisis,* and the chronology attached thereto (Washington, D.C.: Henry L. Stimson Center, 2006).

15. "30 Killed in Jammu Suicide Attack," *The Hindu,* May 14, 2002.

16. Luv Puri, "Be Ready for Decisive Battle, PM Tells Jawans," *The Hindu,* May 22, 2002.

17. Bureau of Consular Affairs, US Department of State, "India Travel Warning," May 31, 2002.

18. Bureau of Consular Affairs, US Department of State, "India Travel Warning," June 5, 2002, http://statelists.state.gov/scripts/wa.exe?A2+ind0206A&L=DOSTRAVEL&P=R1872.

19. Author's interview with Michael Gadbaw, February 15, 2010.

20. Thomas Friedman, *The World Is Flat: A Brief History of the Twenty-First Century* (New York: Macmillan, 2005).

21. Author's conversation with Nandan Nilekani.

22. Friedman, *World Is Flat.*

23. Ibid.

24. Teresita C. Schaffer, *India and the United States in the 21st Century* (Washington, D.C.: CSIS Press, 2009), 177; Nyak and Krepon, *US Crisis Management,* 36; Alex Stolar, *To the Brink: Indian Decision-Making and the 2001–2002 Standoff"* (Washington, D.C.: Henry L. Stimson Center, 2008), 26.

25. Thom Shanker, "Rumsfeld, in India, Offers Linked Ideas but No Peace Plan," *New York Times,* June 12, 2002, http://nytimes.com/2002/06/12/world/.

26. Friedman, *World Is Flat,* 429.

27. See Kenneth Waltz, in *The Spread of Nuclear Weapons: A Debate Renewed,* by Scott D. Sagan and Kenneth N. Waltz (New York: W. W. Norton, 2002); and Sumit Ganguly and Devin Hagerty, *Fearful Symmetry: India-Pakistan Crises in the Shadow of Nuclear Weapons* (Seattle: University of Washington Press, 2005), as cited by Stolar, *To the Brink.*

28. See Friedman, *World Is Flat,* 428.

29. Schaffer, *India and the United States,* 177.

30. Somini Sengupta, "India's Circumscribed Options," *New York Times,* December 12, 2008, http://www.nytimes.com/2008/12/12/world/asia/12-iht-assess.1.18624355.html?pagewanted=all.

31. Aziz Haniffa, "CIA Chief's Visit to India to Institutionalize Intel Cooperation," Rediff.com, http://news.rediff.com/report/2009/apr/04/mumterror-cia-chief-visit-to-institutionalize-intel-cooperation.

32. This endeavor was "FICCI Frames," a conference and trade show focusing on Bollywood and the business of entertainment. The author was a leader of the US participation in this event, which included a US congressional delegation led by Representative John Lewis (D-Ga.) and entertainment professionals featuring the American actor Danny Glover.

33. NASSCOM, "Mumbai Terror Attack," http://www.nasscom.org/Nasscom/templates/NormalPage.aspx?id=55245.

34. Neena Vyas, "BJP: Chidambaram's Statement Objectionable," *The Hindu,* January 6, 2009, 1.

35. "Home Minister Patil Resigns, 'Too Late' Says BJP," Expressindia.com, November 30, 2008, http://www.expressindia.com/latest-news/Home-Minister-Patil-resigns-too-late-says-BJP/392430/.

36. "Chidambaram Gets Security Lessons from US Officials in New York," *Times of India,* September 9, 2009, http://timesofindia.indiatimes.com/India/Chidambaram.

37. Emily Wax, "Despite Promises to Bolster Defenses, India Remains Vulnerable; Months after Terrorists Shocked Mumbai, Experts Cite Persistent Gaps in Security," *Washington Post,* August 22, 2009.

38. Press Trust of India, "US Ready to Support India to Modernize Its Armed Forces," *The Hindu,* October 19, 2009, http://beta.thehindu.com/news/national/article 35777.ece.

39. "Pentagon Announces Plans to Lease Reconnaissance Planes to India," *Defence Talk,* November 15, 2005, http://www.defencetalk.com/pentagon-announces-plans-to-lease-reconaissance-planes-to-india-4651/.

40. Indo-Asian News Service, "US Offers to Lease Choppers to India for Coastal Security," *SiliconIndia,* June 5, 2009, http://www.siliconindia.com/shownews/.

41. Indo-Asian News Service, "US Clears $2.1 Billion Sale of Naval Patrol Aircraft to India," March 17, 2009, http://news.boloji.com/2009/03/29108.htm.

42. Ritu Sharma, "India Works on To-Do List to Revamp Homeland Security," NewKerala.com, http://www.newkerala.com/nkfulnews-1-150519.html.

Chapter 5

1. "Externality costs" may generally be defined as "societal costs that are not reflected in market transactions." Jonathan Koomey and Krause Florentine, "Introduction to Environmental Externality Costs," Lawrence Berkeley Laboratory, 1997, 2, http://enduse.lbl.gov/info/Externalities.pdf.

2. See Shefali Rekhi, "Fast Track to Darkness," *India Today,* May 4, 1998, http://www.India-Today.com/itoday/04051998/biz.html

3. Abhay Mehta, *Power Play: A Study of the Enron Project* (New Delhi: Orient Longman Limited, 2000), 17.

4. Ron Somers, "India's Quest for Energy: The Domestic Picture," in *Foreign Addiction: Assessing India's Energy Security Strategy,* Asia Program Special Report (Washington, D.C.: Woodrow Wilson International Center for Scholars, 2008), 35; and Rekhi, "Fast Track."

5. See "Report of the Cabinet Sub-Committee to Review the Dabhol Power Project" (the so-called Munde Report), 13, reproduced as appendix B to *The Enron Corporation: Corporate Complicity in Human Rights Violations,* edited by Human Rights Watch (New York: Human Rights Watch, 1999), http://www.hrw.org/legacy/reports/1999/enron/enron-b.htm.

6. For descriptions of the MOU, see Paul Lejot and Frederik Pretorius, "Politics, Institutions and Project Finance: The Dabhol Power Project," Asia Case Research Centre, University of Hong Kong, 2007, 4; Indian Center for Management Research (ICMR) Case Study "The Enron Saga," 2001, http://icmrindia.org/casestudies/catalogue/Business

percent20Ethics/The percent20Enron percent20Saga.htm; and Human Rights Watch, *Enron Corporation,* 10.

7. See Human Rights Watch, *Enron Corporation,* 11–12.

8. This is my impression. According to the former chief executive officer of Dabhol Power Company, Salve reasoned that because consumer pricing was on a pooled basis, the increased cost of Dabhol Power Company electricity would be diluted by the lower cost from existing plants so that average cost to the consumers would only be increased by a manageable 10 percent. Author's interview with Sanjay Bhatnagar, February 27, 2010.

9. Human Rights Watch, *Enron Corporation,* 10.

10. Letter from Heinz Vergin, director, India Country Department, International Development Association to M. S. Ahluwalia, secretary, Department of Economic Affairs, Ministry of Finance, April 30, 1993, Reproduced as appendix D in *Enron Corporation,* ed. Human Rights Watch, 159.

11. Minority Staff, Committee on Government Reform, US House of Representatives, "Background on Enron's Dabhol Power Project," February 22, 2002, 13; Girish Sant, Shantanu Dixit, and Subodh Wagle, "The Power Purchase Agreement (PPA) between Dabhol Power Company and Maharashtra State Electricity Board: The Structure and Its Techno-Economic Implications," Prayas Energy Group Report, June 1995, http://www.pryaspune.org/peg/publications/ppa_dpc_epw_002A01.pdf.

12. Sant, Dixit, and Wagle, "Power Purchase Agreement," 3–9.

13. The author chaired this Working Group.

14. Pachauri would go on to accept the Nobel Peace Price in 2007 in his capacity as chairman of the Intergovernmental Panel on Climate Change. He has retained his role as director-general of The Energy and Resources Institute (TERI).

15. See Naunidhi Kaur, "Mumbai: A Decade after Riots," *Frontline* 20, issue 14 (July 5–18, 2003); and Edward A. Gargan, "Hindu Storm: A Special Report—Trust Is Torn: Police Role in Bombay Riots," *New York Times,* February 4, 1993.

16. See John F. Burns, "Riot Scars Are Gone, but Bombay Is Still Healing," *New York Times,* April 17, 1994, www.nytimes.com/1994/04/17/world/riot-scars-are-gone -but-bombay-is-still-healing.html.

17. See Julia M. Eckert, *The Charisma of Direct Action: Power, Politics and the Shiv Sena* (New York: Oxford University Press, 2003).

18. See John-Thor Dahlburg, "Column One: This Power Game Has High Stakes for India—Rocks Fly as a US Consortium Begins to Build a Huge Utility Plant. If Newly Elected Officials Scratch the Project, Billions in Foreign Investment May Be Jeopardized," *Los Angeles Times,* June 22, 1995, http://articles.latimes.com/1995-06-22/news/ mn-16009_1_dabhol_power-plant.

19. See Minority Staff, Committee on Government Reform, US House of Representatives, "Background on Enron's Dabhol Power Project," 6, citing "The Enron Affair: Shadowy Path to State Approval," *Financial Times,* January 12, 2002. Also see S. Padmanabhan, "Dabhol Project: Politics of Power," *Business Line,* May 28, 2001, http:// www.hindunet.com/businessline/2001/05/28/stories/042856pd.htm.

20. "Enron's Rebecca Mark: 'You Have to Be Pushy and Aggressive,'" *Business Week,* February 24, 1997, http://www.businessweek.com/1991/08/b351586.htm.

21. C. W. L. Hill, "Enron International in India," *International Business: Competition in the Global Marketplace,* 2005, 124–27, http://highered.mcgraw-hill.com/sites/ dl/free/0072873957/Hill4e_124-127.pdf.

22. Human Rights Watch, *Enron Corporation,* 29–37.

23. Lejot and Pretorius, "Politics, Institutions and Project Finance," 8–10.

24. See varying estimates of the actual uptake given by Celia W. Dugger, "High-Stakes Showdown: Enron's Fight over Power Plant Reverberates Beyond India," *New York Times,* March 20, 2001; and A. Inkpen, "Enron and the Dabhol Power Company," Case Study, Thunderbird School of Global Management, 2002, as referenced by Lejot and Pretorius, "Politics, Institutions and Project Finance," 11.

25. See Tony Allison, "Enron's Eight-Year Power Struggle in India" *Asia Times,* January 18, 2001, http://www.atimes.com/reports/CA13Ai01.html.

26. Dugger, "High-Stakes Showdown."

27. Mark Kantor, "Arbitration Award May Alter Dabhol Debate," *Transnational Dispute Management* 1, issue 2 (May 2004), http://www.transnational-disput-management .com/samples/freearticles/tv1-2article179b.

28. See International Finance Corporation, "Tata Ultra Mega Summary of Proposed Investment," April 24, 2008, http://www.ifc.org/ifcext/spiwebsite1.nsf/1ca07340e47 a35cd85256ef00700cee/1584EA74DA3979ABB852573A0006847BB.

29. The author was asked to look into the basis for the political problems of the project on a trip to India in November 1994 to advance Secretary Brown's business development mission. While in Bangalore, the capital of Karnataka, he was informed that many attributed Cogentrix's difficulties to the steadfast refusal of Cogentrix to pay bribes. These bribes were represented as the "normal" course of action in doing business with the state. The Cogentrix project was placed on the list of matters to be discussed by Secretary Brown with the Karnataka chief minister, which Brown did in January 1995.

30. "Cogentrix Told to Win Friends and Influence People," *Rediff on the Net,* May 22, 1998, http://www.rediff.com/business/1998/may/22cogent.htm.

31. "World Business Briefing: Asia; Cogentrix Cleared in India," *New York Times,* December 14, 1999.

32. "Orissa Government Expresses Inability to Buy Power from the AES Transpower Project," *Projects Today,* August 26, 2000, http://www.projectstoday.com/News/ NewsDetails.aspx?nid=502.

33. See Pryas, *India Power Sector Reform Update,* Issue II, January 2002, 7, http:// www.psiru.org/IndiaIRU2-0102.pdf.

34. See Ernest H. Preeg, *India and China: An Advanced Technology Race and How the United States Should Respond* (Arlington Va.: Manufacturers Alliance / MAPI, 2008), 47.

35. Niupam Bajpai and Nandita Dasgupta, *What Constitutes Foreign Direct Investment? Comparison of India and China,* Working Papers Series (New York: Center on Globalization and Sustainable Development, Earth Institute at Columbia University, 2004).

36. See the Power Finance Corporation Ltd. Web site for documents on Ultra Mega Power Projects, http://pfc.gov.in/UMPP.html.

37. "No Cap on Ultra Mega Power Project Allocation to Single Firm," *Hindu Business Line,* July 7, 2009, http://www.thehindubusinessline.com/2009/07/08/stories/ 2009070851851500.htm.

38. For a review of the project, see International Finance Corporation, "Tata Ultra Mega Summary."

39. Press Trust of India, "RFQ for at Least One UMPP Soon: Officials," *Business Standard,* July 12, 2009, http://www:business-standard.com/india/news/rfq-for-at-least -one-umpp-soon-officials/363634/.

40. See Ministry of Power, "Year End Review—2009," http://www.powermin.nic.in/what's_new/pdf/review_MoP_2009.pdf.

41. Al Gore, "Gore Statement on US Signing of Kyoto Protocol," Press Release, Office of the Vice President, November 12, 1998, http://www.commondreams.org/press releases/Novpercent2098/111298c.htm.

42. See Government of India, "Joint Statement on Cooperation in Energy and Related Environmental Aspects," New Delhi, October 26, 1999, http://www.indianembassy.org/pr detail1292/joint-statement-on-cooperation-in-energy-and-related-environmental-aspects.

43. William J. Clinton, "Remarks in Agra at the Signing Ceremony for the Indo-United States Joint Statement on Energy and the Environment," March 22, 2000, http://www.presidency.ucsb.edu/ws/index.php?pid=58280&st=&st1=.

44. Ibid.

45. See David E. Sanger and Katherine Q. Seelye, "The 2000 Campaign: The Incumbent, Gore Meets with India Leader and Prods Senate on Test Ban," _New York Times,_ September 16, 2000, http://www.nytimes.com/2000/09/16/us/2000-campaign-incumbent-gore-meets-with-india-leader-prods-senate-test-ban.html. The author was present at this event.

46. The White House press secretary argued that the signature was dependent on Senate ratification of the protocol so there was nothing to withdraw. See "Press Briefing by Ari Fleischer," March 28, 2001, in _The American Presidency Project_ [online], edited by John T. Woolley and Gerhard Peters (Santa Barbara: University of California, Santa Barbara, n.d.), http://www.presidency.ucsb.edu/ws/?pid=47500.

47. George W. Bush, "Remarks on Global Climate Change," June 11, 2001, in _American Presidency Project,_ ed. Woolley and Peters, http://www.presidency.ucsb.edu/ws/index.php?pid=45985&st=&st1=.

48. Aziz Haniffa, "India Must Enact N-Liability Protection," _Rediff India Abroad,_ October 16, 2008, http://.rediff.com/money/2008/oct/16aziz1.htm.

49. Ironically, this was a modified version of a forum founded by President George W. Bush in 2007. See Rie Jerichow, "Obama Resurrects a Disputed Bush Climate Forum," http://en.cop15.dk/news/view+news?newsid+1161.

50. See Office of the Press Secretary, the White House, "Declaration of the Leaders of the Major Economies Forum on Energy and Climate," July 9, 2009, http://www.whitehouse.gov/the_press_office/.

51. Ibid.

52. "13-Year-Old Indian to Address UN Climate Change Summit," _Economic Times_ (New Delhi), September 21, 2009, http://economictimes.indiatimes.com/new/news-by-industry/et-cetera/ Accessed September 23, 2009.

53. See Juliet Eilperin and Colum Lynch, "Nations Appear Headed toward Independent Climate Goals," _Washington Post,_ September 23, 2009.

54. "Leaders' Statement on the Pittsburgh Summit, September 24–25, 2009," September 25, 2009, 4, http://www.pittsburghsummit.gov/documents/organizational/129853.pdf.

55. Ibid., 3.

56. See "India Ensures Say for Emerging Economies at G20," _Times of India,_ September 26, 2009, http://timesofindia.indiatimes.com/articleshow/msid-5060387,prtpage-1.cms.

57. Ibid.

58. HR 2454, 112, 111th Congress.

59. See Juliet Eilperin, "Firms Start to See Climate Change as Barrier to Profit," *Washington Post,* September 21, 2009.

60. Randeep Ramesh, "India Won't Accept Emissions Limits, Says Envoy," *Guardian,* December 8, 2008, http://www.guardian.co.uk/environment/2008/dec/08/poznzn -climate.

61. See US Department of State, "Transcript of Signing Ceremony for the US-China Memorandum of Understanding on Climate Change, Energy, and the Environment," July 28, 2009, http://www.state.gov/secretary/rm/2009a/july/126575.htm.

62. "Jairam for Major Shift at Climate Talks," *Times of India,* October 19, 2009, http://timesofindia.com/india/Jairam-for-major-shift-at-climate-talks.htm.

63. "Agreement on Cooperation on Addressing Climate Change between the Government of the Republic of India and the Government of the People's Republic of China," October 21, 2009, Ministry of the Environment and Forests Web site, http:// moef.nic.in/index.php.

64. "PM's Address at the New Delhi High-Level Conference on 'Climate Change: Technology Development and Transfer,'" Prime Minister's Office Web site, http://pm india.nic.in.

65. Jairam Ramesh, "Jairam Ramesh Statement on Copenhagen Accord in Rajya Sabha," *The Hindu,* December 22, 2009, http://beta.thehindu.com/news/national/article 69893.ece.

66. Manmohan Singh, "PM's Remarks at the Informal Plenary of HOS/Gs at the 15th COP at Copenhagen," Prime Minister's Office Web site, January 18, 2009, http:// pmindia.nic.in/copenhagen_visit.htm.

67. Ramesh, "Jairam Ramesh Statement."

68. Barack Obama, "Remarks by the President during Press Availability in Copenhagen," December 18, 2009, http://www.whitehouse.gov/the-press-office/remarks -president-during-press-availability-copenhagen.

69. Juliet Eilperin, "Climate Treaty Realities Push Leaders to Trim Agendas," *Washington Post,* April 13, 2010.

70. "Clinton Foundation to Set Up 3,000-MW Solar Plant," *Times of India,* September 8, 2009, http://timesofindiaindiatimes.com/articleshow/msid-4984301,prtpage-1.cms.

71. Abhay Singh, "India's Gujarat to Give Contracts for Solar Project," *Bloomberg.com,* September 18, 2009, http://www.bloomberg.com/apps/news?pid +206020918&sid+a8Eaa7f_xBU#.

72. See "India's Wind Power Boom Is Failing to Deliver," *National Wind Watch,* August 12, 2008, http://www.wind-watch.org/news/2008/08/12/india-wind-power-boom-is -failing-to-deliver.

73. See Keith Bradsher, "The Ascent of Wind Power," *New York Times,* September 28, 2006, http://www.nytimes.com/2006/09/28/business/worldbusiness/28wind.html.

74. "CDM Projects in India," *Indiascan,* http://indiascanblog.com/sectors/wind-farm/.

75. Sushilkumar Shinde, "Speech on US-India Business Council's 'Green India' Summit at Washington," October 16, 2008, http://pibmumbai.gov.in/scripts/detail.asp ?releaseID=E2008PR654.

76. Ibid.

77. See Institute for Global Environmental Strategies, "CDM Country Fact Sheet: India," August 1, 2009, http://envirosope.iges.or.jp/modules/envirolib/upload/984/attach/ india_final.pdf.

78. See Mamuni Das, "India Leads in CDM Project Rejections," *Hindu Business*

Line, September 6, 2007, http://www.thehindubusinessline.com/2007/09/06/stories/2007090652321000.htm.

79. "India Ready to Share CDM Experiences with SAARC," *Commodity Online,* September 1, 2009, http://www.commodityonline.com/news/India-ready-to-share-CDM -experiences-with-SAARC-20832-3-1.html.

Chapter 6

1. Energy Information Administration, US Department of Energy, *India,* Country Analysis Brief, March 2009, www.eia.doe/emeu/cabs/India/Full.html.

2. Ibid.

3. Ministry of Petroleum and Natural Gas, Government of India, *Basic Statistics on Indian Petroleum and Natural Gas,* September 2009, http://petroleum.nic.in/total.pdf.

4. Ibid.

5. Energy Information Administration, US Department of Energy, *International Energy Outlook 2009* (Washington, D.C.: US Government Printing Office, 2009), chap. 3, http://www.eia.doe.gov/oiaf/leo/nat_gas.html.

6. See "India, China to Strengthen Energy Cooperation," *Peoples Daily Online,* January 10, 2006, as quoted at the Chinese Business Council for Sustainable Development's Web site, http://english.cbcsd.org.cn/dynamic/proseminar/3173.shtml; also see "India and China: Oil-Patch Partners?" *Business Week,* February 7, 2005.

7. See the list of ONGC Videsh properties and projects at the ONGC Videsh Web site, http://www.ongcvidesh.com/Assets.aspx?tab=0.

8. Energy Information Administration, US Department of Energy, "International Petroleum (Oil) Production," http://www.eia.doe.gov/emeu/international/oilproduction.html.

9. PetroStrategies, Inc., "World's Largest Oil and Gas Companies," http://www .petrostrategies.org/Links/worlds_largest_oil_and_gas_companies.htm. Interestingly, ExxonMobil is now larger than PetroChina.

10. Sudha Ramachandran, "India Promotes 'Goodwill' Naval Exercises," *Asia Times,* August 14, 2007, http://www.atimes.com/atimes/South_Asia/IH14Df01.html.

11. P. S. Suryanarayana, "Raising Profile as a Maritime Power in East Asia," *The Hindu,* May 2, 2009, http://www.thehindu.com/2009/05/02/stories/2009050255150900 .htm.

12. For a review of the ways in which Iran oil affects US interests, see Roger Howard, *Iran Oil: The New Middle East Challenge to America* (London: I. B. Tauris, 2007).

13. See A. M. Rosenthal, "On My Mind; The US-Iran Oil Scam," *New York Times,* July 16, 1993, http://www.nytimes.com/1993/07/16/opinion/on-my-mind-the-us-iran-oil -scam.html.

14. "Factbox: Iran's Major Oil Customers, Energy Partners," Reuters, August 19, 2009, http://www.reuters.com/article/gca-oil/idustre57124z20090819.

15. See Asad Cheema, "Efforts Underway to Import Crude Oil from Iran," *Daily Mail,* December 24, 2008, http://www.dailymailnews.com/200812/24/news/dmcity page06.html.

16. Kenneth Katzman, "Iran Sanctions," Congressional Research Service Report for Congress, October 8, 2009, 13.

17. Energy Information Administration, US Department of Energy, *Independent*

Statistics and Analysis: India, Oil, (Washington, D.C.: US Government Printing Office, 2010), http://www.eia.doe.gov/cabs/India/Oil.html.

18. ONGC Videsh Web site, http://www.ongcvidesh.com/Assets.aspx?tab=1.

19. See "Leyland Arm to Develop Port, Rail Link in Iran," *The Hindu,* July 9, 2004, http://www.hindunet.com/2004/07/10/stories/2004071002551800.htm.

20. See US Government Accountability Office, *Iran Sanctions: Firms Reported to Have Commercial Activity in the Iranian Energy Sector and US Government Contracts,* GAO-10-721T (Washington, D.C.: US Government Printing Office, 2010), 5.

21. "Reliance No Longer Buying Iranian Crude," *Businessworld,* October 14, 2009, http://www.businessworld.in/bw/2009_10_14_Reliance_No_Longer_Buying_Iranian_Crude.html.

22. See R. K. Pachauri, "Atoms for Peace," *Indian Express,* June 19, 2008, http://www.rkpachauri.org/articles.php?sid+435.

23. "Workshop on Networking for Sustainable Development," *Asian Energy Institute Newsletter,* October 2000, 4, http://www.aeinetwork.org/aei16.pdf.

24. Ranjit Devraj, "Iran's Gas Pipeline May Turn South Asia's Peace Pipe," *Antiwar.com,* October 14, 2004, http://www.antiwar.com/ips/devraj.php?articleid=3775.

25. Katzman, "Iran Sanctions," 5.

26. See, e.g., Kimberly Ann Elliott and Gary Clyde Hufbauer, "Ineffectiveness of Economic Sanctions, Same Song, Same Refrain? Economic Sanctions in the 1990s," *American Economic Review* 89, no. 2 (May 1999): 403–8.

27. US Government Accountability Office, *Iran Sanctions: Impact in Furthering US Objectives Is Unclear and Should Be Reviewed,* GAO-08-58 (Washington, D.C.: US Government Printing Office, 2007).

28. Kenneth L. Katzman, "The Iran Sanctions Act (ISA)," Congressional Research Service, June 4, 2009, 2.

29. Ibid., 9–10.

30. Shebonti Ray Dawal and M. Mahtab Alam Rizvi, *US Sanctions on Iran and Their Impact on India* (New Delhi: Institute for Defence Studies and Analyses, 2010), 7, http://www.idsa.in/system/files/IB_USSanctionsonIran.pdf.

31. Library of Congress, "Bill Summary & Status, 111th Congress (2009–2010), HR 2194, All Information," July 1, 2010, http://thomas.loc.gov/cgi-bin/bdquery/D?d111:1:./temp/~bdXP8Y:@@@L&summ2=m&l/home/LegislativeData.php.

32. Kenneth Katzman, "Iran Sanctions," Congressional Research Service Report 7-5700, April 9, 2010, http://fpc.state.gov/document/organization/141587.pdf.

33. See United Nations Security Council, Resolutions 1737 (2006), 1747 (2007), and 1803 (2008), http://www.un.org/sc/committees/1737/resolutions.shtml.

34. See United Nations Security Council, Resolution 1929 (2010), http://daccess-dds-ny.un.org/doc/UNDOC/GEN/N10/396/79/PDF/N1039679.pdf?OpenElement.

35. Prime Minister's Office, "India's Nuclear Energy Programme and the 123 Agreement with the United States," http://pmindia.nic.in/India percentE2 percent80 percent99s percent20Energy percent20Programme percent20and percent20the percent 20123 percent20agreement.pdf.

36. See "PM's Inaugural Address at the International Conference on Peaceful Uses of Nuclear Energy," September 29, 2009, http://pmindia.nic.in/in/speeches.htm.

37. See Jeremy Page, "India Promises 12,000 percent Boost in Nuclear Capacity by 2050," *The Times* (London), September 30, 2009, http://www.timesonline.co.uk/tol/news/world/asoa/artocle6854501.ece.

38. Energy Information Administration, US Department of Energy, *India,* 7.

39. Sanjay Jog, "Gas Price Revision, IPI & TAPI Pipelines to Remain Priority," *Financial Express,* May 19, 2009, http://www.financialeexpress.com/news/gas-price -revision-ipi-&tapipipelines-to-remain-priority/462088/.

40. "Iran-Pak-India Gas Pipeline: India Undecided," Outlookindia.com, http://news .outlookindia.com/item.aspx?660400.

41. See the project description by Inter-State Gas Systems (Pvt) Ltd., http://www .isgs.pk/project_detail.php?project_id=6.

42. "ADB Ready to Provide Finance to Pak for IPI Project," *Thaindian News,* April 22, 2008, http://www.thaindian.com/newsportal/health/abd-ready-to-provide-finance -to-pak-for-ipi-project_10040628.html.

43. Zainab Jeewanjee, "Peace Pipeline Causes Concern for DC," *Foreign Policy Blogs Network,* September 15, 2009, http://pakistan.foreignpolicyblogs.com/tag/iran -pakistan-india-pipeline/.

Chapter 7

1. Mike Moore, "Opening Address to the WTO's 3rd Ministerial Conference," November 30, 1999, http://www.wto.org/english/thewto_e/minst_e/min99-e/english/press _e/pres156_e.htm.

2. Murasoli Maran, "Statement at the Plenary Session of the Third Ministerial Conference of the WTO in Seattle," November 30, 1999, http://www.indianembassy.org/ policy/WTO/maran_WTO_nov_30_99.htm.

3. See the discussion below in chapter 9 regarding economic engagement and health security.

4. T. N. Srinivasan and Suresh D. Tendulkar, *Reintegrating India with the World Economy* (Washington, D.C.: Institute for International Economics, 2003), 82.

5. Ibid., citing Aaditiya Matoo and Arvind Subrimanian, *India and the Multilateral Trading System after Seattle: Toward a Proactive Role* (Washington, D.C.: World Bank, 2000), to point out that in 2000 India bound rates exceeded applied rates by more than 50 percent in 656 of 673 tariff line items.

6. Satya P. Das has documented a phase of absolute decline from 1997 to 2000 relative to other Southeast Asian countries; see Aaditya Matoo and Robert M. Stern, eds., *India and the WTO* (Washington, D.C.: World Bank, 2003), 5, and chap. 7, 150.

7. See Prabir Sengupa, commerce secretary of India, "Preparations for the Fourth Session of the Ministerial Conference: Communication from India," World Trade Organization General Council document WT/GC/W/459, November 6, 2001.

8. WTO, "The Doha Implementation Decision Explained," http://www.wto.org/ english/tratop_E/implem_explained_e.htm.

9. "Murasoli Maran at Doha," *Indian Express.com,* November 25, 2003, http:// www.indianexpress.com/oldStory/35931.

10. WTO, "Doha WTO Ministerial 2001: Ministerial Declaration," document WT/ MIN(01)/Dec/1, adopted November 14, 2001, http://www.wto.org/english/thewto_e/ minst_e/min01_e.htm.

11. See Robert B. Zoellick, "America Will Not Wait," *Financial Times,* September 21, 2003.

12. See "Murasoli Maran, 1934–2003," *The Hindu,* November 25, 2003, http://www

.hindunet.com/thehindu/2003/11/25/stories/2003112500951000.htm; and "From Trade Pooper to Heroic Leader," *Business Standard,* September 23, 2003, http://www.business -standard.com/india/news/from-trade-pooper-to-heroic-leader/138757/.

13. WTO, "Doha Work Programme Ministerial Declaration," December 18, 2005, http://www.wto.org/english/thewto_e/minist_e/final_text_e.htm.

14. Kamal Nath, "TNC Meeting of July 23rd 2008, Statement of Shri Kamal Nath, Minister of Commerce & Industry, India," http://www.wto.org/english/tratop_e/dda_e/ meet08_stat_ind_21jul_e.doc.

15. This is a reference to the "Special Agricultural Safeguard" (SSG) found in the WTO Agriculture Agreement. This safeguard provision applies only in situations where quantitative restrictions have been converted into tariffs. Thus, the developing countries (which largely had refused to convert quantitative agricultural restrictions to tariffs) were unable to take advantage of the SSG. The SSM is a much broader concept that allows safeguards to be invoked even though tariffs may be increased beyond previously bound rates. See WTO, "An Unofficial Guide to Agricultural Safeguards, GATT, Old Agriculture (SSG) and New Mechanism (SSM)," August 5, 2008, http://www.wto.org/english/ tratop_e/agric_e/guide_agric_safeg_e.htm.

16. Nath, "TNC Meeting."

17. Ibid.

18. See Paul Blustein, *Misadventures of the Most Favored Nations* (New York: Public Affairs, 2009).

19. Note that the G-20 under discussion here is not to be confused with the group of twenty or more developing nations led by India, China, Brazil, and South Africa for the purposes of WTO negotiations. This grouping was particularly instrumental in fighting the positions of the United States and EU at the Cancún WTO Ministerial Conference. This grouping is quite fluid in numbers, although it is still often referred to as "G-20."

20. See Raymond E. Vickery Jr., "India's Bid for a New Order," *IP Global Edition, Journal of the German Council on Foreign Relations,* July–August 2010.

21. Of the original twenty-two participants, Hong Kong, Malaysia, Poland, and Thailand were dropped, and Saudi Arabia, Turkey, and the European Union were added. The G-20 now consists of Argentina, Australia, Brazil, Canada, China, France, Germany, India, Indonesia, Italy, Japan, Mexico, Russia, Saudi Arabia, South Africa, South Korea, Turkey, the United Kingdom, the United States, and the European Union.

22. IMF, "A Guide to Committees, Groups, and Clubs," 2008, http://www.inf.org/ external/np/exr/facts/groups.htm. See also G-20 Web site: http://www.g20.org/about _what_is_g20.aspx.

23. "G20 Chambers of Commerce Send Joint Message to G20 Leaders," November 14, 2008, http://www.eurochambres.be/content/default.asp?PageID=153.

24. Manmohan Singh, "Statement at the Summit of Heads of State or Governments of the G-20 Countries on Financial Markets and the World Economy," November 15, 2008, http://pmindia.nic.in/visits/content.asp?id=241.

25. See http://frwebgate.access.gpo.gov/cgi-bin/getdoc.cg?dbname+2008_presidential _document&docid+pd24n08_Txt-3.

26. George W. Bush, "Remarks at the Summit on Financial Markets and the World Economy," American Presidency Project, November 15, 2008, http://www.presidency .ucsb.edu/ws/index.php?pid=84965&st=&st1=.

27. *New York Times,* November 16, 2008.

28. *Wall Street Journal,* January 12, 2009.

29. See Miglani, Sanjeev, "Obama Calls Pakistan's Zardari, Assures Support," *Reuters Blogs,* November 9, 2008, http://blogs.reuters.com/pakistan/2008/11/09/obama -calls-pakistan percentE2 percent80 percent99s-zardari-assures-support/; Chidanand Rajghatta, "Delhi Shrugs Off Obama Call That Never Came," *Times of India,* November 9, 2008, http://timesofindia.indiatimes.com/world/us/Delhi-shrugs-off-Obama-call-that -never-came/articleshow/3690146.cms.

30. "PM Urges India Inc to Be Sensitive," *Economic Times,* March 28, 2009, http://economictimes.indiatimes.com/News/Economy/Policy/PM-urges-India-Inc-to-be -sensitive/articleshow/4327543.cms.

31. "G20 Chambers Warns against Protectionism," *UPI.com,* March 30, 2009, http:// www.upi.com/Business_News/2009/03/30/G20-Chambers-warns-against-protectionism/ UPI-87841238432075/.

32. "PM's Opening Statement to the Press on the Conclusion of the G-20 Summit," April 2, 2009, prime minister of India's Web site, http://pmindia.nic.in/speeches.htm.

33. See "Why 'India Inside' Spells Quality," *Dataquest,* October 27, 2003, http:// dqindia.ciol.com/content/advantage/103102703.asp.

34. "India Ensures Say for Emerging Economies at G20," *Times of India,* September 26, 2009, http://timesofindia.indiatimes.com/articleshow/msid-5060387.cms.

35. See Prime Minister's Office, "PM's Introductory Statement at Press Conference," September 25, 2009, http://pmindia.nic.in/lspeech.asp?id=824.

36. Surinder Singla, "Our Man in the Middle," *Hindustan Times,* September 29, 2009, http://www.hindustantimes.com/Our-man-in-the-middle/H1-Article1-459453.aspx.

Chapter 8

1. On the morning in question, the author was up early to go duck hunting outside New Delhi with a party that included a member from each group. He spoke that morning with those headed to work.

2. The author's father, Raymond E. Vickery Sr., as head of the Grain and Feed Division of the Foreign Agricultural Service of the US Department of Agriculture, led a mission to India during that period. The mission inspected facilities to determine their capacities to handle US grain.

3. See William F. Hall, "PL 480's Contribution to India's Economic Development," Report ERD-FOR.-8, Economic Research Service, US Department of Agriculture, May 1961.

4. B. R. Shenoy, *PL 480 Aid and India's Food Problem* (New Delhi: Affiliated East-West Press Pvt. Ltd., 1974).

5. Government of India, "Agriculture," in *The National Portal of India,* March 29, 2010, http://india.gov.in/sectors/agriculture/index.php.

6. See Bureau of Labor Statistics, US Department of Labor, "Table 18: Employed Persons by Detailed Industry, Sex, Race Hispanic or Latino Ethnicity," in *Household Data Annual Averages,* http://bls.gov/cps/cpsaat18.pdf.

7. All numbers are from Economic Research Service, US Department of Agriculture, *State Fact Sheets,* 2008, http://www.ers.usda.gov/StateFacts/US.htm.

8. See Bureau of Labor Statistics, US Department of Labor, "Table 19: Employment

Status of the Experienced Civilian Labor Force by Industry," *Estimates for States Geographic Profile,* 2009, http://bls.gov/opub/gp/gpsec2.htm.

9. See Dennis Kux, *India and the United States: Estranged Democracies* (Honolulu: University Press of the Pacific, 2002), 240–47.

10. See Kristin L. Ahlberg, *Transplanting the Great Society* (Columbia: University of Missouri Press, 2009), 120–21.

11. US Department of State, *Foreign Relations of the United States,* 1964–1968, vol. 25 (Washington, D.C.: US Government Printing Office, 1969), document 253, http://state.gov/www/about_state/history/vol_xxv/v.html.

12. Kux, *India and the United States,* 244.

13. See Henry A. Kissinger, "Memorandum for the President, Subject: Economic Aid for India," July 18, 1969.

14. See Kux, *India and the United States,* 293–307.

15. See Shenoy, *PL 480 Aid,* xi–xii.

16. See Clifton R. Wharton Jr., "The Green Revolution: Cornucopia or Pandora's Box?" *Foreign Affairs* 47 (April 1969): 464–76; Wolf Ladejinsky, "Ironies of India's Green Revolution," *Foreign Affairs* 48 (July 1970): 758–68.

17. See Dominique Lapierre and Javier Moro, *Five Past Midnight in Bhopal* (New York: Warner Books, 2002), 197.

18. See Richard C. Lugar and Norman Borlaug, "Lugar/Borlaug: A New Green Revolution," *Washington Times,* April 5, 2009, http://www.washingtontimes.com/news/2009/apr/05/a-new-green-revolution.

19. Manmohan Singh, "PM Condoles the Passing Away of Dr. Norman Borlaug," Prime Minister's Office, September 14, 2009, http://pmindia.nic.in/message/mcontent.asp?=260.

20. "Pawar Mourns Death of Norman Borlaug," *India eNews,* September 13, 2009.

21. Foreign Agricultural Service, US Department of Agriculture, "Fact Sheet: US-India Agricultural Knowledge Initiative," November 2006, http://www.fas.usda.gov/ICD/India_knol_int/factsheet.asp.

22. World Bank, *India: Agricultural R&D Is Critical to Enhance Productivity* (Washington, D.C.: World Bank, 2006), http://www.worldbank.org.in/wbsite/external/countries/southasiaext/indiaextn/0,,contentMDK:21019792~pagePK:141137~piPK:141127~theSitePK:295584,00.html.

23. See Hillary Rodham Clinton, "Remarks Following Tour of Indian Agricultural Research Institute Research Field," July 19, 2009, http://www.state.gov/secretary/rm/2009a/july/126207.htm.

24. The White House, "The Pittsburgh Summit: Partnering on Food Security," *Pittsburgh Summit 2009 Fact Sheet,* September 25, 2009, http://whitehouse.gov/files/documents/g20/Pittsburgh_Fact_Sheet_Food_Security.pdf.

25. Food and Agriculture Organization of the United Nations, "FAO Welcomes G8 Food Security Initiative," July 10, 2009, http://www.fao.org/news/story/en/item/24457/icode/.

26. Kristi Heim, "Behind the G8 Food Security Initiative: Gates Foundation Role," *Seattle Times,* April 5, 2009, http://seattletimes.nwsource.com/htm/thebusinessofgiving/2009450410_gates_foundation_moves_behind.html.

27. "Africa: US Wants to Spotlight "Successful Models" and Be an 'Effective Partner'–Obama," *allafrica.com,* http://allafrica.com/stories/200907021302.html.

28. Hillary Rodham Clinton, "Remarks at Food Security Event Co-Hosted with UN Secretary-General Ban Ki-moon during the UN General Assembly," *US Department of State Diplomacy in Action,* September 26, 2009, http://www.state.gov/secretary/rm/2009a/09/129673.htm.

29. The White House, "Joint Statement by President Obama and Prime Minister Singh of India," November 8, 2010, http://www.whitehouse.gov/the-press-office/2010/11/08/joint-statement-president-obama-and-prime-minister-singh-india.

30. Jairam Ramesh, response to a question from the author, New Delhi, March 30, 2007.

31. US Wheat Associates, "India Paying High Price for US Wheat Quarantine," *Wheat Letter,* June 14, 2007, http://wwww.uswheat.org/wheatLetter/doc/430D78FD2163EBB852572FA0068C021?.

32. See "Wheat Imports: A Tool for Re-shaping India's Agriculture," *Aspects of India's Economy* 42 (December 2006), http://www.rupe-india.org/42/regime.html.

33. US Wheat Associates, "India Paying High Price."

34. US Embassy, "Exclusion of US Wheat from Indian Market Increases Costs for Indian Consumers," press release, June 7, 2007, http://newdelhi.usembassy.gov/pr060807.html.

35. Siddharth Zarabi, "Phytosanitary Norms Not to Be Diluted: EGoM," *Business Standard,* September 17, 2007, http://www.business-standard.com/india/news/phytosanitary-norms-not-to-be-diluted-egom.htm.

36. US Embassy, "Indian Wheat Import Requirements Are Costly to Indian Consumers," press release, July 10, 2007, http://newdelhi.usembassy.gov/pr071007.html.

37. US Wheat Associates, "India Paying High Price."

38. Department of Commerce, Ministry of Commerce and Industry, Government of India, "Export of Indian Mangoes," press release, May 15, 2007, http://commerce.nic.in/PressRelease_detail.asp?id=2029.

39. "News: Economic Crisis Is Hurting Alfonso Mango Exports from India to the US," *FoodBizDaily,* April 27, 2009, http://foodbizdaily.com/articles/28961-economic-crisis-is-hurting-Alfonso-Mango-exports-from-India-to-the-US.

40. "India Will Export Mangoes, Import Motorbikes from US," *Hindu Business Line,* April 14, 2007, http://www.thehindubusinessline.com/2007/04/14/stories/2007041403971000.htm.

41. "India, U.S. Agree upon Export of Indian Litchi to American Market," *Fresh-Plaza,* August 26, 2009, http://www.freshplaza.com/news_detail.asp?id=49550.

42. For a description of how this system worked in two states of South India, see Jos Mooij, *Food Policy and the Indian State: The Public Distribution System in South India* (New York: Oxford University Press, 1999).

43. See Vikas Bajaj, "As Sugar Prices Soar, India Is Caught Short," *New York Times,* August 5, 2009.

44. "Protest over India Stores Closure," BBC News, August 24, 2007, http://news.bbc.co.uk/2/hi/south_asia/6961196.stm.

45. R. Jai Krishna, "Update: Bharti Wal-Mart: To Open 15 Wholesale Stores in 3 Years," *Wall Street Journal,* May 30, 2009, http//:online.wsj.com/article/BT-CO-20090530-701130.html.

46. "Parliamentary Panel Recommends 'Blanket Ban' on FDI in Retail and 'Cash and Carry'; Comes Down Heavily on Big Corporates for Foraying into Modern Retail," *India Retail Biz,* June 19, 2009, http://www.indiaretailbiz.com/blog/2009/06/19/.

47. See Carey Gillam, "Timeline: History of Monsanto Co.," Reuters, November 11, 2009, http://www.reuters.com/article/idUSTRE5AA05Q20091111.

48. Jay Shankar and Thomas Kutty Abraham, "India Rejects First GM Vegetable, Hampering Monsanto," *Bloomberg Businessweek,* February 10, 2010, http://www.businessweek.com/news/2010-02-10/india-rejects-first-gm-vegetable-hampering-monsanto-update1-.html.

49. Ibid.

50. See Andrew Malone, "The GM Genocide: Thousands of Indian Farmers Are Committing Suicide after Using Genetically Modified Crops," *Daily Mail,* November 30, 2008, http://www.dailymail.co.uk/news/worldnews/article-1082559/The-GM-genocide-Thousands-Indian-farmers-committing-suicide-using-genetically-modified-crops.html.

51. See Kitila Suneja, "Monsanto Explores Partnership with Govt to Offer New Biotech Traits," *Business Standard,* August 6, 2010, http://www.business-standard.com/commodities/storypage.php?autono=403681.

52. See Arvind Panagariya, *India the Emerging Giant* (New York: Oxford University Press, 2008), 357–59.

53. "Update 2: India Approves New Fertilizer Policy to Lower Prices," Reuters India, June 12, 2008, http://in.reuters.com/article/companyNews/idINDEL32998020080612.

54. Pranab Mukherjee, "Budget Speech 2009–2010," *Union Budget and Economic Survey,* July 26, 2009, http://indiabudget.nic.in/ub2009-10/bs/speecha.htm.

55. See Pranab Mukherjee, "Budget Speech 2010–2011," *Union Budget and Economic Survey,* February 26, 2010, http://indiabudget.nic.in/ub2010-11/bs/speecha.htm.

56. Geeta Anand, "Green Revolution in India Wilts as Subsidies Backfire," *Wall Street Journal,* February 22, 2010, http://online.wsj.com/article/NA_WSJ_PUB:SB10001424052748703615904575052921612723844.html.

57. See Lapierre and Moro, *Five Past Midnight in Bhopal.*

58. See US Agency for International Development, "Partnerships in Agriculture," *USAID/India,* 2009, http://www.usaid.gov/in/Pdfs/agri_ind.pdf.

59. See Organization for Economic Cooperation and Development, "India," in *Agricultural Policies in Emerging Economies 2009: Monitoring and Evaluation* (Paris: Organization for Economic Cooperation and Development, 2009), 95–112.

60. See John Briscoe, *India's Water Economy: Bracing for a Turbulent Future* (Washington, D.C.: World Bank, 2005), http://www.worldbank.org.in/wbsite/external/countries/southasiaext/indiaestn/o,,contentmdk:20668501~pipk:141127~thesitepk:295584,00.

61. Press Trust of India, "Prices May Go Up Due to Erratic Monsoon: RBI," *Business Standard,* August 18, 2009, http://www.business-standard.com/india/news/prices-may-go-up-due-to-erratic-monsoon-rbi/71035/on.

62. "Poor Monsoon Could Lower India's Growth—Ahluwalia," Reuters, August 18, 2009, http://in.reuters.com/article/specialevents1/idINdia-41815420090818.

63. "Mayday! PM Forms GoM on Food Security and Drought," *Economic Times,* August 14, 2009, http://economictimes.indiatimes.com/articleshow/4892306.cms.

64. See S. J. Scherr, "Soil Degradation: A Threat to Developing Country Security by 2020?" in *Food, Agriculture, and the Environment,* Discussion Paper 27 (Washington, D.C.: International Food Policy Research Institute, 1999) as referenced by B.C. Roy et al., *Subsidizing the Food Crisis* (Washington, D.C.: Greenpeace, 2009).

65. See Maitreesh Ghatak and Sanchari Roy, "Land Reform and Agricultural

Productivity in India: a Review of the Evidence," *Oxford Review of Economic Policy* 23, no. 2 (2007): 251–69.

66. Library of Congress, "India," *Country Studies* (1995) http://memory.loc.gov/cgi -bin/query/D?cstdy:4../temp/~frd_TW1d.

67. PepsiCo, "Partnership with Farmers," *PepsiCo India,* 2009, http://www.pepsi india.co.in/Partnership_with_Farmers.html.

68. "Frito-Lay India Builds Warehouse for Potato Storage in West Bengal," *Potato-Pro,* June 22, 2009, http://www.com/Lists/News/DispForm.aspx?ID=2741.

69. Arun Pandit et al., "Socioeconomic Impact of Potato Processing in India," *New Directions,* Central Potato Research Institute.

70. National Institute of Agricultural Extension Management, Ministry of Agriculture, Government of India, "Contract Farming Ventures in India: A Few Successful Cases," *Spice* 1, no. 4 (March 2003).

71. See the ADM Web site http://www.adm.com/en-US/worldwide/india/Pages/ default.aspx.

72. S 384, 112th Congress.

73. "Lugar/Borlaug: A New Green Revolution," *Washington Times,* April 5, 2009.

Chapter 9

1. P. M. Rao, "The Emergence of the Pharmaceutical Industry in the Developing World and Its Implications for Multinational Enterprise Strategies," *International Journal of Pharmaceutical and Healthcare Marketing* (Bingley, U.K.: Emerald Group Publishing) 2, no. 2 (2008): 104, http://www.emeraldinsight.com/1750-1623.htm.

2. The Patents Act, 1970 (Act 39 of 1970), Chapter II, paragraph 5 (1).

3. Sudip Chaudhuri, *The WTO and India's Pharmaceutical Industry: Patent Protection, TRIPS, and Developing Countries* (New Delhi, Oxford University Press, 2005).

4. "Drugs Price Control Order (DPCO)," Pharmaceutical Drug Manufacturers Web site, http://www.pharmaceutical-drug-manufacturers.com/pharmaceutical-policies/ pharmaceutical-policies/drugs-price-control-order.html.

5. See the biographical sketch at http://www.sikh-history.com/sikhhist/personalities/ parvinder.html.

6. Erika Check, "The Treasure of Mumbai," *Wired,* December 2006, http://www.wired .com/wired/archive/14.12/indiadrug.html.

7. See the CIPLA Web site: www.cipla.com.

8. See Dr. Reddy's Web site: http://www.drreddys.com/aboutus/aboutus.html.

9. Abhay Singh and Mrinalini Datta, "Dr. Reddy's Struggles for Homegrown Hit to Escape Rival Clones," *Bloomberg.com,* December 5, 2006, http://www.bloomberg.com/ apps/news?pid+206011098sid+aPXP80nuYooI.

10. See T. N. Srinivasan and Suresh D. Tendulkar, *Reintegrating India with the World Economy* (Washington, D.C.: Peterson Institute for International Economics, 2003), 78–82.

11. See US Department of Justice, "Pharmaceutical Company Eli Lilly to pay Record $1.415 Billion for Off-Label Marketing," press release, January 15, 2009, http:// dodig.mil/iginformation/IGInformationReleases/EliLillyPressRelease.pdf.

12. See the interview with Rajiv Gulati, "Eli Lilly's Rajiv Gulati on Pharma's

Prospects in India and China," *India Knowledge@Wharton,* October 16, 2008, http://knowledge.wharton.upenn.edu/india/articl.cfm?articleid=4325.

13. See "Eli Lilly Buys Ranbaxy's Stake in JV," *The Hindu,* July 6, 2001, http://www.thehindu.com/thehindu/2001/07/06/stories/06060006.htm.

14. See "Notification of Appointment of a Council on Trade and Industry," August 28, 1998, http://indiaimage.nic.in/pmcouncils/tic/noti1.htm.

15. See the Sun Pharmaceuticals Web site: www.sunpharma.com.

16. For a highly detailed and highly critical view of the role played by US companies in the process of TRIPS negotiation, see Peter Drahos and John Braithwaite, *Information Feudalism: Who Owns the Knowledge Economy?* (London: Earthscan, 2002).

17. Annex 1C to the Marrakech Agreement Establishing the World Trade Organization.

18. See TRIPS Agreement, http://www.wto.org/English/docs_e/legal_e/27-trips.pdf; and Chaudhuri, *WTO and India's Pharmaceutical Industry,* 62–63.

19. See "Notice of Motion, in the Matter of the Pharmaceutical Manufacturers' Association of South Africa et al. and the President of the Republic of South Africa et al. in the High Court of South Africa," case 4183/98, http://www.cptech.org/ip/health/sa/pharmasuit.html.

20. Ibid.

21. Jedediah Purdy, *Being America: Liberty, Commerce, and Violence in an American World* (New York: Random House, 2004), 132–33.

22. Consumer Project on Technology, "Time-Line of Disputes over Compulsory Licensing and Parallel Importation in South Africa," August 5, 1999, http://www.cptech.org/ip/health/sa/sa-timeline.txt.

23. Ibid.

24. Gumisai Mutume, "AIDS Activists March against Pharmaceutical Companies," *Third World Network,* March 12, 2001, http://www.twnside.org.sg/title/against.htm.

25. The letters "ddI" are an acronym for didanosine, an antiretroviral drug. "Maker Yielding Patent in Africa for AIDS Drug," *New York Times,* March 15, 2001, http://www.nytimes.com/2001/03/15/health/15AIDS.html.

26. "AIDS-Drug Deal Expected in South Africa Suit," *New York Times,* April 19, 2001, http://www.nytimes.com/2001/04/19/world/19AFRI.html.

27. Paul Hunt, "Mission to GlaxoSmithKline," annex to *Report of the Special Rapporteur on the Right of Everyone to the Enjoyment of the Highest Attainable Standard of Health of the United Nations General Assembly,* A/HRC/11/12/Add. 2 (New York: United Nations, 2009).

28. "Bristol-Myers Squibb Inflates R&D Base in India," *Express Pharma,* April 15, 2007, http://www.expresspharmaonline.com/20070415/market09.shtml.

29. See Pete Engardio, Arlene Weintraub, and Nandini Lakshman, "Outsourcing the Drug Industry," *BusinessWeek,* September 15, 2008, 48–52; and Gunjan Sinha, "Outsourcing Drug Work: Pharmaceuticals Ship R&D and Clinical Trials to India," *Scientific American,* August 16, 2004, http://www.scientificamerican.com/article.cfm?id=outsourcing-drug-work.

30. See "United States–India Joint Leadership Statement on HIV/AIDS," March 24, 2000, *2000–2001 Public Papers of the Presidents,* edited by Office of the Federal Register (Washington, D.C.: US Government Printing Office, 2001), book I, 527.

31. "Access to HIV/AIDS Pharmaceuticals and Medical Technologies," Executive Order 13155, May 10, 2000, *Federal Register* 65, no. 93 (May 12, 2000): 30521.

32. Lawrence K. Altman, "Clinton Group Gets Discount for AIDS Drugs," *New York Times,* October 24, 2003, http://www.nytimes.com/2003/10/24/health/24AIDS.html.

33. "Clinton Foundation Brokers Deal for Discount HIV/AIDS Drugs, Diagnoses," *Philanthropy News Digest,* January 16, 2006, http://www.foundationcenter.org/pnd/news/story,jhtml?id=127900018.

34. See William J. Clinton Foundation, "UK Government and Clinton Foundation to Help Indian Companies Produce Cheaper AIDS Drugs," press release, reproduced by *India PR Wire,* November 17, 2008, http://www.indiaprwire.com/print/?type+press release&id=2008111715574.

35. William J. Clinton Foundation, "What We Have Accomplished," http://www .clintonfoundation.org/what-we-d0/clinton-hiv-aids-initiative/what-we-ve-accomplished.

36. See Bill & Melinda Gates Foundation, "Avahan AIDS Initiative Commitment Increased to $338 Million," press release, July 23, 2009, http://www.gatesfoundation .org/press-releases/Pages/foundation-and-health-minister-azad-reaffirm-commitment-to -hiv-prevention-090723.aspx.

37. UNITAID, "Members of the Executive Board," http://www.unitaid.eu/en/ Members-of-the-executive-board.html.

38. See Patents (Amendment) Act, 2005, no. 15 of 2005, April 4, 2005, http://ipindia .nic.in/ipr/patent/patent_2005.pdf; William Greene, *The Emergence of India's Pharmaceutical Industry and Implications for the US Generic Drug Market,* Working Paper 2007-05-A (Washington, D.C.: Office of Economics, US International Trade Commission, 2007), 3; and P. M. Rao, "The Emergence of the Pharmaceutical Industry in the Developing World and Its Implications for Multinational Enterprise Strategies," *International Journal of Pharmaceutical and Healthcare Marketing* 2, no. 2 (2008): 108.

39. R. Prasad, "India Rejects Patent Claims on Two HIV/AIDS Drugs," *The Hindu,* September 4, 2009, http://beta.thehindu.com/health/article15145.ece.

40. "Patent Revoked on Tenofovir," *Doctors Without Borders,* January 29, 2008, http:// doctorswithoutborders.org/news/article.cfm?id+2484.

41. For the relevant documents, see World Trade Organization, "TRIPS and Public Health," http://www.wto.org/english/tratop_e/trips_e/pharmpatent_e.htm.

42. USAID/India, "HIV/AIDS Health Profile," 2007, http://www.usaid.gov/our _work/global_health?aids/Countries/asia/india_profile.pdf.

43. Family Health International, *IMPACT India Final Report,* November 2007, 7, http://www.fhi.org/NR/rdonlyres/eh2oo5c5zk2pxym7azrl3eyrxxlrxy6w2nx5o7joub7 mvhes7yq653df4nzk3s7t6bfts6udvgwmm/IMPACTFinalReportIndiaHV.pdf.

44. See Strobe Talbott, *Engaging India: Diplomacy, Democracy, and the Bomb* (Washington, D.C.: Brookings Institution Press, 2004), 255, where Talbott writes: "Robert Blackwill, a former foreign service officer who had been one of George W. Bush's foreign policy advisers ('the Vulcans') during the 2000 campaign, made it a constant theme of his public statements and background briefings for the press to trumpet the contrast between Bush's engagement of India and the policy of neglect and patronizing that had come before." The present author's impression is much the same. One of the great strengths of Bush's foreign policy and the source of its most positive achievements was the continuity and enhancement of the Clinton policy toward India. However, Ambassador Blackwill insisted that Bush had "a big new idea" on India that owed nothing to the previous administration. Thankfully, others in the Bush administration did not share this approach.

45. USAID/India, "US Ambassador Robert D. Blackwill Visits Chennai And Speaks

on HIV/AIDS," press release, November 6, 2002, http://www.usaid.gov/in/newsroom/press_releases/nov06a_2.htm.

46. See USAID/India, "Remarks by USAID India Mission Director George Deikun at the Launch of the Samastha HIV/AIDS Initiative, Bangalore," January 10, 2007, http://www.usaid.gov/in/newsroom/speeches/jan10_7s.htm.

47. See USAID/India, "HIV/AIDS Health Profile," http://www.usaid.gov/our_work/global_health?aids?countries/asia/india_profile.pdf.

48. US Department of Health and Human Services, "HHS–India Fact Sheet: Activities in India," http://globalhealth.gov/news/factsheets/fs020409.html; Joe C. Matthew, "USFDA to Set Up Office in India by September 2009," *Business Standard,* November 18, 2008, http://www.business-standard.com/india/storypage.php?autono=340525.

49. Saikat Chatterjee, "Ranbaxy Plant May Get FDA Inspection 'Any Time Now,'" *Bloomberg.com,* July 31, 2009, http://www.bloomberg.com/apps/news?pid=206012028&sid=alvW2VvVaAKA.

Chapter 10

1. Dennis Kux, *India and the United States: Estranged Democracies* (Honolulu: University Press of the Pacific, 2002).

2. Some would argue that the collapse of the Union of Soviet Socialist Republics and the end of the Cold War was the instrumental factor in US-India rapprochement. They would further argue that this development was political-military in nature as opposed to an economic factor. In accordance with the thesis of this book, this collapse and end of the Cold War is best seen as driven by economic factors. The fact that economic engagement with the USSR under socialist principles became demonstratively unproductive and then infeasible for India certainly contributed to the Indian willingness to engage economically with the United States. Thus, the collapse of the USSR and end of the Cold War driven by economic factors strengthened US-India economic engagement as the driving force for greater US-India strategic cooperation.

3. See David Rothkopf, *Running the World: The Inside Story of the National Security Council and the Architects of American Power* (New York: PublicAffairs, 2005), 352.

4. Benn Steil and Robert E. Litan, *Financial Statecraft: The Role of Financial Markets in American Foreign Policy* (New Haven, Conn.: Yale University Press, 2006)

5. See Harry Kreisler, "An Economist Goes to Washington: Conversations with Laura D'Andrea Tyson," in *Conversations with History* (Berkeley: Institute of International Studies, University of California, 1998), http://globetrotter.berkeley.edu/conversations/Tyson/tyson-con7.html, as quoted by Steil and Litan, *Financial Statecraft,* 175. See also The White House, *National Security Strategy, May 2010,* 4, 15, http://www.whitehouse.gov/sites/default/files/rss_viewer/national_security_strategy.pdf. For a discussion of the varying academic views on the relationship of economics and politics in the world arena, see Jeffrey A. Frieden and David A. Lake, eds., *International Political Economy: Perspectives on Global Power and Wealth* (New York: Bedford / St. Martin's Press, 2000).

6. This difficulty seems endemic within the Government of India as well. See Kishan S. Rana, *Asian Diplomacy: The Foreign Ministries of China, India, Japan, Singapore, and Thailand* (Washington, D.C., and Baltimore: Woodrow Wilson Center Press and

Johns Hopkins University Press, 2009), 64 and 200, where Rana recounts the difficulties of adopting a "whole government" approach within the Indian external affairs system. Rana also notes that while the Ministry of External Affairs coordinates with the Ministry of Defence through regularized mechanisms, "nothing comparable takes place in relation to the economic ministries" (p. 76).

7. Graham Allison and Philip Zelikow, *Essence of Decision: Explaining the Cuban Missile Crisis,* 2nd ed. (Reading, Mass.: Longman, 1999).

Index

Abbott, 252, 258
ABN Amro Bank NV, 140
ACES (American Clean Energy and
Security Act), 160
ACT UP (NGO), 256
ADM, 236
Advisory Committee for Trade Policy
and Negotiations: (ACTPN), 111–12
Advocacy Center, 13, 17, 39, 280
AES Corporation, 62, 133, 146, 148–49
Afghanistan, "Af/Pak" conflict in, 22,
203
AFL-CIO, 99
AGRA (Alliance for a Green Revolution
in Africa), 223
Agricultural Knowledge Initiative. *See*
Knowledge Initiative on Agriculture
Agricultural Trade Development and
Assistance Act of 1954, 210. *See also*
Public Law 480
agriculture: and democracy, 212–13; and
food regulations, 227–30; inputs,
supply of, 230–35, 240; political
importance of, 212–20; Special
Safeguard Mechanism for imports,
197–98; subsidies for, 196, 208; trade
disputes, 225–27, 240. *See also* food
security
Ahluwalia, Montek Singh, 23, 107–8,
137, 204, 234

AIDS. *See* HIV/AIDS
AIDS Prevention and Control Project,
266
AIG, 62
Albright, Madeleine, 70
Alliance for a Green Revolution in
Africa (AGRA), 223
Allison, Graham, 281
Al Qaeda, 122
Alumni of the Indian Institutes of
Technology, 62
American Association of Physicians of
Indian Origin, 62
American Bankers Association, 98
American Clean Energy and Security
Act (ACES), 160
American Express, 118–19
American India Foundation, 5, 165
American Recovery and Reinvestment
Act of 2009 (US Stimulus Act), 106,
202
Andersen, Walter, 63
Animal and Plant Inspection Service, 226
antiretroviral drugs, 267
Ardekani, Ali Shams, 180
Armitage, Richard, 122–23
Arms Control Association, 60
Arms Export Control Act (US), 43, 44–45
Asian American Hotel Owners
Association, 62

Asian Development Bank, 5, 45, 186
Asian monetary crisis of 1997, 199. *See
    also* financial meltdown
Asia Society, 203
Aspen Pharmacare, 261
Atomic Energy Act (US), 36, 52, 71, 72,
    78. *See also* 123 Agreement
Atoms for Peace initiative, 28, 33, 35
atoms for war concern, 71–72
Aurigene (drug company), 260
Avahan program, 262–63
AVERT program, 266

Babri Masjid Mosque, 141
"balance of payment" exceptions, 193
Baldwin, David, 8
Bali Road Map, 164
Balochistan province (Pakistan), IPI
    pipeline and, 185
Banerjee, Mamata, 235
Bangladesh, establishment of, 219
Ban Ki-moon, 159, 223
Bank of America, 140
Barbour, Haley, 66
Barbour Griffith and Rogers, 66, 104
Barshevsky, Charlene, 111, 112–13
Basel Committee on Banking
    Supervision, 201, 205, 207
BASIC countries (Brazil, South Africa,
    India, and China), 164
Bayh, Birch, 66
Bayman, Scott, 38–39, 117–18
Bechtel Corporation, 62, 135, 168
Beecham Group, 252
Beier, David, 10
"Benedict Arnold" designation, 25,
    97–98, 99, 104
Berger, Samuel R. ("Sandy"), 9–10,
    42–43, 48–49, 70
Bergner, Jeffrey, 73, 77
Berlusconi, Silvio, 158
Berman, Howard L., 81–82, 184
Bhaba Atomic Research Center, 227
Bharatiya Janata Party (BJP): and civil
    nuclear deal, 88; and Congress Party,
    130; and Hindu nationalism, 42; and

Mumbai terrorist attacks, 125; and
    NDA, 79; and nuclear option
    "induction," 42; power of, 56; and
    Shiv Sena, 141–42, 145; and Singh
    (Manmohan), 109; and Vajpayee, 23,
    42; and WTO, 192
Bharti Enterprises, 229
Bharti-Walmart, 229
Bhopal tragedy of December 1984, 220,
    233
Biden, Joe, 71, 73, 76, 82
Big Emerging Markets initiative, 37–38,
    253
Bilateral Economic Dialogue, 53
Bill & Melinda Gates Foundation. *See*
    Gates Foundation
Biocon (drug company), 260
Birla, C. K., 108
Birla, Kumar Mangalam, 204
BJP. *See* Bharatiya Janata Party
Blackwill, Robert D., 52–53, 66–67, 104,
    120–21, 267, 314*n*44
Blank, Jonah, 71
Blinken, Anthony, 71
Bodman, Sam, 54
Boehringer Ingelheim, 258
Boeing, 10, 46, 62, 84, 127
Bond, Phil, 54
Borlaug, Norman: and Cooperative
    Wheat Research and Production
    Program, 212; and food security,
    220, 241; on green revolution, 210;
    and Nobel Peace Prize, 219; and
    Padma Vibhushan award, 221; and
    Swaminathan, 218, 238; and wheat
    seeds, 225
Bosnia and Croatia mission, 18–21
Boston Tea Party, 28
Boxer, Barbara, 76
Brainard, Lael, 101
Bristol-Myers Squibb, 258, 260
bromus secalinus (rye brome weeds),
    225
Brookings Institution, 101, 104, 108
Brown, Ron: Bangalore visit of, 87–88;
    Big Emerging Markets strategy, 253;

Bosnia and Croatia mission, 18–21; and CEO breakfasts, 262; China, strategic relationship with, 11; and Clinton (Bill), 37, 38; and Cogentrix project, 146–47; and Dabhol project, 140; and electric power, 129; India mission, 23, 38–41, 87–88, 117; and TPCC, 154

Brownback, Sam, 44–45

Brownback I Act, 45

Brownback II Act, 45–46, 50

Brzezinski, Zbigniew, 70

Burns, Bill, 81

Burns, Nicholas, 56, 69, 70, 73

Bush, George H. W.: and pharmaceuticals, 250, 253; and Uruguay Round, 191

Bush, George W.: and civil nuclear matters, 51–53, 68–69, 273; and CPI, 63; and Dabhol project, 145; and dual-use trade, 53; and economic engagement, 9; environmental efforts of, 156–58; and food security, 222; and FutureGen Project, 167; and G-20, 199, 201–2; and HIV/AIDS assistance, 267–68; and Hyde Act, 75; and international trade, 194; and IPI pipeline, 186; and Joint Statement (2005), 2, 56–59, 61, 69, 186; and Knowledge Initiative on Agriculture, 220, 223; and Next Steps in Strategic Partnership initiative, 55–56; and 123 Agreement, 83, 201; and outsourcing, 100, 101; and Portman, 197; and Singh (Manmohan), 73; and terrorism, 8–9, 120

Business Roundtable, 99

"buy America" provisions, 106, 202, 274, 282

Byrd-Hagel Resolution of 1997, 153, 154

call centers, 119

Canadian-Indian Reactor, US (CIRUS), 33, 35

"cap-and-trade" programs, 158, 160

carbon capture schemes, 167–68

Carbon Sequestration Leadership Forum, 167

Carlucci, Frank, 70

Carrefour (retail distributor), 229

Carter, Jimmy: and Hyde Act, 70; India visit of, 49; and sanctions, 181

cash-and-carry businesses, 229

Caterpillar equipment, 178

CDMs. *See* Clean Development Mechanisms

Celeste, Richard, 97, 288*n*12

Centers for Disease Control and Prevention, US (CDC), 267, 268

Central Industrial Security Force, 127

Central Intelligence Agency (CIA), 42, 124

"CEO Breakfasts," 18, 262

CEO Forum, 11, 22, 57, 68, 69

CHAI (Clinton Health Access Initiative), 261–62

Chamber of Commerce, US, 98–99, 251

Chandrasekhar, K. M., 204

Chatterjee, Swadesh, 47, 62, 66, 73, 172–73

Chemical, Industrial, and Pharmaceutical Laboratories (CIPLA): and anti-retroviral drugs, 267; and Clinton Foundation, 261; founding of, 247; as generics company, 248, 256; and HIV/AIDS drug pricing, 258; and TRIPS, 251–52

Cheney, Dick, 73

Chidambaram, Palianappan, 41, 126–27

China, People's Republic of: FDI in, 149–50; and oil and gas production, 176; services share of GDP in, 91–92; strategic relationship with, 10–11

China Light and Power International project, 133

Christman, Dan, 61, 69

Christopher, Warren, 11

CIA (Central Intelligence Agency), 42, 124

CII. *See* Confederation of Indian Industries

CIPLA. *See* Chemical, Industrial, and Pharmaceutical Laboratories

CIRUS (Canadian-Indian Reactor, US), 33, 35
citizen income, 88–90
civil nuclear cooperation, 32–86, 273; bottom line on, 85–86; Bush (G. W.) administration, 51–53; Clinton (Bill) in India, 49–51; Coalition for Partnership with India, 60–63; and economic engagement, 31; and environmental engagement, 167; High-Technology Cooperation Group, 54–55; historical context, 33–41; Hyde Act, 63–78; and IPI pipeline, 184–85, 187; Joint Statement on US-India Strategic Cooperation (2005), 56–63; new approach to India, 48–56; Next Steps in Strategic Partnership initiative, 55–56, 57–58; nuclear option "induction" and sanctions, 42–44, 85; 123 Agreement, 78–85; political uncertainty, 41–48; sanctions relief, 44–47; "separation agreement," 69, 70; Talbott-Singh talks, 47–48, 49; Vajpayee's post-9/11 US visit, 53–55
Civil Nuclear Energy Working Group, 84
Clark, Michael, 44, 46–47, 50–51, 116
Clean Development Mechanisms (CDMs), 155, 167, 168–69, 170
"clean technology," 152, 154
climate change: cooperation on, 165–69; "deniers" of, 170; economic engagement on, 131–46; emissions standards, 153; and G-20, 159–60; "inconvenient truth" of, 156; National Action Plan on, 163; and Obama administration, 158–60
Clinton, Bill: and Advocacy Center, 39; and Berger, 48–49; and Brown, 20, 37, 38; and Brownback acts, 45–46; and climate change, 153, 165–66; Comprehensive Test Ban Treaty, 48; Counterterrorism Joint Working Group, 126; and Dabhol project, 142, 144; and economic engagement, 1, 9–12; environmental efforts, 154–56; and fast-track projects, 146; and Group

of 22, 199; and HIV/AIDS assistance, 260–61, 266–68; India visit of, 49–51; and intellectual property rights, 256–58; and international trade, 191, 194; and Iran, 181; and ISA, 182; and ITA, 113; Kyoto Protocol, 131, 155–56; National Export Policy, 13; and nuclear option "induction," 42–43; and pharmaceuticals, 253; and Rao (Narasimha), 41–42; and "special envoy" on Kashmir, 202; and sustainable growth, 130
Clinton, Hillary Rodham, 17, 84, 126, 161, 222, 223
Clinton Climate Initiative, 165–66
Clinton Foundation, 5, 165, 260–62, 269
Clinton Health Access Initiative (CHAI), 261–62
cloud computing, 119
Clyburn, James, 257
CMS Electric Company, 133, 146, 147–48
Coalition for Economic Growth and American Jobs, 98, 99, 104
Coalition for Partnership with India (CPI), 60–67, 69, 73, 74–75, 81, 83
Coastal Gujarat Power Limited, 151
Coca-Cola, 28
Cogentrix, Inc. project, 133, 146–47, 301n29
Cohen, William S., 63, 65, 70, 72, 84
Colombo Plan, 33
Commerce Department, US, 16–17, 37, 283
"commercial diplomacy," 8, 13, 277
Committee of Participants on the Expansion of Trade in Information Technology Products, 113
Communication Workers of America (CWA), 99–100, 107
competitiveness, definition of, 88–90, 98
Comprehensive Iran Sanctions, Accountability and Divestment Act of 2010 (US), 183
Comprehensive Test Ban Treaty (CTBT), 40, 47–48, 53

compulsory licensing, 255
Confederation of Indian Industries (CII): and Agricultural Knowledge Initiative, 224; and climate change, 156; HIV/ AIDS efforts, 267; and HTCG, 54; and ITA, 112; on Joint Statement (2005), 59; and 123 Agreement, 80; and outsourcing, 108; and pharmaceuticals, 251; and separation agreement, 69; and USIBC, 68; and US-India Commercial Alliance, 41
Congressional Research Service, 100–101
Congress of South African Trade Unions, 258
Congress Party, 56, 89, 145, 146, 161
Consumers Energy, 148
Cooperative Wheat Research and Production Program, 212
Copenhagen Accord, 164, 165
Copenhagen Green Climate Fund, 164
Copps, Michael, 39
Council on International Economic Policy, 11
counterguarantees system, 132, 139–40, 151
Counterterrorism Joint Working Group, 126
CPI. *See* Coalition for Partnership with India
Crime and Criminal Tracking Network, 127
Croatia and Bosnia mission, 18–21
CTBT. *See* Comprehensive Test Ban Treaty
Cutter, Bowman, 10
CWA (Communication Workers of America), 99–100, 107

Dabhol Power Company, 135, 138–39, 140, 143. *See also* Dabhol project
Dabhol project, 2–3, 131–46; conclusion of, 145–49, 169; contract approvals and negotiation, 136–39; counterguarantees, 139–40; difficulties with, 134–36, 142–43; as fast-track project, 2–3, 131–46, 275; Indian political

reaction to, 144–45; resumption of, 143–44; Shiv Sena opposition to, 141–42
Daley, Bill, 50
Das, Tarun, 41, 80, 204
Daschle, Tom, 97
Declaration on the TRIPS Agreement and Public Health, 265
Department for International Development, UK (DFID), 223, 261
Department of Defense Appropriations Act (US), 46
Diouf, Jacques, 222
"dirty tariffication" process, 192
Dobbs, Lou, 100
Doctors Without Borders, 256, 258
Dodd, Christopher, 97
Doha Round: Declaration on the TRIPS Agreement and Public Health, 265; Doha Development Agenda, 110, 194–95; Doha Ministerial Declaration, 193, 194; and G-20, 204, 207; Nath on, 196–97; Obama on, 25; and outsourcing, 110, 114; US-India participation in, 192–98, 208, 224
Dorgan, Byron, 289n16
dot-com bubble, 97
Dow Chemical, 62, 233
Dr. Reddy's Laboratories Ltd., 246, 247–48, 251, 252, 253
drugs. *See* pharmaceuticals
Drugs Price Control Order, 246
dual-use trade, 53–54
Dubrovnik (Croatia), 19–20, 21
due diligence process, 121–23
Dulles, Allen, 33
Dulles, John Foster, 33
Duncan, John J., 97
du Pont de Nemours Foundation, 212
Durbin, Dick, 102–3, 109, 110
Durbin-Grassley bill, 102–3, 109

Eagleburger, Lawrence, 54
economic crisis. *See* financial meltdown
economic engagement, 1–31; bottom line, 30–31; in Clinton administration,

economic engagement (*continued*)
9–12; definition of, 3–6; economic-
political interactions, 25–27, 30;
historical context, 27–30; importance
of, 270–71; and India's foreign policy,
22–25; methodology of book, 6–7;
private sector involvement in, 17–22,
281–83; private-sector resources,
17–22; and public-private partnerships, 14, 17–18, 31, 284; strategic
issues, definition of, 3–6; strategic
issues, political action on, 12–22, 31;
strategic issues, relationship between,
7–9, 13–14, 271–79, 284; and
terrorism, 126–27; and US national
interests, 15–17, 279–84
Economic Report of the President 2004,
100
The Economist on economic engagement,
13
EDF (power company), 133
EGOM (Empowered Group of Ministers),
226
Eisenhower (aircraft carrier), 219
Eisenhower, Dwight D.: and Agricultural
Trade Development and Assistance
Act of 1954, 210; Atoms for Peace
initiative, 33
Eizenstat, Stuart, 16–17
ElBaradei, Mohammed, 69–70, 80
Electoral College (US), 213–14
electricity: FDI for, 131; subsidies for,
233, 239. *See also* environment and
electric power
Electricity Act of 2003 (India), 150
electric power. *See* electricity;
environment and electric power
Eli Lilly, 247, 250–51, 260
Emergency Economic Stabilization Act
of 2008 (US), 202
Empowered Group of Ministers (EGOM),
226
Energy Association, US, 156
Enron Corporation, 2–3, 130, 134–38,
141, 145. *See also* Dabhol project

Enron Power Corporation Project. *See*
Dabhol project
Environmental Protection Agency (EPA),
16, 18, 140, 154, 156
Environmental Trade Working Group, 154
environment and electric power, 129–71;
AES Corporation, 148–49; bottom
line, 169–71; Bush (G.W.)
administration's efforts, 156–58;
climate change, cooperation on,
165–69; Clinton administration's
efforts, 154–56; CMS Electric
Company, 147–48; Cogentrix, 146–47;
Dabhol project, 2–3, 131–46; fast-
track projects, 133–34, 146–52;
Obama administration's efforts,
158–64, 170; Spectrum Technologies
USA, 149; US-India efforts, 152–56
EPA. *See* Environmental Protection
Agency
"equity oil and gas" program, 175–76,
177
Essential Commodities Act (India), 227,
246
"essential" drugs, 246
Esserman, Susan, 112
"estranged democracies" concept, 273
European Union (EU), 182
"evergreen revolution," 223
Executive Order 12959 (banning
investment in Iran), 181
Export-Import Bank, US: and Brownback
I Act, 45; and clean energy projects,
156; and Dabhol project, 139, 140,
142, 144; and economic engagement,
5, 16; and Glenn Amendment
sanctions, 36; guarantees from, 14,
187; and Gujarat refinery complex,
179
Export-Import Bank of Japan, 144
"externality costs," 130, 299n1

Fair Price Shops, 228
FAO (Food and Agriculture
Organization, UN), 216, 222

farming. *See* agriculture
Farsi Offshore Block, 179
fast-track projects, 131–49; aftermath of,
  149–52; and counterguarantees, 139;
  Dabhol project, 2–3, 131–46, 275;
  failure of, 152–53; fates of other
  projects, 146–49; initial projects,
  133–34; optimism about, 129–31; for
  power development, 132
FBI (Federal Bureau of Investigation),
  124, 127
FCS (Foreign Commercial Service),
  16–17
FDA (Food and Drug Administration,
  US), 247, 268
FDI. *See* foreign direct investment
Federal Bureau of Investigation (FBI),
  124, 127
Federal Grain Inspection Service, 226
Federation of American Scientists, 69
Federation of Indian Associations Tri-
  State Area, 62
Federation of Indian Chambers of
  Commerce and Industry (FICCI): and
  Agricultural Knowledge Initiative,
  224; and economic engagement, 111;
  and G-20, 200; and HTCG, 54; and
  ITA, 112; on Joint Statement (2005),
  59; and Kanwar, 251; and Mumbai
  terrorist attacks, 125; and 123 Agree-
  ment, 80; and separation agreement,
  69; and technology controls, 52; and
  US-India Commercial Alliance, 41
"feedback loops," 12, 26–27, 26*f*, 113–14,
  268, 272
Fein, Bruce, 65
Feinstein, Dianne, 126
Fernandes, George, 120, 290*n*30
Fertilizer Prices Committee, 231
fertilizers: market for, 216–17, 240; price
  schemes for, 231–32, 241
FICCI. *See* Federation of Indian
  Chambers of Commerce and Industry
FII (foreign portfolio, institutional or
  indirect investment), 4

filibustering, 214
financial meltdown, 189–209; bottom
  line, 208–9; Doha Round negotiations,
  194–98, 208; G-20 reaction, 198–208,
  209
Financial Stability Forum, 201, 205, 207
Fissile Material Cutoff Treaty, 47, 59
Fitz-pegado, Lauri, 21
five-year plans (India): Fourth (1966–71),
  216; and IPI pipeline, 180; "power to
  all" provision in, 150
Flowserve (US subsidiary), 179
Fluor (US subsidiary), 179
Food and Agriculture Organization, UN
  (FAO), 216, 222
Food and Drug Administration, US
  (FDA), 247, 268
Food Corporation of India, 228
"Food for Peace Program," 210
food regulations, role of Indian, 227–30
food retail operations, reforms to, 228–30,
  239–40
food security, 24, 210–42, 275–76;
  agricultural and food regulations,
  227–30; agricultural inputs supply,
  230–33, 240; agricultural trade
  disputes, 225–27, 240; agriculture,
  political importance of, 212–20;
  bottom line, 241–42; changes in
  approach to, 237–41; "food security
  initiative," 222–23; green revolution,
  second, 57, 209, 220–25, 233–37;
  natural inputs for, 233–35; and
  private-sector engagement, 235–37,
  241; and Public Law 480, 215–20;
  reforms in, 237–41
Ford, Gerald, 44
Ford corporation, 62
"Foreign and Domestic Investment in
  Retail Sector" report, 229–30
Foreign Commercial Service (FCS),
  16–17
Foreign Corrupt Practices Act (US), 226
foreign direct investment (FDI), 4, 130,
  131, 144, 146, 149–50

Foreign Investment Approval Board, 136
Foreign Investment Promotion Board
  (FIPB), 136, 146, 149
foreign policy, economic engagement
  and, 15–17, 22–25, 270–71
foreign portfolio, institutional or indirect
  investment (FII), 4
Forest Labs, 260
Fortune 500 companies, 119
Foster Wheeler, 178
Freeman, Orville, 215–16
Friedman, Thomas L., 115, 123
Frito-Lay, 236
Fuerth, Leon, 10
Fukuyama, Francis, 12
FutureGen Industrial Alliance, Inc., 167
FutureGen Project, 167
Future Group (retailer), 229

G-7. *See* Group of Seven
G-8. *See* Group of Eight
G-13 (Group of Thirteen), 201
G-20. *See* Group of Twenty
G-22 (Group of Twenty-Two), 199
G-77 (Group of Seventy-Seven), 162
Gadbaw, Michael, 44, 121
Gandhi, Indira, 28, 218–19, 238, 245–46,
  247
Gandhi, Mahatma, 76
Gandhi, Mohandas, 41, 213
Gandhi, Rajiv, 29
Gandhi, Sonia, 79
GAO. *See* Government Accountability
  Office
Garten, Jeffrey, 37, 38, 40, 41, 253
Gates, Bill, 262
Gates, Melinda, 262
Gates, Robert M., 12
Gates Foundation, 5, 222–23, 262–63,
  269
GATT (General Agreement on Tariffs
  and Trade), 249
Gazprom, 182
GDP (gross domestic product), 91–92
GE. *See* General Electric
GEC (power company), 133

Geithner, Timothy, 108, 126
General Agreement on Tariffs and Trade
  (GATT), 249
General Electric (GE): and CPI, 62; and
  Dabhol project, 135; in India, 117–19;
  and India-Pakistan crisis, 121–23; and
  integrated gasification combined-cycle
  technology, 168; Tarapur nuclear
  plant, 34, 39, 58; and wind energy, 166
General Mills, 237
Generation IV International Forum, 59
generic drugs, 247, 248, 250, 251–52,
  256, 264
genetically modified seeds, 230–31
Gilead Sciences (drug company), 265
Gilman, Ben, 47
GlaxoSmithKline, 252, 259
Glaxo Wellcome, 252, 258
Gleevac (leukemia drug), 264
Glenn, John, 36, 43
Glenn Amendment sanctions: and
  Brownback II act, 46; and civil nuclear
  cooperation, 36–37, 156; and eco-
  nomic engagement, 15, 49; lifting of,
  32; 9/11 terrorist attacks, 51–52; and
  nuclear option "induction," 43–44;
  and Talbott, 47
Global Alliance of Hindus (VHP, Vishwa
  Hindu Parishad), 108
Global Issues Forum, 157
Godrej, Adi, 204
Goenka, R. P., 204
Gonzales, Emilio T., 103
goods and services, production of, 90–91
Gore, Al: and Brown, 20; and economic
  engagement, 10; and environmental
  cooperation, 156; and HIV/AIDS
  efforts, 256–57; and Kyoto Protocol,
  129, 153; and Working Group on
  Environmental Technology Exports,
  140
Government Accountability Office, US
  (GAO), 94, 181, 187
Gowda, H. D. Deve, 142, 147
Grassley, Charles, 101–3, 107, 109, 110
Grassley-Sanders Amendment, 107

Green India initiative, 157–58
green revolutions: and agricultural
  inputs, 230–35; criticism of, 219–20;
  "evergreen revolution," 223; failure of,
  223–25; and "food security initiative,"
  222–23; and PL 480 program, 211,
  215–19; reform in, 237–41; and
  "saving India," 210; second, 57, 209,
  220–25, 233–37. *See also* food
  security
"green technology," 275
Gridco (power company), 149
gross domestic product (GDP), 91–92
groundwater, overexploitation of, 233
Group of Eight (G-8), 30, 158, 199, 201,
  222, 277
Group of Seven (G-7), 198–200, 201,
  277
Group of Seventy-Seven (G-77), 162
Group of Thirteen (G-13), 201
Group of Twenty (G-20): and climate
  change, 159–60; and economic
  engagement, 5, 277; financial meltdown response of, 202–8; London
  meeting of, 203–4; Pittsburgh Summit,
  159, 205–7; reform of, 198–202, 209;
  and stimulus measures, 204–5, 208;
  and WTO, 198, 204
Group of Twenty-Two (G-22), 199
"Group Pricing Scheme" for fertilizers,
  232
Gutierrez, Carlos, 157–58
GVK Power, 133

Hadley, Steve, 54
Hamas, 181
Hamid, Yusuf, 247, 252
Hamied, Khwaja Abdul, 247
Harley Davidson motorcycles, importa-
  tion of, 227
"harmonization" process, 265
Harrison, Selig "Sig," 63, 69, 81
Hastert, Dennis, 100
Hathaway, Robert, 63
heavy water, 33, 74, 288n4
Helms, Jesse, 48

Henik, Ingrid Belton, 288n1
Henry J. Hyde United States–India
  Peaceful Atomic Energy Cooperation
  Act of 2006 (US), 77. *See also* Hyde
  Act
Henry L. Stimson Center, 60
Heritage Foundation, 104
Hewlett-Packard, 119
Hezbollah, 181
High-Technology Cooperation Group
  (HTCG), 54–55, 57–58
Hinduja (oil firm), 179
Hindu nationalism ("Hindutva"), 42
Hindustan Antibiotics Ltd., 245
Hiring American Workers in Companies
  Receiving TARP Funding provision,
  107
HIV/AIDS, 243–69, 276–77; bottom
  line, 268–69; confronting challenge
  of, 243–44; governmental engagement
  on, 266–68, 269; Indian pharmaceu-
  tical companies, 246–48; intellectual
  property rights in drugs, 244–46; legal
  engagement on, 263–66, 269; non-
  governmental organizations, role of,
  260–63; pharmaceuticals, commercial
  engagement over, 259–60; pharma-
  ceutical sector engagement before
  TRIPS, 250–54; South Africa and
  TRIPS, 254–59; WTO founding and
  TRIPS, 248–49
Hoagland, Jim, 13
Hobbes, Thomas, 7
Hoffmann–La Roche, 258
Holbrooke, Richard, 19, 108, 203
Holder, Eric, 126
Hollings, Ernest "Fritz," 39
H-1B and L-1 Visa Fraud and Abuse
  Prevention Act of 2007 (US), 102
H-1B and L-1 Visa Reform Act of 2009
  (US), 109
H-1B visas: and Doha Round, 110; and
  outsourcing, 100, 104–7, 121; political
  repercussions of, 109; prohibition on,
  102–3, 202
Honeywell, 62

House International Relations Committee, 65, 74, 77
HR 5682 bill, 75, 76
HTCG (High-Technology Cooperation Group), 54–55, 57–58
Hu Jintao, 158, 159, 162
Hume, David, 7
Hyde, Henry, 70, 71, 73, 77
Hyde Act (US), 63–78; atoms for war concern, 71–72; impact of, 83; implementing legislation for, 77–78; introduction of bill, 69–71; Lantos's proposal, 72–74; and Obama, 81, 82; and 123 Agreement, 82–83; passage of bill, 75–77, 173; prerequisites to, 67–69; redrafted bills, 74–75

IAEA. *See* International Atomic Energy Agency
IAFPE (Indian American Forum for Political Education), 62
IBM, 28, 119
Ibrahim, Dawood, 141
ICICI Bank, 267
ICI Pharmaceuticals, 247
IGCC (integrated gasification combined-cycle), 168
IMF. *See* International Monetary Fund
Immigration and Nationality Act (US), 102
Implementation Force (IFOR) in Bosnia, 21
Implementing AIDS Prevention and Care (IMPACT), 266
Inderfurth, Karl F. "Rick," 63, 82
Indian Agricultural Research Institute, 218
Indian American Council, 99
Indian American Forum for Political Education (IAFPE), 62
Indian Central Electricity Authority, 135
Indian Council of Medical Research, 268
Indian Drugs and Pharmaceuticals Limited, 245, 247
Indian Oil Corporation Limited, 179

India-Pakistan Relief Act of 1998 (US), 45
"India Shining" slogan, 55–56
Indo-Soviet Friendship Treaty, 219
Indo-US Corporate Fund, 267
Industrial Development Bank of India, 140, 144
Industry Sector Advisory Committee, 112
Information Technology Agreement (ITA), 111–13, 114, 192, 208
Information Technology Association of America, 98–99
information-technology-enabled services (ITES), 4, 92–96, 95*f*, 97, 104, 110, 114
Infosys Technologies, 105, 109, 119
Infrastructure Limited, 133
inputs, agricultural, 230–35, 240
integrated gasification combined-cycle (IGCC), 168
intellectual property rights: compulsory licensing, 255; and GATT, 249; in HIV/AIDS drugs, 244–46, 254–61; legal engagement for, 263–66, 269; and pharmaceuticals, 259–60
International Atomic Energy Agency (IAEA), 59, 68, 79–81, 173, 184, 273
International Finance Corporation, 151
International Military Education and Training program, 45
International Monetary Fund (IMF), 198, 199–201, 205, 206–7, 209, 278
International Rice Institute, 212
International Thermonuclear Experimental Reactor, 59
Iran-Pakistan-India (IPI) gas pipeline, 172–88, 273–74; bottom line, 186–88; civil nuclear initiative, 184–85, 187; economic factors, additional, 185–86; "equity oil and gas" ambitions, India's, 175–76, 177; foreign oil and natural gas interests, 177–80; history and progress of, 180–86; and India's oil and natural gas needs, 174–75, 186;

sanctions, 180–83, 186–87; strategic planning for, 171; and US oil and natural gas needs, 176–77, 186
Iran Sanctions Act, US (ISA), 181–83, 187
irrigation systems, 216
Ispat Group (power company), 133
ITA. *See* Information Technology Agreement
ITES. *See* information-technology-enabled services
Itron (US subsidiary), 179
ITT corporation, 62

Jaish-e-Mohammed (terrorist organization), 115, 120
Jaitly, Arun, 195
Janata Dal Party, 147
Jaya Food Industries, 133
Jefferson, Thomas, 215
Jindal, Sajjan, 204
John F. Welch Technology Center, 118
Johnson, Lyndon B.: and food security, 238; and green revolution, 237; India relations under, 34; and PL 480 program, 28, 211, 215–16, 217–18; "short rein" policy, 219
Joint Statement (US-India) of July 18, 2005, 56–63; Bush (G.W.) and Singh (Manmohan) on, 2, 56–59, 61, 69, 186; and civil nuclear cooperation, 56–63, 157, 220; and Doha Round, 197; Indian commitment to, 67; obligations under, 69; praise and criticism of, 59–60; and USIBC, 59, 61
Joint Statement on Cooperation in Energy and Related Environmental Aspects, 155
Joint Terror Task Force Center, 126, 127
Jones, James, 85, 126
Jones, Ted, 62
Joseph, Robert G., 70
J. P. Morgan, 62
Jubilant Biosys, 260
Juster, Kenneth, 54

Kalyani, Baba, 204
Kamath, K. V., 204
Kantor, Mickey, 18–19, 20, 21, 111, 191
Kanwar, Omkar, 251
Karnik, Kiran, 104
Kashmir: Line of Control, 48, 116, 120, 123; special envoy on, 202–3
Kaye, Charles "Chip," 61, 78, 108
Kennedy, John F., 34, 210
Kerry, John, 25, 97–98, 99, 100, 104
Khanna, Tejendra, 112
Kimball, Daryl, 60, 82
King, Martin Luther, Jr., 41
King, Robert, 71
Kirk, Ron, 207
Kissinger, Henry, 44, 70, 219
Knoll Pharmaceutical, 252
Knowledge Initiative on Agriculture, 57, 220–21, 223–24, 241
Krepon, Michael, 60
Krishna, S. M., 162
Krishnakumar, N., 122
Kulkarni, Vivek, 122
Kumaramangalam, P. Rangarajan, 147
Kux, Dennis, 273
Kyoto Protocol: Bush (G.W.) administration, 156–57; Clean Development Mechanism, 155, 167, 168–69, 170; Clinton administration, 131; and Copenhagen Accord, 165; and developing countries, 153; expiration of, 170; "two-track" process, 164; US-India cooperation on, 154–56, 162

Lake, Tony, 10
lame duck sessions, 75
land grant college–agricultural extension service model, 233
land ownership, 234–35
Lantos, Tom, 70, 72–74, 77, 81, 172–74, 187
Lashkar-e-Taiba (terrorist organization), 115, 120
Lasswell, Harold, 7

Lay, Kenneth, 134, 145, 250
Left Parties, 79, 80, 109
Lenin, Vladimir, 7
Levine, Edward, 71
Lewis, Jerry, 46
Lewis, John, 298*n*32
Line of Control. *See* Kashmir
liquefied natural gas (LNG): and Dabhol
    project, 133, 134, 136, 144; India,
    importation to, 175; and IPI pipeline,
    180; in US, 177. *See also* natural gas
Litan, Robert, 8, 277
Lockheed Martin, 62, 84, 126
L-1 visas, 102–3, 109
Lugar, Richard, 32, 70–71, 76, 241
Lugar-Casey Global Food Security Act
    (US), 241

Magaziner, Ira, 165
Maharashtra province (India), political
    change in, 140–41
Maharashtra State Electricity Board
    (MSEB), 135, 137–39, 143, 144–45
Major Economies Forum on Energy and
    Climate Change, 158, 159
majority prosperity concept, 89–90
Malabar 07 (naval exercise), 178
Mandela, Nelson, 255
mangoes, import of, 227
Mankiw, Gregory, 100
Mansingh, Lalit, 122
Maran, Murasoli, 192–93, 195
Mark, Rebecca, 134, 143, 145
Market Access and Compliance Bureau,
    280
Markey, Edward J., 72, 74
Marrakech agreement, 192, 253–54
Matrix Laboratories, 261
McCain, John, 81, 104
McCormick, Brian, 81
McGraw-Hill, 62
Medicines and Related Substances Act
    (South Africa), 255, 257
megapower projects. *See* Ultra Mega
    Power Projects initiative

memoranda of understanding (MOUs),
    132–33, 134–37
Merck, 248, 252, 258, 260
Meteorological Department, Indian, 234
Metro Cash and Carry, 229
Michigan State University–Tamil Nadu
    Agricultural University horticulture
    project, 221
Microsoft, 119, 262
middle class, economic development for,
    89–90
Mill, John Stuart, 7
Missile Technology Control Regime, 59
Mitra, Amit, 41, 80, 189–90
Mittal, Sunil Bharti, 108
Monsanto, 230–31
monsoons, 233–34
Moore, Mike, 190
Moran, Murasli, 190
motorcycles, importation of, 227
Mottur, Ellis, 39, 289*n*22
MOUs. *See* memoranda of understanding
MSEB. *See* Maharashtra State Electricity
    Board
Mukherjee, Pranab, 83, 232
Mulford, David, 57
Mullen, Mike, 124
Multi-Agency Centre, 127
Mumbai terrorist attacks, 1–2, 124–26,
    128, 275
Munjal, Pawan, 108
Munjal, Sunil Kant, 204
Murthy, N. R. Narayana, 119
Musharraf, Pervez, 116, 120, 122

NACO. *See* National AIDS Control
    Organization
Nandigram incident of 2007, 235
Napolitano, Janet, 126
NASSCOM. *See* National Association of
    Software and Services Companies
Natco Group, 178
Nath, Kamal, 110, 195–98, 207
National Action Plan on climate change,
    163

National AIDS Control Organization (NACO), 244, 249, 262, 266, 267
National AIDS Control Program, 244
National Association of Software and Services Companies (NASSCOM): and anti-outsourcing legislation, 99, 108; and Blackwill, 104; and Brown, 87–88; and HTCG, 54; and ITA, 112; and ITES, 93, 96; Nilekani on, 122; and US Southwest border security, 110
National Clean Development Mechanism Authority, 168–69
National Democratic Alliance (NDA), 55, 79, 125, 150, 192
National Economic Council (NEC), 10, 11, 12, 281
National Export Policy, 13
National Institutes of Health (NIH), 267, 268
National Intelligence Grid, 127
National Organization of Indian Associations, 62
National Pharmaceutical Pricing Authority, 246
National Power Plc, 133
National Security Council (NSC), 10, 15, 281
National Security Strategy, 12
National Solar Mission, 166
National Thermal Power Corporation, 149
natural gas: "equity oil and gas" program, 175–76, 177; India's need for, 174–75, 186; and US-India relations, 177–80; US need for, 176–77, 186. *See also* liquefied natural gas
Naval War College, US, 116–17
NDA. *See* National Democratic Alliance
NEC. *See* National Economic Council
Negroponte, John, 124
Nehru, Jawaharlal, 28, 33, 125, 218, 245
New and Renewable Energies Ministry, 170
Next Steps in Strategic Partnership initiative, 55–56, 57–58

NGOs. *See* nongovernmental organizations
NIH (National Institutes of Health), 267, 268
Nilekani, Nandan, 119, 122
9/11 terrorist attacks, 9, 32–33, 51–52, 288n1
Nixon, Richard, 11, 218
Nobel Prize, 69, 180, 219
"no-first-strike" policy, 117
nonaligned policy, 33–34
nongovernmental organizations (NGOs), 143, 224, 256, 260–63
Non-Proliferation Treaty (NPT), 67, 72
Novartis (drug company), 264–65
NSC. *See* National Security Council
nuclear cooperation. *See* civil nuclear cooperation
Nuclear Nonproliferation Act of 1978 (US), 36
Nuclear Proliferation Prevention Act of 1994, 36. *See also* Glenn Amendment sanctions
Nuclear Suppliers Group: and civil cooperation, 273; guidelines of, 59, 79, 81; and IAEA, 173; India's membership in, 85; and NPT, 36
Nuclear Threat Initiative, 60, 70
nuclear war, 116–17
Nunn, Sam, 60, 70
Nunn-Lugar legislation, 70
"Nutrient Based Subsidy" policy, 232
Nye, Joseph, 11

Obama, Barack: on competitiveness, 89; and economic engagement, 8, 11, 25, 189; environmental efforts, 158–64, 167, 170; and food security, 222–23; and green revolution, 224; and Hyde Act, 81, 82; India relations, 202–3; Iowa, political importance of, 214; National Security Strategy, 12; and 123 Agreement, 82–85; and outsourcing, 90, 101, 110–11; and Singh (Manmohan), 22, 108, 202, 203, 206, 208; and stimulus measures, 204–5,

Obama, Barack (*continued*)
207–8; on tax reform, 25, 87, 88, 105;
and 2008 presidential campaign,
104–6
OECD (Organisation for Economic
Co-operation and Development), 37
oil: "equity oil and gas" program,
175–76, 177; India's need for, 174–75,
186; and US-India relations, 177–80;
US need for, 176–77, 186
Oil and Natural Gas Corporation Ltd.
(ONGC), 175–76
Oil India Limited, 179
O'Leary, Hazel, 129, 139
Omnibus Consolidated and Emergency
Supplemental Appropriations Act of
1999 (US), 45
123 Agreement, 78–85; Berman on, 184;
Congressional approval, 81–83; delays
in, 79; impact of approval, 83–85; and
Indian businesses, 79–80; and Indian
politics, 172–73; and Lantos, 73;
Singh's (Manmohan) political deal,
80–81; and US-India relations, 201
ONGC (Oil and Natural Gas Corporation
Ltd.), 175–76
ONGC Videsh Ltd. (OVL), 175–76, 179
OPEC (Organization of the Petroleum
Exporting Countries), 177
OPIC. *See* Overseas Private Investment
Corporation
Oracle, 119
"organizational behavior" model, 281
Organisation for Economic Co-operation
and Development (OECD), 37
Organization of the Petroleum Exporting
Countries (OPEC), 177
Orissa Power Generation Company, 146
outsourcing, 87–114, 274–75; bottom
line, 114; of call centers, 119;
competitiveness and citizen income,
88–90, 98; criticism of, 98–100;
definition of, 293n6; economic reality
of, 100–101; and H-1B visas, 100,
104–7, 121; Indian reaction to, 107–9;

and India-Pakistan crisis, 122;
information-technology-enabled
services, 92–96, 95*f*, 97, 110, 114; of
pharmaceuticals, 259–60; of plastics,
118; political revival of, 101–3;
production of goods and services,
complexity of, 90–91; services, 91–96;
trade in goods and services, 93, 94*f*;
and trade liberalization, 111–14; and
US businesses' response, 98–100;
US-India cooperation, effect on,
109–11; US political concerns about,
96–98; and US presidential campaign
(2008), 103–6
Overseas Private Investment Corporation
(OPIC): and Brownback I Act, 45; and
Dabhol project, 139, 140, 142, 144;
and economic engagement, 16; and
Glenn Amendment sanctions, 36;
insurance from, 14
Overseas Shipholding Group, 178–79
OVL (ONGC Videsh Ltd.), 175–76, 179

Pachauri, Rajendra K., 70, 140, 159, 180
Pacific Council on International Policy,
111, 113
Padma Vibhushan award, 221
Pakistan: "Af/Pak" conflict, 22, 203;
crisis with India, 1–2, 121–24, 128;
and East Pakistan, 219; Iranian oil
imports to, 178; Mumbai attack,
reaction to, 124–26; and nuclear
war, 116–17; and terrorism, 115–16,
119–20
Palestine Islamic Jihad, 181
Parasiliti, Andrew, 66
Parke Davis, 252
Parker Drilling (US subsidiary), 179
Parsons Brinckerhoff, 62
Partnerships for Innovation and
Knowledge in Agriculture, 221
patent rights. *See* intellectual property
rights
Patents Act of 1970 (India), 245, 246,
263–64

Patton Boggs, 67
Paul, Vivek, 122
Pawar, Sharad, 141, 221, 222
Pelosi, Nancy, 82
PEPFAR (President's Emergency Plan
  for AIDS Relief), 267, 268
PepsiCo, 235–36
Persian Gulf, oil from, 176, 177
pesticides, 232–33, 240
Petronas (oil company), 182
Pfizer, 252
Pharmaceutical Research and
  Manufacturers of America, 251
pharmaceuticals: antiretroviral drugs,
  267; commercial engagement over,
  259–60; compulsory licensing, 255;
  "essential" drugs, 246; generic drugs,
  247, 248, 250, 251–52, 256, 264;
  Indian companies, development of,
  246–48; intellectual property rights
  in, 244–46; legal engagement for,
  263–66, 269; US-India engagement
  before TRIPS, 250–54
phytosanitary norms, 225–27
Pickering, Tom, 63, 65
Pillsbury brand, 237
Pirimal Life Sciences, 260
Pittsburgh Summit of G-20, 159, 205–7
"Plant Quarantine (Regulation of Import
  into India) Order, 2003" (Indian
  Agriculture Ministry), 225
plastics business, outsourcing by, 118
"polluter pays" concept, 153
Poneman, Dan, 84
Portman, Robert, 195, 196–97
potato production, 236
Powell, Colin, 120, 122, 123
Power Finance Corporation, 150–51
power production. *See* environment and
  electric power
power purchase agreements (PPAs),
  137–39, 144
"power to all" initiative, 150
PPPs. *See* public-private partnerships
Prabhu, Suresh, 150

Premji, Azim, 118
Presidential Business Development
  Mission, 18, 23, 38, 41, 87–88, 117
presidential campaign of 2008 (US),
  103–6
President's Commission on Industrial
  Competitiveness, 89, 98
President's Emergency Plan for AIDS
  Relief (PEPFAR), 267, 268
price control regimes, 246, 247, 259
Prime Minister's Council on Trade and
  Industry, 251
private sector: agricultural development,
  role in, 224; and economic engagement, 17–22, 281–83; and second
  green revolution, 233–37, 241. *See
  also* public-private partnerships
  (PPPs)
Public Distribution System, Indian,
  227–28
Public Law (PL) 480: and agriculture,
  political importance of, 215; aid flows
  under, 5, 28, 34; and food security,
  210–11; and green revolution, 215–19;
  Indian withdrawal from, 219–20; and
  weed seeds, 225
public-private partnerships (PPPs): and
  economic engagement, 14, 17–18, 31,
  284; and food security, 241; High-
  Technology Cooperation Group, 54–55;
  and IPI pipeline, 186. *See also* private
  sector
Punjab Agriculture University, 235
Punjab Agro Industries Corporation,
  235

Ralph Nader Consumer Project on
  Technology, 256, 258
Raman, Siva, 218–19
Ramesh, Jairam, 161–62, 163–64
Ramon Magsaysay Award for
  Community Leadership, 219
Ranbaxy: and antiretroviral drugs, 267;
  banning of drugs from, 268; and
  Clinton Foundation, 261; commercial

Ranbaxy (*continued*)
engagement of, 250–51, 253, 259–60;
development of, 246–47, 248; political
influence of, 252
Rao, Mohan, 149
Rao, P. V. Narasimha: and Brown, 23;
and Clinton (Bill), 41–42; and Dabhol
project, 142; and economic engage-
ment, 9, 29; and HIV/AIDS, 244; and
power developers, 132; and Uruguay
Round, 191–92; and WTO, 248–49
Ray, S. S., 40
Raytheon, 62, 84
Reagan, Ronald, 191
Reddy, Kallam Anjil, 247, 251
Reddy's Laboratories. *See* Dr. Reddy's
Laboratories Ltd.
"regime change," 22
Reid, Harry, 76
Reliance–Anil Dhirubhai Ambani Group,
151
Reliance Fresh, 229
Reliance Industries Ltd., 174, 179, 187,
229
Reliance Jamnagar (oil refinery), 174
Reliance Power Ltd., 151–52
Renfrew, Charles, 146
Repsol (oil company), 182
Reserve Bank of India, 234
retail operations, reforms to, 228–30,
239–40
"Retention Price Scheme" for fertilizers,
231–32
Reyes, Silvestre, 126
Rice, Condoleezza, 53, 56, 70–71, 82,
83, 124
Richardson, Bill, 155
Riedel, Bruce, 82
rioting, Hindu-Muslim, 140–41
Roach, Stephen, 91
Rockefeller Foundation, 210, 211–12,
222–23
Rome Agreement of 1965, 215–18, 220,
231
Rood, John, 69
Roosevelt, Franklin D., 219

Rothkopf, David, 10, 277
Rove, Karl, 81
Royal Dutch Shell, 182
RPG, 229
Rubin, Robert, 10
Ruia, Shashi, 204
Rumsfeld, Donald, 123
Russia, IPI pipeline and, 186
rye brome weeds (*bromus secalinus*),
225

Salve, N. K. P., 129–31, 132, 135–36,
300*n*8
Samastha Initiative, 267
sanctions: Congressional relief from,
44–47; and IPI pipeline, 180–83,
186–87; against Iran, 174; as negative
economic engagement, 15; and nuclear
option "induction," 42–44, 85. *See
also* Glenn Amendment sanctions
Sanders, Bernie, 107
Saran, Shyam, 58–59, 84, 158
Schaffer, Howard, 63
Schaffer, Teresita "Tezie," 63
Schumer, Charles, 109
Schwab, Susan, 110, 197, 207
Scowcroft, Brent, 70
SEBs (State Electricity Boards), 132
Secure Borders, Economic Opportunity
and Immigration Reform Act of 2007
(US), 103
Security Council, UN, 183
seeds: genetically modified, 230–31;
weed dispute, 225–27
SEI Capability Maturity Model
Integration for Systems Engineering
and Software Engineering, 206
Sen, Amartya, 212
Sen, Ronen, 32
Senate Foreign Relations Committee, 65,
70–71, 77
"separation agreements" on civil nuclear
cooperation, 69, 70
services: production of, 90–91; role of,
91–92; trade in goods and services, 93,
94*f. See also* outsourcing

SEZs (special economic zones), 235
Shanghvi, Dilip S., 248
Shankar, Meera, 40
Sharif, Nawaz, 116
Sharma, Anand, 207
Shastri, Lal Badhur, 217–18
Shelby, Richard, 289n16
Sherman, Brad, 72
Shinde, Sushilkumar, 168
Shiv Sena Party, 130, 141–42, 143, 145, 150
"short rein" policy, 219
Sibal, Kanwal, 54
Singh, Bhai Mohan, 250
Singh, J. K., 72
Singh, Jaswant, 47–48, 60, 155
Singh, Manmohan: and Bharatiya Janata Party, 109; and Borlaug, 221; and Bush (G.W.), 73; and climate change, 158; and Dabhol project, 140; and economic engagement, 8, 89, 195; and environmental efforts, 170; and fertilizer subsidies, 232, 241; on green revolution, 220, 223; and G-20, 159, 200, 203–4, 207; and harvest failures, 234; on HIV/AIDS, 243, 267; and Hyde Act, 78; on IMF, 200–201; and IPI pipeline, 186; on Iranian gas, 172; and Joint Statement (2005), 2, 56–57, 59, 61; "Manmohan Singh Doctrine," 23; and Mumbai terrorist attacks, 125; and Obama, 22, 108, 202, 203, 206, 208; and 123 Agreement, 79, 80–81, 84, 184, 201; and power developers, 132; and Ramesh, 162; on stimulus measures, 204–5; and WTO, 248–49
Singh, Natwar, 56
Singh, Parvinder, 246, 250–51
Singhania, Harsh Pati, 204
Skilling, Jeffrey, 145
Smith Kline Beecham, 252
Software Engineering Institute (SEI), 206
Somers, Ronald S., 60–61, 68, 69
South Africa, HIV/AIDS in, 254–59

South Asia Association for Regional Cooperation, 169
South Pars natural gas field, 182
Southwest Border Security Bill (US), 109
Special Agricultural Safeguard (SSG), 307n15
special economic zones (SEZs), 235
special envoy on Kashmir, 202–3
Special Safeguard Mechanism (SSM) for agricultural imports, 197–98, 307n15
"Special 301 watch list," 257
"specialty occupations" designation, 102
Spectrum Technologies USA, 133, 149
SSG (Special Agricultural Safeguard), 307n15
Standard Organics Ltd., 248
State Department, US, 16–17, 279
State Electricity Boards (SEBs), 132
State Food and Civil Supplies Corporations, 228
Steil, Benn, 8, 277
Steinberg, James, 108
Stern, Todd, 158
S 3709 legislation (US), 74
Stimson Center, Henry L., 60
stimulus measures, economic, 204–8. *See also* American Recovery and Reinvestment Act of 2009
strategic issues: definition of, 3–6; economic engagement, relationship between, 7–9, 13–14, 31, 271–79, 284; political action on, 12–22, 31. *See also specific issues (e.g., civil nuclear cooperation)*
Strides Arcolab, 261
Subbarao, D., 204
Subramaniam, Chidambaram, 216, 218–19, 238
subsidies: agricultural, 196, 208; for electricity, 233, 239; for fertilizers, 231–32, 241. *See also* tariffs
sugar, regulations on, 228
suicides among farmers, 231
Summers, Lawrence, 108
Sun Microsystems, 119

Sun Pharmaceuticals Industries, Ltd., 246, 248, 251–52
Suven Life Sciences, 260
Swaminathan, M. S., 218–19, 221, 238

Talbott, Strobe, 47–48, 49, 60, 155, 314*n*44
Taliban, 22, 30, 122, 185
Tamil Nadu State Electricity Board (TNSEB), 148
Tarapur nuclear plant, 34, 35, 39, 58, 59
tariffs: "balance of payment" exceptions, 193; and Dabhol project, 138, 143; "dirty tariffication" process, 192; and ITA, 208. *See also* subsidies
TARP (Troubled Asset Relief Program), 107
Tata, Ratan, 204
Tata Consultancy Services, 105, 119
Tata Energy Research Institute, 140
Tata power plant, 151
tax reforms, 25, 87, 88, 105
Tellis, Ashley J., 72
terrorism, 115–28, 274–75; departure notices and travel restrictions, 120–21, 128; and economic engagement, 127–28; GE's due diligence during India-Pakistan crisis, 121–23; growing crisis, 119–20; Mumbai attacks, reaction to, 124–26, 128; and nuclear war, 116–17; and US-India strategic cooperation, 126–27; "war on terror," 8–9, 12. *See also specific attacks; specific organizations*
Tesco (retail distributor), 229
Texas Instruments, 88, 89
Textron, 62
Thackery, Bal, 143
TIBCO Software, 119
Tibotec Pharmaceuticals, 265
Times of India, Mitra in, 80
Tinna Group, 236–37
Tinna Oils & Chemicals Ltd., 236–37
TNSEB (Tamil Nadu State Electricity Board), 148
Tobias, Randy, 250

tomato production, 236
Total SA (investor), 182
"Towards Faster and More Inclusive Growth" (Congress Party), 89
TPCC. *See* Trade Promotion Coordinating Committee
Trade and Development Agency, 14, 16, 36, 45
trade disputes in agriculture, 225–27, 240
Trade Promotion Coordinating Committee (TPCC), 13, 17, 140, 154
Trade-Related Aspects of Intellectual Property Rights (TRIPS Agreement): and Doha Round, 194; and drug companies, 252–53; flexibility in, 194, 254, 255, 265; and HIV/AIDS drugs, 254–59, 261; Marrakech agreement, 253–54; and patented drugs, 263–65; US position on, 257; and WTO, 248–49, 251
travel restrictions in response to terrorism, 120–21, 128
Treasury Department, 11–12, 17, 280
TRIPS Agreement. *See* Trade-Related Aspects of Intellectual Property Rights
Troubled Asset Relief Program (TARP), 107
Turkey, gas pipeline with Iran and, 182
2008 presidential campaign, 103–6
"two-track" process, 164
Tyson, Laura, 279

Ultra Mega Power Projects initiative, 150–51, 152, 167, 170
UNFCCC. *See* United Nations Framework Convention on Climate Change
Uniloids Ltd., 247
Union Carbide, 220, 233
UNITAID (drug purchasing facility), 263
United Front, 42
United Nations Climate Change Conference, 131
United Nations Framework Convention on Climate Change (UNFCCC): and Bush (G.W.) administration, 157; and

CDM, 168–69; developing countries under, 161; India's position on, 163; and Kyoto Protocol, 155; and Obama administration, 158; "two-track" process, 164

United Progressive Alliance (UPA): and Congress Party, 56, 195, 232; and 123 Agreement, 79; "power to all" initiative, 150; trust vote for, 184, 197

United States and India Nuclear Cooperation Promotion Act of 2006 (US), 73

United States–India Joint Leadership Statement on HIV/AIDS, 260–61

Unocal Corporation, 60–61

UOP (Honeywell subsidiary), 179

UPA. *See* United Progressive Alliance

Uruguay Round, 190, 191–92, 193, 249, 253

US Agency for International Development (USAID), 18, 221, 233, 266, 267

US Citizenship and Immigration Services (USCIS), 103

US Climate Change Initiative, 157

US First Solar Inc., 166

US-India Business Council (USIBC): and CII, 68; and CPI, 61–62; and Dabhol project, 144; "Green India" initiative, 157; and G-20, 203; and Hyde Act, 75–76; on Joint Statement (2005), 59, 61; and Mumbai terrorist attacks, 125; and outsourcing, 108; and sanctions relief, 44–45; and separation agreement, 69; and Somers, 60–61; and WTO, 189

US-India Commercial Alliance, 41, 57, 112

US-India Commercial Dialogue, 51

US-India Economic Dialogue, 57

US-India Energy Dialogue, 157

US-India Financial and Economic Forum, 51

US-India Friendship Council, 62–63, 66, 73

US-India Working Group on Trade, 51

US-South Africa Binational Commission, 257

US Trade Representative (USTR), 15, 17, 253, 257

Vajpayee, Atal Bihari: and BJP, 23, 42, 142; and Blackwill, 121; and Cogentrix project, 147; Comprehensive Test Ban Treaty, 48; and economic engagement, 9; and environmental cooperation, 156; HIV/AIDS efforts, 260–61; and NDA, 55, 79; Next Steps in Strategic Partnership initiative, 55–56; and Pakistan, 120; post-9/11 US visit, 53

Vantage Energy Services (US subsidiary), 179

Verma, Richard, 76

Vickery, Raymond E., Sr., 308*n*2

Vietnam War, US involvement in, 218, 219

visas. *See* H-1B visas; L-1 visas

Vishwa Hindu Parishad (VHP, Global Alliance of Hindus), 108

"vote of trust" campaign, 184, 197

"Vulcans" advisers group, 52–53

Wall Street Journal, Fein's access to editorial management at, 65

Wal-Mart, 229

Warburg Pincus (investment firm), 108

"war on terror," 8–9, 12

Washington Times, Fein's access to editorial management at, 65

Weatherford (US subsidiary), 179

weed seeds, dispute over, 225–27

Welch, Jack, 117–18

Welch Technology Center, 118

WestBridge Capital Partners, 119

Westinghouse, 62

wheat, 225–27

Wheat Associates, 226

William J. Clinton Foundation. *See* Clinton Foundation

Wilson, Charlie, 46

wind energy production, 166–67

Wipro Technologies, 105, 118

Wisner, Frank G., 40, 62, 63, 65, 142, 203

Wisner, Graham, 66–67
Wolin, Neal, 11–12
Workadia, 119
Working Group on Civil Nuclear Energy, 80
Working Group on Environmental Technology Exports, 140
World Bank: and AES project, 149; and agriculture innovation, 222; and Dabhol project, 135, 137, 142; and economic engagement, 5; and financial meltdown, 198; and Glenn Amendment sanctions, 37; and G-20, 199–200, 207; India assistance from, 45; infrastructure development, 201; and ITES exports, 96; reform of, 209, 278; and stimulus measures, 205; and technology exports, 92
World Trade Organization (WTO): founding of, 191–92, 208, 248–49; and G-20, 198, 204, 207; harmonization through, 265; and ITA, 113; Marrakech agreement, 192, 253–54; Ministerial Conference, 189–91, 192–93; and outsourcing, 99; and sanctions, 182; and TRIPS Agreement, 248–49, 251; Uruguay Round, 190, 191–92, 193, 249, 253; US-India cooperation in, 192–94; US interest in, 278. *See also* Doha Round
Wyeth, 252

Xerox, 62

"Y2K" problem, 96–97, 294n22

Zardari, Asif Ali, 202
Zelikow, Philip, 281
Zoellick, Robert, 195